Montenegro

Peter Dragičević

BIOGRADSKA GORA NATIONAL PARK (p141)
Primeval forest mirrored in a tranquil alpine lake

TARA CANYON (p143)
Kilometre-high walls provide a sublime backdrop to a rafting trip through paradise

DURMITOR NATIONAL PARK (p142)
Numerous paths criss-cross the craggy peaks, littered with glacial lakes

PIVA CANYON ROAD (p136)
Breathtaking riverside drive clinging to the canyon walls

SERBIA

BOSNIA & HERCEGOVINA

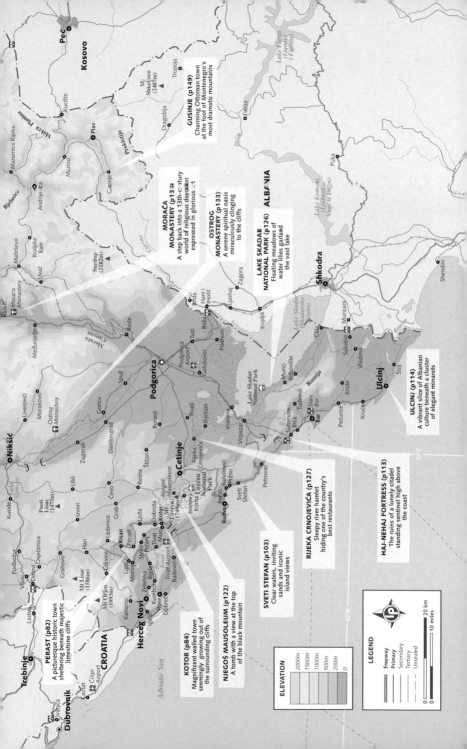

PERAST (p82)
A picturesque historic town sheltering beneath majestic limestone cliffs

KOTOR (p84)
Magnificent walled town seemingly growing out of the surrounding cliffs

NJEGOŠ MAUSOLEUM (p122)
A tomb with a view at the top of the black mountain

SVETI STEFAN (p103)
Clear waters, inviting sands and iconic island views

RIJEKA CRNOJEVIĆA (p127)
Sleepy river hamlet hiding one of the country's best restaurants

HAJ-NEHAJ FORTRESS (p113)
The ruins of a lonely citadel standing sentinel high above the coast

ULCINJ (p114)
A vibrant slice of Albanian culture beneath a cluster of elegant minarets

LAKE SKADAR NATIONAL PARK (p126)
Floating meadows of water lilies garland the vast lake

OSTROG MONASTERY (p133)
A serene spiritual oasis miraculously clinging to the cliffs

MORAČA MONASTERY (p13■)
A step back into a 13th-century world of religious devotion expressed in glorious art

GUSINJE (p149)
Charming Ottoman town at the foot of Montenegro's most dramatic mountains

LEGEND

ELEVATION
2000m
1500m
1000m
500m
200m
0

Freeway
Primary
Secondary
Tertiary
Unsealed

0   20 km
0   10 miles

Adriatic Sea

On the Road

PETER DRAGIČEVIĆ

If you think that driving around the Bay of Kotor is beautiful, just wait until you take the numerous hairpin turns of the old Austrian road to Lovćen (p122) and look down on it from the slopes of the black mountain itself. There were numerous 'wow' moments while researching this book, but this one was hard to top.

MY FAVOURITE TRIP

The tour bus had left Budva at the crack of dawn so by the time I boarded in Nikšić the charming tour guide had already spent a couple of hours keeping everyone entertained with interesting anecdotes, disco music and shots of *rakija*. An awed silence settled as we headed through the astonishing Piva Canyon (p136) and by the time we had disembarked by the banks of the Tara River (p143) in Šćepan Polje everybody was pretty excited. Before long my new best friends and I were splashing through the rapids on an inflatable raft, admiring an impossibly beautiful landscape untainted by human hand.

For full author biographies see p184.

Montenegro Highlights

Most travellers consider Montenegro a new discovery, and they sure do like what they're discovering. The string of impossibly charming seaside villages and pristine beaches backed by striking mountains were the first to catch travellers' attention. Now the rich offerings of the mountainous interior and the warm welcome of the Montenegrins also have people making repeat visits. We asked our authors, staff and readers what they love most about Montenegro. Share your Montenegro highlights at lonelyplanet.com/montenegro.

TIM HUGHES

1 ENJOYING KOTOR VIEWS

A highlight of our trip was climbing the 1500 steps to the old fortification overlooking not only Kotor (p84) but the majestic fjord that this sleepy town is nestled in. We tackled this early in the morning on a perfect summer's day before the searing heat kicked in. Afterwards we rewarded ourselves with a dip in the emerald-coloured fjord.

Jason Shugg, Lonely Planet staff

DURMITOR PEAKS

Climbing Bobotov Kuk (2523m), considered the highest peak of Montenegro, was the greatest challenge of my amateur mountaineering experience. Though demanding, the climb is incredibly colourful, a combination of rocky terrain and scented pastures. After three hours we reached the summit, and I could truly say it was worth it! The view from above the clouds is divine, and standing there at the very top of Montenegro you are over-whelmed by the power of Durmitor (p142).

Sanja Manitašević, traveller, Serbia

3

2 ATMOSPHERIC BUDVA

Budva's walled Old Town (p97) is simply gorgeous, rising from the Adriatic like a miniature, less glamorous Dubrovnik. There's an atmosphere of romance and a typically Mediterranean love of life in every corner. You can spend hours exploring the labyrinth of narrow cobbled streets with tiny churches and charming galleries, and reflect on the inspiring sea views from the ancient Citadel.

**Branislava Vladisavljević,
Lonely Planet staff**

4 SVETI STEFAN

The beach near Sveti Stefan peninsula (p103) is sandy and pretty busy, but visiting the hotel on the island itself reminded me of scenes from a Bond film. The entrance fee was nominal and wandering through the narrow streets with numerous nooks and crannies acting as apartments, with a beautiful restaurant terrace facing the open seas, was a few hours well spent. Highly recommended.

Maja Thompson, traveller, UK

ROCKY MOUNTAIN HIGHS

Montenegro's steep mountain roads give plenty of opportunities for sweeping views. Leaving the Podgorica–Cetinje highway for what turned out to be a sublime fish lunch in the speck of dust on the map that is the village of Rijeka Crnojevića (p127), an incredible panorama opens up. Far below, the river winds sluggishly through the water lilies on its journey to Lake Skadar and the conical pair of mountains that the locals affectionately call Sofia Loren. No Italian actress ever looked so sublime.

Peter Dragičević, Lonely Planet author

PETER DRAGIČEVIĆ

5

LAKESIDE RELAXATION

Lake Skadar (p126) is a great place to spend a day cruising with friends. You can relax on the beach surrounded by forested hills and have lunch at the rustic restaurant with local specialities. If you're lucky you might get to see a pelican!

Ranka Tijanić, traveller, Montenegro

PATRICK HORTON

6

VISITING THE BLACK LAKE

You should visit the glacial Black Lake (p142), a 30-minute walk from Žabljak, in summer, when it isn't covered in ice. Because it's surrounded by black pine forest, the water really looks black – it's a surreal image!

Ranka Tijanić, traveller, Montenegro

8

7

SOLITUDE IN BIOGRADSKA

I once spent a day in the Biogradska Gora (p141), hiking in the forest and rowing on the lake. There was such a peaceful, solitary, untouched-by-the-world feel to it, that I could have happily stayed a year.

Branislava Vladisavljević, Lonely Planet staff

9

WHITE-KNUCKLE RIDES

My all-time Montenegro highlight is the simple joy of travelling around. Driving along the Podgorica–Kolašin road through the Morača Canyon (p138), in particular, is often a white-knuckle ride with countless cliffside bends and tunnels, but the beauty and power of the landscape are such that you find you're in no hurry to reach your destination.

Branislava Vladisavljević, Lonely Planet staff

PETER DRAGIČEVIĆ

10 THE FOG CLEARING ON PERAST

On paper the tiny village of Perast (p82) on Montenegro's Bay of Kotor sounded like our ideal of a romantic getaway. But pouring rain and thick fog when we arrived meant we could barely see a thing. No worries: the village's one little bar-cafe gave us exactly the physical and emotional warm-up we needed as we slowly became locals and ended up joining a 'jam' of impromptu Montenegrin folk music. Then on the third evening the fog cleared. We sat on the little quayside with a bottle of local bubbly gaping at the glories that were finally unveiled…

Dani Systermans, traveller, Belgium

PATRICK HORTON

11 MORAČA MONASTERY

Coming down out of the mountains we hit a traffic jam – a six-hour, stand-still beast of a thing. As luck would have it, we drew up next to the 11th-century Morača Monastery (p138), something that wasn't on our itinerary. We couldn't have asked for a more serene spot, and whiled away the hours gazing at its gorgeous paintings and icons and kicking back in the heart of the Morača Canyon.

Neal Bedford, Lonely Planet author

WITOLD SKRYPCZAK

12 ISLAND TOKENS

We loved the tiny island deep inside the Bay of Kotor – its Our-Lady-of-the-Rock Church (p82), with charming tokens of the old days (that's where brides used to leave their wedding bouquets and sailors silver plaques for good luck), was an unexpected gem.

Dragana Vojinović, traveller, Canada

SHANNON BRUCE N/

13 THE RUINS OF STARI BAR

It's easy to mistake Bar for just an industrial port town, but that would be missing out on a hidden treasure: tucked away in the hills and sheltered by olive trees, some of them hundreds of years old, the ruins of Stari Bar (p113) leave a powerful impression and are a delight to explore.

Dragana Vojinović, traveller, Canada

VIEWS FROM A BALCONY

The sweeping bay view from a Herceg Novi (p76) balcony awakens your sense of space. The architecture blends perfectly with the hillside setting: try counting hundreds of stone steps leading from the Old Town to the beach, or concentrating on the performance at the open-air stage atop a medieval tower. In the evening join the vibrant promenade along the coast, past beautiful girls chatting in cafes and local boys playing water polo in the sea.

Aleksandra Vladisavljević, traveller, Serbia

14

RAFAEL ESTEFANIA

CIRCUITING THE BOKA

The Bay of Kotor (p73) must be one of the most enticing introductions to a country anywhere. Heading south from Herceg Novi the combination of lavender-grey mountains, glassy green sea, stony villages and blooming pomegranate trees is awe-inspiring. Perast was the perfect spot for a laid-back coffee stop, and Kotor's mighty walls and narrow streets were ideal for exploring.

Will Gourlay, Lonely Planet staff

15

PETER DRAGIĆEVIĆ

Св. преп. Исаије от Оногошта

16 **THE TEMPTATIONS OF OSTROG**

WITOLD SKRYP

The famous 17th-century Orthodox monastery Ostrog (p133) attracts the faithful from all over the Balkans. Carved into steep cliffs, it seems unreachable as you try to make it there along the curved mountain path. A true temptation, even if you're not a believer!

Ranka Tijanić, traveller, Montenegro

Contents

On the Road   4

Montenegro Highlights 5

Destination
Montenegro   15

Getting Started   16

Itineraries   20

History   24

The Culture   36

Food & Drink   44

Landscape & Lifestyle 53

The Environment   61

Gateway City:
Dubrovnik   66

Bay of Kotor   73
Herceg Novi   76
Around Herceg Novi   80
Morinj   81
Risan   81
Perast   82
Dobrota   83
Kotor   84
Prčanj   89
Stoliv   89
Lastva   89
Tivat   90
Around Tivat   92
Luštica Peninsula   92

Adriatic Coast   94
Budva   96
Around Budva   102
Sveti Stefan   103
Around Sveti Stefan   106
Petrovac   107
Around Petrovac   109
Bar   110
Around Bar   113
Ulcinj   114
Around Ulcinj   118

Central Montenegro 120
Lovćen National Park   122
Cetinje   123
Lake Skadar National Park 126
Podgorica   129
Danilovgrad   133
Ostrog Monastery   133
Nikšić   134
Around Nikšić   136

Northern Mountains 137
Morača Canyon &
Monastery   138
Kolašin   138
Biogradska Gora
National Park   141
Mojkovac   142
Durmitor National Park   142
Bijelo Polje   145
Rožaje   146
Plav   147
Around Plav   149

Directory   151
Accommodation   151
Activities   152
Business Hours   155
Children   155
Climate Charts   158
Customs Regulations   158
Dangers & Annoyances   158
Discount Cards   159
Embassies & Consulates   159
Festivals & Events   159
Food   159
Gay & Lesbian Travellers   159

Holidays 160
Insurance 160
Internet Access 160
Legal Matters 160
Maps 161
Money 161
Post 161
Shopping 161
Solo Travellers 161
Telephone 161
Time 162
Tourist Information 162
Travellers with Disabilities 162
Visas 162
Women Travellers 162

Transport 163
GETTING THERE
& AWAY 163
Entering the Country 163
Air 163
Land 167
Sea 169
GETTING AROUND 170
Bicycle 170
Bus 170
Car & Motorcycle 170
Hitching 172
Local Transport 172
Train 172

Health 173
BEFORE YOU GO 173
Insurance 173
Recommended
Vaccinations 173
Internet Resources 173
IN TRANSIT 173
Deep Vein
Thrombosis (DVT) 173
Jet Lag & Motion Sickness 174
IN MONTENEGRO 174
Availability &
Cost of Health Care 174
Infectious Diseases 174
Traveller's Diarrhoea 174
Environmental Hazards 174
Travelling with Children 174

Regional Map Contents

Language 176

Glossary 182

The Authors 184

Behind the Scenes 185

Index 189

Map Legend 196

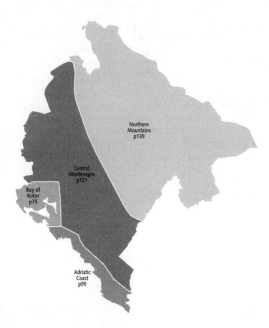

Northern
Mountains
p139

Central
Montenegro
p121

Bay of
Kotor
p75

Adriatic
Coast
p95

Destination Montenegro

Imagine a place with sapphire beaches as spectacular as Croatia's, rugged peaks as dramatic as Switzerland's, canyons nearly as deep as Colorado's, palazzos as elegant as Venice's and towns as old as Greece's, then wrap it up in a Mediterranean climate and squish it into an area two-thirds the size of Wales and you start to get a picture of Montenegro.

Going it alone is a brave move for a nation of this size – its entire population of 678,000 would barely fill a medium-sized city in many parts of the world – but toughing it out is something this gutsy people have had plenty of experience in. Their national identity is built around resisting the Ottoman Empire for hundreds of years in a mountainous enclave much smaller than the nation's current borders.

After negotiating a reasonably amicable divorce from an unhappy state union with Serbia in 2006, relations between the exes have recently taken a turn for the worse. At the time of writing, Serbia had expelled Montenegro's ambassador after Montenegro officially recognised the former Serbian province of Kosovo as an independent country, joining around 50 other nations who had already done so. It was particularly galling for Serbia, coming a day after it had won a vote at the UN to ask the International Court of Justice for a ruling on the legality of Kosovo's declaration of independence (a vote that Montenegro supported).

Recognising Kosovo was a particularly difficult decision for Montenegro to make given their shared history with Serbia and the fact that a third of Montenegro's population is Serbian. In doing so, Montenegro is clearly setting its sights towards Europe and potentially a future less defined by ethnicity and religion.

Given the country's natural assets, tourism is vitally important to Montenegro's future. In that respect it's done spectacularly well in filling its tiny coast with Eastern European sun-seekers for two months of each year, while serving up the rest of the country as bite-sized day trips. The upshot for intrepid travellers is that you can easily sidestep the hordes in the rugged mountains of Durmitor, the primeval forest of Biogradska Gora or in the many towns and villages where ordinary Montenegrins go about their daily lives. This is, after all, a country where wolves and bears still lurk in forgotten corners.

Montenegro, Crna Gora, Black Mountain: the name itself conjures up romance and drama. There are plenty of both on offer as you explore this perfumed land, bathed in the scent of wild herbs, conifers and Mediterranean blossoms. Yes, it really is as magical as it sounds.

FAST FACTS

Named after Mt Lovćen (ie 'black mountain' or *monte negro* in Italian; Crna Gora in Montenegrin)

Population: 678,000

Area: 13,812 sq km

Capital: Podgorica

President: Filip Vujanović

Prime Minister: Milo Đukanović

GNI (per capita): €3900 (2007 estimate)

Inflation: 9.2%

Unemployment: 12%

Currency: euro

Official language: Montenegrin

Famous for: being really beautiful

Getting Started

Relax, Montenegro is easy. If you're the type who gets caught up in the excitement of planning every step of your journey in advance, by all means go ahead. If you'd prefer to wing it, that should be fine as well – provided you're a) avoiding the busy months of July and August; b) not planning a major mountain-biking, mountaineering or multi-day hiking adventure; and c) not hoping to cram everything into two days. Those sorts of factors will all require more in the way of organisation.

If you're a 'go with the Montenegro flow' sort of person it would still pay to flick through the destination chapters of this book in advance and see which places take your fancy. If you wait until you're there and take the advice of the locals, chances are you'll find yourself under one of a line of hundreds of beach umbrellas in Budva, being pressured into booking expensive coach tours. The presumption is that tourists – especially those from outside the region – have extravagant tastes, like crowded places with loud music and generally need their hands held. The idea that some people might prefer intrepid, independent travel isn't widely understood in these parts. During our research for this book we were constantly dissuaded from visiting towns slightly off the beaten track where there might not be a three-star hotel to stay in. Don't be put off or you'll miss out on some gems.

> The number of tourists visiting Montenegro annually is double the country's resident population.

> See Climate Charts (p158) and the beginning of each destination chapter for more information.

WHEN TO GO

Montenegrin tourism is hung up with the idea of 'the season', which in most places is July and August. Wherever possible, these months should be avoided as prices skyrocket, accommodation options dry up, traffic snarls along the coastal road, insanely loud music thumps through the streets at night and hordes of tourists blanket the beaches. Worse still, some coastal areas experience water shortages.

The best months to visit are May, June, September and October. You'll still get plenty of sunshine and the average water temperature is over 20°C. The downside of avoiding 'the season' is that you will find some places closed (especially camping grounds and beachside bars and restaurants) and activities harder to track down.

The ski season is roughly from December to March. Winter can be a lovely time to visit the coast if you relish peace and quiet and the opportunity to hang out with locals in the few cafes that remain open. Many hotels also close their doors, but accommodation shouldn't be difficult to find.

> **HOW MUCH?**
>
> Short taxi ride €5
>
> Internet access per hour €1
>
> Cup of coffee €1
>
> Bottle of *vranac* (local red wine) from the market €2.50
>
> Postcard €0.50
>
> See Quick Reference on the inside front cover for more examples.

COSTS & MONEY

Montenegro is desperately trying to make a transition from mass-market tourism to attracting the glitterati. Basically it's a case of 'Goodbye Serb and Kosovar families; welcome pretentious gits in multimillion-dollar yachts'. At the moment the balance is still tipped slightly more towards the former than the latter, but things are quickly changing.

By European standards it's still a relatively cheap place to visit but there's a sense that perhaps you should get in quick. Budget travellers renting private rooms and eating pizza and street snacks could comfortably get by on €30 per day. If you're staying in a three-star hotel and eating three proper sit-down meals, this jumps up to €70 per day. If your priorities are fancy sheets and fish meals that stare back at you while they're served, allow at least double this.

DON'T LEAVE HOME WITHOUT...

- checking whether you need a visa (p162)
- ensuring your passport has six months left on it
- your driver's licence and/or an International Driving Permit (p171)
- something to wear while swimming, unless it's winter or you're sticking to nudie beaches
- warm clothes if you're visiting the mountains
- some clothes that won't scare the monks (p133)
- decent walking shoes (flip-flops aren't much use if you trod on a viper)
- a trashy novel (it's hard to find English-language books here)
- earplugs, especially if you're staying in one of the Old Towns
- an open mind and a modicum of patience
- a healthy appetite
- this book

TRAVELLING RESPONSIBLY

Since our inception in 1973, Lonely Planet has encouraged our readers to tread lightly, travel responsibly and enjoy the magic independent travel affords. International travel is growing at a jaw-dropping rate, and we still firmly believe in the benefits it can bring – but, as always, we encourage you to consider the impact your visit will have on both the global environment and the local economies, cultures and ecosystems.

Getting There & Away

If you're coming from within Europe, it's quite possible to reach Montenegro without flying or driving. Montenegro's solitary passenger railway line dissects the country from south to north and continues through to Belgrade. From the Serbian capital, Europe's web of rail lines connects to all corners of the continent including Britain. Italy's east-coast port cities of Bari and Ancona are plugged into the same network and linked to Montenegro via regular ferry services. See the boxed text on p169 for more tips on flight-free travel, p168 for details of train services and p169 for ferries. If you do choose to fly, the boxed text on p164 has information about carbon-offset schemes.

Slow Travel

Once you're there, what's the rush? Montenegro is a small enough country to be explored by 'slow' means. Flying between destinations isn't an option as there are no internal flights. The bus network is very good and the train services, while limited, can also prove useful. The mountainous terrain may dissuade everyone but the fittest or most devout eco-warriors from taking advantage of the excellent hiking (see p154) and mountain-biking (see p153) trails, but they really do provide a wonderful way to see the country and they're well supported with resources from the National Tourist Office. Kayaking (see p155) is a fun option for exploring the Bay of Kotor and Lake Skadar. If you're an experienced sea kayaker you can tackle the entire coast this way.

Accommodation & Food

The 'eco' label is bandied around a lot in Montenegro but it's not always clear what is meant by it. All you can take for granted in an ecolodge

TOP PICKS

MONTENEGRO
Podgorica ●

BEACHES

From sandy stretches to rocky coves, Montenegro's clear-watered beaches are its biggest drawcard. See the Adriatic Coast chapter (p94) for more options.

- Pržno on the Luštica Peninsula (p93)
- Sveti Stefan (p103)
- Murići in Lake Skadar National Park (p128)
- Morinj in the Bay of Kotor (p81)
- Miločer Beach at Sveti Stefan (p106)
- Drobni Pijesak near Petrovac (p109)
- Dobreč on the Luštica Peninsula (p93)
- Lučice Beach at Petrovac (p107)
- Ladies' Beach in Ulcinj (p116)
- Pržno near Sveti Stefan (p106)

ACTIVITIES

If you can scrape yourself off the sand, Montenegro's not short on active pursuits to get your pulse racing. See p152 for more details.

- Rafting on the Tara River (p143)
- Kayaking around the Bay of Kotor (p78)
- Cruising on Lake Skadar (p126)
- Hiking in Biogradska Gora National Park (p141)
- Mountain biking around Lovćen National Park (p122)
- Skiing in Durmitor National Park (p144)
- Birdwatching in Lake Skadar National Park (p126)
- Paragliding from above Bečići (p103)
- Diving near Budva (p153)
- Parasailing from Herceg Novi (p78)

FESTIVALS & EVENTS

In the warm months there's almost always something going on somewhere around the country, ranging from centuries-old traditions to all-out parties. See p159 for more information.

- Adventure Race Montenegro (p159)
- Fašinada, Perast (p82)
- Boka Navy Day, Kotor (p86)
- Traditional Kotor Carnival, Kotor (p86)
- Lake Skadar Day, Virpazar (p127)
- Boka Night, Kotor (p86)
- International Folklore Festival, Budva (p100)
- River Zeta Festival, Danilovgrad (p133)
- International Fashion Selection, Kotor (p86)
- International Klapa Festival, Perast (p82)

is that it will be surrounded by nature. Don't expect solar power, composting toilets, ecofriendly materials, water-reduction practices or even recycling (Herceg Novi is currently trialling recycling, the first and only Montenegrin town to do so). Still, these are generally small-scale operations benefiting the local people in remote areas. Some, such as Eco Katun Vranjak (p140), make an effort to preserve and encourage traditional folk activities and crafts.

With so many gargantuan resorts being thrown up on the coast, many of them foreign-owned, you can choose to put your money directly into local hands by staying in smaller, family-run hotels and private accommodation. The same goes for restaurants. Outside the large resorts, they're almost always independently run by local families.

You won't find an organic section in local shops, but much of the local fruit, vegetables and meat would come close to qualifying for this category.

Responsible Travel Organisations

The Podgorica-based Centre for Sustainable Tourism Initiatives (p131) works to develop responsible- and sustainable-tourism products in the country. This nongovernment, nonprofit organisation was founded in 2006 with money from the United States Agency for International Development (USAID) and CHF International. Much of its focus has been in the north of the country, working with small local operators to set up profitable and sustainable businesses which bring employment to the area. Their commercial wing, Montenegro Adventures (p131), organises tours and accommodation.

It's fair to say that some of the tourist businesses run by expats are more likely to fulfil Western expectations of environmental standards. Good examples are Black Mountain (p78) and Kayak Montenegro (p78), both of which have strong eco-credentials.

READING UP

There aren't a huge number of books specifically about Montenegro available in English, although many include the fledgling country in a wider discussion of the region. Rebecca West's *Black Lamb and Grey Falcon* (1941) is one of the classics of travel literature. This wordy but often hilarious travelogue provides wry observations on the peoples and politics of pre-WWII Yugoslavia.

For an interesting and exceptionally detailed dissection of the convoluted history of this land, you can't do better than *Realm of the Black Mountain: A History of Montenegro* by Elizabeth Roberts (2007). It's not light reading. At the other extreme is *Montenegro: A Novel* by Starling Lawrence (1997). It's an entertaining tale of politics, bloodshed and romance set at the dawn of the 20th century; perfect for the plane or the beach.

Life and Death in the Balkans: a Family Saga in a Century of Conflict by Bato Tomašević (2008) does much to illuminate the nation's recent history through a personal account of one family's journey. Marco Houston achieves a similar thing by looking at the travails of a slightly earlier and much grander family in *Nikola and Milena, King and Queen of the Black Mountain: The Rise and Fall of Montenegro's Royal Family* (2003).

On a more practical note, *The Mountains of Montenegro* by Rudolf Abraham (2007) is a good resource for alpine adventurers.

The character of Jay Gatsby in F Scott Fitzgerald's *The Great Gatsby* boasts of a Montenegrin military medal awarded to him by King Nikola.

INTERNET RESOURCES

Destination Montenegro (www.destination-montenegro.com)
Montenegro Smiles (www.montenegrosmiles.com)
Montenegro Times (www.themontenegrotimes.com)
National Tourist Organisation (www.montenegro.travel)
So Montenegro (www.somontenegro.co.uk)
Visit Montenegro (www.visit-montenegro.com)

Itineraries
CLASSIC ROUTES

THE BEST BITS
One Week / Kotor to Budva

Base yourself somewhere in the vicinity of **Kotor** (p84) and spend three days exploring the nooks and crannies of the Bay of Kotor. Take the dazzling drive to **Cetinje** (p123) through **Lovćen National Park** (p122), stopping to visit the **Njegoš Mausoleum** (p122) on the way. Spend the next morning working up an appetite in Cetinje's museums and monastery, before heading to **Rijeka Crnojevića** (p127) for lunch. Lay off the wine though, as you'll need a clear head for the drive to **Ostrog Monastery** (p133) that afternoon. Continue on to **Šćepan Polje** (p143) and book a cabin at one of the rafting camps. Hit the **Tara River** (p143) the next morning, then head back down to **Podgorica** (p129) to celebrate your achievement in the capital's bars. The following morning continue to **Virpazar** (p127) for a chilled-out half-day cruise on **Lake Skadar** (p126). Carry on down to **Sveti Stefan** (p103) and spend your last days chilling out on the beach and exploring the surrounding towns such as **Pržno** (p106) and **Budva** (p96).

Taking in the country's most iconic sights, this 425km trip focuses mainly on the Bay of Kotor and the Adriatic Coast. Montenegro is teensy-weensy, so a short journey clear across the country is suggested, giving you a taste of the mountains and a day's rafting.

THE FULL MONTE
Two to Three Weeks / Herceg Novi to Petrovac

Start off in **Herceg Novi** (p76) and take a boat or kayak trip to **Rose** (p93), **Mamula Island** (p81), the **Blue Grotto** (p93) and possibly the beaches of the **Luštica Peninsula** (p93). Stop at **Morinj** (p81) for a swim and **Risan** (p81) for a gander at the Roman mosaics on your way to **Perast** (p82). Consider staying overnight and don't miss **St George's** (p82) and **Our-Lady-of-the-Rock Islands** (p82). Continue to **Kotor** (p84) and use this as a base to discover **Dobrota** (p83), **Prčanj** (p89) and **Stoliv** (p89). Then follow the previous itinerary through **Lovćen National Park** (p122), **Cetinje** (p123), **Rijeka Crnojevića** (p127), **Ostrog Monastery** (p133) and **Šćepan Polje** (p143) for rafting. Instead of heading straight back to Podgorica, continue on to **Žabljak** (p143) and spend some time exploring **Durmitor National Park** (p142). Follow the road along the Tara River to the isolated **Dobrilovina Monastery** (p144). Keep the nature buzz going with a trip to **Biogradska Gora National Park** (p141) – you can stay in the cabins here or continue on to the upmarket hotels in **Kolašin** (p138). Stop at the **Morača Monastery** (p138) on your way to **Podgorica** (p129), then hang out in the capital for a day. Continue down to **Virpazar** (p127) for a morning's cruise on **Lake Skadar** (p126), then head on to **Murići** (p128). Skirt the Rumija Mountains until the road shies away from the Albanian border and hooks down to **Ulcinj** (p114). Head down to **Velika Plaža** (p118) before continuing back up the coast. Stop to check out **Stari Bar** (p113) and **Haj-Nehaj fortress** (p113) before continuing on to **Sveti Stefan** (p103). Use this as base to explore **Budva** (p96), **Pržno** (p106), **Petrovac** (p107) and the surrounding monasteries.

All of Montenegro's big-hitting beauty spots are covered in this 770km itinerary, which can be accomplished in two weeks or stretched out to a leisurely three. Starting with the amazing Bay of Kotor, you'll then visit all four national parks before hitting the Adriatic beaches.

ROADS LESS TRAVELLED

BREATHTAKING BYWAYS & BACKWATERS

Four Weeks /
Morinj to Buljarica Beach

Wend your way around the wonderful Bay of Kotor road, staying at smaller spots such as **Morinj** (p81), **Perast** (p82), **Prčanj** (p89) or **Krtole** (p92). Continue around the **Luštica Peninsula** (p92), allowing time to get lost amongst the olive groves. Cut through the tunnel towards Kotor and take the glorious back road through **Lovćen National Park** (p122) to **Cetinje** (p123). Check out **Rijeka Crnojevića** (p127), **Danilovgrad** (p133) and **Ostrog Monastery** (p133) on the way to **Nikšić** (p134), then take the dramatic road along the Piva River to **Šćepan Polje** (p143) for a rafting expedition. Cut through on the back road to **Žabljak** (p143) and consider staying in one of the remote mountain huts in **Durmitor National Park** (p142). Another stunning drive will take you along the Tara River to **Dobrilovina Monastery** (p144). Cut down to **Biogradska Gora National Park** (p141), then check out **Mojkovac** (p142) and **Bijelo Polje** (p145) en route to **Rožaje** (p146). Double back slightly and head down to **Plav** (p147), making sure you fit in a quick visit to **Gusinje** (p149). Take the awe-inspiring back road through Andrijevica to **Kolašin** (p138), then call in at the peaceful **Morača Monastery** (p138) before being wowed by the road along the Morača Canyon. Stop off at the obscure ancient ruins of **Žabljak Crnojevića** (p129) before continuing to **Virpazar** (p127). Head along Lake Skadar to **Murići** (p128). Stop at **Lake Šas** (p119) on the way to the coast, where you might find a relatively uncrowded spot on **Velika Plaža** (p118). Check out the enigmatic ruins of **Stari Bar** (p113) and remote **Haj-Nehaj fortress** (p113), then beat the crowds at the uncluttered south end of **Buljarica Beach** (p107).

Here's one for those of you who want to lose yourselves and your fellow travellers in hidden corners. You'll definitely need a car to get to all the tucked-away spots on this 1000km itinerary, but you'll be rewarded with some of Europe's most beautiful drives.

TAILORED TRIPS

CARBON CAUTIOUS

There's only one train route through Montenegro and while it misses some of the iconic sights it does take in a good cross-section of what the country has to offer. **Bar** (p110) is at the end of the line and although it's not the highlight of the coast you can walk to good rugged beaches within half an hour. Get off the train at **Virpazar** (p127) to explore **Lake Skadar National Park** (p126). The museums and bars of **Podgorica** (p129) are in walking distance of the station. The Bjelasica mountain range can be accessed from several stops: you can go skiing if you alight at **Kolašin** (p138); head straight into **Biogradska Gora National Park** (p141) from Štitarička Rijeka; or access walking tracks from **Mojkovac** (p142). From Mojkovac a reasonably flat hike in the other direction will take you to **Dobrilovina Monastery** (p144) on the edge of **Durmitor National Park** (p142). **Bijelo Polje** (p145) has an interesting mix of monasteries and mosques.

It's quite possible to explore the **Bay of Kotor** (p73) by kayak from **Herceg Novi** (p76). If you're really fit and reasonably experienced you could kayak along the entire coast.

The 138km Coastal Mountain Traversal walking route links Herceg Novi with **Murići** (p128) via **Mt Orjen** (p80) and **Lovćen National Park** (p122); spur routes lead to **Kotor** (p84), **Budva** (p96) and Bar.

BEACH YOURSELF

If you plan to spend your holiday as near to horizontal as possible, Montenegro offers plenty of opportunities. For our money, the best beaches are **Pržno** (p93) on the Luštica Peninsula for its clean water and natural beauty, and **Sveti Stefan** (p103) for the iconic views of the fortified island.

For a buzzy Riviera feel, plant yourself amongst the rows of sun umbrellas at **Budva** (p96), **Ulcinj** (p114) or **Herceg Novi** (p76). If you've got the kids in tow, they'll love **Petrovac** (p107) and the other **Pržno** (p106), near Sveti Stefan. For the chance of your own empty patch of sand, try **Velika Plaža** (p118) or **Buljarica Beach** (p107).

Much of Lake Skadar is edged by water lilies, but **Murići** (p128) offers a nice clear swimming spot. You can avoid the underwater foliage of **Lake Plav** (p147) by taking to the deeper waters off the pier. The slow-moving waters of the inner part of the Bay of Kotor are like swimming in a lake. **Morinj** (p81) offers decent swimming from a pretty little beach.

You'll catch people sunbathing on little beaches along the rivers but fewer braving the bracing waters. Still, if you're rafting along the **Tara River** (p143) on a scorching hot day, you might find its pristine appeal hard to resist.

History

For a small and little-known country, Montenegro has a long, convoluted and eventful history. Its rugged terrain and shoreline have witnessed movements of peoples, momentous events and idiosyncratic characters aplenty.

THE ILLYRIANS & THE ROMANS

The Illyrians were the first known people to inhabit the region, arriving during the late Iron Age. By 1000 BC a common Illyrian language and culture had spread across much of the Balkans. Interaction amongst groups was not always friendly – hill forts were the most common form of settlement – but distinctive Illyrian art forms such as amber and bronze jewellery evolved. In time the Illyrians established a loose federation of tribes centred in what is now Macedonia and northern Albania.

The Adriatic Sea is named after the ancient Illyrian tribe Ardeioi.

Maritime Greeks created coastal colonies on the sites of some Illyrian settlements around 400 BC. Thereafter Hellenic culture gradually spread out from Greek centres, particularly from Bouthoe (Budva). The Romans eventually followed. The initial impetus for the Roman incursion came when, in 228 BC, the Greeks asked for Roman protection from an Illyrian, Queen Teuta. The feisty sovereign tempted fate when she murdered two Roman envoys. She fled to Risan, forced from her stronghold by the Romans who determined to stay in the region, attracted by its natural resources.

The Illyrians continued to resist the Romans until 168 BC, when the last Illyrian king, Gentius, was defeated. The Romans capitalised on this entrée to fully absorb the Balkans into their provinces by 100 BC. They established networks of forts, roads and trade routes from the Danube to the Aegean, which further accelerated the process of Romanisation. However, outside the towns Illyrian culture remained dominant.

ROME IN DECLINE

The Romans established the province of Dalmatia, which included what is now Montenegro. The most important Roman town in this region was Doclea, founded around AD 100. Archaeological finds from Doclea (eg jewels and artwork) indicate that it was a hub in a lively and extended trade network.

Even with its extensive trade networks, Rome was in decline by the early 4th century, when Emperor Diocletian split the empire into two administrative halves. Invaders from north and west were encroaching on Roman territory and in 395 the Roman Empire was formally split, the western half retaining Rome as capital and the eastern half, which eventually became the Byzantine Empire, centred on Constantinople. Modern Montenegro lay on the fault line between these two entities.

TIMELINE

300 BC	231–228 BC	AD 100
Illyrian tribes achieve supremacy in the Balkans founding city states (including one at Lake Skadar near the modern Montenegro-Albania border) and establishing themselves as maritime powers in the Adriatic.	Illyrian Queen Teuta establishes her base at Risan and pirates under her command roam the Adriatic, harrying the Romans, among others. Eventually the Romans bring her reign to an end.	Doclea, a settlement established by the Illyrians, grows to become a significant city under Roman rule. It is home to up to 10,000 people.

After the Ostrogoths rolled through the Balkans and took the previously Roman-controlled parts of the region, Emperor Justinian re-established Byzantine control of the Balkans after 537 and brought with him Christianity.

THE SLAVS ARRIVE

Some time earlier a new group, the Slavs, had begun moving south from the broad plains north of the Danube. It is thought that they moved in the wake of a nomadic Central Asian people, the Avars, who were noted for their ferocity. The Avars tangled with the Byzantines, razing Doclea while roaring through the Balkans. They had too much momentum, however, rolling on and besieging the mighty Byzantine capital at Constantinople in 626. The Byzantines duly crushed them and the Avars faded into history.

Controversy remains as to the role the Slavs played in the demise of the Avars. Some claim that Byzantium called on the Slavs to help stave off the Avar onslaught, while others think that the Slavs merely filled the void left when the Avars disappeared. Whatever the case, the Slavs spread rapidly through the Balkans, reaching the Adriatic by the early 7th century.

Two main Slavic groups settled in the Balkans, the Croats along the Adriatic coast and the Serbs around Hercegovina and Doclea, which came to be known as Duklja. Byzantine culture lingered on in the towns of the interior, thus fostering the spread of Christianity amongst the Slavs.

For all their ferocity, the Avars disappeared swiftly from the annals of history. To 'die away like Avars' is a common Balkan saying.

FIRST SLAVIC KINGDOMS

Meanwhile, the Bulgarians created the first Slavic state in the Balkans. By the 9th century, the Bulgarian Prince Boris was advocating that the Slavonic language be used for the church liturgy. The subsequent spread of the Cyrillic script allowed various other Slavic kingdoms to grow as entities separate from Byzantium.

One such polity was the Raška, a group of Serbian tribes that came together near Novi Pazar (in modern Serbia) to shake off Bulgarian control. This kingdom was short-lived, being snuffed out by Bulgarian Tsar Simeon around 927, but not before Raška recognised the Byzantine emperor as sovereign, further speeding the spread of Christianity in the region.

Soon another Serbian state, Duklja, sprang up on the site of the Roman town of Doclea. Under its leader, Vladimir, Duklja swiftly expanded its territory to take in Dubrovnik and what remained of Raška. By 1040, Duklja (under a new princeling, Vojislav) was confident enough to rebel against Byzantine control and expand its territory along the Dalmatian coast and establish a capital at Skadar (modern Shkodra in Albania).

Around 1080, under Bodin, Duklja achieved its greatest extent, absorbing Raška and present-day Bosnia, while simultaneously becoming known as Zeta. This zenith was temporary, however, as civil wars and various intrigues led to its downfall and power shifted back to Raška during the 12th century.

It seems that the Byzantines' first impressions of the Slavs weren't entirely positive. The Byzantine historian John of Ephesus remarked that they were 'rude savages'.

395	614	800s
Theodosius the Great dies. The Roman Empire is divided into two. Present-day Slovenia, Croatia and Bosnia fall into the Western Roman Empire; Serbia, Montenegro and Macedonia go to the Byzantine Empire.	The Avars sack the Roman cities of Salona and Epidaurum. Some contend that Slavic tribes followed in their wake; others say the Slavs were invited into the region by Emperor Heraclius to fend off the Avars.	The first Serbian entity, Raška, arises near modern Novi Pazar. Ruled by a *župan*, it is squeezed between the Byzantine and Bulgarian empires.

THE NEMANJIĆI & THE GOLDEN AGE

Stefan Nemanja, born in Zeta, was to establish the dynasty that saw Serbia reach its greatest territorial extent. After first leading the Serbs to victory over the Byzantines, he was captured and taken to Constantinople. He later formed an alliance with Hungarian King Bela III and by 1190 had regained Raška's independence from Byzantium, also claiming Zeta and present-day Kosovo and Macedonia for his kingdom.

Nemanja later retired as a monk to Mt Athos in Greece, while his sons conquered further territory. After his death Nemanja was canonised by the Orthodox church. Meanwhile, the Fourth Crusade in 1204 had hobbled the Byzantines and Venetian influence began spreading through the Adriatic.

In 1219, Sava, one of Nemanja's sons, made an agreement with a weakened Byzantium that the Serbian church should be autocephalous (self-ruling), and appointed himself its first archbishop. Later, Uroš I made first mention of Serbia as a political entity, declaring himself 'king of all Serbian lands, and the coast'. However, this era was marked by power shifting between the Bulgarians and Byzantines.

Byzantium: The Surprising Life of a Medieval Empire by Judith Herrin is an accessible and engaging account of the empire that controlled the Balkans before the coming of the Slavs.

Around 1331 Dušan, who had earlier distinguished himself fighting the Bulgarians, was proclaimed the 'young king'. He was to prove a towering figure in Serbian history, both physically (he was around 2m tall) and historically. He swiftly confirmed he was in control by chasing the Bulgarians out of Macedonia and capturing territory from the Byzantines. In expanding so rapidly under Dušan, Serbia became an 'empire', its territory doubled taking in Serbs, Albanians, Bulgarians and Greeks. More than just an aggressive campaigner, Dušan also codified the Serbian law (known as the *Zakonik*) and established the Serbian Patriarchate. In linking the Orthodox church with the Serbian royal line, Dušan also created a sense of cohesion amongst previously fractious Serbian tribes.

Nonetheless, throughout this period Zeta, the more forbidding coastal realm that was to become the kernel of the Montenegrin state, remained distinct from Serbia. Zetan nobles displayed a reluctance to submit to the Raškan rulers of Serbia, while the Raškan rulers themselves generally appointed their sons to oversee Zeta, further indicating the separation of the two entities.

When Dušan died in 1355 he was succeeded by his son Uroš who singularly lacked the leadership qualities of his father and was derided as 'the Weak'. Wanting for charisma, Uroš was unable to stem infighting amongst Serbian nobles and saw Greeks, Albanians and Hungary capturing lands that Dušan had brought within the realm.

THE ARRIVAL OF THE TURKS

During Uroš's reign various factions tussled for power and the Balšić family rose to prominence. The Balšići established a base near Skadar and began claiming territory along the Adriatic coast. In the north the Venetians

869	1015	1054
At the behest of Byzantium, Macedonian monks Methodius and Cyril create the Glagolitic alphabet, precursor of the Cyrillic alphabet, specifically with a view to speeding the spread of Christianity among the Slavic peoples.	With the decline of the Bulgarian empire, following the death of Tsar Samuil, Duklja arises as a Serb-controlled principality in the place of the recently departed Raška.	The Great Schism irrevocably splits the churches into (eastern) Orthodox and (western) Catholic realms. Modern-day Montenegro lies on the fault line between the two.

reappeared. By the time Uroš died Serbian barons were busy squabbling amongst themselves, oblivious to a greater threat that was steadily advancing through the Balkans: the Ottoman Turks.

At their first meeting, in 1371, the Turks smashed the Serbs in the battle of Marica. Meanwhile the Balšići were distracted struggling with other noble families, and the Albanians were encroaching. Uroš's successor Lazar Hrebeljanović, a Serbian noble, avoided the entanglement at Marica and began taking the fight to the previously invincible Ottomans. Despite some success, Lazar was distracted by scheming among the Balšići and neighbouring Bosnian nobles. Disaster was in the offing: the Turks were poised to take Serbia.

Of those who survived the Turkish onslaught, the Crnojević family rose to the fore. As the Ottomans continued to expand their territory, they established Skadar as their regional capital, forcing out the Crnojevići. In the early years of the 15th century the Ottoman tide receded temporarily, due to entanglements in Turkey, and the persistent Venetians began encroaching on the Adriatic coast again. Thus ensued another era where different groups tussled for power and parts of Montenegro alternated between Ottoman vassalage and Venetian control, while Stefan Lazarević (Lazar's successor and Turkish vassal in Serbia) also made attempts to claim Zeta. However, by 1441 the Ottomans had fully regained control and had rolled through Serbia. In the late 1470s they lunged at the previously unbowed region of Zeta. At that point Zeta as a political entity came to an end. Ivan Crnojević, the leader of the Crnojevići clan, led a beleaguered group to the easily defendable and inaccessible heights near Mt Lovćen and in 1482 established a court and a monastery at what was to become Cetinje. In so doing he established the future Montenegrin capital.

The Balkans by noted historian Mark Mazower is a readable short introduction to the region. It offers clear and incisive overviews of the cultures and geography of the Balkans in general.

KOSOVO POLJE & AFTER

In 1386 the Ottoman Turks took Lazar's stronghold at Niš, then in 1389 at Kosovo Polje the amassed armies of Lazar and Ottoman Sultan Murat met. This proved to be one of the most pivotal events in Balkan history. Both leaders were killed, and while neither side could conclusively claim victory the Serbian empire was emphatically brought to an end. The Serbian army, the largest resisting force in the Western Balkans, was incapacitated and with greater manpower the Ottomans were free to sally forth and continue their march into central Europe. Lazar's widow accepted Ottoman suzerainty and the battle entered Serbian legend, portrayed as a noble and ultimately hopeless act of Serbian bravery in the face of overwhelming odds.

In the wake of the battle of Kosovo the power of the Balšić family declined and a group of nobles fled to inaccessible and easily defendable territory in Zeta. Some see this as a decisive moment in Montenegrin history. This group (led by the Crnojević family) is seen as the core of modern Montenegro in that they were determined to avenge the battle of Kosovo Polje, unlike Serbia which succumbed to the Ottoman juggernaut.

1166	**1208**	**1331**
Stefan Nemanja establishes the Nemanjić dynasty, a Serbian line which is to reign for over 200 years. He is later recognised as an Orthodox saint.	Sava returns to the Balkans from the Orthodox monasteries at Mt Athos and begins to organise the Serbian Orthodox Church as a distinct ecclesiastical entity.	Allegedly the tallest man alive at the time, Dušan assumes the leadership and raises Serbia to be one of the largest kingdoms in Europe.

Ivan died in 1490 and was succeeded by his son Đurađ. It was during this time that Venetian sailors began calling Mt Lovćen the Monte Negro (meaning 'black mountain'), which lends its name to the modern state. Under Đurađ, Montenegro enjoyed a brief golden age. Đurađ was noted as a lover of books, and aside from being an inspiring military leader he was responsible for establishing the first printing press in the Balkans and overseeing the first publication of printed matter by any of the southern Slavs. Meanwhile, the Ottomans continued assailing Cetinje and succeeded in overrunning it in 1514.

Two hefty scholarly volumes, The Early Medieval Balkans and The Late Medieval Balkans, by John VA Fine cover demographic, political and religious changes in the wider Balkan region from the 6th to the 16th centuries.

OTTOMAN CONTROL OF THE BALKANS

Despite taking Cetinje the Ottomans withdrew. This remote corner was inhospitable and barren; in any case the Turks were more intent on controlling the Adriatic. Under Süleyman the Magnificent, the Turks took Belgrade in 1521, putting beyond doubt their dominance of the Balkans. That one rocky eyrie, Mt Lovćen and environs – later referred to as Old Montenegro – became the last redoubt of Serbian Orthodox culture holding out against the Ottomans.

Indeed, the Montenegrins retained a degree of autonomy. Innately warlike and uncontrollable, their behaviour was such that the Ottomans opted for pragmatism and largely left them to their own devices – the territory was too rugged and people too unruly. The Turks merely collected taxes and allowed the Montenegrins concessions that were not extended to other subjugated peoples.

Miguel de Cervantes, author of Don Quixote, spent five years as a prisoner of Algerian pirates. It is thought that he spent some time imprisoned in Ulcinj.

At the same time, with the Venetians extending their control in the Adriatic, taking Kotor and Budva, the Montenegrins found themselves at the fault line between the Turkish and Venetian empires. In 1571 an alliance of European powers destroyed the Ottoman navy at the battle of Lepanto. This was not a happy outcome for Montenegro, however, as some elements of the Ottoman navy escaped to Ulcinj, where they established a pirate base from which they harassed the rest of the Adriatic coast for several centuries.

Through the 17th century a series of wars in Europe exposed weaknesses in the previously invincible Ottoman war machine. At one stage, the Ottomans determined to remove the concessions which the Montenegrins had long enjoyed and which they now considered rightfully theirs. Montenegrin resistance to the Turkish attempt to enforce a tax regime was violent and the Turkish retribution horrific. As Turkish reactions grew more violent, the bonds between previously unruly Montenegrin clans became stronger.

During the 1690s the Ottomans took Cetinje several times – in 1692 they destroyed the monastery that Ivan Crnojević had built – but each time they were forced to retreat due to persistent harrying from Montenegrin tribesmen. At the conclusion of the Morean War in 1699 the Ottomans sued for peace for the first time ever, ceding territory at Risan and Herceg Novi. The Montenegrins' enthusiastic and effective participation in the

1355	1389	1482
The Balšići come to the fore. Although they assume a position amongst the Serbian nobility, it is likely that the family actually came from a Vlach background.	At the battle of Kosovo Polje the cream of the Serbian nobility is killed by the invading Ottoman Turks. In time the Ottomans regroup and expand further into the Balkans.	After a series of Ottoman attacks against Zeta during the late 1470s, Ivan Crnojević leads the remaining nobility to Cetinje, which will become the kernel of the Montenegrin state.

war had brought them – and their martial virtues – to the attention of the Habsburgs and the Russians while also furthering a sense of common purpose amongst the previously squabbling tribes.

It was then that the Ottomans finally realised they would not be able to control Old Montenegro; nonetheless they were clearly reluctant to give up their claim. To encircle it, they built a string of fort towns that attracted the Muslim population of the region. In the countryside remained the Orthodox tribes and peasants, who developed a sense of solidarity and separateness from the relatively well-off town populations. For the locals, identity was tied to the notion of tribe and the Serbian Orthodox Church, rather than Serbia or Montenegro. Nonetheless, distinct Serbian and Montenegrin identities were evolving: the Serbs were directly ruled by the Ottomans, while the Montenegrins retained a degree of autonomy in their mountain fastness and had managed to avoid being entirely weighed down by the Ottoman 'yoke'.

Božidar Jezernik's *Wild Europe* is a fascinating collage of travellers' impressions of the Balkans over 500 years. Two lively chapters record Western perceptions of Montenegro.

THE VLADIKAS

In 1697 Danilo was elected *vladika*, previously the position of metropolitan within the Orthodox church hierarchy. Danilo, however, had more than ecclesiastical matters on his mind. Ambitious and warlike, he declared himself 'Vladika of Cetinje and Warlord of all the Serb lands'. In so doing, Danilo presumed a role as the leader of the Serbs, perhaps a reflection of Montenegrins dubbing themselves 'the best of the Serbs' during years of battles against the Turks. Beyond this, Danilo succeeded in elevating the role of church leader into that of a hereditary 'prince-bishop' – a political (and military) leader as

---

MONTENEGRO & RUSSIA'S SPECIAL RELATIONSHIP

In the early 18th century a newly assertive Russia, under Peter the Great, was looking to modernise. Peter's agents appeared in the Adriatic and encountered the Montenegrins. As fellow adherents of the Orthodox faith and fellow combatants against the Ottomans, the Russians immediately recognised the fighting abilities of the Montenegrins. Vladika Danilo, realising his small realm needed larger allies, approached the Russian tsar for support in the struggle against the Turks. Travelling to St Petersburg, Danilo established an alliance with Russia that was to prove significant for Montenegro.

Subsequent *vladika*s, upon achieving office, made a point of visiting Russia to cement their relationships with the tsar. Petar II Petrović Njegoš, in 1833, went so far as to travel to St Petersburg to have himself consecrated by Tsar Nicholas I. Several *vladika*s were educated in Russia, primarily as there were virtually no teaching institutions in Montenegro; *vladika*s invariably returned to Montenegro with new ideas to modernise their relatively undeveloped state.

Throughout the Montenegrins' struggle against the Ottomans, Russia provided tactical and financial support, although Montenegrin independence always took a back seat to Russia's wider strategic interests.

1521	**1593–1606**	**1667**
The Ottomans take Belgrade, thereby confirming their control of Serbia. Meanwhile, the Venetians have been expanding along the Adriatic coast for over a century.	During the Austrian-Ottoman wars the pope attempts to incite the Montenegrins, as fellow Christians, to fight against the Ottomans, but with limited success.	A devastating earthquake hits the Adriatic coast, destroying much of Kotor, which is under Venetian control. The city has also recently endured an outbreak of plague.

well. Under the Ottoman imperial administration to which the Montenegrins were nominally beholden such a development was possible, because the *millet* system allowed subject peoples to elect religious but not civil leaders.

Under Danilo's leadership, interactions with the Ottomans remained on the antagonistic course previously set. In 1711 the Ottomans rumbled through Cetinje yet again, but were forced to withdraw. The following year at the battle of Carev Laz a vastly outnumbered Montenegrin force commanded by Danilo engaged and inflicted heavy losses on an Ottoman army. The reputation of the Montenegrins as fearsome fighters was only heightened.

Danilo died in 1735 after declaring that he alone would choose his successor. As his position determined that he must be celibate, he decreed that he would be succeeded by his cousin Sava, another monk. Sava was pensive and indecisive where Danilo had been impetuous and resolute. In 1750 Danilo's nephew Vasilije manoeuvred himself into a position whereby he could gently assume the role of co-*vladika*. Vasilije promptly decamped to St Petersburg to seek further Russian support for the struggle against the Ottomans. While in Russia, Vasilije wrote the first-ever history of the Montenegrins.

In 1766 the Ottomans established the Ecumenical Patriarchate in Constantinople responsible for all of the Orthodox churches in the Ottoman domain, and the Serbs later set up their own patriarchate in Habsburg territory, beyond the reach of Ottoman authorities. These moves effectively led to the creation of separate Montenegrin and Serbian Orthodox churches, and while the Montenegrins retained some sense of community with the Serbs this was another factor in the divergent experience and evolution of separate national consciousness of the Montenegrins.

One of the more bizarre characters in Montenegrin history is Šćepan Mali, who emerged in 1767 claiming to be the Russian Tsar Peter III. In fact, Tsar Peter had been murdered years earlier, but Šćepan hoodwinked the Montenegrins and succeeded in getting himself voted in to lead the *zbor* (council). Despite his dubious claim, Šćepan, also known to be brutal and erratic, had some success in quelling the chronic infighting that bedevilled the Montenegrin tribes, while also creating the first population register, regulating markets and instituting road-building. His luck run out in 1773 when he was murdered by a Montenegrin and Sava was able to retain control.

Sava was succeeded in 1784 by Petar I Petrović who promptly decamped to Russia to curry favour. No sooner had he left than Kara Mahmud, an Ottoman maverick, sacked Cetinje in an attempt to carve out a personal fiefdom in Montenegro and Albania. Petar subsequently took on Kara Mahmud, winning two significant victories despite being at a distinct disadvantage. Petar's final victory over Kara Mahmud resulted in the beheading of the Ottoman renegade and won international recognition of the Montenegrins for their fearlessness in battle. At the same time the Montenegrins were able to expand into the mountains, thus for the first time spreading out of their last redoubt

Petar I was not only a social and ecclesiastical leader; he is also credited with introducing the potato to Montenegro.

1697	1784	1797–1815
Danilo becomes *vladika* (prince-bishop) and establishes the Petrović dynasty. He mediates disputes between tribes and clans and within 15 years begins the fightback against the Ottomans.	Petar I is consecrated as *vladika*, eventually to become the most enduring military and spiritual leader of all the Petrovići. In 1796 he defeats the Ottoman renegade Kara Mahmud and expands Montenegrin territory considerably.	Napoleon brings the Venetian Republic to an end; Venetian dominions are initially given to the Habsburgs, but in 1806 Napoleon gains the Adriatic coast, which he dubs the Illyrian Provinces.

of Old Montenegro. This victory fostered a sense of unity amongst the tribes, and Petar instituted his legal code, the *Zakonik,* and increased the power of his role as *vladika.* Now, while Serbia remained firmly under Ottoman control, the Montenegrins were on the offensive.

NAPOLEON & FOREIGN INTERESTS

Meanwhile, Napoleon appeared in 1797 claiming Venice's Adriatic territories, thus removing Montenegro's main rival for power in the Adriatic. The years to come saw Napoleon tangling with the Montenegrins, British and Austrians in the Adriatic. The Montenegrins operated with military support from the Russians and briefly captured Herceg Novi, a long hoped-for Adriatic coastal town, but in the washup they were forced to abandon it due to diplomatic horse-trading. After the Napoleonic Wars international observers remarked that the Montenegrins were 'born warriors', a reputation only enhanced after the defeat of an Ottoman force at Morača in 1820.

Petar I lived to a ripe old age and was succeeded by his nephew Petar II Petrović Njegoš. Two meters tall, Njegoš fulfilled the requirement that the *vladika* be striking, handsome and dashing, and while not as successful a military leader as his predecessors he abandoned the monk's robes traditionally associated with the role of *vladika* and got about in the regalia of the mountain chief. Njegoš made further unsuccessful attempts to gain access to the sea. In other aspects of nation-building he was more successful. He increased the role of government and developed a system of taxation for Montenegro. He also canonised his predecessor Petar I, thus bringing a saintly aspect to the role of *vladika,* in emulation of the saintly kings of medieval Serbia.

Njegoš made the now traditional trip to St Petersburg in search of military and monetary support from the Russian tsars and set about modernising his nation, which by all accounts was primitive and undeveloped. He introduced the first printed periodical and built the first official residence in Cetinje, replacing the previous earthen-floored home with a 25-room edifice that became known as the Biljarda in honour of the billiard table that it contained.

Succeeding Petrović rulers continued the process of modernisation, albeit gradually. Danilo came to power in 1851 and promptly declared himself prince, thus bringing an end to the ecclesiastical position of *vladika* as leader of the Montenegrins. In 1855 he won a great victory over the Ottomans at Grahovo and he skilfully steered a course between the interests of the Great Powers – Austria-Hungary, Russia, France and Britain – all of whom had designs on Montenegro and the broader Balkan region.

Nikola, who became prince after Danilo, pressed on with a road-building program and introduced the telegraph to Montenegro. He was also responsible for founding a school for girls in Cetinje, the first-ever such institution in Montenegro. During the 1860s Nikola established contact with Mihailo Obrenović, ruler of the Serbian principality (by then de facto independent

Elizabeth Roberts' lively and detailed history of Montenegro, *Realm of the Black Mountain,* is a must for anyone interested in the goings-on of this fascinating country.

1800s	**1830–51**	**1876–78**
Petar I continues courting Russia in the hope of military and financial support in the struggle against the Ottomans. Russia's interest waxes and wanes in the wake of other diplomatic priorities, which continues until WWI.	Njegoš transforms Montenegro into a secular state. He is most famous for his epic poem *The Mountain Wreath,* which resonates as a call to arms for peoples to resist foreign oppression.	Wars of independence across the Balkans see Serbia, Bulgaria and Montenegro win their freedom from the rapidly shrinking Ottoman Empire. Montenegro is eulogised across Europe as a nation of indomitable souls.

A ROMANTIC VIEW OF THE 'PETRIFIED OCEAN'

The Montenegrins' feats during their ultimate defeat of the Ottomans brought them to the attention of Western Europe. Their achievements in the face of perceived Ottoman thuggishness were extolled as the feats of a 'race of heroes' by, amongst others, British Prime Minister Gladstone and in a sonnet by Alfred Lord Tennyson. Diplomats, soldiers and foreign correspondents during the age of romanticism were quick to extol the virtues of the Montenegrins, who had bravely held out for centuries while surrounded by encroaching Turks. The country's history was retold in distinctly rose-coloured shades. The mountainous landscape, too, was rapturously described, one observer depicting it as a 'petrified ocean'.

The Montenegrins themselves took this in their stride, and chimed in calling themselves the freest of all peoples. Foreign observers' romantic accounts of the culture and history of Montenegro were only somewhat mitigated by the Montenegrin warrior habit of removing and displaying the heads of their enemies...

from the Ottoman rule). The two leaders signed an agreement to liberate their peoples and create a single state. Most significantly, Nikola reorganised the Montenegrin army into a modern fighting force.

FREEDOM FROM THE OTTOMANS

A rebellion against Ottoman control broke out in Bosnia and Hercegovina in 1875. Both Serbs and Montenegrins joined the insurgency, Montenegrins (under Nikola) again excelling themselves and making significant territorial gains. In the wake of the struggle for Bosnia, the Congress of Berlin in 1878 saw Montenegro and Serbia achieve independence from the Ottomans. Montenegro won control of upland territories in Nikšić, Podgorica and Žabljak and territory around Lake Skadar and the port of Bar, effectively tripling in size.

The Serbs, meanwhile, were suspicious of Montenegrin intentions and the expansionist Austrians annexed Bosnia and Hercegovina, thus stymying any further Montenegrin expansion to the north. In fact, the Austrians were the main strategic interest in the region at the time, claiming Skadar (Shkodra, in modern Albania) and parts of the Sandžak region of Serbia. The Montenegrins, however, managed to take control of the Ulcinj region of the Adriatic coast, which had a significant Albanian population.

After 1878 Montenegro enjoyed a period of ongoing peace. The process of modernisation continued with the program of road-building and the construction of a railway. Nikola's rule, however, became increasingly autocratic. His most popular move during these years was marrying off several of his daughters to European royalty. In 1910, on his 50th jubilee, he raised himself from the role of prince to king.

In the early years of the 20th century there were increasing calls for union with Serbia and rising political opposition to Nikola's rule. The Serbian King

1910	1918	1920–39
Nikola Petrović anoints himself as king, raising eyebrows across Europe that such a diminutive and impoverished territory, home to only 200,000 souls, could really qualify as a kingdom.	The Kingdom of Serbs, Croats and Slovenes is created after the Serbs, among others, break away from Austria-Hungary. The Serbian Prince Aleksandar Karađorđević assumes the monarchy. Montenegro is included within his domains.	The interwar years are an unhappy time for Montenegro, marked by the dismantling of Montenegrin institutions, squabbles about organisation of the Yugoslav entity and socio-economic stagnation.

Petar Karađorđević in fact made an attempt to overthrow King Nikola and Montenegrin-Serbian relations reached their historical low point.

The Balkan Wars of 1912–13 saw the Montenegrins patching things up with the Serbs to join the Greeks and Bulgarians in an effort to throw the Ottoman Turks out of Europe. During the wars, the Montenegrins gained Bijelo Polje, Berane and Plav and in so doing joined their territory with that of Serbia for the first time in over 500 years. The idea of a Serbian-Montenegrin union gained more currency. In the elections of 1914 many voters opted for union. King Nikola pragmatically supported the idea on the stipulation that both the Serbian and Montenegrin royal houses be retained.

WWI & THE FIRST YUGOSLAVIA

Before the union could be realised WWI intervened. The Serbs, keen to fend off the Austrians, entered the war on the side of the Great Powers and the Montenegrins followed in their footsteps. Austria-Hungary invaded shortly afterwards and swiftly captured Cetinje, sending King Nikola into exile in France. In 1918 the Serbian army reclaimed Montenegro and the French, keen to implement the Serbian-Montenegrin union, refused to allow Nikola to leave France, formally bringing an end to the Petrović dynasty. The same year Montenegro was incorporated in the newly created Kingdom of Serbs, Croats and Slovenes – the first Yugoslavia.

Throughout the 1920s some Montenegrins, peeved at their 'little-brother' to Serbia status, as well as the loss of their sovereignty and distinct identity, put up spirited resistance to the union with Serbia. This resentment increased after the abolition of the Montenegrin church, which was subsumed into the Serbian Orthodox Patriarchate in Belgrade. Taking advantage of fears of a Serb-Croat civil war, on 6 January 1929 King Aleksandar in Belgrade proclaimed a royal dictatorship, abolished political parties and suspended parliamentary government, thus ending any hope of democratic change. In 1934, while on a state visit in Marseilles, King Aleksandar was assassinated by the fascist-inspired Croatian Ustaše.

Meanwhile, during the mid-1920s the Yugoslav Communist Party arose; Josip Broz Tito was to become leader in 1937. The high level of membership of the Communist Party amongst Montenegrins was perhaps a reflection of their displeasure with the status of Montenegro within Yugoslavia.

WWII & THE SECOND YUGOSLAVIA

During WWII Hitler invaded Yugoslavia on multiple fronts. The Italians followed on their coat-tails. After routing the Yugoslav army, Germany and Italy divided the country into a patchwork of areas of control. The Italians controlled Montenegro and parts of neighbouring Dalmatia. Some anti-union Montenegrins collaborated with the Italians in the hope that the Petrović

For a quirky, or perhaps reverent (who can tell) look at Tito visit www .titoville.com. Enjoy pictures of him striking statesman-like poses, scripts from his speeches, lists of his 'wives' and jokes about him.

Eastern Approaches by British diplomat and swashbuckler Fitzroy Maclean includes chapters detailing Maclean's time fighting alongside Tito's Partisans. Breathless, exciting stuff.

1941	1943	1945–48
Hitler invades Yugoslavia and divides it into areas of German and Italian control. Mussolini occupies Montenegro with plans to absorb it as an Italian protectorate.	Tito's communist Partisans achieve military victories and build a popular antifascist front. They reclaim territory from retreating Italian brigades. The British lend military support and the Partisans eventually take control of Yugoslavia.	Founding of the Federal People's Republic of Yugoslavia. In time, Tito breaks with Stalin and steers a careful course between Eastern and Western blocs, including establishing the nonaligned movement.

dynasty would be reinstated. Meanwhile, Tito's Partisans and the Serbian Četniks (royalists) engaged the Italians, sometimes lapsing into fighting each other. The most effective antifascist struggle was conducted by National Liberation Army Partisan units led by Tito. With their roots in the outlawed Yugoslav Communist Party, the Partisans attracted long-suffering Yugoslav intellectuals, groups of Montenegrins and Serbs, and antifascists of all kinds. They gained wide popular support with an early manifesto which, although vague, appeared to envision a postwar Yugoslavia based on a loose federation.

In 1946 the Montenegrin capital was moved from Cetinje to Podgorica and renamed Titograd. (All Yugoslav republics had one town named after Tito, but Montenegro was the only to have the capital so named.) In 1992 Titograd was changed back to Podgorica, which remained the capital.

Although the Allies initially backed the Serbian Četniks, it became apparent that the Partisans were waging a far more focused and determined fight against the Nazis. With the diplomatic and military support of Churchill and other Allied powers, the Partisans controlled much of Yugoslavia by 1943. The Partisans established functioning local governments in the territory they seized, which later eased their transition to power. Hitler made several concerted attempts to kill Tito and wipe out the Partisans, but was unsuccessful. As the tide of the war turned, the Italians surrendered to the Allies and, with the Partisans harassing them, the Germans withdrew. On 20 October 1944 Tito entered Belgrade with the Red Army and was made prime minister.

The communist federation of Yugoslavia was established. Tito was determined to create a state in which no ethnic group dominated the political landscape. Montenegro became one of six republics – along with Macedonia, Serbia, Croatia, Bosnia and Hercegovina, and Slovenia – in a tightly configured union. Tito effected this delicate balance by creating a one-party state and rigorously stamping out all opposition whether nationalist, royalist or religious. He decreed that Montenegro have full republic status. The border of the modern state was set too: Montenegro won Kotor, but lost some areas of Kosovo in the horse-trading that Tito used in order to establish a balance between the various Yugoslav republics.

Montenegrin-born Milovan Đilas was part of Tito's closest circle and considered his successor, only to become one of the most famous dissidents in Europe, spending years in prison and writing a raft of books, including *Land Without Justice* and *Memoirs of a Revolutionary*.

In 1948 Tito fell out with Stalin and broke off contacts with Russia. This caused some consternation in Montenegro given its historical links with Russia. Of all the Yugoslav republics, Montenegro had the highest per capita membership of the Communist Party, and it was highly represented in the army.

During the 1960s, the concentration of power in Belgrade became an increasingly testy issue as it became apparent that money from the more prosperous republics of Slovenia and Croatia was being distributed to the poorer republics of Montenegro and Bosnia and Hercegovina. Unrest reached a crescendo in 1971 when reformers within the Communist Party, intellectuals and students called for greater economic autonomy and constitutional reform to loosen ties within the Yugoslav federation, but nationalistic elements manifested themselves as well. Tito fought back, clamping down on the liberalisation that had previously been gaining momentum in Yugoslavia. The stage was set for the rise of nationalism and the wars of the 1990s, even though Tito's 1974 constitution afforded the republics more autonomy.

1980	1991	1997
Death of President Tito prompts a genuine outpouring of grief. Tributes flow, but Yugoslavia is beset by inflation, unemployment and foreign debt, setting the scene for the difficulties to come.	Yugoslavia splits. As Slovenia, Croatia, Bosnia and Macedonia seek their independence, the question of Montenegrin independence is raised, but a year later Montenegrins vote to remain a Yugoslav republic.	Milo Đukanović wins a further election victory. Relations with Milošević cool. Montenegro adopts a pro-Western stance and distances itself from the Serbian position during the NATO raids in defence of Kosovo in 1999.

Tito left a shaky Yugoslavia upon his death in May 1980. The economy was in a parlous state and a presidency rotating amongst the six republics could not compensate for the loss of his steadying hand at the helm. The authority of the central government sank with the economy, and long-suppressed mistrust among Yugoslavia's ethnic groups resurfaced.

UNION WITH SERBIA, THEN INDEPENDENCE

With the collapse of communism, Slobodan Milošević used the issue of Kosovo to whip up a nationalist storm and ride to power on a wave of Serbian nationalism. The Montenegrins largely supported their Orthodox coreligionists. In 1991 Montenegrin paramilitary groups, in conjunction with the Serb-dominated Yugoslav army, were responsible for the shelling of Dubrovnik and parts of the Dalmatian littoral. These acts appeared to serve no strategic purpose and were roundly criticised in the international press, and in fact were a particular propaganda disaster for Milošević and the Yugoslav army. In 1992, by which point Slovenia, Croatia, Bosnia and Hercegovina and Macedonia had opted for independence, the Montenegrins voted overwhelmingly to remain in the rump Yugoslav state with Serbia. Admittedly there was some Montenegrin edginess about their place within 'Greater Serbia', and Montenegrins raised the issue of the Montenegrin autocephalous church in 1993.

As the war in Bosnia that Milošević had largely instigated wound down with the signing of the Dayton accords in 1995, Milo Đukanović began distancing himself from Milošević. Previously a Milošević ally, Đukanović had been elected Montenegrin prime minister in 1991, but he now realised that Montenegrin living standards were low and discontent was rising. He decided that Montenegro would fare better if it adopted a more pro-Western course. In doing so he became the darling of Western leaders, who were trying to isolate and bring down Milošević. As the Serbian regime became an international pariah, the Montenegrins increasingly moved to re-establish their distinct identity. Relations with Serbia rapidly cooled, with Đukanović winning further elections in Montenegro despite spirited interference from Belgrade.

In 2000 Milošević lost the election and Koštunica came to power in Serbia. With Milošević toppled, Montenegro was pressured to vote for a union of Serbia and Montenegro. In theory the union was based on equality between the two members, but in practice Serbia was such a dominant partner that the union proved unfeasible from the outset. Again, this rankled given the Montenegrins' historic self-opinion as the 'best of the Serbs'. In May 2006 the Montenegrins voted for independence. Since then the divorce of Serbia and Montenegro has proceeded relatively smoothly. Montenegro has rapidly opened up to the West and instituted economic, legal and environmental reforms with a view to becoming a member of the EU. In late 2006 Montenegro was admitted to NATO's Partnership for Peace program and in early 2007 made steps towards EU membership by signing a 'stabilisation and association' agreement.

Misha Glenny's *The Balkans: Nationalism, War & the Great Powers, 1804–1999* explores the history of outside interference in the Balkans; his *The Fall of Yugoslavia* deciphers the complex politics, history and cultural flare-ups that led to the wars of the 1990s.

2002	2006	2007
Yugoslavia expires. With the EU guiding events, it is to be replaced by the union of Serbia and Montenegro. The union is intended to be an equal partnership but it rapidly proves unworkable.	In May, Montenegrins vote in a referendum for independence from Serbia. With a slim majority (55%) voting in the affirmative, Montenegro declares independence in June.	Having the previous year become a member of the UN, Montenegro is admitted to the IMF and, continuing its pro-Western stance, signs a 'stabilisation and association' agreement with the EU.

The Culture

THE NATIONAL PSYCHE

A staple feature of nearly every museum in Montenegro is a display of weapons. These aren't any old guns and swords. Inlaid with mother-of-pearl and set with precious jewels, these are finely crafted objects that have been handled with obvious love and care. The period architecture was solid and perfunctory and the paintings largely devotional, but when it came to making guns, the Montenegrins were happy to indulge in a bit of bling. Men weren't properly dressed without a pair of fancy pistols protruding from their waistbands; one can only imagine what kind of accidental injuries were sustained.

Gunshots can still be heard here but only in celebration. It's the traditional accompaniment to weddings and other festivities, as a flight from Ljubljana to Podgorica discovered when it took an accidental hit during celebrations for Orthodox Christmas Eve in 2008. There were no casualties.

The warrior spirit may traditionally have been at the heart of Montenegrin society but today most people are keen to get on with their lives and put the turbulence of the last two decades behind them. The peaceful split from Serbia was symbolic of that, as were the arrests in August 2008 of four people accused of war crimes during the conflict with Croatia and six on charges relating to Kosovo.

Tied in with the warrior culture is the importance of *čojstvo i junaštvo*, which roughly translates as 'humanity and bravery' – in other words, chivalry. In the past it inspired soldiers to fight to the death rather than abandon their mates to the enemy or face the shame of being captured. While it might not have exactly the same practical application today, don't expect a Montenegrin to back down from a fight, especially if the honour of their loved ones is at stake. Luckily Montenegro doesn't (yet) attract stag-party groups – it doesn't take much to imagine the sort of reception that drunken louts would get if they were stupid enough to be disrespectful to the local women.

A popular self-belief is that Montenegro has a better tolerance of ethnic and religious minorities than many of its neighbours. This is possibly true, although you may still hear some mutterings from locals about the threat of a Greater Serbia/Albania/Croatia. The issue of identity is a thorny one, particularly with regard to Montenegrin-Serb relations. Pro-Serbian graffiti cover the country and while most Montenegrins feel a strong kinship to their closest siblings, this is coupled with a determination to maintain their distinct identity.

At the same time, many young people are focused on the prospect of joining the EU and the opportunities they hope it will present with regard to their pay packets. Montenegro may well lose many of its professionals if that happens, although one suspects that this beautiful country will always draw a good many of them back in time. Much frustration comes from the restrictions on travel that ironically have increased since the fall of communism. Yugoslav citizens didn't even need visas to visit their western neighbours, whereas now a holiday to London or Paris requires a considerable amount of hoop-jumping.

Montenegrin society has traditionally been clannish, with much emphasis placed on extended family groupings. This can create the potential for nepotism; accusations that major employers and public officials favour family, friends or business associates are commonplace. A 2008 survey by the Employers' Union of its members revealed that 86% of respondents

It's said that the first prison in Cetinje didn't need to lock the doors: confiscating the prisoners' pistols was enough to keep them inside as it was considered shameful to walk around unarmed.

believed there was corruption in Montenegro, with the most affected areas being public administration, health care and the judiciary. In October 2008 10 managers of the Port of Bar were arrested on corruption allegations.

However, the main impression of the Montenegrin people that travellers will leave with is that of warm hospitality and a genuine lust for life.

LIFESTYLE

On a warm summer's evening the main street of every town fills up, as they do throughout the Balkans, with a constant parade of tall, beautiful, well-dressed people of all ages, socialising with their friends, checking each other out and simply enjoying life. In summer, life is lived on the streets and in the cafes.

The enduring stereotype of Montenegrins is that they are lazy, an accusation that they themselves sometimes revel in. Certainly the cafes and bars are always full, but perhaps no more so than in the neighbouring countries. As a young Montenegrin recently discussing the topic on an internet forum put it, 'Man is born tired and lives to rest'. This typecasting goes back a long way; Rebecca West in her classic *Black Lamb and Grey Falcon* (1941) heard it from her Serbian travelling companion in the 1930s. Today's visitors may find it surprising, as most Montenegrins you'll meet in hotels and restaurants seem to put in about 10 hours a day, seven days a week. Mind you, many of the same people will find themselves with lots of time on their hands once summer ends.

Family ties are strong and people generally live with their parents until they are married. This makes life particularly difficult for gays and lesbians or anyone wanting a taste of independence. Many young people get a degree of this by travelling to study in a different town.

> The most common graffiti you'll spot in Montenegro is a cross with the letter 'c' in each of its quadrants. This is actually the Cyrillic version of the letter 's' and it stands for *samo sloga Srbina spasava*, meaning 'only unity saves the Serbs'.

ECONOMY

Since independence, Montenegro's economy has been booming. The International Monetary Fund (IMF) estimated economic growth of 7.5% in 2008, making it the fastest growing economy in the Balkans. At the time of research, this was expected to drop back to 5% in 2009; still a healthy result given the problems facing the world economies.

The adoption of the euro along with a conscious alignment towards Europe (while maintaining close ties with Russia) has helped to attract significant foreign investment. A lack of capital gains tax and an income tax rate of 9% for both individuals and companies make it even more attractive. The Central Bank of Montenegro (CBCG) estimated net capital income from abroad to be €914 million in 2008, mainly from Russia, Hungary, Great Britain, Switzerland, Austria and Cyprus.

However, it's not all wine and roses. An inconsistent electricity supply costs business dearly, especially in energy-intensive operations such as KAP (Kombinat Aluminijuma Podgorica), the country's major aluminium producer. The plant and associated bauxite mine accounts for more than 50% of Montenegrin exports, 17.5% of GDP and is the country's largest single employer, but there are fears for its future given its substantial annual losses.

Power and water shortages also affect tourism, yet despite the creaking infrastructure, visitor numbers now reach around 1.2 million annually – almost double the country's resident population. Tourism is one of the country's main industries, along with the production of steel, aluminium, consumer goods and agricultural products.

The annual trade deficit is growing sharply, standing at around €1.2 billion. Exports earn the country €273 million while imports are around five times that. Italy and Switzerland are Montenegro's leading export destinations, while imports come mainly from Serbia, Italy, Greece, Croatia and Slovenia.

For the average citizen, increases in wages haven't kept up with retail prices (according to figures from CBCG), and the affordability of living is decreasing compared to their neighbours. The IMF estimated 2008's inflation rate to be 9.2% in 2008, due in part to the global hike in food and oil prices. At the time of writing, this was expected to drop back to 5.2% in 2009. The average salary in Montenegro was €426 a month in August 2008. The Montenegrin Confederation of Unions estimates the minimum monthly living expenses for a family of four to be €740. Unemployment may be the lowest in the region but it still affects around 12% of the population.

Eighty per cent of Montenegro's poor live in the north of the country. The European Agency for Reconstruction has been involved in supporting potential growth in this region in industries such as agriculture, wood processing, mining, energy and tourism.

According to a study released by the Business Software Alliance in 2008, Montenegro ranks in the top 20 countries in the world for software piracy. It's estimated that 83% of the country's software is bootlegged.

POPULATION

What maketh a Montenegrin? Throughout the Balkans people tend to identify more by ethnicity than citizenship. Hence an Albanian, Bosniak (Slavic Muslim) or Serb is unlikely to call themselves Montenegrin, even if their family has lived in the area that is now Montenegro for generations. This is hardly surprising as a family which has never left its ancestral village may have children born in Montenegro, parents born in Yugoslavia, grandparents born in the Kingdom of Serbs, Croats and Slovenes, and great-grandparents born in the Ottoman or Austro-Hungarian Empires.

In the 2003 census 43% of the population identified as Montenegrin, 32% as Serb, 8% as Bosniak (with a further 4% stating Muslim as their ethnicity), 5% as Albanian, 1% as Croat and 0.4% as Roma. Montenegrins are in the majority along most of the coast and centre of the country, while Albanians dominate in the southeast (around Ulcinj), Bosniaks in the far west (Rožaje and Plav), and Serbs in Herceg Novi and in the north.

To get an idea of the population changes caused by the recent wars you need only look at the changes since the 1981 census, when Montenegrins made up 69% of the population and Serbs only 3%. There are now 10 times more people identifying as Serbs living in Montenegro than before the wars.

Although people have drifted away from the more remote villages, Montenegro isn't particularly urbanised, with more than half of the populace living in communities of less than 10,000 people. Roughly a third of the population live in the three cities that have more than 20,000 people (Podgorica, Nikšić and Pljevlja).

RELIGION

Religion and ethnicity broadly go together in these parts. Over 74% of the population is Orthodox (mainly Montenegrins and Serbs), 18% Muslim (mainly Bosniaks and Albanians) and 4% Roman Catholic (mainly Albanians and Croats). Protestants barely registered (0.06%) and only 12 people in the entire country identified as Jewish in the 2003 census.

In 1993 the Montenegrin Orthodox Church (MOC) was formed, claiming to revive the autocephalous church of Montenegro's *vladika*s (prince-bishops) that was dissolved in 1920 following the formation of the Kingdom of Serbs, Croats and Slovenes (later Yugoslavia) in 1918. Furthermore, they claim that all church property dating prior to 1920, and any churches built with state funds since, should be returned to it. The Serbian Orthodox Church (SOC) doesn't recognise the MOC and neither do the other major Orthodox churches. The SOC still controls most of the country's churches and monasteries. When work commenced on the construction of a new MOC monastery in Nikšić in September 2008, protesters blocked the road and pelted both MOC supporters and police with eggs; 65 were arrested.

Islam is strongest in the east of the country (there are major mosques in Ulcinj, Plav, Gusinje, Rožaje, Bijelo Polje and Pljevlja) and Catholicism in the Bay of Kotor. In the Catholic areas there's a history of cooperation with the Orthodox Church, including the unusual situation of several early churches having an Orthodox and a Catholic altar side by side. The Catholic Church in the Bay of Kotor is still tied to Croatia, while the rest of the country falls under the archdiocese based in Bar.

MEDIA

For a tiny country, Montenegro sure has a lot of news media. Two local daily newspapers are published in Cyrillic and two in the Latin alphabet, while dailies from neighbouring countries are also readily available. While this level of competition coupled with a constitutional guarantee of a free press might be seen to point to a healthy media environment, the situation for Montenegro's editors is troubled. Freedom House, a non-government organisation that's largely funded by the US government, rated Montenegro's press as only 'partly free' in 2008. The country was tied with East Timor and Mongolia at number 81 of the 195 countries rated, placing it behind Croatia but ahead of Serbia, Bosnia and Albania.

In 2004 Duško Jovanović, the editor-in-chief of *Dan* (The Day) newspaper, a critic of both the government and Montenegrin independence, was murdered on the street outside his office. Despite an initial arrest the crime had not been solved at the time of writing.

Amnesty International has been following the case of Željko Ivanović, the director of the only other independent newspaper *Vijesti* (The News), who was badly beaten on the street by three men in September 2007. In an interview he claimed that the attack was politically motivated due to the newspaper's investigation of political corruption and mafia influence. He was subsequently ordered to pay €20,000 to Prime Minister Milo Đukanović after accusing the politician's 'biological or criminal family' of being involved. Đukanović also (unsuccessfully) sued the newspaper's editor-in-chief and publisher. Two men were eventually sentenced for the crime but Ivanović believes that they were paid to confess and weren't the perpetrators, a claim which is allegedly supported by some eyewitnesses.

The government holds a controlling stake in *Pobjeda* (Victory), the third daily newspaper, although they are considering selling some of their shares in the loss-making publication.

Other assaults on journalists noted by Amnesty International include an attack by two masked men armed with baseball bats on Radio Berane editor-in-chief Tufik Softić in 2007, as well as the May 2008 attack on sports journalist Mladen Stojović weeks after he spoke out about mafia involvement in football.

The International Press Institute (IPI) expressed concern that reporters covering protests surrounding the building of an MOC church in Nikšić in September 2008 had their cameras confiscated by the police. In response to the incident the Secretary General of the Vienna-based South East Europe Media Organisation (SEEMO) said: 'It is intolerable that journalists are prevented from performing their professional duties... This incident demonstrates that Montenegrin journalists continue to operate in an often hostile environment'.

'There's a history of cooperation with the Orthodox Church, including the unusual situation of several early churches having an Orthodox and a Catholic altar side by side.'

WOMEN IN MONTENEGRO

Montenegrin society has traditionally been rigidly patriarchal and despite major advances in education and equality for women during the communist years, distinct gender roles remain. If you're invited to a Montenegrin home for dinner, for example, it's likely that women will do all the cooking, serving of the meal and cleaning up, and it's quite possible that an older hostess may not sit down and eat with you but spend her whole time fussing around the kitchen.

These days you'll see plenty of younger women out and about in cafes and bars, although perhaps fewer in the Muslim areas in the east. Literacy and employment levels are relatively equal, and basic rights are enshrined in law including (since 1945) the right to vote.

Women are underrepresented in management roles and make up only 8% of Members of Parliament. However, the constitution includes a guarantee of equality and a commitment to develop an equal-opportunity policy. The government has established a Gender Equality Office and is working with the United Nations Development Programme (UNDP) on a national action plan for gender equality. The country's highest-ranking woman is Gordana Đurović, one of two deputy prime ministers.

Montenegro has been identified as both a transit point and a destination for women trafficked for the purposes of sexual exploitation. In 2008 the country was downgraded by the US State Department to the third tier of a list which divides countries into four categories reflecting their efforts to combat such activities. Montenegro now sits only one rung up from the 14 worst-ranked nations and below all the other countries of the former Yugoslavia.

Women's associations that have formed to assist the victims of trafficking and domestic violence – which the United Nations Development Fund For Women (UNIFEM) believes is widespread – include ANIMA (Association for a Culture of Peace and Non-Violence) based in Kotor. There are now safe houses in Podgorica and Nikšić.

> In his 1848 book 'Dalmatia and Montenegro', Englishman Sir John Gardner Wilkinson noted that Montenegrin men were akin to 'despots' with women as their 'slaves': 'She is the working beast of burden and his substitute in all laborious tasks'.

SPORT

Montenegrins are crazy, bordering on certifiable, about sport. Luckily they are also very good at it, particularly for a country of their size.

Football (soccer) is the national obsession and the country's most famous citizens include Dejan Savićević (Montenegrin Football Federation president and former winner of the European Cup with Red Star Belgrade and AC Milan) and Predrag Mijatović (part of the Champions League–winning Real Madrid team in 1998 and now the club's sports director). Current big-name players include Mirko Vučinić (AS Roma), Stevan Jovetić (ACF Fiorentina) and Simon Vukčević (Sporting Lisbon). At the time of writing the country was beginning its first World Cup qualification campaign (for 2010 FIFA World Cup).

Basketball is also extremely popular and at the time of writing Montenegro was to enter international competition for the first time in 2009. A handful of Montenegrins have made American NBA squads.

Montenegro's first Olympic appearance in Beijing in 2008 didn't net them any medals despite them being the favourites in water polo. The 2008 European Championship–winning Montenegrin team beat its western neighbours Croatia to compete for a medal, only to lose the bronze to its northern neighbours Serbia.

One to watch out for is young swimmer Matija (Matt) Jauković, who has been nudging the world-record time for the 50m butterfly. Unfortunately for Montenegrin Olympic aspirations, he's recently been naturalised as an Australian.

ARTS
Literature
Towering over Montenegrin literature is Petar II Petrović Njegoš (1813–51); towering so much, in fact, that his mausoleum overlooks the country from the top of the black mountain itself (p122). This poet and prince-bishop produced the country's most enduring work of literature, *Gorski vijenac* (The Mountain Wreath; 1847), a verse play romanticising the struggle for freedom from the Ottomans. It's not without controversy as the story glorifies the massacre of Muslims on Orthodox Christmas Eve in 1702, known as the Montenegrin Vespers. It's not certain whether it actually happened, but according to the story Vladika Danilo, Njegoš's great granduncle, ordered the leaders of the Montenegrin tribes to kill all of their kinspeople (men, women and children) who had converted to Islam. Some commentators have drawn a parallel between this story of ethnic cleansing and the atrocities that took place in Bosnia in the 1990s.

Following in the same epic tradition was Avdo Međedović (1875–1953), a peasant from Bijelo Polje who was hailed as the most important *guslar* (singer/composer of epic poetry accompanied by the *gusle,* a one-stringed folk instrument) of his time. If you think that 'Stairway to Heaven' is too long, it's lucky you didn't attend the marathon performance over several days where Međedović is said to have recited a 13,331-line epic.

Danilo Kiš (1935–89) was an acclaimed author of the Yugoslav period who has several novels translated into English, including *Hourglass* (1972) and *A Tomb for Boris Davidovich* (1976). He was born in what is now Serbia but moved to Cetinje with his Montenegrin mother after his Hungarian Jewish father was killed in the Holocaust.

Miodrag Bulatović (1930–91) was known for his black humour and graphic portrayals of dark subjects. His most famous books such as *Hero on a Donkey* (1967), *The Red Rooster Flies Heavenward* (1959) and *The Four-Fingered People* (1975) are available in English.

He may have been born a Bosnian Croat but Ivo Andrić (1892–1975), Yugoslavia's greatest writer, had a home in Herceg Novi. Andrić was awarded the Nobel Prize in 1961 for his brilliant *Bridge over the Drina* (1945). While you're rafting along the Tara River (p143), it's worth remembering that the Tara becomes the Drina just over the Bosnian border.

Montenegrin-born Borislav Pekić (1930–92), who lived in Belgrade and spent years in emigration in London, was another significant name in Yugoslav literature. His huge opus includes novels, dramas, science fiction, film scripts, essays and political memoirs. His work has been translated into a number of languages but at present only the early novels *The Time of Miracles* (1965), *The Houses of Belgrade* (1970) and *How to Quiet a Vampire* (1977) are available in English.

Cinema
In the few years since independence, Montenegrin cinema has yet to set the world alight. Someone that's working hard to change that is Marija Perović, who is credited with being the country's first female film and TV director. She followed up her 2004 debut *Opet pakujemo majmune* (Packing the Monkeys, Again!) with *Gledaj me* (Look at Me) in 2008.

Veljko Bulajić has been directing movies since the 1950s, with his most recent being *Libertas* in 2006. His *Vlak bez voznog reda* (Train Without a Timetable) was nominated for the Golden Palm at Cannes in 1959, while *Rat* (War) was nominated for the Golden Lion at the 1960 Venice Film Festival. Another noteworthy Yugoslav-era director was Živko Nikolić (1941–2001), who directed 24 features from the 1960s to 1990s.

The Montenegrin language lends itself to poetry and it was once commonplace to frame formal language in verse. A British diplomat from the time of King Nikola reported that a government minister once delivered an entire budget in verse.

Montenegro's biggest Hollywood success is cinematographer Bojan Bazeli, whose titles include *King of New York* (1990), *Kalifornia* (1993), *Mr & Mrs Smith* (2005) and *Hairspray* (2007).

Ironically, the movie that springs to most people's minds when they think of Montenegro is the 2006 Bond flick *Casino Royale;* the Montenegrin scenes were actually shot in the Czech Republic. The Golden Palm–nominated *Montenegro* (1981), directed by Serb Dušan Makavejev, was set in Sweden.

Music & Dance

If anyone doubts the relevance of the Eurovision Song Contest they should travel through Montenegro. Montenegrins love their local pop, particularly if it's a gut-wrenching power ballad or a cheesy ditty played loud and accompanied by a thumping techno beat. Popular artists include Sergej Ćetković, Vlado Georgiev and up-and-coming pretty boy Bojan Marović.

In the 1990s the excruciatingly named Monteniggers carried the torch for home-grown hip hop. Continuing on the unfortunate name theme, Rambo Amadeus is Montenegro's answer to Frank Zappa. He's been releasing albums since the late 1980s, flirting with styles as diverse as turbofolk, hip hop and drum and bass.

Jumping back a few years, Archbishop Jovan of Duklja was producing religious chants in the 10th century, making him the earliest known composer in the region. The first reference to secular musical instruments is contained in 12th-century military instructions outlining tactics to create an illusion of greater numbers in battle. Traditional instruments include the flute and the one-stringed *gusle* which is used to accompany epic poetry.

The unusual *oro* is a circle dance accompanied by the singing of the participants as they tease each other and take turns to enter the circle and perform a stylised eagle dance. For a dramatic conclusion, the strapping lads form a two storey circle, standing on each other's shoulders.

> 'The unusual *oro* is a circle dance accompanied by the singing of the participants as they tease each other and take turns to enter the circle.'

Architecture

Traditional Montenegrin houses are sturdy stone structures with small shuttered windows and terracotta-tiled pitched roofs. In the mountainous regions a stone base is topped with a wooden storey and a steeply pitched cut-gable roof designed to let the snow slide off. The *kula* is a blocky tower-like house built for defence that's most common in the country's far eastern reaches. They are usually three to four stories tall with no windows on the lowest floor, and they sometimes have ornate overhanging balconies in wood or stone on the upper level.

The influence of Venice is keenly felt in the walled towns of the coast, which echo the spirit of Dubrovnik and other Dalmatian towns. Cetinje's streets include late-19th-century mansions and palaces remaining from its days as the royal capital.

It's easy to be dismissive of the utilitarian socialist architecture of the Yugoslav period, yet there are some wonderfully inventive structures dating from that time. James Bond would have been quite at home settling in with a martini beneath the sharp angles and bubbly light fixtures of some of the 1970s hotels. It would be a shame if those that haven't already been bowled over or modernised aren't restored to their period-piece glory.

As for the concrete apartment blocks of the cities, they may look grim but they're hardly the slums you'd expect of similar-looking housing projects in the West. While nobody seems to be charged with the upkeep of the exteriors, inside they're generally comfortable and well looked after.

Visual Arts

Montenegro's artistic legacy can be divided into two broad strands: religious iconography and Yugoslav-era painting and sculpture.

The nation's churches are full of wonderful frescoes and painted iconostases (the screen that separates the congregation from the sanctuary in Orthodox churches). A huge number were produced by members of the Dimitrijević-Rafailović clan from Risan in the Bay of Kotor, who turned out 11 painters between the 17th and 19th centuries.

Earlier Serbian masters (predating Montenegro) include Longin, a monk from 16th-century Peć (in present-day Kosovo), whose unique approach to colour created otherworldly scenes of saints and Serbian royalty backed by blue mountains and golden skies. You'll find his work at Piva Monastery (see the boxed text, p136).

Following him half a century later was Đorđe Mitrofanović from Hilandar (now in northern Greece), whose accomplished icons and frescoes feature in the Morača (p138) and Pljevlja (see the boxed text, p145) monasteries. A talented contemporary of his was Kozma, who also worked at Morača and Piva.

Among the modern painters, an early great was Petar Lubarda (1907–74) whose stylised oil paintings included themes from Montenegrin history. Miodrag (Dado) Đurić is now in his seventies but still creates accomplished surrealist musings. Other names to look out for include Milo Milunović, Filip Janković, Jovan Zonjić, Vojo Stanić, Dimitrije Popović and sculptor Risto Stijović. The best places to see the works of these and others are at Cetinje's Art Museum (p123) and the Podgorica Museum & Gallery (p131).

Of the contemporary crop, one to watch is Jelena Tomašević, whose paintings and video installations have been exhibited in New York, Berlin and Venice.

Northern Montenegro and other parts of the Western Balkans are a treasure trove of carved medieval tombstones known as *stećci*. These mysterious monuments often bear ornaments and philosophical inscriptions. Their origins and symbolism continue to puzzle archaeologists.

Food & Drink

Loosen your belt, you're in for a treat. Eating in Montenegro is generally an extremely pleasurable experience. By default, most of the food is local, fresh and organic, and hence very seasonal.

The food on the coast, especially around the Bay of Kotor, is virtually indistinguishable from Dalmatian cuisine: lots of grilled seafood, garlic, olive oil and Italian dishes. Inland it's much more meaty and Serbian-influenced.

The only downside is the lack of variety. Restaurants tend to come in three types: traditional (serving the aforementioned fish or meat grills), pizza and pasta joints, or a mixture of the two. By the time you've been here a week, menu déjà vu is likely to have set in.

STAPLES & SPECIALITIES

The village of Njeguši in the Montenegrin heartland is famous for its *pršut* (smoke-dried ham) and *sir* (cheese). Anything with 'Njeguški' in its name is going to be a true Montenegrin dish and stuffed with these two goodies; this might be pork chops, veal, steak or spit-roasted meat *(Njeguški ražanj)*.

In 1951, when acclaimed Croatian sculptor Ivan Meštrović was given the commission to create the models for the magnificent statues in the Njegoš Mausoleum on the top of Mt Lovćen (p122), it's said that all he asked for by way of payment was cheese and *pršut* from Njeguši.

In the mountains, meat roasted *ispod sača* (under a metal lid covered with hot coals) comes out deliciously tender. Lamb may also be slowly poached in milk with spices and potato *(brav u mljeku)*. Beef is cooked with cabbage-like *raštan*, rice and pepper to make a rich stew called *japraci*. You might eat it with *cicvara* (a cheesy, creamy cornmeal or buckwheat dish) or *kačamak* (similar but with potato) – they're heavy going, for sure, but comforting on those long winter nights. The best honey is also produced in the mountains.

On the coast, be sure to try the fish soup *(riblja čorba)*, a delicious clear broth usually including rice. Grilled squid *(lignje na žaru)* is always an excellent choice, the crispy tentacles coated in garlic and olive oil or stuffed with *pršut* and *sir*. Nearly 400 years of Venetian rule in parts of the coast has left a legacy of excellent risotto and pasta dishes. Black risotto *(crni rižoto)* gets its rich colour and subtle flavour from squid ink and includes pieces of squid meat. Seafood risotto can also be white or red (with a tomato-based sauce) and served hot or cold.

While all of these dishes make filling mains in themselves, at a formal dinner they're just a precursor to the grilled fish. In most fish restaurants, whole fish *(riba)* are often presented to the table for you to choose from and sold by the kilogram according to a quality-based category. Local varieties tend to be small but tasty; the bigger ones are probably fresh but imported. Eel is a speciality, particularly on Lake Skadar. Fish dishes are flavoured with wild herbs such as laurel and parsley as well as lemon and garlic.

Various types of grilled meat are common throughout the former Yugoslavia, including *ćevapčići* (pieces of minced meat shaped into small skinless sausages), *pljeskavica* (spicy hamburger patties) and *ražnjići* (pork or veal kebabs). Grills are often served with fried chips and salad.

For dishes that have more than just meat (although they're by no means vegetarian-friendly) try *musaka* (layers of aubergine, potato and minced meat), *sarma* (minced meat and rice rolled in sour-cabbage leaves), *kapama* (stewed lamb, onions and spinach with yogurt) and *punjene tikvice* or *paprike* (courgettes or capsicum stuffed with minced meat and rice). Other dishes from the region that have crept onto Montenegrin menus include spicy Hungarian goulash *(gulaš)* and Turkish kebabs *(kebap)*.

TASTY TRAVEL

Nothing in Montenegro is particularly challenging to the Western palate, although some dishes may be challenging the arteries. Here are some of the more unusual items:

- **cheese in oil** – a bit like a firmer fetta
- **cheese in wheat** – the love child of parmesan and cheddar
- **cicvara and kačamak** – cheesy, creamy cornmeal porridge
- **kajmak** – somewhat sour, creamy cottage cheese, traditionally set in animal skin
- **popara** – a mixture of bread, milk, cheese and oil served for breakfast
- **pršut** – thinly sliced dried ham similar to Italian *prosciutto*
- **rakija** – lighter fluid in the guise of fruit brandy
- **raštan** – a slightly bitter, dark green vegetable from the cabbage family
- **slane palačinke** – a heart attack disguised as a crumbed, deep-fried, cheese-filled pancake

---

Breakfast usually consists of fresh bread with slices of cheese and cured meat (salami or *pršut*) or perhaps a sweet pastry. Locals often skip breakfast and grab something like a *burek* (see p47) on their way to work. Omelette *(omlet)* is the most common cooked breakfast, although some places will offer variations on a Full English (sausages, eggs and possibly ham). Toast is fairly uncommon.

Lunch, served mid-afternoon, has traditionally been the main family meal, but with Western working hours catching on, this is changing. A family lunch might consist of a soup followed by a salad and a cooked meat or fish dish of some description. Dinner would then be lighter, possibly just bread with cured meats, cheese and olives. However, if you're heading out for a proper sit-down evening meal, you'll probably start late (after 8pm) and eat a similar meal to the typical lunch.

Fresh seasonal fruit is the usual closer to a meal. The most typical Montenegrin sweet dish is *priganice* (fritters) served with honey, cheese and jam. Incredibly sweet cakes and tortes are offered with coffee, including delicious *baklava* (a Turkish slice made of chopped nuts and raisins layered between filo pastry and soaked in honey). The local ice cream *(sladoled)* is also excellent.

DRINKS

Montenegro's domestic wine is eminently drinkable and usually the cheapest thing on the menu. *Vranac* is the indigenous red grape, producing excellent, full-bodied wines. It's traditionally aged in walnut rather than oak barrels and its history goes back an extremely long way. Illyrian Queen Teuta is said to have been particularly fond of the drop and encouraged its production in the 3rd century BC. Locally produced whites include the native *krstač*, chardonnay and sauvignon blanc.

Nikšićko Pivo (try saying that after a few) is the local beer and a good thirst quencher. It comes in light and dark varieties.

Many people distil their own *rakija* (brandy), which is considered a cure for all ills, including stomach ache, poor digestion, coughs and colds, cleansing wombs or just for starting the day with a bang (it ranges from 40% to 60% alcohol). It's offered as a sign of hospitality, so you're likely to be given a shot if you're visiting or staying in a private home and sometimes even on bus tours. The purpose of this isn't solely to watch the tourists' eyes glaze over, although we suspect that's part of the fun. The most common variety in

In the late 19th century, patients in Cetinje hospital were prescribed a glass of wine per day as a tonic.

Montenegro is *loza*, made out of grapes, but it can be made from just about anything: pears *(kruškovača)*, apples *(jabukovača)*, walnuts *(orahovača)* etc. They're all pretty close to rocket fuel but the plum variety *(šljivovica)* seems the most lethal. The highest-grade *rakija* is called *prvijenac*. *Pelinkovac* is a bitter-sweet herbal aperitif that tastes like medicine with a kick – a bit like Jägermeister.

The coffee *(kafa)* is universally excellent. In private houses it's generally boiled up Turkish-style, 'black as hell, strong as death and sweet as love'. At cafes, espresso is the norm and it comes short *(mala)* or long *(velika)* and with or without milk *(mlijeko)*. A large coffee with milk is called a German *(Njemačka)* coffee. Don't expect an inch of overfrothed milk on a cappuccino – they usually come silky and smooth like an antipodean flat white.

The wild herbs that abound in the mountains are made into a profusion of herbal teas, including peppermint, chamomile, thyme, primrose and nettle. If you want anything other than herbal teas, ask for Indian tea. Asking for a white tea will confuse matters completely, so request a small jug of milk to go with it. It's easiest not to ask for a cup of tea if you're visiting someone's house as it's likely to send your hosts into quite a flap.

Keep an eye out for interesting fruit juices, especially *šipak* made from wild pomegranate.

People here take their *rakija* seriously. A waiter in a Kotor tavern was sentenced to seven months in jail for watering down the national spirit.

CELEBRATIONS

It doesn't take much of an excuse to get the *rakija* flowing. It's an integral part of weddings, funerals and just about everything. Food also plays a big part in all community events.

In the lead-up to Orthodox Christmas it's common to fast or abstain from meat and dairy products. On Christmas Day a special round bread *(česnica)* with a coin hidden in it is broken by hand and shared amongst the household. Whoever finds the coin can look forward to a lucky year ahead. Christmas feasts often include roast pork.

Another type of bread called *slavski kolač* is prepared to celebrate a Serbian Orthodox family's patron saint's day, along with *žito,* a sweet made from honey, walnuts and boiled wheat. At Easter, eggs are dyed and elaborately painted.

WHERE TO EAT & DRINK

The country abounds with eating options, so you won't go hungry – unless you want to eat anything that doesn't have meat as the main ingredient. Meat in pastry, meat with potatoes, meat on its own, vegetables stuffed with meat, meat stuffed with meat – the list goes on.

Any place that attracts tourists will have a selection of restaurants and *konoba*s (small family-run eateries). Most hotels will have a decent restaurant and many offer full- or half-board options. In less tourist-frequented towns such as Nikšić, Mojkovac and Plav, proper restaurants are rare but fast food is easy to find. There's usually no distinction between a cafe and a bar, except in the Muslim areas where some cafes may not sell alcohol. Cafes don't usually serve food apart from cakes and sometimes ice cream. Restaurants open at around 8am and close around midnight, while cafe-bars may stay open until 2am or 3am. Bookings are only required at the swankiest places.

Silver service is standard at the nicer fish restaurants. If you order a whole fish by the kilogram, the waiters (they're usually men at such places) will make quite a show of slicing it up in front of you and arranging it on the plate. Generally it will be served with a complementary vegetable dish such as the delicious combination of silverbeet *(blitva)*, mushy potato, olive oil and garlic.

MONTENEGRO'S TOP CULINARY SPOTS

Combining wonderful food with atmospheric waterside settings, the following restaurants are our pick of the bunch. Some of them are a little pricier than the average, but with restrained ordering (fish soup with complementary bread is always great value) they're enjoyable at any budget.

- **Konoba Ćatovića Mlini** (p81) Combines seafood dishes with Njeguši treats in an old mill by a bubbling stream.
- **Restoran Stari Mlini** (p84) The name actually means Old Mill, so expect a similarly gurgling stream and more emphasis on Dalmatian dishes.
- **Riblja Čorba** (p118) You could fish from your table in this wooden construction jutting over the Bojana River, but fortunately someone else has already gone to the trouble.
- **Ristorante Tramontana** (p89) Sublime Italian food served on a terrace overlooking the Bay of Kotor.
- **Stari Most** (p127) A tranquil riverside location and a well-focused seafood menu make this a candidate for Montenegro's best restaurant.

Tipping isn't expected but it's customary to round up the bill to the nearest euro or to leave some coins. Service is usually pleasant but can be incredibly frustrating, especially when it comes time to leave. For every week in Montenegro expect to spend about eight hours waiting to pay the bill. Once it's finally delivered to your table don't let the waiter disappear again or you'll be waiting for another 15 minutes for them to take your money. By this stage any desire to leave a big tip will probably have dissipated.

Quick Eats

The cheapest and most ubiquitous Balkan snack is *burek,* a filo-pastry pie made with *sir* (cheese), *meso* (meat), *krompir* (potato) or occasionally *pečurke* (mushrooms), most commonly consumed with yogurt. Savoury or sweet *palačinke* (pancakes) are served from kiosks in busy areas. Toppings include chopped walnuts and almonds, jam and banana. For a major artery clog, go for a *slane* (salty) *palačinke* – pancakes stuffed with ham and cheese, then crumbed, deep-fried and served with lashings of yogurt, tomato sauce and mayonnaise. Yes, it really is as disgustingly unhealthy as it sounds.

Fast-food outlets and *pekaras* (bakeries) serving *burek, ćevapčići,* pizza slices and *palačinke* are easy to find, especially around bus and train stations. The standards of hygiene are generally good and the prices very reasonable.

VEGETARIANS & VEGANS

Eating in Montenegro can be a trial for vegetarians and almost impossible for vegans. Pasta, pizza and salad are the best fallback options. Many menus have bread *(hljeb),* olives *(masline)* and cheese as starters, so you can usually tailor your own antipasto platter. Beware of ordering stuffed vegetables as they're likely to be stuffed with meat.

Standard salads include the *srpska salata* (Serbian salad) of raw peppers, onions and tomatoes, seasoned with oil, vinegar and maybe chilli, and *šopska salata,* consisting of chopped tomatoes, cucumber and onion, topped with grated soft white cheese. Also look for *zeljanica* (cheese pie with spinach), *sirnica* (cheese and egg pie), *krompiruša* (potato and onion pie) or *pasulj prebranac* (spiced beans). Unfortunately these traditional dishes are more often cooked at home than in restaurants – when the locals head out for a special dinner they expect meat.

Montenegro is a McDonalds-free zone. You won't find a single set of golden arches in the entire country. The same goes for KFC, Burger King, Starbucks and all the other icons of American take-away hegemony.

There isn't a lot of comprehension about vegetarianism in these parts, so expect to get a few confused or incredulous looks. In this book we've used the Ⓥ symbol in reviews for restaurants with at least a couple of vegetarian options. At the time of research there were no strictly vegetarian restaurants in the country.

EATING WITH KIDS

Children are warmly welcomed almost everywhere in Montenegro. On the long summer evenings you'll see lots of kids with their parents in restaurants, beachside cafes and sometimes even in bars and open-air nightclubs. You may not find children's menus or highchairs, but with plenty of pasta and pizza on the menu there shouldn't be a problem finding something to fill them up. It may be a challenge to find a table away from people smoking. For more information on visiting Montenegro with children, see p155.

HABITS & CUSTOMS

Eating in Montenegro is a slow, social affair and many dishes are large enough to be shared. However, you won't get strange looks if you're eating alone. Table manners and cutlery aren't markedly different from those in the West, although it's perfectly acceptable to use your hands to pick the bones out of small fish. Smoking at the table is common and it wouldn't occur to locals that this might be offensive to some people.

Table settings usually include bottles of vegetable oil and red-wine vinegar. Better establishments will also offer olive oil and balsamic vinegar. The local olive oil is delicious and a great accompaniment to the bread that's served free of charge with most meals. In some places, especially around Lake Skadar and the Bojana River, a scone-like corn damper is offered.

Wine is a part of life here and served with most meals. There seems little point in ordering expensive imported bottles when the domestic produce works so well with the cuisine – and it's cheap! Mixing wine with water is very common and you may even come across more disturbing combinations such as red wine with coke. Red wine is often served chilled in summer.

If you're lucky enough to be invited to someone's house for dinner, it's best to do so on an empty stomach. Force-feeding guests is a regional hobby and you're likely to be greeted with a chorus of 'eat, eat' from your hosts if you look like you're finishing. A good trick is to eat slowly, as there's always another course around the corner when you least expect it.

If you're invited to someone's house for dinner, it's considered good manners to bring a small gift for the hostess, such as flowers – but keep in mind that an even number of stems is bad luck.

EAT YOUR WORDS

As any student of French will know, restaurants are a good place to practise or show off your language skills. For those less linguistically blessed, this section will help if you get caught out by a menu without English translations. Refer to the Language chapter (p176) for further tips on pronunciation.

Useful phrases

I'm hungry.
Ja sam gladan/gladna. (m/f)   ya sam *gla*·dan/*glad*·na
I'm a vegetarian.
Ja sam vegetarijanac/vegetarijanka. (m/f)   ya sam ve·ge·ta·ri·*ya*·nats/ve·ge·ta·*ri*·yan·ka
I don't eat meat (or fish).
Ne jedem meso (ili ribu).   ne *ye*·dem *me*·so (*ee*·lee *ri*·bu)
I'm allergic to (nuts).
Alergičan/Alergična sam na (orahe). (m/f)   a·*ler*·gi·chan/a·*ler*·gich·na sam na (*o*·ra·he)
Waiter!
Konobar!   *ko*·no·bar

What's the speciality of the house?
Šta je specijalitet kuće?   shta ye spe·tsi·ya·*li*·tet *ku*·che
What would you recommend?
Šta biste preporučili?   shta *bi*·ste pre·po·*ru*·chi·li
Please bring the menu/bill.
Molim vas donesite jelovnik/račun.   *mo*·lim vas do·*ne*·si·te ye·lov·nik/*ra*·chun
Enjoy your meal!
Prijatno!   *pri*·yat·no

Food Glossary
BASICS

biber	*bi*·ber	pepper
čaša	*cha*·sha	glass
čokolada	cho·ko·*la*·da	chocolate
doručak	*do*·ru·chak	breakfast
džem	jem	jam
hljeb	hlyeb	bread
jaja	*ya*·ya	eggs
jelovnik	ye·lov·nik	menu
kašika	*ka*·shi·ka	spoon
konoba	*ko*·no·ba	small, usually family-run restaurant
margarin	mar·*ga*·rin	margarine
marmelada	mar·me·*la*·da	marmalade
med	med	honey
nož	nozh	knife
pekara	*pe*·ka·ra	bakery
pirinač	*pi*·ri·nach	rice
puter	*pu*·ter	butter
račun	*ra*·chun	bill/cheque
restoran	re·*sto*·ran	restaurant
ručak	*ru*·chak	lunch
šećer	*she*·cher	sugar
sir	sir	cheese
so	so	salt
tanjir	*ta*·nyir	plate
užina	*u*·zhi·na	snack
večera	*ve*·che·ra	dinner
viljuška	*vi*·lyush·ka	fork

DRINKS

čaj	chai	tea
crna kafa	*tsr*·na *ka*·fa	black coffee
crno/bijelo vino	*tsr*·no/*bye*·lo *vi*·no	red/white wine
jabukovača	*ya*·bu·ko·va·cha	apple brandy
jardum	*yar*·dum	slightly salted sheep's milk, drunk cold
jogurt	*yo*·gurt	yogurt
kafa sa mljekom	*ka*·fa sa *mlye*·kom	coffee with milk
krstač	*krs*·tach	white-wine variety
kruškovača	*krush*·ko·va·cha	pear brandy
loza	*lo*·za	grape brandy
mineralna voda	*mi*·ne·ral·na *vo*·da	mineral water
mljeko	*mlye*·ko	milk
Njemačka kafa	*nye*·mach·ka *ka*·fa	long white coffee
orahovača	*o*·ra·ho·va·cha	walnut brandy
pelinkovac	pe·*lin*·ko·vats	herbal liqueur

piće	*pi*·che	drink
pivo	*pi*·vo	beer
prvijenac	*pr*·vi·ye·nats	highest-grade brandy
rakija	*ra*·ki·ya	brandy
šljivovica	*shlyi*·vo·vi·tsa	plum brandy
topla čokolada	*top*·la cho·ko·*la*·da	hot chocolate
vinjak	*vi*·nyak	cognac
voćni sok	*voch*·ni sok	fruit juice
voda	*vo*·da	water
vranac	*vra*·nats	red-wine variety

FISH & MEAT

bakalar	ba·*ka*·lar	cod
ćuretina	*chu*·re·ti·na	turkey
dagnje	*dag*·nye	mussels
govedina	*go*·ve·di·na	beef
jagnjetina	*yag*·nye·ti·na	lamb
jastog	*ya*·stog	lobster
kobasica	ko·*ba*·si·tsa	sausage
lignje	*lig*·nye	squid
losos	*lo*·sos	salmon
meso	*me*·so	meat
oslić	*o*·slich	hake
pastrmka	*pas*·trm·ka	trout
piletina	*pi*·le·ti·na	chicken
računi	*ra*·chi·chi	crabs
riba	*ri*·ba	fish
šaran	*sha*·ran	carp
škampi	*shkam*·pi	prawns
školjke	*shkoly*·ke	oysters
šunka	*shun*·ka	ham
svinjetina	*svi*·nye·ti·na	pork
teletina	*te*·le·ti·na	veal

VEGETABLES & FRUIT

banana	ba·*na*·na	banana
bijeli luk	*bye*·li luk	garlic
blitva	*blit*·va	silverbeet
boranija	bo·*ra*·ni·ya	green beans
breskva	*bres*·kva	peach
crni luk	*tsr*·ni luk	onion
cvekla	*tsve*·kla	beetroot
dinja	*di*·nya	melon
grašak	*gra*·shak	peas
grožđe	*grozh*·je	grapes
jabuka	*ya*·bu·ka	apple
jagoda	*ya*·go·da	strawberry
kajsija	*kai*·si·ya	apricot
karfiol	*kar*·fi·ol	cauliflower
krastavac	*kra*·sta·vats	cucumber
krompir	*krom*·pir	potato
kruška	*kru*·shka	pear
kupus	*ku*·pus	cabbage
limun	*li*·mun	lemon
ljute papričice	*lyu*·te pap·ri·*chi*·tse	chillies

lubenica	lu·*be*·ni·tsa	watermelon
masline	*mas*·li·ne	olives
nar	nar	pomegranate
paprika	pa·pri·ka	capsicum
paradajz	pa·ra·*daiz*	tomato
pasulj	pa·suly	kidney beans
pečurke	pe·chur·ke	mushrooms
plavi patlidžan	*pla*·vi pat·*li*·jan	eggplant
pomorandža	po·*mo*·ran·ja	orange
povrće	po·vr·che	vegetables
raštan	*rash*·tan	cabbage-like vegetable
šargarepa	shar·ga·re·pa	carrot
šljiva	*shlyi*·va	plum
smokva	*smok*·va	fig
spanać	spa·nach	spinach
tikvice	*tik*·vi·tse	courgettes
višnja	*vish*·nya	cherry
voće	*vo*·che	chefruit
zelena salata	ze·le·na sa·*la*·ta	lettuce

Menu Decoder
STARTERS

ajvar	*ai*·var	a spicy mixture of fried peppers and eggplant, chopped and seasoned with garlic, salt, vinegar and oil
burek	*bu*·rek	a flaky pastry with layers of cheese, spinach or minced meat
cicvara	*tsits*·va·ra	porridge-like mix of cream, cheese and buckwheat or cornflour
gibanica	*gi*·ba·ni·tsa	a dish made of layers of filo pastry filled with eggs and white cheese and baked in the oven
kačamak	ka·*cha*·mak	porridge-like mix of cream, cheese, potato and buckwheat or cornflour
kajmak	*kai*·mak	a kind of soft cheese made out of the salted cream from boiled milk
kulen	*ku*·len	paprika-flavoured sausage served with cottage cheese, peppers, tomatoes and pickled vegetables
miješana salata	mi·ye·sha·na sa·*la*·ta	mixed salad
pihtije	*pih*·ti·ye	jellied pork with garlic
pogačice sa čvarcima	*po*·ga·chi·tse sa *chvar*·tsi·ma	similar to scones, containing pieces of fried pork fat
popara	*po*·pa·ra	a mixture of bread, milk, cheese and oil
pršut	*pr*·shut	smoked dried ham
salata od hobotnice	sa·*la*·ta od ho·bot·ni·tse	octopus salad
slane palačinke	*sla*·ne pa·la·*chin*·ke	a crumbed, deep-fried, cheese-filled pancake
turšija	*tur*·shi·ya	pickled vegetables
ukljeve	*uk*·lye·ve	small fish eaten fried or smoked

MAIN DISHES

brav u mljeku	brav u *mlye*·ku	lamb poached in milk with spices and potato
ćevapčići	che·*vap*·chi·chi	minced pork, beef or lamb shaped into small sausages then grilled
crni rižoto	*tsr*·ni *ri*·zho·to	squid risotto coloured black by squid ink
đuveč	*ju*·vech	stew of carrots, potatoes, tomatoes, peppers, onions, rice and meat topped with grated cheese
gulaš	*gu*·lash	goulash
jagnjetina ispod sača	*yag*·nye·ti·na *is*·pod *sa*·cha	lamb meat cooked under a metal lid covered with hot coals (often with potatoes)

japraci	*ya·pra·tsi*	rich beef stew with *raštan,* rice and pepper
kapama	*ka·pa·ma*	stewed lamb, onions and spinach with yogurt
kebap	*ke·bap*	kebab
lignje na žaru	*lig·nye na zha·ru*	grilled squid
musaka	*mu·sa·ka*	layers of aubergine, potato and minced meat
Njeguški ražanj	*nye·gush·ki ra·zhany*	spit-roasted meat stuffed with cheese and dried ham
omlet	*om·let*	omelette
pljeskavica	*plye·ska·vi·tsa*	spicy hamburger patty
prženi krompir	*pr·zhe·ni krom·pir*	roast potatoes
punjene paprike/ tikvice	*pu·nye·ne pap·ri·ke/ tik·vi·tse*	capsicums/courgettes stuffed with minced beef or pork and rice in a fresh tomato sauce
raštan	*rash·tan*	dark green cabbage cooked with smoked ribs
ražnjići	*razh·nyi·chi*	small cubes of pork or veal grilled on a skewer
riblja čorba	*rib·lya chor·ba*	fish soup
riblji paprikaš	*rib·lyi pap·ri·kash*	fish stew with paprika
sarma	*sar·ma*	cabbage leaves stuffed with ground meat and rice

DESSERTS

baklava	*ba·kla·va*	a flaky pastry with nuts, soaked in sugar syrup
palačinke	*pa·la·chin·ke*	pancakes
priganice	*pri·ga·ni·tse*	fritters served with honey, cheese or jam
sladoled	*sla·do·led*	ice cream
štrudla sa jabukama/ višnjama/ orasima	*shtrud·la sa ya·bu·ka·ma/ vish·nya·ma/ o·ra·si·ma*	a blend of pastry and fruit with apples/cherries/nuts
torta	*tor·ta*	cake

LANDSCAPE & LIFESTYLE

When you're this little it's easy to be overlooked, so Montenegro over-compensates by being crammed full of extraordinary sights. The coastline is so beautiful that even the mountains can't resist dipping their toes in the clear waters. They push up behind each other, filling most of the land, with only a scattering of sparkling lakes to give them breathing space. The local people, far from being cowed by the exuberant landscape, match it stroke for stroke – filling the country's innumerable street cafes with passionate conversation and Balkan bravado.

Beaches, Bays & Lakeside

Lord Byron described this coastline as 'the most beautiful encounter between the land and the sea'. Wherever you choose to splash about in the crystalline waters, chances are there will be a mountainous backdrop proving the great Romantic poet right. The ancient settlements hugging the shoreline only add to the enchantment.

❶ Kotor by Night
In the evening the fortifications arching high up on the cliffs behind Kotor are spectacularly illuminated, forming a halo from their reflections in the still, dark waters of the bay (p84).

❷ Sveti Stefan
A picture-perfect island village anchored to the coast by the narrowest of causeways, Sveti Stefan has survived its transformation into a luxury resort with all of its historic charm intact (p103).

❸ Ulcinj
Ulcinj's buzzy Mala Plaža (Small Beach) is framed by a skyline where minarets compete with oversized socialist sculpture and the imposing walls of an ancient town (p114).

❹ Kayaking in the Bay of Kotor
Exploring the Boka Kotorska (Bay of Kotor) by paddle power gives you access to all the secluded beaches, waterside villages and tiny islands within the surreal fjordlike walls of the bay (p78).

❺ Birdwatching
Lake Skadar is one of the most important wetland habitats in Europe and home to hundreds of species. The star of the show is the endangered Dalmatian pelican (p126).

❻ Pržno
Sheltered within a green horseshoe of Mediterranean foliage, Pržno's clear waters and sandy beach provide the perfect setting for lazy days in the sun (p93).

Cultural Life

Millennia of human habitation and waves of invaders have left a rich legacy of art, architecture, music, food and tradition. This is not a place where people hide themselves away in their homes. Life is lived loudly on the streets and no opportunity for a celebration is allowed to escape.

❶ Perast
The perfect setting for a romantic dinner by the serene waters of the Bay of Kotor, Perast is an oversized village comprised almost entirely of elegant baroque palazzos and churches (p82).

❷ Cafe Society
In Montenegro, this includes everybody. Join the throngs supping and socialising on the streets of every city and town throughout the country (p37).

❸ Cetinje's Museums
The former royal capital has found a good use for its grand historic buildings, filling them with interesting museums devoted to the nation's art, history and culture (p123).

❹ Ostrog Monastery
Seemingly sprouting out of the surrounding cliffs, this gleaming white monastery is the country's spiritual heart for its Orthodox population as well as a popular place of pilgrimage (p133).

❺ Frescoes
Affecting images of doe-eyed saints with otherworldly elongated bodies cover the walls of the nation's historic churches. Some of the best examples can be found at Morača Monastery (p138).

❻ Kotor's Old Town
Kotor's marbled streets, stone palazzos, many churches and imposing fortifications combine to form Montenegro's most beautiful town – one which will transport you back in time (p84).

Mountain Majesty

Much of Montenegro's surface looks like it's been dug up by a giant puppy out of freshly laid concrete. A lunar landscape of craggy peaks gives way to lush forests, high plains and twinkling glacial lakes known as 'mountain eyes'. It's a terrain suited for skiing, hiking, ooh-ing and aah-ing.

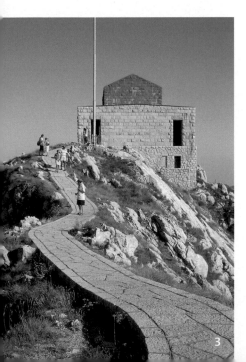

① Rafting

The Tara River (also famous for its magnificent bridge) slices deeply through the Durmitor range, providing one of the world's most dramatic rafting routes and the nation's most popular active attraction (p143).

② The Kotor–Cetinje road

One of the world's great drives, the back road from Kotor to Cetinje loops up and up, providing ever more jaw-dropping views of the Bay of Kotor and the Adriatic Sea beyond (p88).

③ Njegoš Mausoleum

At the top of one of Mt Lovćen's highest peaks, this tomb for the nation's hero echoes the grandeur of the black mountain itself through imposing sculpture, solemn architecture and awe-inspiring views (p122).

④ Biogradska Gora National Park

If you're on the hunt for wood nymphs or satyrs, the 1600 hectares of virgin forest at the heart of the Bjelasica Mountains would be a good place to start (p141).

⑤ Comfort Food

Being cold is one thing but being cold and hungry just won't do. In the mountains, fill up on tender lamb roasted *ispod sača* (under a metal lid covered with hot coals) accompanied with artery-clogging creamy, cheesy porridges (p44).

⑥ Skiing

Savin Kuk within Durmitor National Park never quite sheds its cap of snow and in the winter its 3.5km run is adored by enthusiastic skiers and snowboarders (p144).

1

The Environment

'Wild Beauty', crows Montenegro's enduring tourism slogan, and indeed the marketing boffins are right to highlight the nation's extraordinary natural blessings. A lot of focus is placed on the clear coastal waters, but journey into the mountainous interior and you'll still find pockets of virgin forest and large mammals long since hunted out of existence on most of the continent.

Much of the credit for this lies with the terrain itself. Its rugged contours haven't just hindered foreign invaders, they've limited the population spread and the worst excesses of development. For millennia the highest regions have supported seminomadic shepherds in a sustainable fashion. Now these reaches are being put to new economic use as a setting for adventure and ecotourism. The Montenegrin government has realised the value of this by declaring the country the world's first 'ecological state', yet it remains to be seen what this means in a country where hunting is popular, recycling is virtually unknown and people litter as a matter of course. The harder battle lies with educating businesses and individuals as to the impact of their everyday actions on this beautiful land.

THE LAND

Montenegro is comprised of a thin strip of Adriatic coast, a fertile plain around Podgorica and a whole lot of mountains. These are part of the Dinaric Alps, a 645km continuous stretch that runs along the eastern side of the Adriatic from the Julian Alps in Slovenia to Mt Korab in Macedonia. They're formed of sedimentary rocks such as dolomite and limestone that were once part of the sea bed but were thrust up by the movement of continental plates somewhere around 50 million to 100 million years ago. Major earthquakes still rip through periodically, including the 1979 disaster that measured 6.9 on the Richter scale, destroying Budva's Old Town and killing 156 people. Montenegro's highest peak is Kolac (2534m) in the Prokletije range near the Albanian border. You might also find Bobotov Kuk (2523m) in the Durmitor range listed as the highest peak; Kolac is often not taken into account because of its location along the country's border.

Most of Montenegro's mountains are karstic in nature with craggy grey-white outcrops, sparse vegetation and, beneath, caves. Water disappears into the rock and bubbles up elsewhere to form springs and lakes. Rivers such as the Tara, Piva and Morača have cut deep canyons, not due to sheer force but rather through the carbon dioxide in the water reacting with the hard limestone (calcium carbonate) to form soluble calcium bicarbonate.

The oddly shaped Bay of Kotor is technically a drowned river canyon although it's popularly described as a fjord (which falsely implies glacial action). Ancient glaciers did, however, form the Plav Valley on the edge of Prokletije Mountains, and glacial lakes are common in Durmitor National Park. Lake Visitor, in the mountain of the same name above Plav, has the unusual quirk of a floating island. Local legends say that it was once a raft used by the ancient shepherds to transport stock. Because it was well fertilised it developed soil and foliage and now drifts around the lake.

Lake Skadar, the largest in the Balkans, spans Montenegro and Albania in the southeast. It's mainly fed by the Morača River and drained into the Adriatic by the Bojana River at its opposite corner. It's a cryptodepression, meaning that the deepest parts are below sea level.

Montenegro's crumpled terrain means that the bulk of the population lives in the fertile plains of the Morača and Zeta Rivers or clings to the coast.

Over half of Montenegro is more than 1000m above sea level and 15% is higher than 1500m.

WILDLIFE

Many species of animal and bird have managed to find solace in Montenegro's hidden nooks. Precisely because those nooks are so hidden you're unlikely to see any of the more dramatic mammals. Birdwatchers are more likely to have their tendencies gratified with plenty of rare wetland birds congregating around Lake Skadar and flashy birds of prey swooping over the mountains.

Animals

MAMMALS

Let's start with the big fellows. Brown bears like to hang out in the forests at altitudes of 900m and higher. In 2000 there were estimated to be less than 130 remaining in Montenegro, concentrated in the northern and eastern mountains. Despite the male bears weighing up to 200kg, they pose little threat to humans unless they're protecting a cub or are startled. There have only been three known bear-caused fatalities in Europe in the last hundred years (mainly in Scandinavia). The odds aren't so good the other way around. Despite the 'ecological state' declaration, bears are only protected from recreational hunters in summer. Females with cubs under two years old may not be hunted at any time. Once this species could be found anywhere between Ireland and Japan; they survived in Britain until the year 500.

Likewise grey wolves don't pose much of a threat unless they're rabid or starving. They too fancy forest living but may venture out into the meadows to make closer acquaintance with the odd bit of livestock. For this reason there's still a price on their head in some areas. Wolves are fairly widely spread around the interior.

The Eurasian lynx is a medium-sized species of wild cat that stands about 90cm high and is recognisable by distinctive black tufts on its ears. You're unlikely to see or hear them as they're nocturnal, very quiet and highly endangered. There are estimated to be less than 100 left in the Balkans, including Montenegro's northern regions, and conservation projects have been established to protect them.

Its canine compatriot, the golden jackal, stands slightly higher and is related to the wolf. While they're not common in Montenegro, they're known to live around Bar and Ulcinj with three packs spotted on Ada Bojana.

Look out for European otters going about their unspeakably cute business around Lake Skadar and the Tara River. Badgers hang out in Durmitor and Biogradska Gora National Parks. Balkan chamois join roe deer in Durmitor, while the latter also wander the Lovćen and Bjelasica Mountains. Foxes, weasels, moles, groundhogs, hares, shrews, bats, wild boar, red squirrels and dormice complete the diverse mammalian picture.

BIRDS

Of the 300-odd species of bird that live in Montenegro, the superstars of the avian world are the birds of prey that nest in the many mountains. A two-headed species has even made it onto the nation's flag, along with those of neighbouring Serbia and Albania. The golden eagle has a wingspan of up to 240cm and can sometimes supplement its rodent diet with lambs and small goats. Its smaller cousin, the eastern imperial eagle (wingspan 200cm), is listed as a vulnerable species on the IUCN (International Union for Conservation of Nature) Red List along with the spotted eagle and white-headed vulture. Even more endangered are the Egyptian vulture and the saker falcon that jets in for the summer from Central Asia. Others include the booted eagle, white-tailed eagle, peregrine falcon, goshawk, sparrowhawk, Eurasian eagle owl, griffon vulture and buzzard.

The Bojana River occasionally performs the unusual trick of flowing upstream. This happens in winter when the swollen waters of its Albanian tributary the Drim cut across it and the volume of water forces part of the flow back into its source, Lake Skadar.

Other glamorous flappers include the Dalmatian pelican, which is the spokesmodel of Lake Skadar National Park. This is the largest of all pelican species and is also on the vulnerable list, with only 1000 breeding pairs remaining in Europe. Lake Skadar is recognised by an international treaty, the Ramsar Convention, as a 'wetland of international importance'. It is home to a quarter of the world's population of pygmy cormorants, which are listed as 'near-threatened'. They're joined by 262 other, mainly migratory species including the near-threatened great snipe and the vulnerable great bustard (mind how you read that).

REPTILES, AMPHIBIANS & SNAKES

If you're wandering the remote trails you'll often catch sight of something reptilian scurrying off the path. Montenegro has an impressive collection of lizards, newts, frogs, turtles and snakes. The isolated glacial lakes of the karstic mountain ranges harbour species such as the *serdarski triton*, a type of alpine newt that only exists in one small lake in Durmitor. Another vulnerable species endemic to the Balkans, the mosor rock lizard, hides out in Durmitor and Lovćen National Parks. The European pond terrapin (or turtle) is listed as near-threatened but can still be spotted in both Lovćen and Lake Skadar National Parks.

Of more interest or concern to most visitors are Montenegro's snakes. Commonly spotted and often mistaken for a snake is the harmless slow-worm (sometimes called blindworm), a 50cm-long brown legless lizard. Rather less harmless is the horned viper. Reaching up to 95cm, this is possibly the largest and most venomous snake in Europe. It likes rocky habitats (which doesn't rule out much in Montenegro) and has a zigzag stripe on its body and a distinctive scaly 'horn' on its nose. If you're close enough to spot the horn you're probably a little too close. The good news is that this guy isn't at all aggressive and will only bite with extreme provocation, so mind where you tread.

If you're a fan of Greek mythology you should keep an eye out (especially in the Bjelasica Mountains) for the harmless – unless you're a mouse – Aesculapian snake. Asclepius was the Greek god of healing, whose symbol is a staff with a snake twisted around it – you may recognise it as the logo of the World Health Organization. Greek and Roman temples dedicated to the god traditionally had these critters slithering all over them, so it's quite possible that Montenegro's specimens may be the descendants of holy serpents.

FISH

Lake Skadar alone is home to 48 species of fish, including eels, an endemic type of bleak known as *ukljeva* and the unfortunately named *krap* (a variety of carp). There may well be more as in the past 20 years 10 new species have been discovered. *Mladica* is a type of trout that's endemic to the Balkans. One giant specimen, weighing in at 41.5kg when it was snagged at Lake Plav, has the dubious honour of being the biggest fish ever caught in Montenegro. The nearby Ljuca River was once well known for having excellent stocks of grayling, a popular game fish, but water pollution due to sewerage run-off has hurt its reputation.

Plants

The coastal strip is classic Mediterranean botanical heaven: bushy oleanders covered in pink and white flowers; headily scented daphne; gnarled olive trees draped in silver-green leaves; mimosa, laburnum and broom all breaking into yellow flowers in spring; pomegranates heavily laden with crimson fruit; hardy wild fig colonising ruined houses; fragrant laurels and elegant palms.

One of Montenegro's more curious species is the olm, a blind amphibian that can be found in Biogradska Gora National Park and is listed on the IUCN Red List as vulnerable. Its Montenegrin name, *čovječja ribica*, means 'human fish' because of its human-like skin.

In parts of the coast it was traditional for a man to plant olive trees before he could be married – an early form of carbon crediting, perhaps. There are estimated to be 100,000 olives in the vicinity of Bar alone, the most famous of which is the massive 2000-year-old *stara maslina* (see the boxed text, p114). It's now thought that there are whole groves in the vicinity pushing the two millennia mark.

Heading up Mt Lovćen, the lower slopes are covered in forests of black beech. Once these deciduous trees lose their leaves and their distinctive black trunks are bared, you'll understand why the Venetians named it the 'black mountain'. Higher up, the beech are joined by an endemic pine called *munika*. Healing and sweet-smelling herbs poke out from the rocky slopes, including sage, rosemary, balm, mint, chamomile and St John's wort.

This type of vegetation is typical of much of the mountainous north, although you'll also find oak, ash, fir, juniper, maple and hazel trees on the lower slopes (below 850m) and birch among the conifers in the higher reaches (above 1600m). The mountain meadows and scree slopes are often blanketed with white and yellow saxifrage, violets and gentian, named after Illyrian king Gentius who once ruled from nearby Skadar. *Edraiathus glisicii* is an endemic herbaceous perennial that breaks into violet bell-like flowers in summer. It's joined by edelweiss and the pale flowers of fuzzy *Verbascum durmitoreum*, the name giving it away as a native of Durmitor.

The marshy edges of Lake Skadar are carpeted with white and yellow water lilies, reeds, willows and edible water chestnuts. Rare endemic species of orchids may also be found.

Sailors from what is now Montenegro once travelled the globe, returning with many of the interesting botanical specimens that you'll see today in places like Herceg Novi and Bar. These include bamboo, eucalyptus, *Ginkgo biloba*, and the agave (for which Bar was once famous).

> As far back as 1888 Montenegro passed a law banning fishing with dynamite. Unfortunately this practice still goes on in some other parts of the Balkans.

NATIONAL PARKS

Montenegro's first three national parks were declared in 1952: Lovćen (p122), Durmitor (p142) and Biogradska Gora (p141). In 1983 Lake Skadar (p126) joined them as the country's first nonmountainous national park. In total they cover an area of 90,870 hectares.

Sometime during the life of this book it's possible that Montenegro will declare a section of the Prokletije Mountains bordering Albania its fifth national park. This area contains the country's highest peak and is part of a proposed cross-border Balkans Peace Park.

Montenegro's most interesting and popular national park is Durmitor, a truly magnificent place for nature-lovers, blessed with springs of clear mountain water and glacial lakes that mirror the heavens. Spread over 39,000 hectares, Durmitor National Park has 48 peaks over 2000m, with its highest, Bobotov Kuk, coming in at 2523m. The Tara River is raftable and is hidden in the deepest canyon in Europe (1300m at its apogee). Durmitor is under Unesco protection, as is the Tara River.

Biogradska Gora National Park covers 5650 hectares of the Bjelasica Mountains and includes 1600 hectares of virgin forest – one of the most significant untouched stands remaining in Europe. Here you'll find groves of juniper, wild rose, pine, beech, maple, fir and elm trees, the tallest of which reach 45m.

Lovćen National Park's 6220-hectare offering is cultural as well as natural, encompassing the old Montenegrin heartland and the impressive mausoleum of the national hero, Njegoš.

The 40,000-hectare Lake Skadar National Park is spread around the Montenegrin side of the largest lake in southern Europe on the border with

Albania (where it is called Shkodra). It counts as one of the largest bird reserves in Europe, with rarities such as the Dalmatian pelican residing on its shores.

ENVIRONMENTAL ISSUES

For a new country, especially one recovering from recent wars in the region, Montenegro has made some key moves to safeguard the environment, not least declaring itself an 'ecological state' in its constitution. Yet in the rush to get bums on beaches the preservation of the nation's greatest selling point sometimes plays second fiddle to development. An example is the offering for tender of 680 hectares of land on the beautiful and relatively untouched Luštica Peninsula, which forms the southern headland of the Bay of Kotor. The prospective buyer will be expected to contribute at least €100 million for tourism development. At the same time major developments are in the works for Velika Plaža, Ada Bojana and various sites in the mountainous north.

Water shortages continue to affect the coast and in 2008 high salinity levels rendered Tivat's supply undrinkable for a spell. A new desalination plant has been constructed near Budva but these operations are notoriously energy-intensive.

The country currently imports 40% of its electricity. The major hydroelectric station on the Piva River feeds into the Serbian grid, with Serbia supplying that same amount of output back into the Montenegrin grid. At the time of research contracts were being signed by private companies to create eight new minihydroelectric power plants on various rivers. After these have commenced, 10 more projects will be offered for tender. While this form of generation is low in emissions, it requires the building of dams to flood river canyons and permanently alter the river flow.

There's little awareness of litter as a problem. It's not just the ubiquitous practice of throwing rubbish out of car windows; we've seen waitresses clear tables by throwing refuse straight into the river and we've heard reports of train employees doing the same. It's particularly bad in places like Rožaje and Plav, where the rivers are clogged with household refuse. Along the coast, fly-tipping of rubble from building sites is a problem. On an encouraging note, recycling is being trialled in Herceg Novi – it's not currently available anywhere else in the country.

An invasive form of Red Sea algae that has blanketed large sections of the Mediterranean has started to establish itself in Montenegrin waters. By and large the water quality for swimming is good.

At the World Congress for the Protection of Nature in Barcelona in 2008, the Montenegrin Environment Minister Predrag Nenezić emphasised the need for a regional approach to the protection of ecosystems that cross political boundaries. Certainly for a country of this size the environmental successes and failures of its neighbours will have a direct impact on its ecological health. Montenegro's coastal waters are relatively uncontaminated compared to those of neighbouring Albania, for example, where crumbling infrastructure allows oil to seep into rivers and out to sea. Montenegro also shares Lake Skadar with Albania and while the Montenegrin side is largely protected by a national park, the Albanian side has no such safeguard.

The mooted Balkans Peace Park in the Prokletije Mountains bordering Albania and Kosovo is an example of a cross-border zone that would benefit from a combined approach to its protection. Certainly a move from Montenegro to declare its section a national park would be a good start, but it remains to be seen how much political issues will hamper effective cooperation.

Montenegro has 500 types of herbs with medicinal properties, many of which are harvested for essential oils and ingredients for natural remedies. Wormwood is an ingredient of absinthe and was once exported to Italy to make the bitter liqueur Amaro Montenegro.

Gateway City: Dubrovnik

What can one say about Dubrovnik that hasn't been said already? Lord Byron's 'jewel of the Adriatic' has been quoted endlessly, George Bernard Shaw's 'paradise on Earth' is a well-worn saying by now. Dubrovnik leaves most people speechless, its beauty gobsmacking, its setting a knockout. Not that it's a secret – quite the contrary; too many people know of its beauty and thousands of tourists walk squashed along the main street throughout the year, gazing, gasping, snapping. It's one of the world's hottest tourist destinations.

Although the shelling of Dubrovnik in 1991 horrified the world, the city has bounced back with characteristic vigour to again enchant its visitors. The hedonistic can pamper themselves in one of the city's fine hotels or enjoy a refreshing plunge into the sea. History buffs can trace the rise and fall of Dubrovnik's commercial empire in museums replete with art and artefacts. A local symphony orchestra and a busy concert season delight music-lovers.

Dubrovnik is an easy place to visit from Montenegro, and the perfect introduction to Croatia, plus it's a great launching place for expeditions to the surrounding region which is equally, though less famously, gorgeous.

Orientation

Čilipi international airport is 24km southeast of Dubrovnik. The Jadrolinija ferry terminal and the bus station are next to each other at Gruž, several kilometres northwest of the Old Town, which is closed to cars. The main street in the Old Town is Placa (better known as Stradun).

Information

You can change money at any travel agency or post office. There are numerous ATMs in town and near the bus station and the ferry terminal.

Algoritam (Map p68; ☎ 322 044; www.algoritam.hr; Placa 8; ⏲ 9am-8.30pm Mon-Fri, to 3pm Sat) Has a good selection of English-language books, including guidebooks.

Hospital (Map p67; ☎ 431 777; Dr Roka Mišetića bb) Emergency services are available 24 hours.

Lapad post office (Map p67; Šetalište Kralja Zvonimira 21; ⏲ 9am-6pm Mon-Sat)

Main post office (Map p68; cnr Široka & Od Puča; ⏲ 9am-6pm Mon-Sat)

Netcafé (Map p68; ☎ 321 125; www.netcafe.hr; Prijeko 21; per hr 30KN; ⏲ 9am-11pm) A wonderfully friendly cafe with a fast connection and good services.

Tourist office (www.tzdubrovnik.hr; ⏲ 8am-8pm daily Jun-Sep, 8am-3pm Mon-Fri, 9am-2pm Sat, closed

Sun Oct-May) Bus Station (Map p67; ☎ 417 581; Obala Pape Ivana Pavla II 44a); Gruž Harbour (Map p67; ☎ 417 983; Obala Stjepana Radića 27); Lapad (Map p67; ☎ 437 460; Šetalište Kralja Zvonimira 25); Old Town (Map p68; ☎ 323 587; Široka 1); Pile Gate (Map p68; ☎ 427 591; Dubrovačkih Branitelja 7) Maps, information and the indispensable *Dubrovnik Riviera* guide.

Sights
OLD TOWN

You will probably begin your visit of Dubrovnik's World Heritage-listed Old Town at the city bus stop outside **Pile Gate** (Map p68). As you enter the city, Dubrovnik's wonderful pedestrian promenade, Placa, extends before you all the way to the **clock tower** (Map p68) at the other end of town.

Just inside Pile Gate is the huge 1438 **Onofrio Fountain** (Map p68), and the **Franciscan Monastery** (Franjevački Samostan; Map p68; ☎ 321 410; Placa 2; ⏲ 9am-5pm) with a splendid cloister and

DUBROVNIK

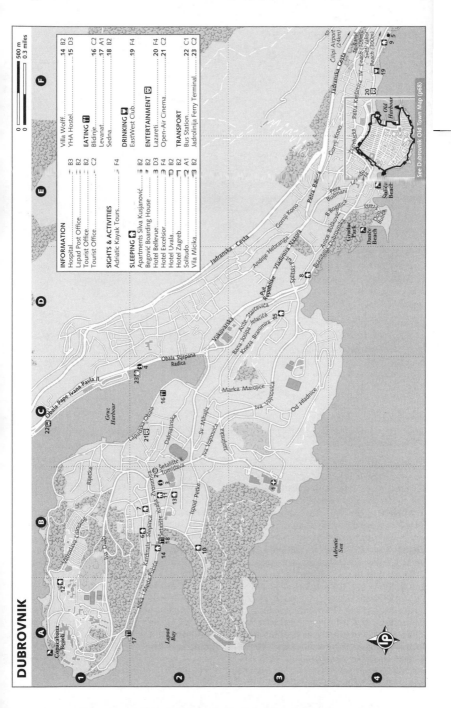

0 ——— 500 m
0 ——— 0.3 miles

INFORMATION		
Hospital............................	1	B3
Lapad Post Office..............	2	B2
Tourist Office...................	3	B2
Tourist Office...................	4	C2
SIGHTS & ACTIVITIES		
Adriatic Kayak Tours...........	5	F4
SLEEPING		
Apartments Silva Kusjanović..	6	B2
Begović Boarding House......	7	B2
Hotel Bellevue..................	8	D3
Hotel Excelsior.................	9	F4
Hotel Uvala.....................	10	B2
Hotel Zagreb....................	11	B2
Solitudo.........................	12	A1
Vila Micika......................	13	B2
Villa Wolff......................	14	B2
YHA Hostel......................	15	D3
EATING		
Bilidnje.........................	16	C2
Levanat..........................	17	A1
Sedna............................	18	B2
DRINKING		
EastWest Club...................	19	F4
ENTERTAINMENT		
Lazareti.........................	20	F4
Open-Air Cinema................	21	C2
TRANSPORT		
Bus Station.....................	22	C1
Jadrolinija Ferry Terminal......	23	C2

See Dubrovnik Old Town Map (p68)

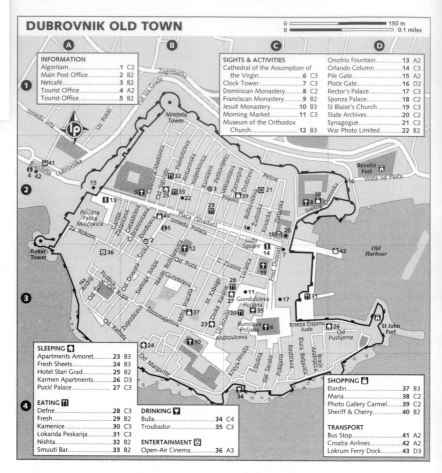

DUBROVNIK OLD TOWN

0 — 150 m
0 — 0.1 miles

INFORMATION
Algoritam......................1 C2
Main Post Office.............2 B2
Netcafé........................3 B2
Tourist Office................4 A2
Tourist Office................5 B2

SIGHTS & ACTIVITIES
Cathedral of the Assumption of
  the Virgin..................6 C3
Clock Tower..................7 C3
Dominican Monastery.......8 C2
Franciscan Monastery......9 B2
Jesuit Monastery...........10 B3
Morning Market.............11 C3
Museum of the Orthodox
  Church.....................12 B3

Onofrio Fountain............13 A2
Orlando Column.............14 C3
Pile Gate.....................15 A2
Ploče Gate...................16 D2
Rector's Palace..............17 C3
Sponza Palace...............18 C2
St Blaise's Church..........19 C3
State Archives...............20 C2
Synagogue....................21 C2
War Photo Limited..........22 B2

SLEEPING
Apartments Amoret..........23 B3
Fresh Sheets.................24 B3
Hotel Stari Grad.............25 B2
Karmen Apartments.........26 D3
Pucić Palace.................27 C3

EATING
Defne..........................28 C3
Fresh...........................29 B2
Kamenice.....................30 C3
Lokanda Peskarija...........31 C3
Nishta.........................32 B2
Smuuti Bar...................33 B2

DRINKING
Buža...........................34 C4
Troubadur.....................35 C3

ENTERTAINMENT
Open-Air Cinema............36 A3

SHOPPING
Đardin.........................37 B3
Maria..........................38 C2
Photo Gallery Carmel.......39 C2
Sheriff & Cherry.............40 B2

TRANSPORT
Bus Stop......................41 A2
Croatia Airlines..............42 A2
Lokrum Ferry Dock..........43 D3

the third-oldest functioning **pharmacy** (🕑 9am-5pm) in Europe; it's been operating since 1391. The **church** (🕑 7am-7pm) has recently undergone a long and expensive restoration to startling effect. The monastery **museum** (adult/concession 20/10KN; 🕑 9am-5pm) has a collection of liturgical objects, paintings and pharmacy equipment.

In front of the clock tower at the eastern end of Placa (on the square called Luža) is the 1417 **Orlando Column** (Map p68) – a popular meeting place. On opposite sides of the column are the 16th-century **Sponza Palace** (Map p68) – originally a customs house, later a bank, and now housing the **State Archives** (Državni Arhiv u Dubrovniku; Map p68; ☎ 321 032; admission 15KN; 🕑 8am-3pm Mon-Fri, 8am-1pm Sat) – and **St Blaise's Church** (Map p68), a lovely

Italian baroque building built in 1715 to replace an earlier church destroyed in the 1667 earthquake. At the end of Pred Dvorom, the wide street beside St Blaise's, is the baroque **Cathedral of the Assumption of the Virgin** (Map p68). Located between the two churches, the 1441 Gothic **Rector's Palace** (Knežev Dvor; Map p68; ☎ 321 437; Pred Dvorom 3; adult/student 35/15KN; 🕑 9am-2pm Mon-Sat Oct-May, 9am-6pm daily Jun-Sep) houses a museum with furnished rooms, baroque paintings and historical exhibits. The elected rector was not permitted to leave the building during his one-month term without the permission of the senate. The narrow street opposite opens onto Gundulićeva Poljana, a bustling **morning market** (Map p68). Up the stairs south of the square is the 1725

Jesuit Monastery (Jezuitski Samostan; Map p68; Poljana Ruđera Boškovića).

As you proceed up Placa, make a detour to the **Museum of the Orthodox Church** (Muzej Pravoslavne Crkve; Map p68; ☎ 323 283; Nikole Božidarevića; adult/concession 10/5KN; ⏱ 9am-1pm Mon-Fri) for a look at a fascinating collection of 15th- to 19th-century icons.

By now you'll be ready for a leisurely walk around the **city walls** (Map p68; adult/child 50/20KN; ⏱ 9am-7.30pm Apr-Oct, 10am-3.30pm Nov-Mar), which have entrances just inside Pile Gate, across from the Dominican monastery and near St John Fort. Built between the 13th and 16th centuries, these powerful walls are the finest in the world and Dubrovnik's main claim to fame. They enclose the entire city in a protective veil over 2km long and up to 25m high, with two round and 14 square towers, two corner fortifications and a large fortress. The views over the town and sea are great – this walk could be the high point of your visit.

Whichever way you go, you'll notice the 14th-century **Dominican Monastery** (Dominikanski Samostan; Map p68; ☎ 322 200; adult/child 20/10KN; ⏱ 9am-6pm), which is located in the northeastern corner of the city. Its forbidding fortress-like exterior shelters a rich trove of paintings from Dubrovnik's finest 15th- and 16th-century artists.

Dubrovnik has many other sights, such as the unmarked **synagogue** (Sinagoga; Map p68; ☎ 321 028; Žudioska 5; admission 10KN; ⏱ 10am-8pm Jun-Sep, 9am-3pm Mon-Fri Oct-May) near the clock tower, which is the second-oldest synagogue in Europe. The uppermost streets of the Old Town below the north and south walls are pleasant to wander along.

One of the better photography galleries you're likely to come across, **War Photo Limited** (Map p68; ☎ 326 166; www.warphotoltd.com; Antuninska 6; admission 30KN; ⏱ 9am-9pm daily May-Sep, 10am-4pm Tue-Sat, 10am-2pm Sun Oct & Apr) has changing exhibitions that are curated by the gallery owner and former photojournalist Wade Goddard. It's open in summer only, and has up to three exhibitions in that period, relating to the subject of war seen from various perspectives.

BEACHES
Banje (Map p67), the closest beach to the Old Town, is just beyond the 17th-century **Lazareti** (p71; a former quarantine station) outside **Ploče Gate** (Map p68). Another nearby, good local beach is **Sveti Jakov** (Map p67), a 20-minute walk down Vlaho Bukovac street or a quick ride on bus 5 or 8 from the northern end of the Old Town. Other beaches past Pile Gate are **Šulići** and **Danče** (Map p67), a pebbly and rocky beach respectively. Another excellent place for swimming is underneath the **Buža bar** (p71), on the outside of the city walls. Diving is off the rocks, there are steps to help you get in and out and some cemented space between the rocks for sunbathing. There's not much shade here, so bring a hat and strong sun protection. There are also hotel beaches along the **Lapad Peninsula** (Map p67), which you can use without a problem. The largest is Copacabana Beach outside the Hotel Kompas.

An even better option is to take the ferry that shuttles half-hourly in summer to lush **Lokrum Island** (return 80KN), a national park with a rocky nudist beach (marked FKK), a botanical garden and the ruins of a medieval Benedictine monastery.

Activities
Adriatic Kayak Tours (Map p67; ☎ 312 770; www.kayakcroatia.com; Frankopanska 6) offers a great series of kayak tours for experienced and beginner kayakers. Tours cover nearby Lokrum Island and the Elafiti Islands, but you can also go white-water rafting on the Tara River (p143) and kayaking in the Bay of Kotor (p73) in Montenegro.

Sleeping
Private accommodation is generally the best option in Dubrovnik, but beware of the scramble of private owners at the bus station or Jadrolinija wharf. Some provide what they say they offer, others are rip-off artists. The owners listed below meet you at the station if you call in advance. Otherwise head to any of the travel agencies or the tourist office. Expect to pay about €28 to €50 for a room in the high season.

OLD TOWN
Fresh Sheets (Map p68; ☎ 091 799 2086; beds@igot fresh.com; Sv Šimuna 15; per person €25; ⏱) A brand new place, this is a collection of four individually decorated apartments – Lavender, Rainforest, Sunshine, Heaven – each sleeping two to four people (plus a sofa), and one double room. The location is excellent (in the heart of Old Town), you get free internet and wi-fi and, when the Fresh bar's kitchen is open, a free smoothie every day.

Apartments Amoret (Map p68; ☎ 091 530 4910; www
.dubrovnik-amoret.com; Dinke Ranjine 5 & Restićeva 2; apt €50-
120; 🖳) Six artistically appointed apartments
and rooms are tucked away within two Old
Town houses (Amoret 1 and Amoret 2) that
date back to the 16th century. Each is different
but all are lovingly decorated to create some of
the most charming accommodation anywhere
in Dubrovnik.

ourpick Karmen Apartments (Map p68; ☎ 323
433, 098 619 282; www.karmendu.com; Bandureva 1; apt
€55-145; 🖳) Set inside an old stone house in
the middle of the Old Town, the four apartments are beautifully decorated with original
artwork and imaginative use of recycled materials. There are small, one- to two-person
apartments, as well as two for three or four
people. Book well in advance because it all
gets whipped up by June.

Hotel Stari Grad (Map p68; ☎ 322 244; www.hotel
starigrad.com; Palmotićeva; low-high s 650-1180KN, d 920KN-
1580KN; 🖳) Staying in the heart of the Old
Town in a lovingly restored stone building is
an unmatchable experience. The eight rooms
are elegantly and tastefully furnished to feel
simple and luxurious at the same time.

Pucić Palace (Map p68; ☎ 326 222; www.thepucicpal
ace.com; Od Puča 1; low-high s €206-315, d €290-505; 🖳)
Right in the heart of the Old Town and inside
what was once a nobleman's mansion, this
five-star hotel is Dubrovnik's most exclusive
and hottest property. There are only 19 rooms,
all exquisitely decorated and featuring Italian
mosaics, Egyptian cotton and baroque beds.

ourpick Hotel Bellevue (Map p67; ☎ 330 000; www
.hotel-bellevue.hr; Petra Čingrije 7; d from €250; 🖳 🖳 🖳)
Although not strictly speaking within the borders of the Old Town, but a five-minute walk
west from Pile Gate, Hotel Bellevue's location –
on a cliff that overlooks the open sea and
the lovely bay underneath – is pretty much
divine. The rooms are beautifully designed,
the balconies overlook the said sea and bay.
Its restaurant, Vapor, is top-notch too, with
excellent seasonal products, fish, meat and a
wide range of Croatian wines.

OUTSIDE THE OLD TOWN
Solitudo (Map p67; ☎ 448 200; www.camping-adri
atic.com; Iva Dulčića 39; per person/campsite €5.40/10.20;
🕑 mid-May–mid-Oct) This pretty and renovated
camping ground is within walking distance
of the beach.

YHA Hostel (Map p67; ☎ 423 241; dubrovnik@hfhs
.hr; Vinka Sagrestana 3; low-high per person B&B 85-120KN)

Basic in decor, the YHA Hostel is clean and,
as travellers report, a lot of fun. If you are allowed to choose a bed (rare), the best dorms
are rooms 31 and 32, for their 'secret' roof
terrace with a refreshingly lovely view.

Apartments Silva Kusjanović (Map p67; ☎ 435
071, 098 244 639; silva_dubrovnik@yahoo.com; Kardinala
Stepinca 62; per person 100KN) Sweet Silva has four
large apartments that can hold four to eight
beds. All have terraces with gorgeous views
and barbecues.

Begović Boarding House (Map p67; ☎ 435 191;
http://begovic-boarding-house.com; Primorska 17; low-high
dm €14-19, s €25-32, d €32-40; 🖳) A long-time favourite with our readers, this friendly place in
Lapad has three rooms with shared bathroom
and three apartments. There's a terrace out
the back with a good view. Breakfast is an
additional 30KN.

Vila Micika (Map p67; ☎ 437 332; www.vilamicika
.hr; Mata Vodapića; low-high s 150-210KN, d 300-420KN) A
simple, well-run establishment with rooms
painted in soft and pleasant colours and
equipped with TVs and modern bathrooms.
There's a pleasant outdoor terrace, and it's
only 200m to the Lapad beaches.

ourpick Hotel Zagreb (Map p67; ☎ 430 930; www
.hotels-sumratin.com; Šetalište Kralja Zvonimira 27; low-high
s 400-660KN, d 700-1060KN; 🖳) Under the same
ownership as Hotel Sumratin, Hotel Zagreb
is the more stylish sister, set inside a lovely,
salmon-coloured 19th-century building.
The rooms are large, with marine motifs and
large bathrooms.

ourpick Villa Wolff (Map p67; ☎ 438 710; www.villa
-wolff.hr; Nika i Meda Pucića 1; low-high s 1533-1879KN, d
1606-1898KN; 🖳 🖳) A gorgeous boutique hotel
right on the lovely seaside promenade, Villa
Wolff has six rooms, all beautifully outfitted,
bright and airy. There is a verdant garden that
guests use for sunbathing.

Hotel Uvala (Map p67; ☎ 433 580; www.hotelimaes
tral.com; Masarykov Put 6; d €120-170; 🖳 🖳) A newly
renovated four-star hotel that's decked out
with a lovely reception, indoor and outdoor
pools and a comprehensive spa. It's unfortunate, however, that the rooms in Uvala are a
bit of a let-down with their glum browns and
whites. The service is friendly and the place is
comfortable, very close to the beach.

Hotel Excelsior (Map p67; ☎ 353 353; www.hotel
-excelsior.hr; Frana Supila 12; s/d from 1640/1890KN; 🖳 🖳)
This is possibly Dubrovnik's biggest hotel
extravaganza – after a €10 million refit, the
legendary Excelsior opened again in 2008 to

many bated breaths. The adjacent boutique villa, Villa Odak, has gorgeously understated rooms. There is also an indoor and outdoor swimming pool and a palm-tree terrace.

Eating

OLD TOWN

Weed out tourist traps and choose carefully, and you'll find fabulous food in the Old Town.

Smuuti Bar (Map p68; ☎ 091 896 7509; Palmotićeva 5; smoothies 18-25KN) This place is perfect for breakfast smoothies and nice big mugs of coffee (at a bargain 10KN).

Fresh (Map p68; ☎ 091 896 7509; www.igotfresh.com; Vetranićeva 4; wraps from 20KN) A mecca for young travellers who gather here for the smoothies, wraps and other healthy snacks, as well as drinks and music in the evening.

Nishta (Map p68; ☎ 091 896 7509; Prijeko 30; mains from 30KN) When they opened this unprecedented case of a 100% vegetarian restaurant in Dubrovnik, the baffled locals asked the owners what they served. 'Everything except meat', the owners said, and the locals concluded: 'Well, then you're serving nothing.' Hence the name Nishta ('nothing' in Croatian). Alas, you're in the Balkans, what do you expect? Head here for a refreshing gazpacho, a heart-warming miso soup, Thai curries, veggies and noodles, and many more veggie delights.

Kamenice (Map p68; ☎ 421 499; Gundulićeva Poljana 8; mains from 40KN) It's been here since the 1970s and not much has changed: the socialist-style waiting uniforms, the simple interior, the massive portions of mussels, grilled or fried squid, griddled anchovies and *kamenice* (oysters). The terrace is on one of Dubrovnik's most gorgeous squares.

our pick **Lokanda Peskarija** (Map p68; ☎ 324 750; Ribarnica bb; mains from 40KN) Located on the Old Harbour right next to the fish market, this is undoubtedly one of Dubrovnik's best eateries. The quality of the seafood dishes is unfaltering, the prices are good and the location is gorgeous. The locals queue along with the tourists for the wonderful baby squid, the substantial risottos and the juicy mussels.

Defne (Map p68; ☎ 326 200; Od Puča 1; mains from 70KN) Pucić Palace's top-floor restaurant, it's one of Old Town's classiest. Try the octopus carpaccio starter, served with black *tagliolini* and truffle – a piece of heaven in your mouth – or the gorgeous lobster with white risotto dish. The wine list is impeccable.

LAPAD

Sedna (Map p67; ☎ 352 000; www.hotel-kompas.hr; Petra Čingrije 7; pizzas from 26KN; omelettes 30-35KN) The Hotel Kompas bar-pizzeria is a great and unpretentious spot for breakfast, lunch or dinner. You can sit on a terrace overlooking the beach and Lapad Bay while the locals buzz around, drinking their coffee and chatting on sunny mornings and afternoons.

our pick **Levanat** (Map p67; ☎ 435 352; Nika i Meda Pucića 15; mains 45-120KN) One of the best spots in the whole city, Levanat overlooks the sea from the pine-laden hill between Lapad Bay and Babin Kuk. The food is equally gorgeous as well as innovative, with seafood and unusual sauces, fresh ingredients and delicious vegetarian options.

Blidinje (Map p67; ☎ 358 794; Lapadska Obala 21; mains from 70KN) A great local that's not frequented by many tourists, Blidinje has fabulous views of Gruž Harbour from its terrace. The food is aimed primarily at carnivores, so use the opportunity to taste lamb or veal slow-cooked under hot coals – but make sure you ring in and order at least two hours in advance.

Drinking

EastWest Club (Map p67; ☎ 412 220; Frana Supila bb) By day this outfit on Banje Beach rents out beach chairs and umbrellas and serves drinks to the bathers. When the rays lengthen, the cocktail bar opens.

Troubadur (Map p68; ☎ 412 154; Bunićeva Poljana 2) Come to this legendary Dubrovnik venue for live jazz concerts in the summer.

our pick **Buža** (Map p68; Ilije Sarake) The Buža is a no-fuss place on the outside of the city walls, facing out onto the open sea, with simple drinks and blissful punters.

Entertainment

The summer months are chock-full of concerts and folk dancing. The tourist office has the full schedule.

Lazareti (Map p67; ☎ 324 633; www.lazareti.du-hr.net; Frana Supila 8) Dubrovnik's best art and music centre, Lazareti hosts cinema nights, club nights, live music, masses of concerts and pretty much all the best things in town. Come here for the free art-film seasons hosted by a group of local film-enthusiasts throughout the year. International and local films are projected onto the 19th-century walls of the Lazareti complex, once a quarantine barracks.

Open-Air Cinema (Map p67; Kumičića, Lapad) In two locations, it's open nightly in July and August with screenings starting after sundown (9pm or 9.30pm). The other location is at Za Rokom in the Old Town (Map p68).

Shopping

You'll find souvenir stores all over Stradun, selling Dalmatian marine details, stripy tops, anchors and the like.

Maria (Map p68; ☎ 321 330; www.maria-dubrovnik .hr; Svetog Dominika bb) Take a few deep breaths before you step into this shop, for you are sure to swoon at the sight of soft Miu Miu leather bags, lacquered Alexander McQueen shoes and gorgeous Marni dresses. The prices are international of course, and the service is friendly too, which is always a pleasant surprise.

Sheriff & Cherry (Map p68; ☎ 324 888; www.sherif fandcherry.com; Đorđićeva 4; ☺ 10am-5pm Mon-Fri, to 3pm Sat) One of the few trendy boutiques in town, this Zagreb-based shop stocks all the major fashion labels, such as Paul & Joe, Cheap Mondays, Anya Hindmarch and Dries Van Noten, among many, many others.

Photo Gallery Carmel (Map p68; ☎ 091 577 7157; www.phototgallerycarmel.com; Zamanjina 10; ☺ 9am-4pm Mon-Sat) A newly opened photography gallery that hosts work by local and international artists. Prints are for sale.

Djardin (Map p68; ☎ 324 744; Miha Pracata 8; ☺ 9.30am-6pm Mon-Fri, to 12.30pm Sat) A sprawling jewellery shop in which you can get lost for hours.

Getting There & Away

AIR

Daily flights to and from Zagreb are operated by **Croatia Airlines** (Map p68; ☎ 413 777; www .croatiaairlines.hr; Brsalje 9; ☺ 8am-4pm Mon-Fri, 9am-noon Sat). The fare runs from 400KN one-way, higher in peak season; the trip takes about an hour.

There are also nonstop flights to Rome, London and Manchester in the period between April and October.

TO/FROM THE AIRPORT

Čilipi international airport is 24km southeast of Dubrovnik. The Croatia Airlines airport buses (25KN, 45 minutes) leave from the main **bus station** (Map p67; ☎ 357 088; Obala Pape Ivana Pavla II 44a) 1½ hours before flight times. Buses meet Croatia Airlines flights but not all others. A taxi costs around 200KN.

TO/FROM MONTENEGRO

Buses head between Dubrovnik and Herceg Novi (€8, two hours) twice a day, continuing on to Kotor and Budva. In a busy summer season and at weekends buses out of Dubrovnik can be crowded, so book a ticket well before the scheduled departure time. A taxi from Dubrovnik to Herceg Novi will cost around €60.

Bay of Kotor

Coming from Herceg Novi, the Boka Kotorska (Bay of Kotor) starts simply enough, but as you progress through fold upon fold of the bay and the surrounding mountains get steeper and steeper, the beauty meter gets close to bursting.

It's often described as southern Europe's most spectacular fjord and even though the geological label is not strictly correct, the sentiment certainly is. The combination of rugged mountains plummeting to an opalescent sea, lush Mediterranean vegetation, historic towns and cute-as-a-button villages is pretty hard to beat. Lord Byron, the English Romantic poet, certainly thought so, describing it in 1872 as 'the most beautiful encounter between the land and the sea'.

It's not just the visual sense that's stimulated here. More fragrant than the ground floor of a department store, the Boka is subtly infused with the scent of wild herbs, perfumed flowers and aromatic trees. Local restaurants don't rest on their sublime surroundings but tantalise the taste buds with delicious seafood concoctions. Auditory pleasure can be as gentle as the lapping of the waves, or if your tastes stretch to ear-bleeding techno, that's catered for too.

The bay's compact size means that you can find yourself a base and put down roots for a week or two, spending your days exploring its hidden nooks. Active types can try their hand at kayaking, diving, mountain biking or hiking. Culture vultures can search out interesting art in the museums and numerous churches. History buffs can soak in the ambience of the remnants of the various empires that have passed through. Whatever your angle, there's no escaping the romance of this breathtaking bay.

HIGHLIGHTS

- Randomly roaming the atmospheric laneways of **Kotor's Old Town** (p84)
- Winding your way to dizzying views on the **Kotor–Lovćen back road** (p88)
- Marinating in the baroque beauty of historic **Perast** (p82)
- Cooling off in the shade with an icy beverage on Herceg Novi's **Belavista Sq** (p76)
- Hiking up to peaceful views and heartbreaking ruins in **Gornji Stoliv** (p89)
- Losing yourself within the olive groves of the remote reaches of the **Luština Peninsula** (p93)
- Paddling your way to paradise on a **kayaking day tour** (p78)

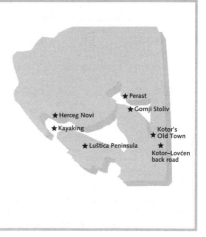

History

While they overlap at times, this geographically compact area's history stands at a slight remove from the rest of Montenegro. Like most of the eastern Adriatic, the Boka was populated by the Illyrian tribes. Their famous Queen Teuta retreated to Risan, the Boka's oldest town, in the course of her war with the Romans in 228 BC. Teuta was the Balkan equivalent of Britain's Boudica (Boadicea) and popular tradition has it that she committed suicide by leaping to her death rather than falling into the hands of the conquerors.

The bay subsequently became part of the Roman province of Dalmatia and before long lavish Roman villas sprang up along Risan's waterfront. When the empire was split into western and eastern sections over 500 years later, the Boka found itself near the fault line, on the very edge of the Western Roman Empire. By the end of the 5th century, with the empire crumbling under barbarian incursions from the north, the Bay of Kotor briefly fell into the hands of the Ostrogoths and then the Slavic tribes.

The Slavic clans of the Boka lived in virtual city states, maintaining allegiances to both the west (Rome) and east (Byzantium). Kotor was eventually incorporated into the principality of Duklja (later Zeta), considered a forerunner of modern Montenegro. At the time of the momentous split between the western (Catholic) and eastern (Orthodox) churches in 1054, Duklja was politically tied to Rome, but by 1190 Raška (soon to be known as Serbia) had annexed Duklja (which was by now known as Zeta) and an Orthodox bishopric was established on the Island of Flowers. Kotor and Perast, however, continued to have a largely Catholic population and to exercise a degree of autonomy.

Attacks from the Ottoman Turks weakened Serbia, and in 1379 Bosnian King Tvrtko assailed the Bay of Kotor. Kotor resisted by aligning itself with Venice but the Bosnians took large parts of the bay and in 1382 founded the port town of Sveti Stefan (later called Novi, meaning 'new') and then Herceg Novi). By 1463 Bosnia, together with its territory in the Boka, had fallen to the Ottomans, while Venice retained control of Kotor.

Kotor survived a siege by the Ottomans in 1538 with the assistance of supplies from Montenegro (now established in the mountains behind it). Risan wasn't so lucky, falling

the following year. In 1570 the bubonic plague hit, killing upwards of 3500 people in Kotor, but the hardy citizens were still able to resist another Ottoman attack in 1572, once again with the help of Venice and Montenegro. The Ottomans tried again in 1657, this time with 10,000 men, but were forced to abandon the siege after only 22 days. The people of Kotor had a brief respite, but 10 years later they were hit by the worst earthquake in the town's history, destroying many buildings and killing scores of people throughout the Boka.

It took a *hajduk* (outlaw) chieftain, Bajo Pivljanin, to put an end to 145 years of Ottoman occupation of Risan. Pivljanin lost his life in 1685 while leading a Venetian contingent to assist Montenegro during an Ottoman assault on Cetinje. Shortly after, the Ottomans were completely pushed out of the Boka, with the control of the entire bay passing into the hands of the Venetians where it remained until Napoleon's dismantling of the republic in 1797. Austria stepped into the vacuum until they too were defeated by the French eight years later.

Unhappy with the prospect of falling under French rule, in 1813 the people of the Boka joined for the first time with Montenegro and their allies Russia. This only lasted a year until Russia agreed to hand the Boka back to the French. A few years later Montenegro, with the aid of Britain this time, succeeded in wrestling the Boka off them but again Russia intervened, this time passing the control back to Austria.

Throughout the period of Venetian and Austrian rule the Boka was considered part of Dalmatia, as it was in Roman times. Before the advent of nationalism in the 19th century, the people of the bay were more likely to be described as 'Bokelj' than by terms such as Serb or Croat. Religion gradually became the defining factor of ethnicity, with Orthodox Christians identifying as Serbs and the Catholics looking towards Croatia. The Boka had always accommodated a mixed population – some churches even had dual Catholic and Orthodox altars – so the emerging pan-Slavic movement found fertile ground and the post-WWI formation of the Kingdom of Serbs, Croats and Slovenes (later Yugoslavia) was generally welcomed by the locals.

It wasn't until after WWII that the Boka became part of the Republic of Montenegro, one of the six that constituted the Socialist

BAY OF KOTOR

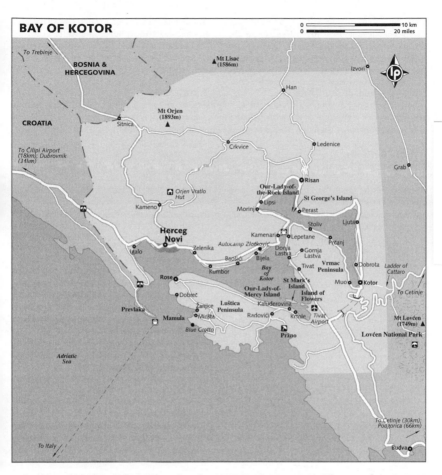

Federal Republic of Yugoslavia. Since then the Catholic population has reduced substantially, especially since the wars of the 1990s. In 1910 Herceg Novi, Perast, Dobrota, Kotor, Prčanj, Tivat and Budva all had a Catholic majority. Today Catholics number only 11% of the Bay of Kotor's population.

Climate

The weather in the outer section of the bay isn't markedly different from the pleasant Mediterranean climate of the coast. Southwest-facing Tivat has a reputation for being one of the sunniest spots. Cloud often drapes the high cliffs of the inner bay. Crkvice in the Orjen massif above Risan is said to have the highest rainfall in Europe, averaging 5300mL per annum. The record was in 1937 when it hit 8065mL. Luckily the karstic nature of the terrain causes the water to disappear into the limestone rather than flooding the towns below.

Getting There & Away

Jadranski put (Adriatic highway) connects the Bay of Kotor to Dubrovnik and to Budva. At the time of research a new highway was being constructed to link the bay (at Lipsi) to Nikšić. Tolls apply to the road connecting Herceg Novi to Trebinje in Bosnia and Hercegovina (€3 each way). A scenic back road links Kotor to Cetinje (see the boxed text, p88).

Buses head between Herceg Novi and Dubrovnik (€8, two hours) twice a day. A taxi from the Croatian side will cost around €60. Montenegrin taxis heading into Croatia are sometimes held up at the border, but you can arrange a transfer to Čilipi airport through a travel agency for about €35.

There are frequent buses to Budva and Podgorica from all around the bay.

For international flights to Tivat airport and ferries between Italy and Kotor, see the Transport chapter at the back of this book.

Getting Around

A road wends its way around the entire coast, narrowing considerably after it passes Kotor. From Kotor the main road takes a tunnel and comes out near Tivat airport. A car ferry crosses backwards and forwards across the bay's narrowest point (see the boxed text, below).

There are three main bus routes in the Boka. There are frequent services on the coastal road from Herceg Novi to Kotor, stopping in all the towns along the way. Buses also connect Herceg Novi to Tivat via the car ferry and Kotor to Tivat via the tunnel.

Taxi boats are a useful form of transportation and in summer they're easy enough to find in the busy marinas. Another option is to rent a kayak.

HERCEG NOVI ХЕРЦЕГ НОВИ

☎ 031 / pop 12,739

It's easy to drive straight through Herceg Novi without noticing anything worth stopping for, especially if you've just come from Croatia with visions of Dubrovnik dazzling your brain. However, just below the uninspiring roadside frontage hides an appealing Old Town with ancient walls, sunny squares and a lively atmosphere. The water's cleaner here near the mouth of the bay, so the pebbly beaches and concrete swimming terraces are popular.

Orientation

Herceg (pronounced 'her·tseg') Novi sprawls along the coast, absorbing former villages on either side of the Old Town. Pedestrian-friendly Šetalište Pet Danica runs along the waterfront, lined with summer bars and shops. The main commercial strip is Njegoševa, which ends just outside the Old Town's walls at Trg Nikole Đurkovića. Herceg Novi is extremely hilly and the fastest way from the highway to the beach is via one of the numerous sets of stairs. Charming as the stairways are, they make Herceg Novi one of the most challenging towns in Montenegro for the mobility-impaired.

Information

There's a cluster of banks with ATMs around Trg Nikole Đurkovića.

Pizzeria Una Storia (☎ 322 844; Njegoševa bb; per hr €1) There are two internet terminals and two scarily well-patronised poker machines.

Post office (Njegoševa 31)

Tourist office (☎ 350 820; www.hercegnovi.travel; Jova Dabovića 12; ☽ 8am-3pm Mon-Fri) On the 1st floor above a house.

Sights

Novi means 'new' and Herceg Novi is indeed one of the newer towns on the bay, but at 620-plus years it's no spring chicken. The

---

VIEW OR QUEUE?

The Bay of Kotor is a very peculiar shape. The entrance is guarded by two peninsulas that shelter the first section of the bay incorporating Herceg Novi and Tivat. The waters then narrow into a thin channel before the spectacular inner bay opens up. **Car ferries** (car/motorcycle/passenger €4/1.50/free; ☽ 24hr) wend their way across the narrowest point from Kamenari (15km northeast of Herceg Novi) to Lepetane (5km north of Tivat).

The road along the bay to Kotor is truly spectacular and should be travelled at least once, whether by car or bus. The distance between Herceg Novi and Kotor is only 43km but it can easily take an hour, longer if you get stuck behind a truck on the narrow winding road.

There's no doubt that the ferry ride is quicker for Tivat or Budva, but in the height of summer there can be horrendous queues, sometimes stretching for kilometres. If there are no queues and you've already travelled the scenic route, you might consider catching the ferry and heading to Kotor via the tunnel south of the town. You're unlikely to gain more than about 10 minutes but you will save a bit of petrol.

Buses to Budva take both routes.

HERCEG NOVI

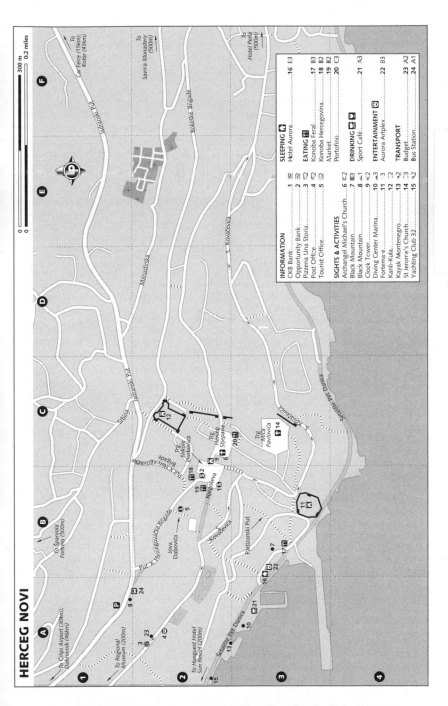

INFORMATION	
CKB Bank	1 B2
Opportunity Bank	2 B2
Pizzeria Una Storia	3 C2
Post Office	4 C2
Tourist Office	5 C2

SIGHTS & ACTIVITIES	
Archangel Michael's Church	6 C2
Black Mountain	7 B3
Black Mountain	8 A1
Clock Tower	9 C2
Diving Center Marina	10 A3
Fortemare	11 C3
Kanli-Kula	12 C2
Kayak Montenegro	13 A2
St Jerome's Church	14 C3
Yachting Club 32	15 A2

SLEEPING	
Hotel Aurora	16 E3

EATING	
Konoba Feral	17 B3
Konoba Hercegovina	18 B2
Market	19 B2
Portofino	20 C3

DRINKING	
Sport Café	21 A3

ENTERTAINMENT	
Aurora Artplex	22 B3

TRANSPORT	
Budget	23 A2
Bus Station	24 A1

Herceg part refers to Herceg (Duke) Stjepan Vukčić of Hercegovina fame who fortified the town in the 15th century. The most dramatic of the remaining fortifications are a little younger.

The big fort visible from the main road is the **Kanli-Kula** (Bloody Tower; admission €1; ☺ 8am-midnight), a notorious prison during Turkish rule (roughly 1482–1687). You can walk around its sturdy walls and enjoy views over the town.

The bastion at the town's seaward edge, **Fortemare**, was rebuilt by the Venetians during their 110-year stint as overlords (before the Austrians, French, Russians, Montenegrins, Austro-Hungarians, Serbs, Germans and Italians all had their turns). In the sea below you can see the ruins of the **Citadella**, the victim of the 1979 earthquake.

The elegant crenulated **clock tower**, built in 1667, was once the main city gate. Just inside the walls is Trg Herceg Stjepana (commonly called Belavista Sq), a gleaming white piazza that's perfect for relaxing, drinking and chatting in the shade. At its centre is the Orthodox **Archangel Michael's Church** (Crkva Sv Arhanđela Mihaila; built between 1883 and 1905), its lovely proportions capped by a dome and flanked by palm trees. The archangel is pictured in a mosaic above the door under an elegant rose window. Its Catholic counterpart, **St Jerome's Church** (Crkva Sv Jeronima; 1856), is further down the hill, dominating Trg Mića Pavlovića.

From its hillside location in the town's eastern fringes, **Savina Monastery** (Manastir Savina; ☎ 345 300; Manastirska 21; ☺ 6am-8pm) enjoys wonderful coastal views. This peaceful complex is dominated by the elegant 18th-century Church of the Dormition (Crkva Uspenja Bogorodice, literally 'the falling into sleep of the Mother of God'), carved from pinkish stone from the island of Korčula in Croatia. Inside there's a beautiful gilded iconostasis, but you'll need to be demurely dressed to enter (no shorts, singlets or bikinis).

The smaller church beside it has the same name but is considerably older (possibly 14th century) and has the remains of frescoes. The monastery is well signposted from the highway.

Apart from the building itself (which is a fab bougainvillea-shrouded baroque palace with absolute sea views), the highlight of the **Regional Museum** (Zavičajni muzej; ☎ 322 485; www .rastko.org.yu/rastko-bo/muzej/; admission €1.50; ☺ 9am-6pm Mon-Sat winter, 9am-8pm Tue-Sun summer) is its impressive icon gallery.

High above the town, on the other side of the main road, is the **Španjola fortress**, which was started and finished by the Turks but named after the Spanish (yep, in 1538 they had a brief stint here as well). If the graffiti and empty bottles are anything to go by, it's now regularly invaded by local teenagers. There's a signpost on the main road, but you'll need to take an unmarked left turn not far past Srbina 34.

Activities

Herceg Novi is shaping up as the country's best base for arranging active pursuits, largely due to a network of expats running professional, customer-focused, environmentally aware businesses. A good place to start is **Black Mountain** (☎ 321 968; www.montenegroholiday.com; Šetalište Pet Danica 41), an agency that can arrange pretty much anything adventurous, including diving, rafting, hiking and paragliding. It offers mountain-bike tours (about €20 per head), hires bikes (€15 per day) and has a second office at the bus station.

Another excellent outfit run by British expats, **Kayak Montenegro** (☎ 067-887 436; www .kayakmontenegro.com; Šetalište Pet Danica bb) rents out kayaks (€5/15/25 per one-/four-/eight-hour hire) and offers paddling tours across the bay (€45 including equipment), as well as day trips to explore Lake Skadar from Rijeka Crnojevića (price on application). In October it works with Black Mountain to stage the Adventure Race Montenegro (see p159).

From May to September **Diving Center Marina** (☎ 069-637 915; www.dcmarina.com; Škver bb) organises dives to about 20 sites in the vicinity of the bay and Budva, including various wrecks and caves. A two-dive trip costs €55 including tanks, weights and the boat trip.

Yachting Club 32 (☎ 069-333 011; Šetalište Pet Danica bb) offers parasailing (single/double €40/60 per 10 minutes) and hires jet skis (€50 per 20 minutes), paddle boats (€8 per hour) and mountain bikes (€3/6/15 per one hour/three hours/day).

Various travel agencies, including Black Mountain, offer day trips to Ostrog (€15 to €40), Dubrovnik (€12 to €20) and other hot spots. Montenegro Adria Tours cruises can all be joined at Herceg Novi – the prices are within €5 of the Tivat price (see p91).

Festivals & Events

Running from late January until March, the **Mimosa Festival** is a mash of yellow blooms, marching majorettes, concerts and a swimming carnival. The three-day **Sunčane Skale** (Sunny Steps) music competition, a kind of low-rent Eurovision, is held in the Kanli-Kula in the second week of July. Held in the same venue in early August, the week-long **Film Festival** showcases movies from the region.

Sleeping

In summer there are often people around the bus station touting private accommodation. The going rate is between €12 and €20 per person for accommodation right on the water, €10 for the centre of town and €7 for rooms on the slopes north of the main road. **Black Mountain** (opposite) can fix you up with rooms starting from around €15 per person, although most of its apartments start at a higher level.

Hotel Perla (☎ 345 700; www.perla.cg.yu; Šetalište Pet Danica 98; low-high s €61-104, d €76-130, tr €111-189, apt €140-210; 🕸) It's a fair stroll from the centre but if it's beach you're after, Perla's possie is perfect. The helpful staff speak excellent English and the front rooms of this medium-sized modern block have private terraces and sea views.

Hunguest Hotel Sun Resort (☎ 355 000; www .hunguesthotels.hu; Sveta Bubala bb; low-high s €62-196, d €96-252, apt €106-280; 🕸 🖭) A Hungarian chain has taken over this sprawling seaside resort and while the facilities have been lifted to four stars, the attitude of some of the staff still belongs to an earlier era. There's secure parking, a tennis court, a large outdoor pool and a spa centre.

ourpick **Hotel Aurora** (☎ 321 620; www.auroramon tenegro.com; Šetalište Pet Danica 42; low-high tw €70-100, d €80-100, tr €105-120; 🕸) You'd never suspect that this handsome stone building was once the railway station, especially given its prime waterfront location at the foot of the Old Town. Oscar-nominated filmmaker Emir Kusturica was behind its loving transformation into a chic and comfortable eight-room boutique hotel, hence the cinemas below (right).

Eating & Drinking

If you want to take on the local women in a tussle for the best fresh fruit and vegetables, get to the market on Trg Nikole Đurkovića by around 8am.

Konoba Hercegovina (☎ 322 800; Trg Nikole Đurkovića; mains €2-6) A firm favourite with the locals, this year-round eatery serves everything from burgers and *ćevapčići* (grilled minced-meat sausages) to traditional meat and fish grills and more exotic dishes like Hungarian goulash.

ourpick **Portofino** (Trg Herceg Stjepana; breakfast €2.50-5, mains €6-16) Its location in Herceg Novi's prettiest square makes it tempting to linger here all day, which is exactly what the town's expat community seems to do. The Italianate menu features creamy pastas and juicy steaks.

Sport Café (☎ 322 018; Šetalište Pet Danica 34; breakfast €3-6, mains €5-17) The massive omelettes make it a good breakfast option, but Sport's smart waterside terrace really steps up to the plate as an arena for competitive cocktail-quaffing. Swizzle sticks shaped like tennis rackets are a winning touch.

Konoba Feral (Šetalište Pet Danica 47; mains €7.50-15) 'Feral' is a local word for a ship's lantern, so it's seafood, not wild cat, that takes pride of place on the menu. The grilled squid is amazing and comes with a massive serving of seasonal vegetables and salads.

Entertainment

In summer there's an outdoor cinema in Fortemare (opposite).

Aurora Artplex (☎ 321 620; Šetalište Pet Danica 42; admission €3) Three tiny cinemas, each no bigger than a typical living room.

Getting There & Around

BOAT

Taxi boats ply the coast during summer, charging about €10 for a trip to the beaches on the Luštica Peninsula (p92).

BUS

At the time of research the **bus station** (☎ 321 225; Jadranski put; 🕑 6am-9pm) was on the main highway above the centre, but there were plans afoot to move international services to the western approach to town. Hopefully through-services will continue to stop at the old station. There are frequent buses to Kotor (€3.50, one hour), which stop at all of the small towns around the bay. Buses to Budva either go via Kotor (€5, 1¾ hours) or on the ferry and through Tivat, which is usually quicker depending on the queues (see the boxed text, p76). Regular services head to Podgorica (€9, three hours) via Budva and Cetinje.

GO WILD

The National Tourist Office, in association with local mountain clubs, has developed the resource *Wilderness Hiking & Biking,* which outlines five magical routes for each activity (downloadable from www.montenegro.travel/xxl/en/brochures/index.html). One of the most exciting and gruelling is the **Coastal Mountain Traversal** (Planinarska Transverzala), a 138km hiking route from Herceg Novi to Lake Skadar that passes through the Orjen, Lovćen and Rumija mountain ranges. The green signs pointing to the trail access points are easily spotted from the main road through Herceg Novi, Kotor and Budva. If you're thinking of attempting this or any other major mountain expedition, it's best to consult an agency such as Black Mountain (p78) who can offer advice and arrange tents, guides and access to mountain huts where they're available.

CAR

Herceg Novi is one of the only towns where they charge for parking on the streets. You can either pay the parking wardens in advance for how long you think you'll need or they'll leave a piece of paper on your windscreen. Don't freak out, it isn't a ticket; they'll use this to calculate the charge on your departure. There doesn't seem to be any consequence if you can't find someone to pay when you leave. A torturous, often gridlocked, one-way system runs through the town, so you're best to park in the car parks on the main road if you're day tripping.

Budget (☎ 321 100; www.budget.com; Njegoševa 90) rents out cars from €68 for one day.

Taxi More (☎ 9730)

AROUND HERCEG NOVI

If sky-clad is your preferred attire, **Zelena Banja** (☎ 684 559; www.full-monte.com) is a clothing-optional complex of campsites and cabins that at the time of research was planned to open during the life of this book in the woodland near the Croatian border crossing.

Herceg Novi's coastal sprawl starts at **Igalo** to the west, where the muddy silt from the sea floor is said to have therapeutic qualities. A major medical spa complex dominates the waterfront.

Heading east along the bay you'll pass beachside communities at **Zelenika**, **Kumbor** and **Baošići** before you reach **Bijela** with its dockyard – one of the largest (and ugliest) industrial sites on the bay.

Between Bijela and the Kamenari ferry (try saying that quickly six times) you'll find **Autocamp Zlotković** (☎ 683 401; uroszlo@cg.yu; per adult/child €3.50/3, per small tent/big tent/car/kombi/campervan €1/2/2/3.50/4). Three generations of the Zlotković family have hosted campers under the olive trees leading to the beach. They have

their own water supply, anchorage for boats and run a fish restaurant. Toilets are of the squat variety.

Mt Orjen Орјен

Hulking Mt Orjen (1893m) separates Herceg Novi from Hercegovina and is higher than the more famous Mt Lovćen, the 'black mountain' itself. Patches of evergreen maple and white oak can be found amongst the rugged limestone karst on the lower slopes, giving way to firs and beeches above the winter snowline.

It's a great landscape for hiking and mountain biking, but you'll need to be well stocked with water as any rain that falls here quickly disappears into the porous karst. Marked hiking trails commence near the bus station at Herceg Novi; heading towards Kotor take the first road to the left, then a right turn and look for the sign pointing to the path near a canary-yellow apartment block. This is the start of the mammoth Coastal Mountain Traversal hiking path (see the boxed text, above) which leads all the way to the shores of Lake Skadar.

A shorter option is the four- to five-hour hike to the **Orjen Vratlo hut** (€8 per person, minimum charge €80). If you want to stay the night you'll need to bring sleeping bags and arrange for the local mountaineering society to open it for you; the nice folks at Black Mountain (p78) can sort this out. This could be the first leg of an 18-hour hike from Herceg Novi to Risan, if you're prepared for a huge slog on the second day. The tracks are rocky and exposed to the elements but not particularly difficult.

For six months of the year there is snow on the mountain and even on a scorching summer's day you should be prepared for a storm.

Mamula Island Мамула

Guarding the entrance to the bay, the circular splat of Mamula is only 200m in diameter. It's named after the Austro-Hungarian general who in the mid-19th century created the fort still standing on the island, which became an infamous Italian prison during WWII. Mamula's now being put to much more pleasant use by day trippers who frequent the beach on its northern edge.

The island's a stop on one of the Kayak Montenegro day tours (p78) as well as many of the boat tours of the bay (p91). Otherwise it's easily reached by taxi boat (p79) or you can hire a kayak and paddle here in about one hour.

MORINJ МОРИЊ

☎ 032

Secluded in the first bend of the inner bay, little Morinj is divided into *gornji* (upper) and *donji* (lower) sections, like many of the coastal villages. The silver dome of Sv Petka Church (Crkva Sv Petke) sparkles above, but the main attraction here is the pretty beach. It's a sheltered nook so you may see algae in places, but the water's mainly clear and the views down the bay are amazing.

There is a darker side to this apparently peaceful spot (it is the Balkans after all). In August 2008 four former Yugoslav army reservists were arrested on war crime charges for the alleged inhumane treatment and torture of 169 Croats who were imprisoned here between 1991 and 1992.

In addition to a post office and store, this village harbours contenders for the titles of best camping ground and best restaurant in the country. Morinj's a 30-minute bus ride from either Herceg Novi or Kotor.

A kilometre further along the road at Lipsi, a large road sign trumpets a prehistoric cave-painting site. Anything that may have been worth seeing here was obliterated by a fire a few years back.

Sleeping & Eating

our pick **Autocamp Naluka** (☎ 373 101; www.autocamp-naluka.com; per adult/child €2.50/1, per tent/car/campervan €3/1.50/5) Pitch your tent under the mandarin trees and next to the stream that bubbles out of a spring at a constant 10°C – the water's too cold for mosquitoes but perfect for keeping your beer cold! There are only squat toilets but the site is immaculately kept by its English-

speaking owner. Water shortages aren't a problem either. Naluka's officially only open from July to August, but phone ahead at other times and you may get lucky.

our pick **Konoba Ćatovića Mlini** (☎ 373 030; mains €7-24; ☽ 11am-11pm) The very same crystalline stream flows around and under this former mill, a rustic stone construction with a picturesque mountain backdrop. It may masquerade as a humble family-owned *konoba* but in reality this is one of Montenegro's best restaurants. Watch the geese idle by as you sample the magical bread and olive oil, which appears unbidden at the table. Fish is the focus but traditional Njeguši specialities (see p44) are also offered. On a hot day we'd heartily recommend the cold fish appetiser – rice salad with prawns, mussel salad, tuna salad, white fish and a delicious fish pâté.

RISAN РИСАН

☎ 032 / pop 2083

Risan has the distinction of being the oldest town on the bay, dating to at least the 3rd century BC when it was a fortified Illyrian town. Their queen Teuta is said to have retreated here during the Roman invasion and made it her capital. When the Romans inevitably took over, they erected sumptuous seaside mansions, one of which is now Risan's main claim to fame.

In 1930 the foundations of a grand villa were discovered, complete with wonderful **mosaics** (admission €2; ☽ 8am-8pm 15 May-15 Oct). A shelter has been erected over the site to protect it from the elements, and English-speaking staff are at hand to explain the building's layout. The dining-room floor is decorated with flowers, herbs, grapevines and squid, while other rooms have intricate geometric patterns. Best of all is the bedroom that features a wonderful depiction of Hypnos, the Greek god of sleep, reclining on a pillow.

While summer holidaymakers still head to its small beaches, Risan has a rundown feel, not helped by the port and large hotel hogging its sea frontage. After checking out the mosaics it's worth a short stroll through the overgrown park, which hides the elegant Orthodox **Church of Sts Peter and Paul** (Crkva Sv Petra i Pavla; 1796), and on to the central square, Trg 21 Novembra. Leading up the hill from here is **Gabela**, an atmospheric lane with interesting diagonal cobbling dating from the Ottoman occupation.

Buses running between Herceg Novi and Kotor stop here.

PERAST ПЕРАСТ
☎ 032 / pop 360

Looking like a chunk of Venice has floated down the Adriatic and anchored itself onto the bay, Perast's streets hum with melancholy memories of the days when it was rich and powerful. Despite only having one real street, this tiny town boasts 16 churches and 17 formerly grand palazzos. While some are just enigmatic ruins sprouting bougainvillea and wild fig, others are caught up in the whirlwind of renovation that has hit the town. Soon the bemused villagers may be rubbing shoulders with the likes of Michael Douglas and Catherine Zeta Jones, who were reported to be looking for real estate here.

Orientation & Information

Perast slopes down from the main road to a narrow waterfront road (Obala Marka Martinovića) that runs along its length. At its heart is a small square lined with date palms and the bronze busts of famous citizens. The **post office** (☯ 8am-2.30pm Mon-Sat) faces the square; there are no banks, ATMs or internet cafes.

Sights

The Bujović Palazzo, dating from 1694, has been lovingly preserved and converted into the **Perast Museum** (Muzej grada Perasta; ☎ 373 519; admission €2.50; ☯ 9am-6pm Mon-Sat, 9am-2pm Sun), showcasing the town's proud seafaring history. It's worth visiting for the building alone and for the wondrous photo opportunities afforded by its balcony.

The imposing 55m bell tower belongs to **St Nicholas' Church** (Crkva Sv Nikole), which also has a **museum** (admission €1; ☯ 10am-6pm) containing the remains of various saints and beautifully embroidered vestments. The church itself is unfinished and given that it was commenced in the 17th century and the bay's Catholic community has declined markedly since then, one suspects it never will be completed.

Just offshore are two peculiarly picturesque islands. The smaller **St George's Island** (Sveti Đorđe) rises from a natural reef and houses a Benedictine monastery shaded by cypresses. Its big sister, **Our-Lady-of-the-Rock Island** (Gospa od Škrpjela), was artificially created in the 15th century and every year on 22 July the

locals row over with stones to continue the task. Its magnificent church was erected in 1630 and also boasts a small **museum** (admission €1; ☯ 7am-7pm). Taxi boats regularly ply to the island for around €3.

Festivals & Events

Hitting a Cock Possibly even more distasteful than it sounds, this tradition (on 15 May) commemorates a 1654 victory by the people of Perast over the Turks. A competition is held to shoot a rooster that is chained to a boat and floated out to sea. The victor gets the dead bird and an embroidered towel, but is required to provide wine for the other contestants. The unfortunate cock was traditionally placed at a distance of 150m but after a couple of years with no feathers ruffled, the distance has been shortened to about 60m. The festivities include a Catholic procession, solemn mass and members of the Boka Navy dancing the *kolo* (wheel dance) in the square.

Fašinada The traditional annual event on 22 July, where male descendents of Perast's leading families row a convoy of decorated and roped-together boats to deposit stones on Our-Lady-of-the-Rock Island. It's now accompanied by a yacht race.

International Klapa Festival (www.festivalklapaper ast.com) Two days of traditional Dalmatian-style unaccompanied singing in July or August.

Sleeping

Perast makes an atmospheric and peaceful base from which to explore the bay. Look out for private rental signs in summer.

Boka Bay B&B (www.bokabay.com; apt €50-75; ☒) There are only two cosy sloped-ceiling apartments here – a studio and a one-bedroom – but they both have water views, en suites and kitchenettes. They only take bookings by email.

Villa Milinović (☎ 373 556; www.milinovic-perast .com; low-high r €50-120; ☒) Dating from 1777, this grand old family palace offers eight rooms of varying sizes within its character-filled walls. The wacky bright linen sits a little uncomfortably with the sober surrounds, but the only real niggle is the lack of shower curtains. Room 101 is the best, offering a Juliet balcony and absolute sea views.

our pick **Hotel Conte** (☎ 373 687; www.hotel-conte .com; low-high apt €90-250; ☒ wi-fi) Hotel Conte is not so much a hotel as a series of deluxe studio to two-bedroom apartments in historic buildings scattered around St Nicholas' Church. The sense of age resonating from the stone walls is palpable, even with the distinctly nontraditional addition of a jacuzzi and sauna in the flashest apartment. The sea views only add to the ambience.

Eating

Konoba Otok Bronza (☎ 373 607; mains €5-11) Dating from the 12th century (yes, you read that right), this memorable place has a cavelike interior with a spring spouting mountain water from its rock walls. Settle in for a reasonably priced traditional meal or just soak up the mood over a glass of local vino under the canopy of grapevines.

Conte Nautilus (☎ 373 687; mains €6,50-14) Meals come with lashings of romance on the flower-bedecked waterside terrace of Conte Nautilus, the restaurant associated with Hotel Conte. This close to the water, how could seafood not be the specialty? You'll be presented with platters of whole fish to select from (€42 per kilogram) and then watch the chosen one return to be silver-served at your table.

Getting There & Away

There's no bus station but buses stop at least hourly on the main road at the top of town. Expect to pay less than €3 for any journey within the bay between Kotor (25 minutes) and Herceg Novi (40 minutes).

Boat tours of the bay invariably stop here (see p86).

DOBROTA ДОБРОТА

☎ 032 / pop 8169

These days Dobrota is effectively a residential suburb of Kotor, connecting up with its famous neighbour a short stroll from the Old Town. Despite this it retains a distinctive feel. While Kotor looks inwards from its walls, Dobrota gazes out to sea, stretching along the shoreline for 5km. Although perhaps not as old as Perast's or Kotor's, Dobrota's mansions are even grander and more decayed. Take the Palazzo Milošević, for example. Its four storeys rise to a graceful pediment and while the bottom floors show obvious signs of inhabitation, you can look straight through the windows of the top floors and see the sky.

There's no doubt that Dobrota, like Perast, is undergoing a spate of re-gentrification at the hands of foreign investors. Yet locals still snigger about its reputation as the site of Montenegro's only psychiatric hospital. At the time of research an elegant paved boardwalk was being constructed at the

Kotor end of Dobrota. Hopefully the works will eventually extend to fixing up the rest of the shamefully potholed road.

Orientation & Information

Dobrota spreads up the coast north from Kotor on the eastern side of the bay. The main section is positioned between Jadranski put (Adriatic highway) and a one-way road that runs along the waterfront south towards Kotor. This road can either be accessed from the top end or from a side road about halfway along. Expect a slow crawl along here in summer and watch out for the potholes.

Accident & Emergency Clinic (Dom zdravlja; ☎ 334 538; Jadranski put bb)

Apoteka Aesulap (☎ 334 699; Jadranski put bb; ☑ 7am-11pm) Pharmacy next to the A&E clinic.

Sights & Activities

Dobrota is Kotor's beach, offering a small pebbly stretch a short stroll from the Old Town.

The town's most distinctive features are its two large Catholic churches. **St Matthew's** (Crkva Sv Mateja; 1670) is the older of the two and wears a baroque frontage, a well-proportioned dome and a tall steeple. **St Eustace's** (Crkva Sv Eustahija) dates from 1773 but has a 19th-century steeple. You'll rarely find them open, which is a shame as St Matthew's apparently contains a painting by Bellini and St Eustace's has a Veronese.

The local **diving club** (☎ 067-358 500) stores its gear near St Matthew's Church but mainly runs trips out of Tivat (€80 for two dives including equipment).

Sleeping & Eating

Dobrota is perfect for exploring Kotor at a decent remove from the noise and flurry of the Old Town.

our pick **Palazzo Radomiri** (☎ 333 172; www.palaz zoradomiri.com; low-high s €60-160, d €100-200, ste €60-280; ✄ ✆ wi-fi) Exquisitely beautiful, this honey-coloured early-18th-century palazzo has been transformed into a first-rate boutique hotel. Some rooms are bigger and grander than others (hence the variation in prices), but all 10 have sea views and luxurious furnishings. Guests can avail themselves of a small workout area, sauna, pool, private jetty, bar and restaurant; half-board is included in the summer prices.

Restoran Ellas (☎ 335 115; meals €8-20) Head upstairs to the rooftop terrace for lovely views of the bay and all the usual traditional dishes. You'll find it beside the waterfront, slightly north of the side road heading into Dobrota.

our pick **Restoran Stari Mlini** (☎ 333 555; Jadranski put, Ljuta; meals €11-21) It's well worth making the trip to Ljuta, just north of Dobrota, for this magical restaurant set in and around an old mill by the edge of the bay. If you have time to spare and don't mind picking out bones, order the Dalmatian fish stew with polenta for two. The steaks are also excellent, as are the bread, wine and attentive service.

KOTOR КОТОР
☎ 032 / pop 5341

Those prone to operatic outbursts may find themselves launching into Wagner at their first glimpse of this dramatically beautiful town, wedged between brooding mountains and a moody corner of the bay. Its sturdy walls – started in the 9th century and tweaked until the 18th – arch steeply up the slopes behind it. From a distance they're barely discernible from the mountain's grey hide, but at night they're spectacularly lit, reflecting in the water to give the town a golden halo. Within those walls lie labyrinthine marbled lanes where churches, shops, bars and restaurants surprise you on hidden piazzas.

In July and August people pour into Kotor and the yachts of the super-rich fill the marina, but this town never gets quite as Euro-trashy as some other parts of the coast – this sheltered arm of the bay just isn't as appealing for swimming. But anyone with a heart for romance, fine food, history and architecture will find Kotor a highlight of their Montenegrin travels.

History

It's thought that Kotor began as Acruvium, part of the Roman province of Dalmatia. Its present look owes much to nearly 400 years of Venetian rule when it was known as Cattaro. In 1813 it briefly joined with Montenegro for the first time, but the Great Powers decided to hand it back to Austria, where it remained until after WWI. There's a strong history of Catholic and Orthodox cooperation in the area, although the number of Catholics has dropped from 51% in 1900 to 13% today. Croats now number only 8% of the population.

Orientation

Kotor's funnel-shaped Stari Grad (Old Town) sits between the bay and Mt Sv Ivan, which is part of the lower slopes of Mt Lovćen (p122). Newer suburbs surround the town, linking up to the old settlements of Dobrota to the north, Muo to the west and, beyond this, Prčanj. The main road to Tivat and Budva turns off the waterfront road at a baffling uncontrolled intersection south of the Stari Grad and heads through a long tunnel.

Information

You'll find a choice of banks with ATMs and the post office on the main square, Trg od Oružja. The Accident & Emergency clinic is in Dobrota (p83).

Dr Oliver Prvulović (☎ 068-738 067) English-speaking doctor who works in both Kotor and Budva.
Forza (☎ 304 352; Trg od Oružja; per hr €2 ; ☯ 7am-midnight) An internet cafe, bookshop, cake shop, ice-cream parlour and a sleek cafe.
Information booth (☎ 325 950; www.kotor.travel; outside Vrata od Mora; ☯ 8am-8pm) Tourist and private-accommodation information, maps and brochures.

Sights

The best thing to do in Kotor is to let yourself get lost and found again in the maze of streets. You'll soon know every corner since the town is quite small, but there are plenty of old churches to pop into and many coffees to be drunk in the shady squares.

The main entrance is the **Vrata od Mora** (Sea Gate), constructed in 1555 when the town was under Venetian rule (1420–1797). Look out for the winged lion of St Mark, Venice's symbol, as you wander around the town. Above the gate the date of the city's liberation from the Nazis is remembered with a communist star and a quote from Tito. As you pass through the gate, look for the 15th-century stone relief of the Madonna and child flanked by St Tryphon and St Bernard. Stepping through onto Trg od Oružja (Square of Arms) you'll see the strange stone pyramid in front of the **clock tower** (1602) that was used as a pillory to shame wayward citizens.

Kotor has a proud history as a naval power and the **Maritime Museum** (Pomorski muzej; ☎ 069-045 447; Trg Bokeljske Mornarice, Stari Grad; admission €4; ☯ 8am-11pm Jul-Aug, 8am-7pm Mon-Sat & 9am-1pm Sun Apr-Jun & Sep, 8am-2pm Mon-Sat & 9am-1pm Sun Oct-Mar) celebrates it with three storeys of displays housed in a wonderful early-18th-century

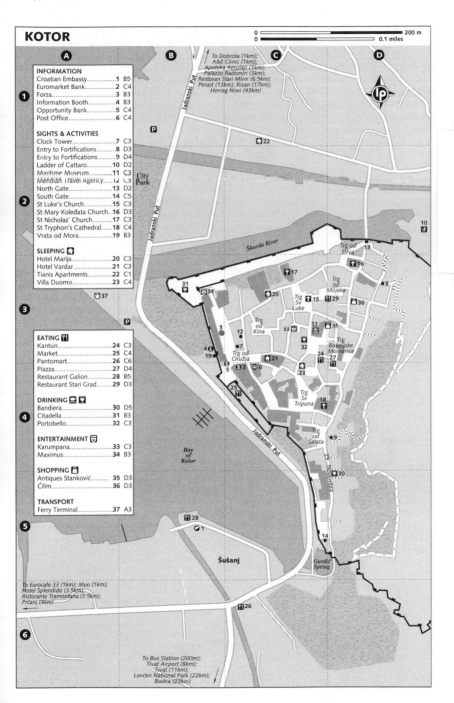

KOTOR

0 — 200 m
0 — 0.1 miles

INFORMATION
Croatian Embassy.................1 B5
Euromarket Bank...................2 C4
Forza......................................3 B3
Information Booth..................4 B3
Opportunity Bank...................5 C4
Post Office.............................6 C4

SIGHTS & ACTIVITIES
Clock Tower...........................7 C3
Entry to Fortifications............8 D3
Entry to Fortifications............9 D4
Ladder of Cattaro.................10 D2
Maritime Museum.................11 C3
Meridian Travel Agency........12 C3
North Gate...........................13 D2
South Gate............................14 C5
St Luke's Church...................15 C3
St Mary Koledata Church....16 D3
St Nicholas' Church..............17 C3
St Tryphon's Cathedral.........18 C4
Vrata od Mora.......................19 B3

SLEEPING
Hotel Marija..........................20 C3
Hotel Vardar.........................21 C3
Tianis Apartments.................22 C1
Villa Duomo..........................23 C4

EATING
Kantun..................................24 C3
Market...................................25 C4
Pantomart.............................26 C6
Piazza....................................27 D4
Restaurant Galion..................28 B5
Restaurant Stari Grad...........29 D3

DRINKING
Bandiera................................30 D5
Citadella...............................31 B3
Portobello.............................32 C3

ENTERTAINMENT
Karumpana............................33 C3
Maximus................................34 B3

SHOPPING
Antiques Stanković...............35 D3
Ćilim.....................................36 D3

TRANSPORT
Ferry Terminal.......................37 A3

To Dobrota (1km); A&E Clinic (1km); Apoteka Aesulap (1km); Palazzo Radomiri (3km); Restoran Stari Mlini (6.5km); Perast (13km); Risan (17km); Herceg Novi (43km)

Škurda River

Bay of Kotor

Šušanj

Gurdić Spring

To Eurocafe 33 (1km); Muo (1km); Hotel Splendido (3.5km); Ristorante Tramontana (3.5km); Prčanj (4km)

To Bus Station (200m); Tivat Airport (8km); Tivat (11km); Lovćen National Park (22km); Budva (23km)

palace. A free audioguide helps explain its collection of photographs, paintings, uniforms, exquisitely decorated weapons and models of ships.

The town's most impressive building is the Catholic **St Tryphon's Cathedral** (Katedrala Sv Tripuna; Trg Sv Tripuna, Stari Grad; admission €1.50; ⊙ 8.30am-7pm), originally built in the 12th century but reconstructed after several earthquakes. When the entire frontage was destroyed in 1667, the baroque bell towers were added; the left one has never been finished. The cathedral's gently hued interior is a masterpiece of Romanesque-Gothic architecture with slender Corinthian columns alternating with pillars of pink stone, thrusting upwards to support a series of vaulted roofs. Its gilded silver-relief altar screen is considered Kotor's most valuable treasure. Up in the reliquary chapel are some lovely icons, a spooky wooden crucifix (1288) and, behind the grill, assorted body parts of saints including St Tryphon. The early martyr's importance to both the Catholic and Orthodox churches makes him a fitting patron for the city.

Sweet little **St Luke's Church** (Crkva Sv Luke; Trg Sv Luke, Stari Grad) speaks volumes about the history of Croat-Montenegrin relations in Kotor. It was constructed in 1195 as a Catholic church but from 1657 until 1812 a Catholic and Orthodox altar stood side by side, with each faith taking turns to hold services here. It was then gifted to the Orthodox Church. Fragments of 12th-century frescoes still survive along with two wonderfully painted iconostases: a 17th-century one in the main church and one from the 18th-century in the chapel of St Spiridon, another saint venerated by both faiths.

Breathe in the smell of incense and beeswax in the relatively unadorned 1909 Orthodox **St Nicholas' Church** (Crkva Sv Nikole; Trg Sv Luke, Stari Grad). The silence, the iconostasis with its silver bas-relief panels, the dark wood against bare grey walls, the filtered light through the dome and the simple stained glass conspire to create a mystical atmosphere.

Tucked in the quiet northern corner of town is the parklike **Trg od Drva** (Wood Sq), hidden behind the Catholic **St Mary Koleđata Church** (Crkva Sv Marije Koleđate; 1221). As it's not usually open you'll probably have to content yourself with admiring the bas-reliefs on the modern bronze doors. Nearby is the 1540 **North Gate**, where a moat is formed by the clear mountain water of the bubbling Škurda River.

Fewer tourists make it to the south end of town, where the houses narrow into a slim corridor leading to the **South Gate** (parts of which date from the 12th century) and the drawbridge over the Gurdić spring. Without the crowds you can easily imagine yourself transported to an earlier time.

Activities

BY FOOT

Looming above Kotor is Mt Sv Ivan (St John), one of the lower peaks of the Lovćen massif. The energetic can make a 1200m ascent via 1350 steps up the **fortifications** (admission €2, charged May-Sep) for unforgettable views and a huge sense of achievement. There are entry points near the North Gate and behind Trg od Salate (Salad Sq). The truly vigorous can climb the ancient caravan trail known as the **Ladder of Cattaro**, which starts near the Škurda River and zigzags up the mountain to join the Coastal Mountain Traversal (see the boxed text, p80) in Lovćen National Park. If you're feeling less hardy you can content yourself with a wonderful drive (see the boxed text, p88).

BY BOAT

Various tour boats leave from opposite the Old Town to explore the bay; expect to pay about €15 for a day tour. If you're keen to potter around the Boka on a boat of your own, you'll be disappointed. A licence is required, so most hire companies supply skippers and cater firmly to the top end. **ProRent** (☎ 305 194) offers two-hour speedboat charters (€150) and five-hour fishing trips (€250). **Avel Yachting** (☎ 325 207; info@avel-yachting.com) charters fancy launches (€720 to €7920 per day) and yachts (€500 to €1190).

Festivals & Events

Traditional Kotor Carnival (www.kotorkarneval.com) Carrying on the Venetian Renaissance tradition with a week of masked balls, parades and performances at the end of February.

Boka Navy Day Dating back to 1420, on 26 June the traditionally clad sailors are presented with the flag and keys of the city and perform the *kolo* (circle dance).

Children's Theatre Festival (www.kfest.cg.yu) Performances by international companies in early July.

Don Branko's Music Days (www.kotorart.com) Classical music festival featuring international artists performing in Kotor's squares and churches from mid-July to mid-August.

International Fashion Selection Some seriously big names (including Romeo Gigli in 2008) send their

---

TOURISM 101

Lots of young Montenegrins rely on tourism for an income. During the high season they often work long hours every day, well aware that the work may dry up in the winter. We spoke to Kotor-based Mickey (Milomir Jukanović) about his job as a tour guide and his favourite places.

Mickey? That's not a very Slavic-sounding name? Actually I'm not Mickey, I'm Milomir. Mickey's just easier to remember. It's usual for people here to have nicknames.

You speak excellent English. I studied English in primary school, high school and faculty (university) and I work with lots of foreign guys. It's quite normal for Montenegrins. I also speak Russian and basic German.

What's your favourite tour? The Boka Bay (Bay of Kotor). I really enjoy working on that tour and being surrounded by one of the prettiest views in my country. Also Lake Skadar. Again, it's peaceful and beautiful.

How do you see tourism in Montenegro today? It is getting better but I have some concerns about the way my country's going. The major thing is that some important things are being forgotten. While trying to get there, you know, people are skipping some steps. The tourist thing just found us completely unprepared and people are not educated as to the levels of service that foreign tourists expect.

That's obviously not the case with you. I studied tourism at the university in Kotor and there was a nonobligatory course on services marketing. We learnt about basic things that may seem obvious but we hadn't really thought about it – like having smiling staff.

What are the top five places that visitors shouldn't miss? Only five? You need to see Tara Canyon, Ostrog Monastery, Boka Bay with Kotor, Lake Skadar...and Cetinje, I think, especially King Nikola's Museum and Cetinje Monastery.

---

collections down a catwalk set up in front of the cathedral at Trg Sv Tripuna in late July.

Summer Carnival (www.kotorkarneval.com) A condensed version of the main carnival staged at a more tourist-friendly time, in late July/early August.

Boka Night Decorated boats take to the bay in mid-August.

Sleeping

Although the Stari Grad is a charming place to stay, you'd better pack earplugs. In summer the bars blast music onto the streets until 1am every night, rubbish collectors clank around at 6am and the chattering starts at the cafes by 8am. Some of the best options are just out of Kotor in quieter Dobrota (p83), Muo and Prčanj (p89).

BUDGET

Enquire about private accommodation at the city's information booth (p84). **Meridian Travel Agency** (☎ 323 448; www.tameridian.cg.yu; near Trg od Oružja, Stari Grad; ⊗ 9am-3pm & 6-9pm Mon-Sat), in the lane behind the clock tower, has rooms on its books at around €15 to €30 per person and can also book hotels.

ourpick **Eurocafe 33** (☎ 069-047 712; lemaja1@cg.yu; Muo 33; r per person €20-25; ⊠) On the Muo waterfront, this traditional stone building with a

small private beach enjoys possibly the best views of Kotor. The top two floors have a scattering of differently configured rooms, some of which share bathrooms. The owner's an ex-footballer turned assistant coach for the national side who speaks excellent English. If there are a few of you, you can enquire about booking a floor.

MIDRANGE & TOP END

Apartments Tianis (☎ 302 178; www.tianis.net; Tabačina bb; r/apt €50/70; ⊠) This newish block offers five large, clean apartments, some of which have a magical view across the Škurda River to the Old Town from their terraces. The rooms are similar but without a kitchenette.

Hotel Marija (☎ 325 062; hotel.marija.kotor@cg.yu; Stari Grad; s/d/tr/q €65/90/103/130; ⊠) Did you remember to bring those earplugs? This little hotel occupies a beautiful palazzo in the centre of the Old Town and although the decor of the rooms is a little dated, it's very comfortable, clean and bordering on grand. One room has a balcony for those Juliet moments.

Hotel Vardar (☎ 325 084; www.hotelvardar.com; Trg od Oružja; low-high s €85-145, d €125-225, ste €123-255; ⊠ wi-fi) Right on the main square, this lovely old place has had a sumptuous modern

---

BACK (ROAD) TO BLACK (MOUNTAIN)

The journey from Kotor to Mt Lovćen, the ancient core of the country, is one of the world's great drives. Take the road heading towards the Tivat tunnel and turn right just past the graveyard (there's no sign). After 5km, follow the sign to Cetinje on your left near the fort. From here there's 17km of good but narrow road snaking up 25 hairpin turns, each one revealing a vista more spectacular than the last. Take your time and keep your wits about you; you'll need to pull over and be prepared to reverse if you meet oncoming traffic. From the top the views stretch over the entire bay to the Adriatic. You can stop for a coffee at the entrance to Lovćen National Park (p122) before heading back; allow two hours for the return trip. Otherwise continue straight ahead for the shortest route to Cetinje (p123) or turn right and continue the spectacular drive on the scenic road through the park.

---

makeover with extremely elegant furnishings. We love the fluffy pillows and swirly marble bathrooms, and the balcony facing the square is more Eva Peron than Juliet. Despite the general swankiness you'll still need the earplugs.

Villa Duomo (☎ 323 111; www.villaduomo.com; Stari Grad; low-high apt €110-280; 🖭) A wonderful blend of modern comforts and traditional ambience, Duomo is the Old Town's most attractive accommodation. Wooden sleigh beds, old-fashioned phones and writing desks are set against the palazzo's bare stone walls, alongside plasma TVs, DVDs and, in some rooms, jacuzzis. Breakfast is served on a lovely internal terrace.

Eating

There are tons of small bakeries and takeaway joints on Kotor's cobbled lanes. For the sweet-toothed, cherry-filled strudel is a speciality of the region. Self-caterers can stock up at the **market** (🕑 7am-2pm) under the town walls, or at the **Pantomart** (Jadranski put; 🕑 6am-11pm) on the road towards the bus station.

Piazza (☎ 069-205 720; Trg Bokeljske Mornarice; mains €2.50-7.50 🕑 8am-late) Serves sandwiches, pancakes and excellent pizzas with thin bases and perfectly measured toppings – great for snacks or an inexpensive sit-down meal.

Kantun (☎ 325 757; Trg Bokeljske Mornarice; mains €5.50-20) Without the sound of techno music this wood-beamed restaurant with a bare stone interior could be a rural *konoba* serving up traditional fare to rough-handed farmers rather than occupying prime Kotor real estate. Make sure you sample the Njeguški cheeses and the *roštiljska kobasica* (grilled homemade sausages).

Restaurant Stari Grad (☎ 322 025; Trg od Mlijeka; mains €8-18; 🖲) Head straight through to the

stone-walled courtyard, grab a seat under the vines and prepare to get absolutely stuffed full of fabulous food – the serves are huge. Either point out the fish that takes your fancy or order from the traditional à la carte menu.

Restaurant Galion (☎ 325 054; Šušanj bb; meals €8-21) With another achingly romantic setting, extremely upmarket Galion gazes directly at the Old Town across the millionaire yachts in the marina. Fresh fish is the focus, served as traditional grills.

Drinking & Entertainment

Kotor's full of cafe-bars that spill into the squares and during the day are abuzz with conversation.

However, all chit-chat stops abruptly in the evening, when speakers are dragged out onto the ancient lanes and the techno music cranked up to near ear-bleeding volumes. On summer nights it's hard to escape it, not that the dolled-up teenagers that pour into town would want to.

Bandiera (29 Novembra) It seems that tourists don't tend to venture down this darker end of town, where you'll find Che Guevara on the wall and rock music on the stereo.

Citadella (☎ 311 000; near Trg od Oružja) This large terrace bar located on top of the old fortifications is fairly touristy, but you can't beat the views of the bay, town and mountain battlements.

Karumpana (☎ 304 912; Stari Grad) Hidden down one of the Old Town's laneways, most of the daytime action happens in the cave-like interior, but come evening the music blasts out with the best of them.

Portobello (☎ 069-407 200; Trg Bokeljske Mornarice, Stari Grad) The bar itself is tiny but on summer nights the DJ lets the music rip outside.

Maximus (☎ 334 342; near Trg od Oružja; admission €2-5; ☒ 11pm-5am Thu-Sat, nightly in summer) Montenegro's most pumping club comes into its own in summer, hosting big-name international DJs and local starlets.

Shopping

Antiques Stanković (☎ 069-071 819; Trg Bokeljske Mornarice) A treasure trove of socialist medals, Roman coins, antique jewellery, traditional garb and other interesting stuff.

Ćilim (near Trg od Mlijeka) Indulge your inner Montenegrin with embroidered folk shirts, knitted socks and locally woven carpets.

Getting There & Away

The **bus station** (☎ 325 809; ☒ 6am-9pm) is to the south of town, just off the road leading to the Tivat tunnel. Buses to Herceg Novi (€3.50, one hour), Budva (€3, 40 minutes) and Podgorica (€7, two hours) are at least hourly.

A taxi to Tivat airport costs around €8.

Azzurra Line ferries connect Kotor with Bari in Italy (see p169).

PRČANJ ПРЧАЊ
☎ 032

Continuing around the bay towards Tivat (rather than taking the tunnel), the road narrows to a single lane despite it being two-way, which makes for lots of fun and plenty of honking when a bus meets a truck coming in the opposite direction. After passing through the village of Muo you'll arrive at Prčanj, 5km from Kotor. This formerly prosperous maritime town has lots of old stone buildings, a couple of restaurants, a bakery, a minimarket, a post office and Catholic churches that come in a choice of small, medium and XXL.

The whopping **Church of the Birth of our Lady** (Crkva Rođenja Bogorodice) – even the name is outsized – was begun in 1789 but not completed until 1908. It's said to be the biggest religious building on the Adriatic coast and it certainly dominates this little town in a God-is-watching-you kind of way. A grand stairway leads up to a terrace offering commanding views of the bay, enjoyed by the slightly bug-eyed statues of St Peter and St Paul standing sentinel on the church's baroque facade.

Back on the flat, the medium-sized 18th-century **St Nicholas' Church** (Crkva Sv Nikole) has a Franciscan monastery attached, while the smaller **St John's** (Crkva Sv Ivana) dates from 1221.

Sleeping & Eating

Hotel Splendido (☎ 301 700; www.splendido-hotel.com; low-high s €65-116, d €93-166, apt €119-199; ☒ ☒ ☐ wi-fi) Negotiating the 4km drive along the narrow waterfront road from Kotor can be stressful but aside from that, Splendido is magnifico. Completely gutted and fitted with comfortable modern rooms, this large stone palazzo still surveys the bay as solidly as it's ever done, although there's now a blissful terrace and swimming pool separating it from the water's edge.

ourpick Ristorante Tramontana (☎ 301 700; mains €4-16) It's hard to top the romantic setting of this Italian restaurant on the terrace of the Hotel Splendido. The food is equally memorable, from sublime pasta to perfectly tender grilled squid.

STOLIV СТОЛИВ
☎ 032

Donji Stoliv is another pleasant seaside village with a huddle of stone houses surmounted by a grand church, 9.5km from Kotor. It's worth stopping here to take the idyllic but steep half-hour's walk through the olive and chestnut trees to the upper village, **Gornji Stoliv**. Most of the families who would have lived here for centuries have now left, with only a few houses remaining occupied and the rest in varying states of picturesque ruin. A church dedicated to the prophet Elijah (Crkva Sv Ilije) dating from 1553 keeps a lonely vigil. At 250m, the views over the bay to Perast are sublime.

Down in Donji Stoliv several houses offer **camping** in July and August (enquire at other times) under their fig and olive trees for around €10 for two people with a car and tent. Facilities are basic (squat toilets with a basket for toilet paper) and water supplies sometimes run out.

LASTVA ЛАСТВА
☎ 032

Continuing on from Stoliv, the road rounds the tip of the Vrmac Peninsula and passes the ferry terminal at Lepetane (see the boxed text, p76) before popping out in the front part of the bay.

Two kilometres further is Lastva, another divided village, but the *gornja* (upper) section of this one has been actively promoted to tourists for its rustic ambience. There's a decent road for starters, leading 3km up the hill. **Gornja Lastva** doesn't offer the same off-the-beaten-track satisfaction as Stoliv, but it's nice to see that this village has been kept alive. Old ladies dressed in black potter about gathering wild herbs, and if you're lucky the parish priest will be around to unlock the 15th-century **St Mary's Church** (Crkva Sv Marije) which reputedly has some accomplished Italian paintings inside. The best time to visit is the first Saturday in August when a village fair is held.

Down in **Donja Lastva** there is a summer **tourist office** (8am-noon & 5-8pm Mon-Sat, 8am-noon Sun) where you can make enquiries about private accommodation in one of the nearby villages. On the tiny village square, next to **St Roko's Church** (Crkva Sv Roka; 1901), **Konoba Giardina** (069-435 496; mains €4-14) dishes up the usual traditional seafood fare as well as substantial cheese and *pršut* (smoke-dried ham) sandwiches.

TIVAT ТИВАТ
032 / pop 9467

Major development is planned for this town, which is not necessarily a bad thing as Tivat has plenty of room for improvement. A row of graceful palm trees lines the waterfront but they do little to disguise the shabby apartment blocks that clutter the centre. At present it's the airport that's the main drawcard, although the town is a useful base to explore the sweet villages of the Vrmac and Luštica Peninsulas.

Aristocratic families from Perast, Dobrota and Kotor once built their summer residences at Tivat to take advantage of its sunny outlook. Canadian businessman Peter Munk hopes to lure the indulged here again with the planned €260-million-plus construction of the massive Porto Montenegro superyacht marina and resort at the old Arsenal shipyard. The complex will include luxury apartments, shops, restaurants and a Four Seasons hotel. There's also likely to be a golf course in the vicinity.

The project isn't without controversy; 3500 locals took to the streets to protest the sale of this state asset to foreign investors and the loss of 480 jobs. Environmental concerns have also been raised, but the developers have argued that the massive cleanup they've committed to undertake on this industrial site will outweigh the impact of the 650 giant yachts that will be able to be berthed at the marina.

Tivat is home to the Bay of Kotor's largest remaining Croat and Catholic community, representing 20% of its population.

Orientation & Information
The centre of Tivat sits between Jadranski put (Adriatic highway) and the sea. Ulica Palih Boraca is the main street and has a post office, a cluster of banks with ATMs, the bus station and a helpful **tourist office** (671 324; www.tivat.travel; Palih Boraca 8; 8am-3pm Mon-Sat, 8am-2pm Sun).

Sights & Activities
The **Town Beach** (Gradska Plaža) is a long concrete platform with a 20m pebbly section reaching from the central promenade southeast towards the marina. There is another pebbly beach, **Belani**, just past the marina.

Tivat's excellent **Gallery & Museum** (Muzejska zbirka i galerija Tivat; 674 591; Nikole Đurkovića 10; admission free; 9am-noon & 6-9pm Mon-Sat, 9am-noon Sun) occupies its most interesting building, the 500-year-old fortified summer residence of the Buća family. The gallery focuses on modern painting and sculpture. Ask the staff to unlock the solid stone defensive tower nearby, which houses a collection of Roman bits and bobs. Next door is a well-presented ethnographical museum with fishing and farming artefacts accompanied by photos of them being put to use. Head upstairs for beautiful jewellery and folk costumes, including little handbags and parasols that the women would wear to ape Western fashion.

Tiny **St Anthony's Church** (Crkva Sv Antuna; Kalimanj bb) dates from the 14th century but is in such a poor state of repair that it turns into a swimming pool when it rains. Inside are some mouldy modern religious prints and the water-damaged remains of frescoes; look out for the 14 coats of arms of Kotor's famous families. From Belani Beach take the gateway through the ruined wall that once protected the summer residence of the Pima family. The church was their private chapel.

North of the centre the **Town Park** (Gradski Park) is a leafy, peaceful retreat. At one edge is the headquarters of Tivat's Arsenal football club. We suspect that the club's North London namesake has nothing to fear if the state of their home ground is anything to go by.

The cruise boat **Vesna II** (tours €15) departs from the esplanade at 9.30am during the tourist season for an expedition that

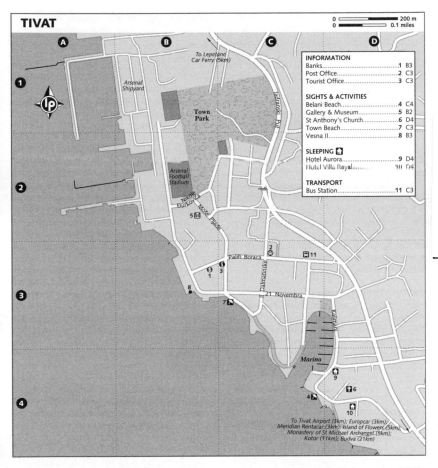

TIVAT

INFORMATION	
Banks.....................................1	B3
Post Office............................2	C3
Tourist Office.......................3	C3

SIGHTS & ACTIVITIES	
Belani Beach.........................4	C4
Gallery & Museum.................5	B2
St Anthony's Church..............6	D4
Town Beach..........................7	C3
Vesna II................................8	B3

SLEEPING	
Hotel Aurora........................9	D4
Hotel Villa Royal.................10	D4

TRANSPORT	
Bus Station.........................11	C3

includes an hour at each of Žanjice beach, Herceg Novi, Perast's islands and Kotor; the return trip is at 7pm.

Montenegro Adria Tours (☎ 674 999; www.monte negroadriatours.com; Župa bb) offers bus tours to Budva (€20), Kotor and Lovćen (€27), Stari Bar (€30), Dubrovnik (€35), Cetinje and Lake Skadar (€40), Ostrog (€40), Albania (€45) and Durmitor (€50), as well as rafting trips on the Tara River (€80) and a range of boat cruises including the following:

- Boka cruise, stopping at Risan, Perast, Our-Lady-of-the-Rock Island, Kotor (€23)
- Budva day cruise, heading down the coast as far as Sveti Stefan (€35)
- Kotor by night (€15)
- Perast and islands half-day cruise (€18)
- Žanjice-Mamula-Blue Grotto day cruise (€24)

Festivals & Events

Like the other bay towns, Tivat's residents don their Venetian masks for a February **carnival**. The Boka Navy gets to dress up and dance the *kolo* at the **Boka Night** in late February. The **Festival of Mediterranean Theatre** offers three weeks of theatre, film and exhibitions from late July, while the **November Culture Days** offer similar fare for those winter nights.

Sleeping & Eating

Enquire at the tourist office (opposite) about private accommodation. Rooms range from €7 to €15 in the high season and from €6 to €10 at other times. Expect to pay €40 to €60 for a two-person apartment. Tivat's eateries aren't very noteworthy but you'll find pizza joints and bakeries scattered around the centre and a row of coffee-and-cake places on the esplanade at the bottom of the main street.

Hotel Aurora (☎ 671 259; aurora@cg.yu; Kalimanj bb; s/d €33/50; 🅿️) Bedecked in flower boxes and bougainvillea, Aurora offers 65 beds in a series of two low-rise blocks near the marina. Parts of its lush gardens were due to be sacrificed for a pool and spa in renovations planned at the time of research.

Hotel Villa Royal (☎ 675 310; www.hotelvillaroyal .cg.yu; Kalimanj bb; low-high s €42-65, d €68-102, apt €102-141; 🅿️ 🖥️) You couldn't accuse this modern block of being drab. Bright blue and orange walls add cheer to the spotless rooms, some of which have balconies and sea views. The friendly staff have a similar effect. Prices include half-board.

Getting There & Around

Tivat sits on the western side of the Vrmac Peninsula, which juts out into the Bay of Kotor and divides it in two. The quickest route to Kotor is to take the main road southeast in the direction of Budva, turn left at the major intersection past the airport and take the tunnel. The alternative is the narrow coastal road. For Herceg Novi, take the ferry from Lepetane, 5km northwest of town (see the boxed text, p76).

From the **bus station** (Palih Boraca bb) there are frequent buses to Budva (€2) via the airport (50c) as well as services to Kotor (€1, six daily) and Herceg Novi (€3, seven daily).

Tivat airport is 3km south of town and 8km through the tunnel from Kotor. Airport minibuses leave when full and head to Budva (€3.50) and Herceg Novi (€8). **Europcar** (☎ 671 894; www.europcarcg.com) and **Meridian Rentacar** (☎ 069-060 525; www.meridian-rentacar.com) have counters at Tivat airport but you may need to call ahead to ensure that they're staffed.

AROUND TIVAT

The overly prosaically named **Island of Flowers** (Ostrvo Cvijeća) is accessed by an unlikely looking road that heads behind the airport and through a rundown area where a former tourist complex still shelters people displaced by the recent wars in the region. At the very end of the potholed road is the

Monastery of St Michael Archangel (Manastir Sv Arhanđela Mihaila). This is the area's most historically significant site. The remains of Roman mosaics have been discovered here, along with the ruins of a 9th-century church and Benedictine monastery. From the early 13th century St Michael's was the seat of the Orthodox bishop of Zeta until it was destroyed by the Venetians in 1452. The sweet little 19th-century **Holy Trinity Church** (Crkva Sv Trojice) stands nearby, shaded by trees and protected by stone walls.

Two more islands stretch out in a line from here but you'll need a boat to access them (a taxi boat from Tivat or Herceg Novi will do the trick). The larger, heavily forested **St Mark's Island** (Sveti Marko) used to be a Club Med and you can still see the huts poking up through the trees. It's a prime spot with a couple of nice beaches so it's bound to be developed sometime soon.

Beyond this the diminutive **Our-Lady-of-Mercy Island** (Gospa od Milosti) was once the residence of Kotor's Catholic bishops and is now a convent. A wooden statue of the Madonna kept in the church is said to have miraculous powers.

LUŠTICA PENINSULA ЛУШТИЦА

Reaching out to form the southern headland of the Bay of Kotor, the gorgeous Luštica Peninsula hides secluded beaches and a dusting of idyllic villages scattered amongst the olive groves of its remote southern edge. If you want to enjoy this magical area while it's still relatively untouched you'd better get in quick. At the time of research tenders were being invited for the privatisation and development of 680 hectares of state and local authority land, a portion of which has its ownership disputed by local villagers.

Krtole & Kaluđerovina
Кртоле и Калуђеровина

The first section of the peninsula facing the bay is already quite developed. At Krtole the beaches look over the green swathe of St Mark's Island and the picturesque Our-Lady-of-Mercy Island that are immediately offshore. If you're looking for a spot to chill out and relax by the beach, you could do a lot worse. This area is cheaper and less frantic than most of the Adriatic coast and some excellent family-friendly mid-sized hotels have sprung up.

Hotel Vizantija (☎ 680 015; www.vizantija.com; Kaluđerovina bb; low-high s €41-58, d €54-76, apt €68-116; ✗ ♨ ▯) Vizantija's three rooms and nine apartments are simply furnished but spick and span. There's a lovely private beach and if the weather turns to custard there's a heated indoor swimming pool as well. Make sure your hire car's got some grunt before you tackle the steep driveway.

Vila Briv (☎ 325 892; yubriv@cg.yu; Obala Đuraševića bb; apt €60-100; ✗ ▯) Step down from the sun deck of this new modern block and straight into the water. There are 24 attractive apartments of differing sizes and configurations on offer, the largest sleeping four comfortably or six at a squeeze. Try for the ones on the ground floor that have large terraces facing the water. You can rent a jet ski or borrow a kayak to paddle out to the islands, and all guests get a free boat cruise of the bay.

ourpick **Vino Santo** (☎ 067-851 662; Obala Đuraševića bb; mains €8.50-18) If different-restaurant-same-menu fatigue is starting to set in, Vino Santo offers the antidote. The traditional seafood favourites are all present and accounted for, but acclaimed chef Dragan Peričić adds a French twist in the delivery. Enjoy the prawns sautéed in cognac and the serene island views as proficient waiters in black bow ties scurry around.

Rose Poce

Continuing west the houses stop, the road gets narrower and the scenery gets greener and prettier. Climbing up the ridge, a panorama of the bay opens up before you. At the peninsula's very tip you'll find the sleepy fishing village of Rose (pronounced with two syllables), a blissful stand of stone houses gazing across the sparkling waters of the bay to Herceg Novi. When we visited a flurry of renovation was in progress but thankfully no sign of any large construction.

Outside summer, village life winds down to near inertia but from May to September a handful of waterside eateries open their doors to day trippers. One of them is **Konoba Adriatic Rose** (☎ 031-687 020; mains €5-11) where you can kick back under the vines with a sandwich (€3) or more substantial seafood meal. If you fancy staying over, ask a local about private accommodation.

If you don't have a car, Rose's easily reached by taxi boat from Herceg Novi (around €10). Kayak Montenegro (p78) stops here on their guided paddle tours or you can hire a kayak and go it alone; it takes about 30 minutes each way.

Southern Hinterland & Beaches

If you have a hire car and you're in the mood for a leisurely drive with a high probability of getting at least temporarily lost, continue on the narrow back roads from Rose that meander through the bucolic olive groves of the southern half of the peninsula. If you see signs for Radovići you're still heading in the right direction.

Along the southern coastline is a string of clean beaches that are popular with day trippers from Herceg Novi. **Dobreč** is reported to have some of the cleanest waters in Montenegro and is only accessible by sea. Kayak Montenegro (p78) day trips head here after visiting Rose. The large white pebbly beach of **Žanjice** sits in a sheltered cove below the olive groves attracting nearly 1000 people in the height of summer. Neighbouring **Mirišta** has a beachside restaurant and can be visited as part of the Kayak Montenegro day trip to Mamula Island (p81).

Another popular boat-tour stop is the **Blue Grotto** (Plava Špilja), so called for the mesmerising effect of the light reflecting through the water. Boats head into the 9m-high cave and usually allow you an opportunity for an iridescent swim. Montenegro Adria Tours (p91) has cruises heading here (combined with Mamula Island and Žanjice), departing from Herceg Novi and Tivat.

At the base of the peninsula, just south of the main town Radovići, is beautiful **Pržno** (not to be confused with the other Pržno near Sveti Stefan). Many of the locals know this beach as Plavi Horizont (Blue Horizon) after the large package-tour hotel it's attached to. This gorgeous scallop of white sand sits within a green horseshoe of scrub, pines and olive trees and is a definite candidate for Montenegro's best beach. Signs advertise a €3 charge for parking, but when we visited (just outside the high season) it wasn't enforced. Facilities include toilets, changing screens, snack stands and a cafe, bar and restaurant.

Adriatic Coast

If coastlines could enter an equivalent of the Eurovision Song Contest, the bookies would surely back the eastern Adriatic – and not just because of Balkan block-voting either. Like the Bay of Kotor, it's the juxtaposition of mountains and sea that sends the spirit soaring, although unlike the bay it's a less closed-in, sunnier vibe that's engendered here and the water's even clearer.

Croatia may hog most of the coast but Montenegro's tiny section packs a lot into a very small area (a bit like the country itself). Without the buffer of Croatia's islands, more of Montenegro's shoreline has developed into sandy beaches, culminating in a 12km continuous stretch leading to the Albanian border.

Unsurprisingly, much of the nation's determination to reinvent itself as a tourist mecca has focused firmly on this scant 100km coastal region. In July and August it seems that the entire Serbian world and a fair chunk of its northern Orthodox brethren can be found crammed into it. Avoid those months and you'll find a charismatic clutch of small towns and fishing villages to explore.

Living on the fault line between various civilisations, the people of the coast have fortified their settlements since ancient times. That legacy can be explored in the lively bars and shops of Budva's Old Town, the surreal glamour of Sveti Stefan's village resort, the ramshackle residences within Ulcinj's fortifications and, most evocatively, the lonely and mysterious ruins of Haj-Nehaj, Stari Bar and Svač. Otherwise just spend your days lazing beside azure waters and supping the local vino in outdoor cafes between the oleanders.

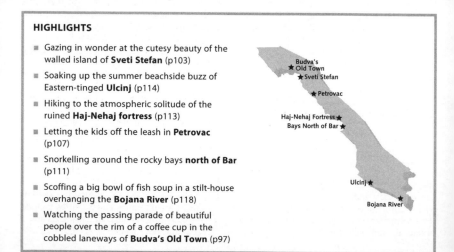

HIGHLIGHTS

- Gazing in wonder at the cutesy beauty of the walled island of **Sveti Stefan** (p103)
- Soaking up the summer beachside buzz of Eastern-tinged **Ulcinj** (p114)
- Hiking to the atmospheric solitude of the ruined **Haj-Nehaj fortress** (p113)
- Letting the kids off the leash in **Petrovac** (p107)
- Snorkelling around the rocky bays **north of Bar** (p111)
- Scoffing a big bowl of fish soup in a stilt-house overhanging the **Bojana River** (p118)
- Watching the passing parade of beautiful people over the rim of a coffee cup in the cobbled laneways of **Budva's Old Town** (p97)

Budva's
★ Old Town
★ Sveti Stefan

★ Petrovac

Haj-Nehaj Fortress ★
Bays North of Bar ★

Ulcinj ★

★
Bojana River

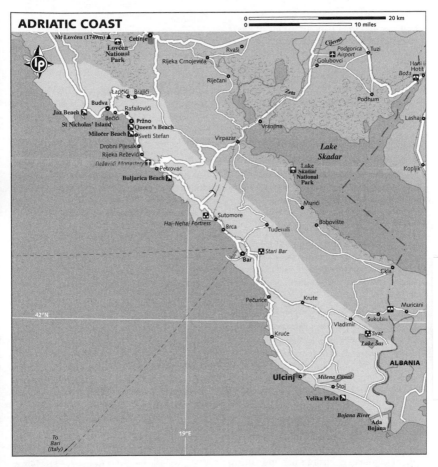

ADRIATIC COAST

History

From the 4th century BC the Ancient Greeks set up colonies along the Illyrian-controlled coast, such as Bouthoe (Budva). Once the Romans had completely smashed Illyria in 168 BC, the region was incorporated into their province of Dalmatia and for over 500 years it benefited from its position near the centre of a great empire. When the decision was made to split the Roman Empire in two, the border-line crossed this section of the coast, leaving most of it within the Greek-influenced eastern (Byzantine) half.

The 'barbarian' Avars poured into the area in the 6th century with only Budva (at the time called Butua) holding out as a bastion of Byzantine culture. The Avars were eventually

defeated and disappeared from human history, but the Slavs were another story. One group, the Serbs, had reached this part of the coast by the 7th century and put down roots, organising into small clans. These eventually became part of the principality of Duklja (later called Zeta), Montenegro's antecedent.

Although beholden to Byzantium, the coastal towns were also influenced by the Latin west due in part to the increasing naval power of Venice. In 1089, only 35 years after the split of Christianity into Catholic (western) and Orthodox (eastern) halves, the rulers of Duklja succeeded in negotiating the creation of a Catholic archdiocese in Bar. Eventually Duklja was brought back into Byzantine control and later incorporated into the Serbian kingdom of Raška. In 1276, Stefan Dragutin overthrew his father to become king of Raška and installed his mother Helen of Anjou as ruler of Zeta, including most of the coast. Helen was a devout Catholic who founded Franciscan monasteries in Bar and Ulcinj.

As Raška became bogged down fighting Byzantium, Bulgaria, Hungary, Venice and the Ottoman Turks, a new force started to gain power in Zeta, the Balšić family. Some historians believe they were originally Orthodox but later converted to Catholicism hoping this would gain them acceptance from the coastal population. In 1368 they had control of Budva, Bar and Ulcinj, but by the end of the century they were forced to oscillate between being a vassal state of the Adriatic's two big players, the Venetians and the Ottomans. By 1443 Venice ruled the coast with the support of powerful families such as the Paštrovići, who were offered a degree of autonomy.

After enjoying a couple of generations of peace, the people of the coast were once again under siege in 1570, this time from the Ottomans who already ruled most of the interior. Once Ulcinj fell, Bar surrendered without a fight. The Paštrovići resisted but couldn't prevent Budva from being sacked. In 1573 Venice signed a peace treaty confirming Ottoman control of the cities south of Budva, much to the detriment of the Paštrovići who continued to oppose their new overlords. In contrast, Ulcinj became a largely Muslim town, as it remains today.

This situation continued until 1877 when King Nikola's Montenegrin army ended 300 years of Ottoman control in Bar and Ulcinj, in the process finally gaining the seaport that they so desperately craved.

Montenegro disappeared completely after WWI as the whole of this coastal region was subsumed into the Kingdom of Serbs, Croats and Slovenes in 1918 (later Yugoslavia). During WWII both this part of Yugoslavia and neighbouring Albania were occupied by the Italians, who planned to redraw the boundaries to include Ulcinj within Albania and annex Budva directly into Italy, leaving only Bar within their planned puppet Montenegrin state. This was never to eventuate and following the Partisan victory, all of the coastal area was incorporated into Montenegro within the federal Yugoslavia, including Budva for the first time.

Climate

Gorgeously Mediterranean is the best way to describe it. Ulcinj is said to be one of the sunniest spots on the Adriatic, notching up 218 sunny days a year.

Dangers & Annoyances

There are no particular dangers but the coast can suffer terribly from water shortages during summer. This is particularly true in Budva, although a new desalination plant may address this in coming years.

Getting There & Away

Budva is connected to the Bay of Kotor by the Jadranski put (Adriatic highway; also known as 'Jadranska magistrala'). The main route to Cetinje and Podgorica leaves Jadranski put between Budva and Bečići and climbs steeply into the mountains. Petrovac is connected to Podgorica via a highway leading through Virpazar and the western edge of Lake Skadar. This route can also be reached by a tunnel starting near Sutomore, north of Bar. A scenic back road links Ulcinj to the southern edge of Montenegro's section of Lake Skadar.

Regular buses connect all coastal towns with the Bay of Kotor and Podgorica, although they're most frequent from Budva.

A railway line links Bar with the centre of the country, including Lake Skadar and Podgorica. For ferries from Bar to Italy and for connections to Albania from Ulcinj, refer to the Transport chapter, page 169.

Getting Around

Jadranski put is the main road connecting all coastal towns and is well served by buses. Olimpia Express (p102) runs especially frequent local services between Budva and Sveti Stefan. Taxi boats are a useful option for short trips between beaches.

BUDVA БУДВА
☎ 033 / pop 10,098

The poster child of Montenegrin tourism, Budva – with its atmospheric Stari Grad (Old Town) and numerous beaches – certainly has a lot to offer. Yet the child has quickly moved into a difficult adolescence, fuelled by rampant development that has leeched much of the charm from the place. Even more is planned, with a 27-storey hotel recently approved. In the height of the season the sands are blanketed with package holidaymakers from Russia

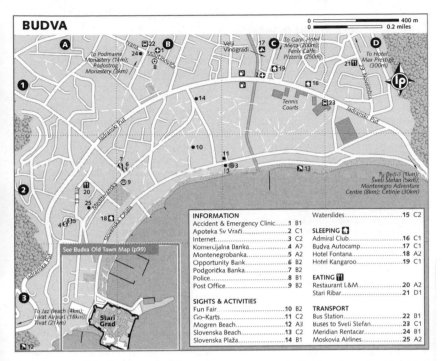

BUDVA

0   400 m
0   0.2 miles

INFORMATION	
Accident & Emergency Clinic......1	B1
Apoteka Sv Vrači........................2	C1
Internet...................................3	C2
Komercijalna Banka....................4	A2
Montenegrobanka.......................5	A2
Opportunity Bank.......................6	B2
Podgorička Banka.......................7	B2
Police......................................8	B1
Post Office................................9	B2

SIGHTS & ACTIVITIES	
Fun Fair.................................10	B2
Go–Karts...............................11	C2
Mogren Beach.........................12	A3
Slovenska Beach......................13	C2
Slovenska Plaža......................14	B1

Waterslides............................15	C2

SLEEPING	
Admiral Club...........................16	C1
Budva Autocamp.....................17	C1
Hotel Fontana.........................18	A2
Hotel Kangaroo.......................19	C1

EATING	
Restaurant L&M.......................20	A2
Stari Ribar..............................21	D1

TRANSPORT	
Bus Station............................22	B1
Buses to Sveti Stefan...............23	C1
Meridian Rentacar...................24	B1
Moskovia Airlines....................25	A2

and Ukraine, while the nouveau riche park their multimillion-dollar yachts in the town's guarded marina. By night you'll run a gauntlet of glorified strippers attempting to cajole you into the beachside bars. It's the buzziest place on the coast so if you're in the mood to party, bodacious Budva will be your best buddy.

Orientation

Jadranski put runs straight through Budva. The Stari Grad isn't visible from the road but juts into the sea near the Tivat approach to town. The marina is immediately north of it, and beyond this Slovenska Beach begins. The main beachside promenade is pedestrianised Slovenska Obala. Apart from the Old Town's lanes, hardly any streets have names and fewer have signs.

Information

There are clusters of banks on and around Ulica Mediteranska.

Accident & Emergency Clinic (Map p97; ☎ 451 026; Ivana Milutinovića bb)

Apoteka Sv Vrači (Map p97; ☎ 453 813; Jadranski put bb; ⏱ 8am-10pm) Pharmacy.

Dr Oliver Prvulović (☎ 068-738 067) English-speaking doctor who works in Budva and Kotor.

Internet (Map p97; Slovenska Obala bb; per 30min €2) Terminals are set up in tents in summer.

Police (Map p97; ☎ 451 183; Ivana Milutinovića bb)

Post office (Map p97; ☎ 402 564; Mediteranska bb)

Tourist office (Map p99; ☎ 452 750; Njegoševa bb, Stari Grad; ⏱ 9am-9pm May-Oct) Brochures about local attractions and accommodation.

Sights

STARI GRAD СТАРИ ГРАД

Budva's best feature and star attraction is its Stari Grad (Old Town) – a mini-Dubrovnik with marbled streets and Venetian walls rising from the clear waters below. You can still see the remains of Venice's emblem, the winged lion of St Mark, over the **main gate** (Map p99). Much of the Old Town was ruined in two earthquakes in 1979 but it has since been completely rebuilt and now houses more shops, bars and restaurants than residences. At its seaward end, the **Citadel** (Map p99; admission €2; ⏱ 8am-midnight May-Nov) offers striking views, a small museum and a library full of rare tomes and maps. Nearby

---

A LOAD OF ANCIENT BULL (& SNAKES)

The founding of Budva is celebrated in the sort of mythical soap opera that the Ancient Greeks loved so much. Cadmus was the son of Agenor, King of Phoenicia (present-day Lebanon, Syria, Israel and Palestine) and the brother of the beautiful Europa, who the great god Zeus took quite a shine to. Europa must have really liked livestock as Zeus turned himself into a bull in order to seduce her. Hiding amongst her father's flocks, he waited until Europa spotted him, caressed his powerful flanks and jumped on his back. He then raced off with her to Crete, thankfully turning himself back into his godly form before having his way with her (when it comes to Zeus, there's a very fine line between seduction and rape). Europa went on to become the first Queen of Crete and give her name to an entire continent.

Cadmus was sent to search for his sister, promising not to return without her. He never did find her and ended up founding the Greek city of Thebes, stocking it with brave men that he grew out of the teeth of a sacred water dragon that he had slain (as you do). He then married Harmonia in the sort of A-list shindig that today's gossip magazines would pay a fortune for, with several immortals as guests.

However, killing a sacred water dragon is very bad luck, so Cadmus and Harmonia hitched up their oxen in order to make a fresh start someplace else. Far to the northwest they founded a new city (with no assistance from dragon teeth), naming it Bouthoe (later Budva) after the Greek word for oxen.

The miserable luck didn't lift and Cadmus was heard complaining that if the gods were so fond of scaly critters then he bloody well wished he was one. The gods, never missing an opportunity for a spot of black humour, obliged – promptly turning him into a snake. Harmonia, perhaps with more qualms about cross-species lovin' than her sister-in-law, begged to be allowed to join him and they both slithered off to live happily every after, or something like that.

---

is the **entry to the town walls** (Map p99; admission €1; ☻ 9am-5pm Mon-Sat).

In the square in front of the Citadel is an interesting cluster of churches. Beautiful frescoes cover the walls and ceiling of the **Holy Trinity Church** (Crkva Sv Trojice; Map p99; ☻ 8am-noon & 5-8pm summer, 8am-noon & 4-7pm winter). Built in 1804 out of stripes of pink and honey-coloured stone, this Orthodox church is the only one that's regularly open. The Catholic **St John's Church** (Crkva Sv Ivana; Map p99), parts of which possibly date from the 9th century, houses the *Madonna of Budva* – a 12th-century icon venerated by Catholic and Orthodox Budvans alike. Tiny **St Mary's in Punta** (Crkva Sv Marije; Map p99) dates from 804 and **St Sava's Church** (Crkva Sv Save; Map p99) from the 14th century, but they're rarely open.

The **Archaeological Museum** (Arheološki muzej; Map p99; ☎ 453 308; Petra I Petrovića 11, Stari Grad; adult/child €2/1; ☻ 9am-10pm) shows off the town's ancient and complicated history – dating back to at least 500 BC – over three floors of exhibits. There's an impressive collection of Greek and Roman jewellery, ceramics and glassware (how it survived in a town so prone to earthquakes and war is anyone's guess) and an ancient helmet with holes in the back, which suggest that the former owner had at least one very bad day.

Also in the Old Town is the **Museum of Modern Art** (Moderna galerija; Map p99; ☎ 451 343; Cara Dušana 19, Stari Grad; admission free; ☻ 8am-2pm & 5-8pm), an attractive gallery staging temporary exhibitions.

BEACHES

With so much construction going on, you might find yourself being lulled by the sound of concrete mixers rather than waves on Budva's beaches – that's if you can find a spot with no Euro-disco blaring. Little **Stari Grad Beach** (Map p99), immediately south of the Old Town, has the ancient walls as an impressive backdrop. If you wander around the headland you'll find quieter double-bayed **Mogren Beach** (Map p97). There's a spot near here where the fearless or foolhardy leap from the cliffs into the waters below.

By the walls on the opposite side of the Old Town, **Maša Beach** (Map p99) is 100m of pebbles leading down from an upmarket cafe. After the marina the long sweep of **Slovenska Beach** (Map p97), Budva's main beach, commences

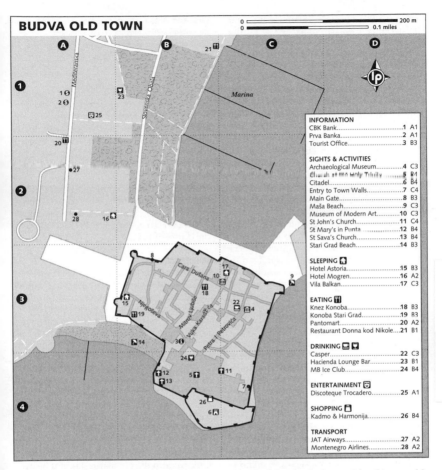

BUDVA OLD TOWN

0 — 200 m
0 — 0.1 miles

Marina

INFORMATION
CBK Bank...................................1 A1
Prva Banka................................2 A1
Tourist Office...........................3 B3

SIGHTS & ACTIVITIES
Archaeological Museum............4 C3
Church of the Holy Trinity........5 B4
Citadel......................................6 B4
Entry to Town Walls.................7 C4
Main Gate.................................8 B3
Maša Beach..............................9 C3
Museum of Modern Art...........10 C3
St John's Church......................11 C4
St Mary's in Punta...................12 B4
St Sava's Church......................13 B4
Stari Grad Beach.....................14 B3

SLEEPING
Hotel Astoria..........................15 B3
Hotel Mogren..........................16 A2
Vila Balkan..............................17 C3

EATING
Knez Konoba............................18 B3
Konoba Stari Grad....................19 B3
Pantomart...............................20 A2
Restaurant Donna kod Nikole...21 B1

DRINKING
Casper.....................................22 C3
Hacienda Lounge Bar................23 B1
MB Ice Club..............................24 B4

ENTERTAINMENT
Discoteque Trocadero...............25 A1

SHOPPING
Kadmo & Harmonija.................26 B4

TRANSPORT
JAT Airways.............................27 A2
Montenegro Airlines................28 A2

with endless rows of sun umbrellas and loungers available for hire (€2 to €3 for each). If you can't get your head around this typically Mediterranean concept, there's no charge for spreading out your towel on the patches of beach set aside for the purpose.

Between the beach and Jadranski put is the sprawling **Slovenska Plaža** (Map p97) tourist village. Anyone with an interest in Yugoslav-era architecture will find its spacious socialism-meets-Spanish-Mission aesthetic fascinating. Mature trees and modern sculpture are scattered between the terracotta-tiled units connected by white colonnades, and there's a swimming pool and tennis courts galore, which are available for hire by nonguests. The lobby is a wonderful period piece, with white marble floors, brass light fixtures, octagonal handrails, boxy white vinyl couches and potted palms. You really wouldn't be surprised if either Roger Moore's James Bond or Marshal Tito swaggered into view at any time. Even their brochures still refer to Yugoslavia! Unfortunately the attitude of the front desk staff dates from the same period.

Activities

In summer a **fun fair** (Map p97) sets up alongside Slovenska Obala, as well as **waterslides** (Map p97; per ride 40c) and **go-karts** (Map p97; per 10min €7). Along the promenade tourist agencies peddle every kind of day tour, including the following (with indicative prices):

Ostrog (€17); Dubrovnik (€30); Cetinje and Mt Lovćen (€23); Lake Skadar (€35); rafting on the Tara River (€60).

You can hire a kayak (€5 per hour) or paddle boat (€6 per hour) from Mogren Beach. A huge range of boats with skippers are available for hire from the marina. A midsized launch might charge €400 for a day's fishing, while a flash one could be €1200 or more.

For underwater adventures try Diving Center Marina (p78) or **Budva Diving** (☎ 069-060 416; www.budvadiving.com).

A walking path starts near the 18th-century **Podmaine Monastery** on the northern edge of the town and leads up the mountains for 2km to the fortified **Podostrog Monastery**. This was once a residence of Montenegro's *vladikas* (prince-bishops). It was here that Petar II Petrović Njegoš wrote *The Mountain Wreath* (p41) and also here that his predecessor Danilo instigated the savage events that inspired it. The complex's smaller church dates from the 12th century and the larger from the 18th. Look above the door for an engraving of the double-headed Montenegrin eagle holding a snake in its claws.

If you continue on the track you'll eventually reach Lovćen National Park (p122) where you can connect with the Coastal Mountain Traversal (see the boxed text on p80).

Festivals & Events

Budva's going all-out to develop a reputation for big events, having hosted the Rolling Stones in 2007 and a Powerboat Grand Prix, Lenny Kravitz and Madonna in 2008. Bringing Madonna to Budva reportedly cost €5 million, most of which was covered by the Budva municipality and the Montenegrin government, which is an indication of the importance the city puts on establishing itself as a venue for these large-scale happenings. An annual beer festival is mooted for June.

Carnival of Budva Venetian masked high jinks in early May.

International Folklore Festival Folk costumes and dances from various European countries in early June.

Busker Fest International street artists show off their skills in Slovenska Plaža in mid-June.

Theatre Town Renowned arts festival happening largely in the Old Town from mid-June to mid-August.

Festival of Mediterranean Song Three-day song competition in late June; Julio Iglesias made an appearance in 2008.

Food and Wine Festival Three days of feasting held in the Slovenska Plaža complex in late September.

Days of Širun A one-day celebration of wine, fish and song on the first Saturday of October.

Sleeping

Budva's tourist office (see p97) produces an excellent hotel directory and private-accommodation booklet. Expect to pay a hefty premium for digs in the Old Town itself, but apartments in the residential Velji Vinogradi neighbourhood are surprisingly reasonable.

BUDGET

Outside the private rooms you won't find too many bargains in Budva these days. Camping is possible at the basic **Budva Autocamp** (Map p97; ☎ 069-062 759; Velji Vinogradi bb; tent & 2 people €8) in the centre of town.

MIDRANGE

Garni Hotel Mena (off Map p97; ☎ 459 310; www.hotel mena.co.me; Velji Vinogradi bb; low-high s €25-40, d €50-80; ✗) Peach-coloured and peachy keen, little Mena has a laid-back attitude to breakfast and checkout times, reasonable rates and nicely furnished rooms. The only downers are all shower-related: raspy towels, no soap and tiny hot-water cylinders.

our pick **Hotel Kangaroo** (Map p97; ☎ 458 653; www.kangaroo.cg.yu; Velji Vinogradi bb; low-high s €29-69, d €39-69, tr €59-104; ✗ ☐ wi-fi) Bounce into a large clean room with a desk, terrace and excellent bathroom at this midsized hotel that's a hop, step and jump from the beach. The owners once lived in Australia, which explains the name and the large mural of Captain Cook's *Endeavour* in the popular restaurant below.

Hotel Max Prestige (off Map p97; ☎ 458 330; www .hotelmaxprestige.com; Žrtava Fašizma bb; low-high s €59-93, d €78-146; ✗ ✉ ☐ wi-fi) If you hadn't guessed from the name, this shiny new minihotel has slight delusions of grandeur. The exterior is a hodgepodge of pretentious turrets and pediments topped by a garish neon sign, yet the vibe inside is smart and comfortable and we love the kidney-shaped pool surrounded by meticulously kept gardens.

Hotel Mogren (Map p99; ☎ 452 041; www.mercursys tem.com; Mediteranska bb; low-high r €60-142, tr €90-213, apt €80-194; ✗ wi-fi) A bit like an elderly aunt you've become fond of, the Mogren has seen better days but traces of a glamorous youth still show through. We hope they never replace the brown vinyl booths, orange vinyl bucket seats and bubbly chandelier in the reception. The rooms are an ode to all things sky-blue: blue built-in wardrobes, blue padded headboards, blue carpet and wispy blue curtains. Ask for a room with a view of the Old Town and the sea.

Admiral Club (Map p97; ☎ 453 627; admiralbd@cg.yu; Jadranski put bb; s/d €71/110; ❄ ☒ wi-fi) There's a cool 1960s vibe to the architecture, even though the stone blocks of the exterior are a little Lego-like. Bougainvillea vines and yellow awnings add a vibrant splash of colour, and ivy-covered walls shelter a lovely tropical swimming pool and restaurant area from the highway outside. Some of the rooms are smallish but they're all fitted with large plasma screens and many have balconies.

Hotel Fontana (Map p97; ☎ 452 153; fontana.lekic@ cg.yu; Slovenska Obala 23; low-high s €72-114, d €90-142, tr €122-192, q €162-256; ☒ wi-fi) Sitting pretty in a park by the beach, Fontana has a holiday-home feel and a terrace cafe for chatting with fellow guests. Rooms are smallish but fine and most of those on the upper levels have sea views.

TOP END

Vila Balkan (Map p99; ☎ 403 564; www.montenegro .com/accommodation/budva/Villa_Balkan.html; Vuka Karadžića 2; apt €90-150; ❄ ☐) The five apartments of this historic Stari Grad house are a good option for a couple or a trio – if the third wheel doesn't mind sleeping on a pull-out bed in the lounge. There's a bit of peeling paint here and there but you'll soon forget about it when you see the sea views and parquet floors. Try for the top floor – it's the same price but a little bigger and has a bathtub.

Hotel Astoria (Map p99; ☎ 451 110; www.hotelasto ria.cg.yu; Njegoševa 4; low-high s €130-190, d €170-230, ste €180-380; ❄ ☐) Water shimmers down the corridor wall as you enter this chic boutique hotel hidden in the Old Town's fortifications. The rooms are on the small side but they're beautifully furnished; the sea-view suite is spectacular. To top it all off, the wonderful guest-only roof terrace is Budva's most magnificent dining area.

Eating
BUDGET

If you're looking for supplies, head to the **Pantomart** (Map p99; ☎ 452 523; Mediteranska 1; ☽ 6am-midnight) near the Old Town. For cheap

fast food and delicious gelato you need only stroll along Slovenska Obala.

Fenix Caffe Pizzeria (off Map p97; Velji Vinogradi bb; sandwiches €2-2.50, pizza €4.50-6) The service can be brusque but the pizzas are excellent. Try the 'Montenegrin': egg, pršut (smoke-dried ham), pancetta, green olives and traditional cheese – you'll need a big appetite to get through a whole one by yourself.

Stari Ribar (Map p97; ☎ 459 543; 29 Novembra 19; mains €3-8) You'll be relieved to learn that the name means Old Fisherman, not Old Fish. This humble eatery in the residential part of town serves grilled fish (fresh, naturally) and meat dishes at local prices. The squid here is definitely worth trying.

Konoba Stari Grad (Map p99; ☎ 454 443; Njegoševa 14; mains €3-12) The small interior looks and smells like an Italian mama's kitchen, with a cosy atmosphere and chequered tablecloths. If the sun's shining, head for the sunny terrace sandwiched between the Stari Grad's walls and beach. All the local specialities are served along with ham-and-eggs or omelette breakfasts.

MIDRANGE

Restaurant L&M (Map p97; ☎ 451 468; 13 Juli bb; mains €5-12) A simple restaurant hidden from most except the discerning local diners who all seem to know each other. It's a great place to fill up on inexpensive pasta and salads.

Restaurant Donna kod Nikole (Map p99; ☎ 451 531; Budva Marina; mains €6-20) You won't have far to wander back to your luxury yacht from this traditional restaurant bedecked unsurprisingly with maritime paraphernalia. Settle in to your brightly coloured table under a canopy of grapevines and fishing nets and enjoy the excellent fish soup. If you're selecting a whole fish, be sure to check how many kilos it is if you don't want to blow the budget.

Knez Konoba (Map p99; Mitrov Ljubiše bb; mains €9-15) Secreted within the Stari Grad's tiny lanes, this atmospheric eatery sports only two outdoor tables and a handful inside. Try the crni rižoto (black risotto) – it's more expensive than most (€10), but they present it beautifully with slices of lemon and orange along with tomato, cucumber and olives.

Drinking & Entertainment

Casper (Map p99; Petra I Petrovića bb) Chill out under the pine tree in this picturesque Old Town cafe-bar. DJs kick off from July, spinning everything from jazz to drum'n'bass.

Hacienda Lounge Bar (Map p99; Slovenska Obala bb) With its tropical foliage, swinging lounges and bright cushions, Hacienda is a swanky spot for a cocktail. Most are around €4 to €8 but €23 for a Bellini seems a bit steep. It sometimes hosts live bands.

MB Ice Club (Map p99; Njegoševa 44) Enjoy coffee, cake or cocktails while soaking in the ambience of the Old Town's main square. There's free wi-fi too.

Discoteque Trocadero (Map p99; ☎ 069-069 086; Mediteranska 4; admission €3-8; ☼ 10pm-4am) DJs hit the decks every night except Saturday, which is folk night. Trocadero has even attracted the odd superstar DJ like Roger Sanchez.

Shopping

Kadmo & Harmonija (Map p99; ☎ 068-553 699; Citadel) Named after Budva's mythical founders, this gallery-like shop sells antiquities, traditional filigree jewellery and beautiful painted icons in silver filigree frames. If you're not a Russian oligarch you may find the prices a little steep (up to €4000 for an icon).

Getting There & Away

The **bus station** (Map p97; ☎ 456 000; Ivana Milutinovića bb) has regular services to Herceg Novi (€5, 1¾ hours), Kotor (€3, 40 minutes), Cetinje (€3, 40 minutes) and Petrovac (€2, 30 minutes).

You can flag down the Olimpia Express (€1.50) from the bus stops on Jadranski put to head to Bečići (five minutes) or Sveti Stefan (20 minutes). They depart every 30 minutes in summer and hourly in winter.

If you're driving in for a day trip, there are plenty of well-marked parking areas but expect to pay about €5 per day or around €1 per hour.

Meridian Rentacar (Map p97; ☎ 454 105; www .meridian-rentacar.com; Popa Jola Zeca bb) Opposite the bus station; one-day hire from €45.

Taxi Association (☎ 9715)

Terrae-Taxi (☎ 9717) Advertises set fares to the following airports: Tivat (€15), Podgorica (€40) and Ćilipi, Dubrovnik (€90).

AROUND BUDVA

Jaz Beach Плажа Jaз

The blue waters and broad sands of Jaz Beach look spectacular when viewed from high up on the Tivat road before rounding the hill to Budva, yet the reality on the ground is a little disappointing. The approach to the beach is marred by potholed roads, swampy fields and a fair bit of scrappy construction. Still, it's quite pretty if you can find a spot away from the blaring music, face the water and not look back. Jaz has become famous as a venue for megaconcerts. The Rolling Stones kicked things off in 2007, with Lenny Kravitz and Madonna following in summer 2008.

Camping is possible between June and September at swampy **Jaz Beach campsite** (☎ 463 545; tent & car €2.50, adult/child €2.50/1).

Bečići & Rafailovići
Бечићи и Рафаиловићи

These two settlements are neighbours, sharing a 1950m sandy beach immediately east of Budva. At the time of research this area was an absolute nightmare, with half of the road dug up and traffic snarled for kilometres. We're sure that this situation will have resolved itself by the time this book is published, yet it's hard to be enthusiastic about the place. Yes, the beach is nice but the Bečići end is completely overshadowed, some would say spoiled, by massive new developments. It's certainly a far cry from its 1935 glory when it won a Parisian prize and was named the most beautiful beach in Europe.

Rafailovići is equally built up but retains the vaguest remnants of a village feel. Older-style apartment hotels hug the cliffs and restaurants line the shore. It's a popular spot for families but at high tide there's hardly any beach.

During summer there's usually someone hiring jet skis, paddle boats and kayaks from the beach, and taxi boats ply the shore for the trip to St Nicholas' Island (opposite). If you fancy a spot of **parasailing** you'll need to keep your eyes open to watch where the boats dock. A short ride costs around €25.

SLEEPING & EATING

Hotel Splendid (☎ 773 777; www.montenegrostars.com; Jadranski put, Bečići; low-high s €127-250, d €194-334, ste €350-7000; ❄ ☂ ☐ wi-fi) Splendid has a reputation as the glitziest resort in Montenegro and it's certainly one of the biggest with 323 rooms and 19 suites. The lobby bar offers panoramic views out to sea, while the 10th-floor restaurant is probably the only place in Montenegro where you'll need to dress up to gain admission. There's a lavish health and beauty spa (treatments €39 to €299; open to nonguests), four swimming pools and various

---

FLY LIKE A DOUBLE-HEADED EAGLE

Montenegro's dramatic craggy peaks make it an obvious candidate for a paragliding hot spot. The sport's still developing but already the launch site at Brajići, 760m above Bečići on the Budva–Cetinje road, is proving popular. The big attraction here is the view across the water to St Nicholas' Island and picture-perfect Sveti Stefan.

Montenegro Adventure Centre (off Map p97; ☎ 067-580 664; www.montenegrofly.com; Lapčići bb), run by a British-qualified senior paragliding instructor, offers tandem flights for €65, landing on Bečići Beach. Their base is at nearby Lapčići where they offer accommodation and can also organise rafting, hiking, mountain-biking and diving trips. If you're already an experienced paraglider, they'll take you up Mt Lovćen where you can make an unforgettable 1740m descent into the Bay of Kotor itself.

---

spots to eat and drink, not to mention the large section of beach that the hotel consumes. It's hard to fault the luxurious rooms, except to say that they have that generic could-be-anywhere kind of feel, which is true of the entire complex.

Tri Ribara (☎ 471 050; Bečićka Plaža 35, Rafailovići; mains €8-18) Sit only metres from the water and have delicious grilled squid and other seafood silver-served to you by deadly serious waiters. The name means 'three fishermen' and inside the stone walls are covered with nautical miscellanea such as anchors, turtle shells and ancient barnacle-encrusted amphorae.

St Nicholas' Island Свети Никола

Known locally as 'Hawaii', St Nicholas' Island (Sveti Nikola) is Montenegro's largest island, stretching to nearly 2km. Fallow deer wander about on this uninhabited green spot, which is only a nautical mile away from Budva or Bečići Beach. Its three sandy beaches and numerous small coves make it a popular destination in summer when taxi boats regularly ferry sunseekers to and fro; expect to pay about €20 return. Local lore has it that the graves scattered around **St Nicholas' Church** (Crkva Sv Nikole) are those of crusaders who died of an unknown epidemic while they camped nearby. The church itself dates to at least the 16th century.

SVETI STEFAN СВЕТИ СТЕФАН
☎ 033

Impossibly picturesque Sveti Stefan, 5km south of Budva, provides the biggest 'wow' moment on the entire coast. From the 15th century to the 1950s this tiny island, connected to the shore by a narrow isthmus and crammed full of terracotta-roofed dwellings, housed a simple fishing community.

That was until someone had the idea to nationalise the whole thing and turn it into a luxury hotel. It became a big hit with both Hollywood and European royalty – guests included Sofia Loren, Doris Day and Queen Elizabeth II – but like so many other things in the former Yugoslavia, it lost its appeal during the 1990s.

The island is a slice of Mediterranean heaven, with oleanders, pines and olives scenting the air and ivy-covered stone buildings growing out of the rocks that support them. Over the last few years tradesmen have replaced screen goddesses on its exclusive streets but at the time of writing the resort was expected to reopen during the lifetime of this book, more bizarrely glamorous than ever. When it does, it's likely that a day rate will once again be charged for mere mortals to wander around. In the meantime, make the most of the lovely beaches facing the island while they're comparatively uncrowded.

Sveti Stefan is also the name of the new township that's sprung up onshore. From its slopes you get to look down at that iconic view all day – which some might suggest is even better than staying in the surreal enclave below.

Information

The nearest post office and ATM are a 20-minute walk away in Pržno (p106). There are no internet cafes.

Activities

The main point of coming to Sveti Stefan is to spend as much time horizontal as possible, with occasional breaks to saunter from your recliner to the sea for a cooling dip. The water here gets deep quickly, as if the

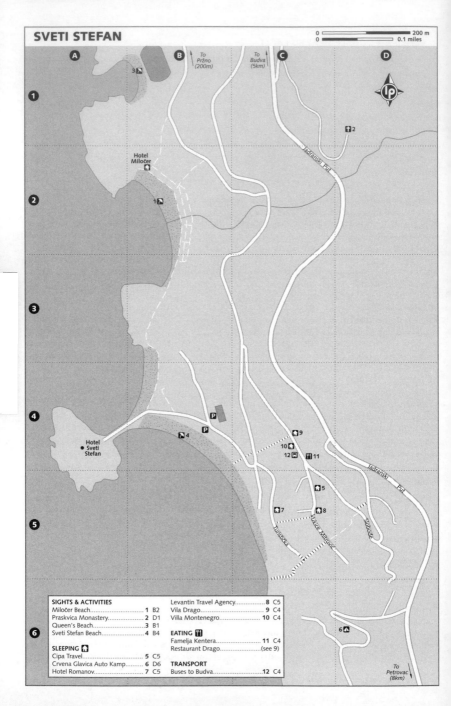

SVETI STEFAN

| 0 | 200 m |
| 0 | 0.1 miles |

To Pržno (200m)

To Budva (5km)

Hotel Miločer

Hotel Sveti Stefan

To Petrovac (8km)

SIGHTS & ACTIVITIES
Miločer Beach	1	B2
Praskvica Monastery	2	D1
Queen's Beach	3	B1
Sveti Stefan Beach	4	B4

SLEEPING
Cipa Travel	5	C5
Crvena Glavica Auto Kamp	6	D6
Hotel Romanov	7	C5

Levantin Travel Agency	8	C5
Vila Drago	9	C4
Villa Montenegro	10	C4

EATING
| Famelja Kentera | 11 | C4 |
| Restaurant Drago | (see 9) |

TRANSPORT
| Buses to Budva | 12 | C4 |

surrounding mountains could hardly be bothered adjusting their slope.

If you insist on breaking the rules, you can take a very pleasant, untaxing walk north past attractive beaches to the cute village of Pržno (p106). From here you can carry on to Praskvica Monastery (p106).

Otherwise you can annoy the shit out of everyone on a jet ski. **Rent-a-Jet Ski** (☎ 069-413 799; per 30min €70) sets up shop on the beach in summer. There are usually kayaks and paddle boats for hire as well. Pržno has a diving operator (p106).

Sleeping

Accommodation fills up quickly in July and August. Private accommodation in the area is summarised in a handy brochure produced by the Budva tourist office (p97).

Cipa Travel (☎ 468 196; www.cipatravel.com; Vukice Mitrović 1; ☺ 8am-3pm) A good agency with English-speaking staff, Cipa has a large selection of apartments on its website, with prices starting from around €10 per person per night.

Levantin Travel Agency (☎ 468 206; www.geocities .com/levantin88/levantin; Vukice Mitrović 3) Not only does the charming, helpful owner bear a striking likeness to Michael Palin c Life of Brian, he can sort you out with private rooms, apartments and other travel arrangements.

BUDGET

Crvena Glavica Auto Kamp (☎ 069-468 070; adult/child/ tent/car €3.50/2/3/2) You don't need to be a movie star or oligarch to enjoy those million-dollar views, as this idyllic and spacious camping site attests. Pitch your tent under the olive trees and stroll past the roving chickens down to the rocky but peaceful shoreline. The outdoor showers and squat toilets are well kept but remember to bring your own paper. The camp is only open from June to September.

MIDRANGE

our pick Vila Drago (☎ 468 477; www.viladrago.com; Slobode 32; low-high d €34-68, tr €58-100, apt €103-170; 🕃) The only problem with this place is that you may never want to leave your terrace as the views are so sublime. Try for room number 5, a spacious double with two terraces; rooms 1, 2 and 6 are cheaper but have limited views. The supercomfy pillows and fully stocked bathrooms are a nice touch, especially at this price.

Hotel Romanov (☎ 033-468 452; www.hotelromanov .com; Turistička bb; low-high s €72-176, d €90-220, ste €115-1000; 🕃 🖵 wi-fi) With a name like this they've clearly got the Russian market in their sights, yet the staff speak excellent English. The rooms are simply but nicely furnished and they all have either a terrace or a Juliet balcony. There are some nice touches, like providing beach towels and expensive Etro products in the bathrooms.

TOP END

Villa Montenegro (☎ 468 802; www.villa-montenegro .com; Vukice Mitrović 2; low-high r €196-700, ste €315-1500; 🕃 🖵 wi-fi) With Hotel Sveti Stefan closed, this discreet cliffside boutique hotel plugs the luxury hole admirably, especially with its two presidential suites. We're talking a private lift, massive living room, three bathrooms, jacuzzi big enough for a hip-hop star's entourage and huge kitchen, not that we can imagine anyone who could afford to stay here actually using it. The regular rooms are also very smart, if a little overpriced. However, the sublime infinite pool and the delightful staff equalise the equation somewhat.

Eating

For more excellent eating options, take the 20-minute stroll to Pržno (p106).

Famelja Kentera (☎ 069-231 922; Slobode 24; mains €3.50-20; 🝢) Ignore the street-level cafe and head upstairs to the terrace for the views. The restaurant menu covers pizza (€4.50 to €8.50) and all the usual seafood dishes, including an excellent black risotto (€6). If you're pining for a breakfast like you'd have at home, this is the place to come. The full English (€5.50) seems a good deal, especially compared to the €4.50 bowl of cornflakes.

Restaurant Drago (☎ 468 477; Slobode 32; mains €4-11) Watch the sunset over the island from the grapevine-covered terrace restaurant of the Vila Drago and enjoy the local Paštrović clan specialities, like roast suckling pig (€15 per kilo). The bread is delicious.

Getting There & Away

Olimpia Express buses head to and from Budva (€1.50, 20 minutes) every 30 minutes in summer and hourly in winter. They leave the highway at Pržno and head past Miločer Beach before stopping on Ulica Slobode near the Vila Drago.

Taxis cost around €13 to Budva, €10 to Bečići, €15 to Petrovac, €35 to Tivat airport,

€120 to Dubrovnik's Čilipi airport and €65 to Podgorica airport.

AROUND SVETI STEFAN
Miločer & Queen's Beaches
Милочер и Краљичина Плажа

At the north end of Sveti Stefan there's a pleasant walk around a headland covered in pines and olive trees looking down to the turquoise waters below. Shortly you'll come to **Miločer Beach** – which is also know as King's Beach (Kraljeva Plaža) – a lovely 280m-long stretch of sand surrounded by beautiful woodland.

Set slightly back from the tranquil bay and fronted by a loggia draped in sweet-scented wisteria is the **Hotel Miločer**. This grand two-storey stone building was built in 1934 as the summer residence of the Karađorđević royal family, the Serbian monarchs who headed the first Yugoslavia.

Amanresorts, who have made a name for their small-scale luxury resorts, has taken over the Miločer's lease along with those of the Hotel Sveti Stefan and the Queen's Beach, a snazzy time capsule further along the road whose brass circular trim may have been designed by a 1970s Yugoslav hobbit. The Miločer is due to be the first of the three to reopen and at the time of research a flurry of activity was under way. Until then, make the most of the beach access – although it may be nicer when someone's paid to pick up the rubbish.

Around the next headland, **Queen's Beach** (Kraljičina Plaža) was a favourite of Queen Marija Karađorđević and it's easy to see why. Cypresses and olive trees provide the backdrop to a pretty 120m curve of reddish sand.

Pržno Пржно

This charming little spot offers a family-friendly red-sand beach and a sufficiently good choice of restaurants to justify a leisurely stroll from Sveti Stefan. An enigmatic ruin rests on a craggy island just offshore, and just enough old stone houses remain to counterbalance the large-scale resort at the northern end of the beach.

Based on the beach side of the Maestral resort, **Pro Dive Hydrotec** (PDH; ☎ 069-013 985; www.prodive-cg.com; Obala bb) offers diving trips to various wrecks, caves and reefs. A three-dive day trip costs from €130 for one person

to €60 per person if you can muster up five friends. It also rents out kayaks (€10 per hour).

INFORMATION

There's an ATM in the lobby of the large Maestral resort at the northern end of town. The **post office** (☎ 468 202) is at the southern end by the main bus stop and taxi stand. If you're driving here, look for signs pointing to Miločer rather than Pržno. Make sure you don't confuse it with the other Pržno on the Luštica Peninsula.

SLEEPING & EATING

Apartments Kažanegra (☎ 468 738; www.kazanegra .com; Obala 12; apt €120-300) This stone villa is as close as you can get to the beach without ending up with sandy toes. It houses a range of tidy one-, two- and three-bedroom apartments, one of which also has a jacuzzi. The owner's adult son speaks excellent English and is an enthusiastic font of knowledge on tucked-away sights.

Konoba Kod Zaga (☎ 069-023 425; Obala 5; mains €7-20) In a country where excellent coffee is the norm, Zaga's is outstanding. Their cappuccinos don't have a trace of bubbly, overheated foam but rather form the silky *crema* that antipodeans would label a 'flat white'. It also serves a small menu of seafood and steak to its mainly local clientele.

Konoba More (☎ 468 255; Obala 18; mains €9-15; ⏰ 11.30am-11.30pm) A stereotypically dreamy Mediterranean restaurant with a terrace that juts out over the beach, serving traditional and Italian-tinged fish dishes.

Konoba Langust (☎ 468 369; Obala 34; mains €9-15) Much the same as More, a little further along the beachfront.

Restaurant Blanche (☎ 068-504 171; Obala 11; mains €9-17) Going for a flash Western-style look that would be hard to spot in a snowstorm, Blanche offers a break from menu monotony with a wide selection of Italian dishes including saltimbocca and truffle-infused pasta. While the Dolce & Gabbana salad may sound a tad pretentious, the Octopussy one suggests they don't really take themselves too seriously.

Praskvica Monastery
Манастир Прасквица

Just off the main road in the hills slightly north of Sveti Stefan, this humble monastery, named after the peach-scented water of a brook that flows nearby, rests amongst an ancient grove of olive trees. It was an important political centre for the Paštrovići, a local tribe of Serbian origin whose distinctive cultural traditions have survived along this section of the coast despite numerous foreign occupations.

The monastery was established in 1413 by Balša III of Zeta, and the main church dedicated to **St Nicholas** (Sv Nikola) has its origins from that time, although it was substantially destroyed by the French in 1812 as punishment for the monks' support of Montenegrin *vladika* Petar I's attempt to overtake the Bay of Kotor. Traces of the original frescoes remain on the left wall. The current gilt-framed iconostasis (1863) features paintings by Nicholas Aspiotis of Corfu.

Further up the hill beside a cemetery are an old schoolhouse and the smaller **Holy Trinity Church** (Crkva Sv Trojice), which has survived from the 15th century although its frescoes date from the 17th.

The monastery is well signposted from the main road and an easy walk from either Sveti Stefan or Pržno. In Pržno the walking track starts near the curved gate leading to the Hotel Miločer. A path behind the monastery connects with the Coastal Mountain Transversal (see the boxed text, p80).

PETROVAC ПЕТРОВАЦ
☎ 033

The Romans had the right idea, building their summer villas on this lovely bay. If only the new crop of developers had a scrap of their classic good taste. Still, once you get down to the pretty beachside promenade where lush Mediterranean plants perfume the air and a 16th-century Venetian fortress guards a tiny stone harbour, the aberrations up the hill are barely visible. This is one of the best places on the coast for families: the accommodation's reasonably priced, the water's clear and kids roam the esplanade at night with impunity.

In July and August you'll be lucky to find an inch of space on the fine reddish pebbles of the **town beach**, but wander south and there's cypress- and oleander-lined **Lučice Beach**, with a kid's waterslide on its far end. Continue over the leafy headland for another 30 minutes and the 2.4km-long sweep of **Buljarica Beach**

comes into view, most of which is blissfully undeveloped – at least for now. At the time of research a development tender process was being initiated.

Information
This seaside village has no street signs.
Accident & Emergency Clinic (Zdravstvena stanica; ☎ 461 055) At the top of town; follow the road from the bus station.
Apoteka Lijek (☎ 462 350; ☼ 8am-9pm Mon-Sat, 8am-1pm & 5-9pm Sun) Pharmacy opposite the clinic.
CKB Bank ATM (Nika Anđusa bb) Outside Voli supermarket.
Internet Café (per hr €2; ☼ 10am-midnight) At the side of the Red Commune Memorial House.
Komercijalna Bank At the side of the large Hotel Palas; no external ATM.
Post office (☎ 461 010) In the very centre of town.

Sights
Apart from the beaches, Petrovac's most interesting attraction is also its most neglected. In 1902 the foundations of a Roman building complete with **mosaics** were discovered in an olive grove in the northern part of town and here they remain in a precarious state of preservation. A section containing a motif of three interlinked fish (which would date it to the Christian period, probably the 4th century) has already disappeared. If you don't mind a spot of cross-country clambering, take the path leading through private land opposite **St Thomas' Church** (Crkva Sv Tome) – which is itself in poor repair but apparently contains some interesting frescoes. Make your way through the olives and undergrowth to the dig site where you will need to watch your footing. A dilapidated glass shed covers a section of mosaic roughly 10m by 15m. If it's locked (as it was when we visited), it's possible to peak through a broken window.

Elijah's Church (Crkva Sv Ilije) is a similar age to St Thomas', dating from the 14th or 15th century.

Directly in front of the town beach is what looks like one sheer rocky outcrop capped with a church and a stand of trees but is actually two islets – **Katič** and **Holy Sunday Island** (Sveta Nedjelja). **Holy Sunday Church** (Crkva Sv Nedjelje) is said to have been built in gratitude by a Greek sailor who was shipwrecked there. The current church replaces one destroyed in the 1979 earthquake.

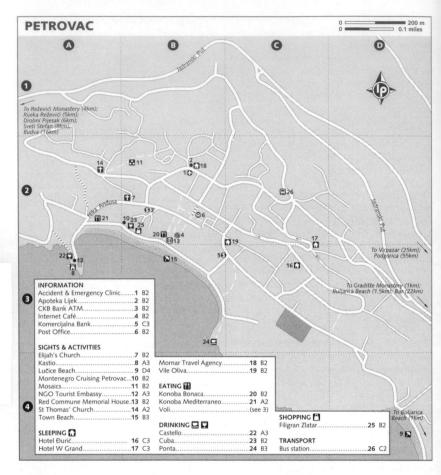

PETROVAC

To Reževići Monastery (4km);
Rijeka Reževići (5km);
Drobni Pijesak (6km);
Sveti Stefan (8km);
Budva (16km)

To Virpazar (25km);
Podgorica (55km)

To Gradište Monastery (1km);
Buljarica Beach (1.5km); Bar (22km)

To Buljarica
Beach (1km)

INFORMATION
Accident & Emergency Clinic.......**1** B2
Apoteka Lijek..............................**2** B2
CKB Bank ATM............................**3** B2
Internet Café..............................**4** B2
Komercijalna Bank.....................**5** C3
Post Office..................................**6** B2

SIGHTS & ACTIVITIES
Elijah's Church...........................**7** B2
Kastio..**8** A3
Lučice Beach..............................**9** D4
Montenegro Cruising Petrovac...**10** B2
Mosaics.....................................**11** B2
NGO Tourist Embassy................**12** A3
Red Commune Memorial House.**13** B2
St Thomas' Church....................**14** A2
Town Beach...............................**15** B3

SLEEPING
Hotel Đurić................................ **16** C3
Hotel W Grand..........................**17** C3

Mornar Travel Agency...............**18** B2
Vile Oliva..................................**19** B2

EATING
Konoba Bonaca.........................**20** B2
Konoba Mediterraneo................**21** A2
Voli..(see 3)

DRINKING
Castello.....................................**22** A3
Cuba...**23** B2
Ponta..**24** B3

SHOPPING
Filigran Zlatar............................**25** B2

TRANSPORT
Bus station................................**26** C2

Kastio, the small Venetian fortress by the harbour, offers gorgeous views of the beach and the dramatic diagonal stratification of the limestone cliffs melting into the turquoise water below. An interesting socialist realist bas-relief remembering the 'socialist revolution' is partly obscured in the foliage. The first commune in the Adriatic was established in this area and is celebrated in the **Red Commune Memorial House** (Crvena Komuna; ☎ 404 877; www.crvenakomuna.com; admission free; ☼ 8am-2pm & 6-10pm) on the waterfront, which houses a modern art gallery and revolutionary museum.

Activities

If you fancy a stroll, Buljarica Beach is about 1km away or you can continue on to Gradište

Monastery (p110). Reževići Monastery (p110) is about 4km in the opposite direction.

NGO Tourist Embassy (☎ 069-687 858) operates from a shed by the harbour. The gregarious self-appointed ambassador offers trips in a 10HP zodiac inflatable (€30 per hour), an eight-seater 30HP version (€50 per hour) or a small outboard (€100 per hour); petrol is extra. Fishing, snorkelling, diving (€30 including equipment) and waterskiing are all options, or you can opt for a tow in a rubber tube.

Montenegro Cruising Petrovac (☎ 069-618 747; www.mcruisingpetrovac.com; ☼ 8am-8pm summer, 8am-2pm winter) offers day excursions to Ostrog Monastery (€17) and Dubrovnik (€30), cruises on the Bay of Kotor (€20) and Lake Skadar (€35) and rafting on the Tara River (€60).

Festivals & Events

Mediterranean Program Folk troupes or brass bands perform every Wednesday night from June to September on the promenade in front of the Red Commune Memorial House.

International Aerobics Weekend Better pack those leg warmers after all. Includes a mini football world cup and beach-volleyball contest, all happening from late July to early August.

Petrovac Night Free fish, wine and beer, majorette parades, performances by Eurovision contestants…who could ask for anything more on the last Saturday in August.

Petrovac Jazz Festival Three nights of finger-snapping faves in late August.

Sleeping

A couple of basic camping grounds operate in summer in Buljarica including one right on the beach.

Mornar Travel Agency (☎ 461 410; www.mornar-travel.com; ☯ 8am-8pm summer, 8am-2pm winter) An excellent local agency, Mornar offers private accommodation from €23 per person.

Hotel W Grand (☎ 461 703; www.wgrandpetrovac.com; low-high s €41-71, d €54-94, tr €81-141; ✖ ▣ wi-fi) The colour scheme simulates the effect of waking up inside an egg yolk, but this modern midsized hotel has roomy rooms with comfy beds and puts on a brilliant breakfast buffet on its view-hungry terrace.

Hotel Đurić (☎ 462 005; www.hoteldjuric.com; low-high d €55-85, tr €70-105, q €80-120; ✖ ▣ wi-fi) There's a vaguely Spanish Mission feel to this smart new minihotel that opens its doors between June and September. All rooms have kitchen facilities and there's a restaurant at the back under a canopy of kiwi fruit and grapevines.

Vile Oliva (☎ 461 194; vileoliva@cg.yu; low-high r €60-100, apt €100-120; ✖ ▣) That's *vi*·le as in 'villa', not 'vile'. In fact, the staff here are lovely. Set in a 400-year-old grove of gnarly olive trees close to the beach, this complex comprises a mixture of older and newer low-rise blocks that were being renovated at the time of research. The apartments sleep up to four people at a push. It's only open from June through to September.

Eating

The esplanade is lined with fast-food joints, ice-cream stands, restaurants and cafe-bars. One street back, **Voli** (Nika Anđusa bb) is a decent-sized supermarket with an excellent deli and fresh-fruit section.

Konoba Mediterraneo (mains €8-16) There are no surprises on the menu (a line-up of the usual seafood and meat suspects), but Mediterraneo offers a lovely leafy setting directly opposite the beach.

Konoba Bonaca (☎ 069-084 735; mains €8-15) Set back slightly from the main beachside drag, this traditional restaurant focuses mainly on seafood but the local cheeses and olives are also excellent. Grab a table under the grapevines on the terrace and try the cheese in oil (a bit like a hard fetta) or the cheese in wheat (like the love child of parmesan and cheddar).

Drinking & Entertainment

Cuba DJs kick off in the summer at this beachside cafe where the staff all wear Che Guevara T-shirts.

Castello (☎ 067-614 423; terrace/club free/€2; ☯ terrace from 6pm, club from midnight) Sip a cocktail and enjoy gorgeous views over the parapets of the Venetian fortress. DJs spark up both on the terrace and inside on summer nights.

Ponta (☯ 8am-1am) Built into the rocks at the south end of the beach, this is a great location for a combination of cafe-bar, club and restaurant.

Shopping

Filigran Zlatar Located near the Red Commune Memorial House, this is a reputable place to buy traditional filigree jewellery – simple necklaces start at about €25.

Getting There & Around

Petrovac's **bus station** (☎ 461 510) is near the top of town. There are regular services to Budva and Bar (each €2, 30 minutes).

Don Street Taxi Service (☎ 069-437 966) has metered cabs.

AROUND PETROVAC

Drobni Pijesak Дробни Пијесак

Hidden in a secluded cove between Sveti Stefan and Rijeka Reževići, Drobni Pijesak is a 240m stretch of 'ground sand' (which is the literal translation of the name) surrounded by green hills and turquoise waters. Every year on 28 June the elders of the 12 Paštrović clans hold the Bankada here, a community court that has its origins in the 16th century. Nowadays its main focus is the restoration and preservation of the tribe's traditions, environmental and cultural conservation and economic development. The day ends with a folk and arts festival.

Rijeka Reževići Ријека Режевићи

Traditional Paštrović-style architecture differs from the rest of Montenegro, favouring rows of terrace houses (or semidetached town houses in real-estate speak) with stone walls, small windows, single pitched roofs and 'hog's back' curved terracotta tiles. This charming village offers some lovely examples and although gentrification is evident, thus far the focus has been on restoration rather than demolition.

A footpath to the left of the car park below the village church leads through the woods to a quiet boulder-strewn beach that offers secluded swimming and good snorkelling. The beachside fish restaurant **Balun** (☎ 069-285 652; mains €12-18) is comparatively pricey (first-class fish €60 per kilogram) but it's highly rated by the locals. You can always just order a coffee and a €5 sandwich and gaze over the oleanders to the clear waters below.

Reževići Monastery & Around
Манастир Режевићи

Hospitality has always been important at this atmospheric stone complex, just off the highway north of Petrovac. Until the 19th century, the Paštrovići would leave a bottle of wine here for passers-by, one of whom in 1226 was King Stefan II of the Serbian Nemanjić dynasty. It was he who founded the smaller church of the complex, the **Church of the Dormition** (Crkva Uspenja Bogorodice). Once your eyes adjust to the dark interior you'll be able to make out fine frescoes covering the walls. The frescoes in the larger **Church of the Holy Trinity** (Crkva Sv Trojice; 1770) are newer and hence much more vivid. The iconostasis was painted by Petrovac local Marko Gregović.

Both churches are holding up well considering that they've survived attacks by Ottoman, French and Italian armies. There's usually an elderly black-robed nun holding the fort in the small gift shop selling religious icons and homemade olive oil and honey. Local tradition tells of a Greek or Roman temple and cemetery that once stood on this site.

Just down the hill from the monastery is **Perazića Do**, a small sandy beach bookended by rocky headlands. Near the highway a stone building (1856) was once a school and now houses a **museum, gallery and library** devoted to

the Paštrović tribe, although you'll be lucky to find it open.

Gradište Monastery
Манастир Градиште

Perched on a hill overlooking Buljarica Beach, Gradište Monastery is a tranquil collection of stone buildings facing onto a central courtyard. The monastery was first mentioned in documents from 1305 although it's believed to date from 1116. Like many Montenegrin monasteries it's had a rough time over the years at the hands of invading armies and it's been rebuilt several times.

The three churches found on the site are renowned for their frescoes. The interior of **St Nicholas' Church** (Crkva Sv Nikole) is completely covered in beautiful paintings of biblical scenes and Serbian royalty dating from 1620. The iconostasis was carved and painted by Vasilije Rafailović of the famous family of artists from Risan (p81). Its neighbour, **St Sava's Church** (Crkva Sv Save), was built in 1864 and has an iconostasis by Nicholas Aspiotis, whose work you'll also see at Praskvica Monastery (p106). Look out for a peculiar image of a saint with the head of a donkey. One school of thought suggests that it was St Christopher who was so blessed after he prayed to be rid of his darned good looks. On a slight elevation is the **Church of the Dormition** (Crkva Uspenja Bogorodice).

Taking the main road south of Petrovac, turn left after the tunnel and park at the base of the hill where there's a steep 300m walk to the monastery.

BAR БАР
☎ 030 / pop 13,790

Dominated by Montenegro's main port and a large industrial area, Bar is unlikely to be anyone's holiday highlight but it is a handy transport hub welcoming trains from Belgrade and ferries from Italy. More interesting are the ruins of Stari Bar (Old Bar) in the mountains behind.

Unlike the northern part of the coast, which remained largely under the rule of Venice and then Austria, the areas from Bar south spent 300 years under Turkish control. From here on you'll start to notice more mosques and Ottoman-looking buildings, although not in modern Bar itself which was only founded in 1908.

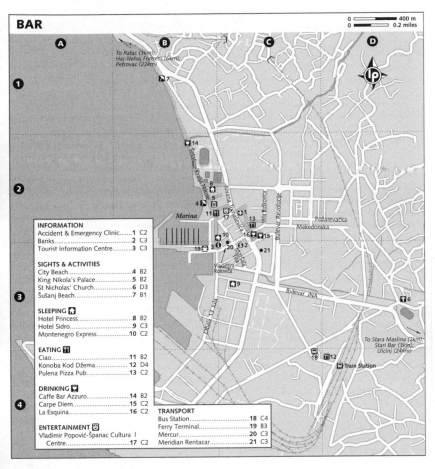

BAR

INFORMATION
Accident & Emergency Clinic.......**1** C2
Banks...**2** C3
Tourist Information Centre..........**3** C3

SIGHTS & ACTIVITIES
City Beach......................................**4** B2
King Nikola's Palace.....................**5** B2
St Nicholas' Church......................**6** D3
Šušanj Beach.................................**7** B1

SLEEPING
Hotel Princess...............................**8** B2
Hotel Sidro....................................**9** C3
Montenegro Express....................**10** C2

EATING
Ciao..**11** B2
Konoba Kod Džema.....................**12** D4
Pulena Pizza Pub..........................**13** C2

DRINKING
Caffe Bar Azzuro..........................**14** B2
Carpe Diem..................................**15** C2
La Esquina....................................**16** C2

ENTERTAINMENT
Vladimir Popović-Španac Cultura l
Centre...**17** C2

TRANSPORT
Bus Station...................................**18** C4
Ferry Terminal..............................**19** B3
Mercur..**20** C3
Meridian Rentacar........................**21** C3

Orientation & Information

Bar's centre is immediately east of the marina and ferry terminal. Beaches stretch north from here, while the port and industrial area are to the south. There are several banks with ATMs around Ulica Maršala Tita and Ulica Vladimira Rolovića.

Accident & Emergency Clinic (☎ 124; Jovana Tomaševića 42)

Police (☎ 311 222; Maršala Tita 18)

Post office (☎ 301 300; Jovana Tomaševića bb)

Tourist Information Centre (☎ 311 633; Obala 13 Jula bb; ⏰ 7am-9pm Jul & Aug, 7am-2pm Mon-Fri Sep-Jun) This office has helpful staff with good English and stocks useful brochures listing sights and private accommodation.

Sights

With a large industrial port and marina on its doorstep, Bar's **City Beach** is not the most appealing option for swimming. Heading north, **Šušanj Beach** is popular with Serbian holidaymakers. Beat the crowds in the succession of rocky coves that follow; they are perfect for snorkelling and sheltered swimming. If you're concerned about the Speedos chafing, you can go the full monty at a stony bay just before the rustic ruins of the 11th-century Benedictine monastery of the **Mother of God of Ratac** (Bogorodica Ratac). Destroyed by the Turks in 1571, the remains of its chapel now have a congregation consisting of wild figs and the occasional old lady in black.

TAKING THE BAR EXAM

One of the legacies of Yugoslavia's communist years is a rigorous education system. We asked English teacher Daniela Đuranović to teach us a thing or two about her home town and country.

Where's a good place to begin? First swim in the sea. Bar's most beautiful beaches are a little out of town. For me, Montenegro's best beach is Pržno near Sveti Stefan. I think that God when he made that place said 'wow, this is one beautiful place'.

What about cultural pursuits? Definitely visit Bar Museum and Stari Bar. I think there are some artists still living there and it comes alive with performances during the Summer Festival.

What else shouldn't be missed? You must visit the mountains. They're beautiful in summer but I like them at winter covered in snow. I don't ski, though. I just drink coffee and tea and enjoy the nature.

You were born and raised in Bar. How has it changed over the years? Bar has developed a lot. One thing I don't like is that they have cut down the trees that gave the centre of town its name: Topolica. In this park (behind the museum) there are some very interesting trees. King Nikola asked sailors to bring them from all around the world.

You seem to have a good life here. I see TV programs about Provence, talking about the nature, the cheese, the produce. I can eat that food every day. I wouldn't change that. In summer I have everything I need here.

Presenting an elegant facade to the water, **King Nikola's Palace** (Dvorac Kralja Nikole; ☎ 314 079; Šetalište Kralje Nikole; admission €1; ☒ 8am-3pm) was built in 1885 and now houses a collection of antiquities, folk costumes and furniture that once supported royal bottoms. Its leafy gardens contain plants cultivated from seeds and cuttings collected from around the world by Montenegro's sailors.

Bar first became the seat of a Catholic diocese in the 9th century and in 1089 it was elevated to an archdiocese, with the archbishop given the title 'Primate of Serbia'. The elegant archbishop's palace sits next to the baroque-style **St Nicholas' Church** (Crkva Sv Nikole; ☎ 344 236; Popovići bb) in the west of town on the route to Stari Bar. These days the archdiocese comprises part of Kosovo and all of Montenegro except for the Kotor diocese, which remains attached to the Croatian arm of the church.

Festivals & Events

Chronicle of Bar Plays, exhibitions, literary events and concerts in July and August.

Summer with Stars A series of concerts by regional pop stars in July and August.

Swimming Marathon A 5km ocean race between Sutomore and Bar in August.

Port Cup International women's volleyball tournament in August.

Old Olive Tree Gatherings Art and literary festival for children in November.

Sleeping

It's surprisingly difficult to find decent accommodation in Bar so unless you've got an early or late transport connection, you're better off heading elsewhere.

Montenegro Express (☎ 311 133; Obala 13 Jula bb; ☒ 8am-8pm Mon-Sat Jul & Aug, 8am-2pm Mon-Sat Sep-Jun) This travel agency can arrange accommodation in local houses, with private rooms starting from €9 per person.

Hotel Sidro (☎ 312 425; www.lukabar.cg.yu/eng /sidro.htm; Obala 13 Jula bb; low-high r €32-72, apt €42-140; ☒ wi-fi) Owned by the port company (the name means 'anchor'), Sidro is best kept as a fall-back option. The cheaper rooms in the older section have crappy bathrooms and no air conditioning. The 'deluxe' rooms are better but they're hardly luxurious and more attention to the cleaning wouldn't go astray.

Hotel Princess (☎ 300 100; www.hotelprincess-mon tenegro.com; Jovana Tomaševića 59; low-high s €80-140, d €100-200, apt €150-450; ☒ ☒ ☒ wi-fi) It's pricey and generic but this resort-style hotel is the best option in Bar by far. Make the most of your money at the private beach, swimming pool and spa centre.

Eating

Ciao (Šetalište Kralja Nikole bb; breakfast €2-4, mains €4.50-10) A pleasant place for an omelette, pizza or pasta on the waterfront.

Pulena Pizza Pub (☎ 312 816; Vladimira Rolovića bb; mains €3-7) Pulena is a busy eating and drinking spot under the outer of the three spaceships that some zany architect designed as the focal point of town. Pizza, pasta and delicious gelato are on offer.

Konoba Kod Džema (☎ 067-888 405; mains €4-10) This atmospheric stone-walled restaurant is an air-conditioned haven midway between the train and bus stations. Nibble on delicious *pršut* (smoke-dried ham) and bread straight off the griddle while you're waiting for your connection.

Drinking & Entertainment

The one thing Bar isn't short of is bars.

Caffe Bar Azzuro (Šetalište Kralja Nikole bb) A funky summer-only bar under the pine trees by the beach with decent music and log seats.

Carpe Diem (Vladimira Rolovića bb) Part of a swanky strip of bars on a pedestrian-only lane just off the main street, Carpe Diem has comfy outdoor furniture, big screens for the football and large photos of jazz and blues men on the walls.

La Esquina (Vladimira Rolovića bb) Carpe Diem's neighbour makes up for its tiny indoor area with stacks of seats under a canopy of trees. The coffee's excellent.

Vladimir Popović-Španac Cultural Centre (Dom kulture; ☎ 311 586; Jovana Tomaševića 57) The main venue for live theatre, classical music and movies with a summer stage outside. Movie tickets are around €2.

Getting There & Away

From Bar the fastest route to Podgorica is via a toll road (€2.50 each way) that leaves the highway past Sutomore, northwest of Bar.

The **bus station** (☎ 346 141) and adjacent **train station** (☎ 301 622; www.zeljeznica.cg.yu) are 1km southeast of the centre. Bus destinations include Podgorica (€5, seven daily), Petrovac (€2, 12 daily) and Ulcinj (€2.50, six daily). Trains to Podgorica (€3, one hour, 14 daily) also stop at Virpazar (€2). Local buses stop in the centre on Ulica Jovana Tomaševića and head to Stari Bar and north along the coast as far as Čanj.

Ferries to Bari and Ancona in Italy (p169) leave from the **ferry terminal** (Obala 13 Jula bb) near the centre of town. You can book your Montenegro Lines ferry tickets here and there's a post office branch and ATM. Azzurra

Line can be booked at **Mercur** (☎ 313 617; Vladimira Rolovića bb).

In summer you can hail a taxi boat from the marina or beach for a short trip up the coast (€2 for Sutomore). **Meridian Rentacar** (☎ 314 000; www.meridian-rentacar.com; Jovana Tomaševića 30; 1-day hire from €45) has a branch in the centre of town.

AROUND BAR

Haj-Nehaj Fortress Xaj-Hexaj

If you wasted your youth playing *Dungeons & Dragons* or you just like poking around old ruins, the lonely battlements of Haj-Nehaj fortress should definitely be added to your itinerary. It was built in the 15th century by the Venetians to defend their southern border from the Ottoman Turks whose conquests had brought them as far as the river that runs into Šušanj Beach in modern Bar.

To get here from Bar, follow the highway north for 6.5km and turn left at the sign pointing towards the Sv Nikola Hotel. After 600m, park near the houses at the bottom of an unsealed road to the right. Walk straight up the road with the castle directly in front of you and turn right at a sign reading УЛИЦА ЗЕЛЕНИ СОКАК (Ulica Zeleni Sokak; the sign actually points left) and immediately look for the path on your left. From here it's a steep but attractive walk through the pines for 30 minutes on a stony path that's often hard to distinguish.

When the gate finally does come into view the fortifications rise so precipitously from the stone that you'll be left wondering how it was ever built. Once you're inside there are extensive ruins to explore, rising charismatically from a blanket of wild sage and flowers. At the very top, looking over Bar, is the shell of the 13th-century **St Demetrius' Church** (Crkva Sv Dimitrija), easily recognised by its vaulted roof and stone altar. It predates the fort itself and once had separate Catholic and Orthodox altars.

Stari Bar Стари Бар

Impressive **Stari Bar** (Old Bar; adult/child €1/50c; ☼ 8am-8pm), Bar's original settlement, stands on a bluff 4km northeast off the Ulcinj road. A steep cobbled hill takes you past a cluster of old houses and shops to the fortified entrance where a short dark passage pops you out into a large expanse of vine-clad ruins and abandoned streets overgrown with grass and wild flowers.

A PEACEFUL OBSERVER

At Mirovica near Stari Bar is a living witness that has stood and mutely waved symbols of peace while the armies of consecutive empires have swept through this land. At 2000 years of age, **stara maslina** (old olive tree) is possibly the oldest tree in Continental Europe and one of the oldest of its species in the world. A ring of white stone protects its personal space from tree-huggers and there's a nominal charge to visit (adult/child €1/50c), but it can be admired nearly as well from the road. You'll find it well signposted from the road to Ulcinj.

There are over 100,000 olive trees in the Bar area, many of which have seen more than a millennium.

Findings of pottery and metal suggest that the Illyrians founded the city around 800 BC. In the 10th century, the Byzantine town was known as Antivarium as it's opposite the Italian city of Bari. It passed in and out of Slavic and Byzantine rule until the Venetians took it in 1443 (note the lion of St Mark in the entryway) and held it until it was taken by the Ottomans in 1571. Nearly all the 240 buildings now lie in ruins, a result of Montenegrin shelling when they captured the town in 1878.

A small **museum** just inside the entrance explains the site and its history. The northern corner has an 11th-century **fortress** with views showcasing Stari Bar's isolated setting amid mountains and olive groves. Nearby are the foundations of the **Cathedral of St George** (Katedrala Sv Ðorđa), Bar's patron saint. Originally a Romanesque church, the Turks converted it into a mosque in the 17th century but the unlucky edifice was yet again in ruins after an accidental explosion of gunpowder. In the western part of the town are the remains of **St Nicholas' Church** (Crkva Sv Nikole) offering glimpses of Serbo-Byzantine frescoes. If you're wondering why **St John's Church** (Crkva Sv Jovana) is in such good nick, it's because it's been completely reconstructed by one of the families associated with the original church.

Ottoman constructions include a solid and charming **Turkish bathhouse** from the 17th or 18th century, the **clock tower** (1753) and the 17th-century **aqueduct** that carried water from a spring 3km away; it was reconstructed after the 1979 earthquake.

Just outside the main gate is the **Omerbašića Mosque** (Omerbašića džamija; 1662), a simple construction with a square stone base and an elegant minaret enclosed by a stone wall. The domed structure near the entrance is the tomb of Dervish Hasan. Many of the Roma people who make a significant proportion of Stari Bar's remaining population practise Islam.

Buses marked Stari Bar depart from Ulica Jovana Tomaševića in the centre of new Bar every hour (€1).

EATING & SHOPPING

The road leading up to Stari Bar has a small strip of idiosyncratic eateries and shops.

Konoba Spilja (☎ 340 353; Stari Bar bb; mains €3-15) So rustic you wouldn't be surprised if a goat wandered through, this is a terrific spot for a traditional meal after exploring Stari Bar.

Opal II Filigren (☎ 340 634; Stari Bar bb) An excellent place to buy silver filigree jewellery – they've been perfecting their craft over 100 years.

ULCINJ УЛЦИЊ
☎ 030 / 10,838

If you want a feel of Albania without actually crossing the border, buzzy Ulcinj's the place to go. The population is 72% Albanian and in summertime it swells with Kosovar holidaymakers for the simple reason that it's a hell of a lot nicer than any of the Albanian seaside towns. The elegant minarets of numerous mosques give Ulcinj a distinctly Eastern feel, as does the lively music echoing out of the kebab stands around Mala Plaža (Small Beach).

Orientation

You're unlikely to a find a single street sign in most Montenegrin towns but in Ulcinj you'll sometimes find three different ones per street: a Montenegrin and an Albanian version of the Yugoslav-era name as well as a new Albanian name. Thus the main boulevard leading east–west at the top of town is either Maršala Tita or Gjergj Kastrioti Skënderbeu, and the main street heading down to the beach is either *ulica* 26 Novembra or *rruga* Hazif Ali Ulqinaku. In this text we've used the name that was most prominently displayed at

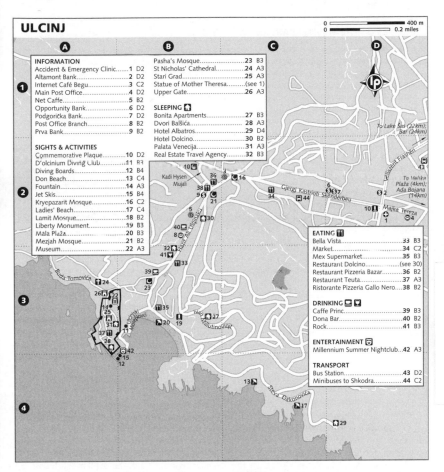

ULCINJ

0   400 m
0   0.2 miles

INFORMATION
Accident & Emergency Clinic.......1 D2
Altamont Bank..........................2 D2
Internet Café Begu....................3 C2
Main Post Office.......................4 D2
Net Caffe.................................5 B2
Opportunity Bank.....................6 D2
Podgorička Bank.......................7 D2
Post Office Branch....................8 B2
Prva Bank................................9 B2

SIGHTS & ACTIVITIES
Commemorative Plaque............10 D2
D'olcinium Diving Club...............11 B3
Diving Boards..........................12 B4
Don Beach...............................13 C4
Fountain.................................14 A3
Jet Skis..................................15 B4
Kryepazarit Mosque..................16 C2
Ladies' Beach..........................17 C4
Lamit Mosque..........................18 B2
Liberty Monument....................19 B3
Mala Plaža..............................20 B3
Mezjah Mosque........................21 B2
Museum..................................22 A3

Pasha's Mosque........................23 B3
St Nicholas' Cathedral...............24 A3
Stari Grad...............................25 A3
Statue of Mother Theresa..........(see 1)
Upper Gate.............................26 A3

SLEEPING
Bonita Apartments...................27 B3
Dvori Balšića...........................28 A3
Hotel Albatros.........................29 D4
Hotel Dolcino..........................30 B2
Palata Venecija........................31 A3
Real Estate Travel Agency..........32 B3

EATING
Bella Vista..............................33 B3
Market...................................34 C2
Mex Supermarket.....................35 B3
Restaurant Dolcino...................(see 30)
Restaurant Pizzeria Bazar..........36 B3
Restaurant Teuta.....................37 A3
Ristorante Pizzeria Gallo Nero....38 B2

DRINKING
Caffe Princ.............................39 B3
Dona Bar................................40 B2
Rock......................................41 B3

ENTERTAINMENT
Millennium Summer Nightclub....42 A3

TRANSPORT
Bus Station.............................43 D2
Minibuses to Shkodra...............44 C2

the time of research (usually the new Albanian names), but be aware that there is a push to return to the old names.

Information

Accident & Emergency Clinic (☎ 412 433; Majka Tereza bb) There's a pharmacy attached.
Altamont Bank (Vëllazërit Frashëri bb)
Internet Café Begu (Hazif Ali Ulqinaku bb; per hr 50c; ☒ 9am-3am)
Main post office (Majka Tereza bb; ☒ 8am-noon & 5-9pm)
Net Caffe (Hazif Ali Ulqinaku bb; per hr 50c)
Opportunity Bank (Gjergj Kastrioti Skënderbeu bb)
Podgorička Bank (Gjergj Kastrioti Skënderbeu bb)
Post office branch (Hazif Ali Ulqinaku bb)
Prva Bank (Hazif Ali Ulqinaku bb)

Sights

The ancient **Stari Grad** (Old Town) overlooking Mala Plaža is still largely residential and somewhat dilapidated – a legacy of the 1979 earthquake. A steep slope leads to the **Upper Gate**, where just inside the walls there's a small **museum** (☎ 421 419; admission €1; ☒ 6am-noon & 5-9pm) containing Roman and Ottoman artefacts. On the site is a 1510 church that was converted to a mosque in 1693; you can still see the ruined minaret. Just outside the museum is a **fountain** (actually, it's now more of a tap) with an Arabic inscription, a crescent moon and flowers carved into the stone.

Below the Upper Gate amongst a picturesque grove of gnarled olive trees is the Orthodox **St Nicholas' Cathedral** (Saborna crkva Sv Nikole; Buda

---

PIRATES OF THE MEDITERRANEAN

Listen up, me hearties, to a swashbuckling tale of murder, theft and slavery. Even before the Venetians took over in 1405, Ulcinj had a reputation as a pirate's lair. That didn't change when the Ottomans wrested control (nominally at least) in 1571. Quite the opposite, in fact. By the end of the 16th century as many as 400 pirates, mainly from Malta, Tunisia and Algeria, made Ulcinj their main port of call – wreaking havoc on passing vessels and then returning to party up large on Mala Plaža.

Legendary leaders became celebrities across the eastern Mediterranean, with stories of the Karamindžoja brothers, Lika Ceni, Ali Hodža and the like fuelling the imaginations of avid listeners. Legendary Spanish writer Cervantes was one victim; he's said to have spent five years in the vaults by the main square before being ransomed. Legend has it that he appropriated the town's name for his character Dulcinea in *Don Quixote*. Others were less lucky, like the pilgrims bound for Mecca robbed then drowned by Lika Ceni – an act that outraged the sultan and landed the pirate a hefty price on his head.

Along with their usual business of pirating, Ulcinj's crews had a lucrative sideline in slavery. Ulcinj became the centre of a thriving slave trade, with people (mainly from North Africa and some as young as two or three) paraded for sale on the town's main square. Ulcinj is perhaps the only place in the Western Balkans to have had a significant black minority.

Tomovića bb). It's a relative newbie, having been built in 1890 shortly after the Ottomans were booted out, although it's believed to stand on the site of a 15th-century monastery.

On the cliff above Mala Plaža is the imposing **Liberty Monument** (Ivan Millutinoviqit bb), a lovely piece of socialist art that's now neglected and covered in graffiti. Its two V-shaped white segments resemble a pair of fighter planes that have crash-landed on their noses. Closer up they're more like stylised wings sprouting from the figures facing each other at the centre.

In better nick is the **statue of Mother Theresa**, the most famous Albanian of recent years (she was actually born in Macedonia), which stands in front of the Clinic on the boulevard named after her. On the adjacent corner there's an interesting **commemorative plaque**: 'In gratitude to the people of Ulcinj for the humanity, solidarity and hospitality they have shown in sheltering and taking care of the persecuted from Kosova during the period March '98 to June '99 – Grateful Kosovars'.

One of Ulcinj's most distinctive features is its many mosques. Most are fairly simple structures and they're generally more interesting from the outside than inside. **Kryepazarit Mosque** (Džamija Vrh pazara; Hazif Ali Ulqinaku bb) was built in 1749 at the intersection of the main streets; its name means 'Top of the Market'. Within the same block but set back slightly from the road is the 1728 **Mezjah Mosque**

(Džamija Namaždjah; Hazif Ali Ulqinaku 71), Ulcinj's main Islamic place of worship. **Pasha's Mosque** (Pašina džamija; Buda Tomovića bb), dating from 1719, is an elegant complex with a *hammam* (Turkish bathhouse) attached. **Lamit Mosque** (Džamija Ljamit; Kadi Hysen Mujali bb) dates from 1689 but was substantially rebuilt after the 1979 earthquake. The ceiling has interesting green-painted geometric wood panelling.

Activities

Mala Plaža may be a fine grin of a cove but it's a little hard to see the beach under all that suntanned flesh in July and August. You are better off strolling south where a succession of rocky bays offers clear water and a little more room to breathe. At **Don Beach** you can either plant yourself on a concrete terrace or find a patch of grass under the pines. **Ladies' Beach** (admission €1.50), true to its name, has a strict women-only policy, while a section of the beach in front of the Hotel Albatros is clothing-optional.

Divers wanting to explore various wrecks and the remains of a submerged town should contact the **D'olcinium Diving Club** (☎ 067-319 100; www.uldiving.com; Mala Plaža). The introductory dive costs €30, and two dives including equipment are €40. It also hires gear for snorkelling (€3) and diving (€15).

In summer you can hire **jet skis** from the paved area below the city walls. Local teenagers show off their skills on the **diving boards** that are set up here.

Sleeping

The strangely named **Real Estate Travel Agency** (☎ 421 609; www.realestate-travel.com; Hazif Ali Ulqinaku bb; ☗ 8am-9pm) has obliging English-speaking staff who can help you find private rooms (from €10 per person), apartments or hotel rooms. It also rents cars, runs tours and sells maps of Ulcinj.

BUDGET

Bonita Apartments (☎ 423 164; bonita-ul@cg.yu; Ivan Milutinovqil 67; s/d/tr/q €20/30/45/60; ☒) Sitting somewhere between private accommodation and a small hotel, Bonita offers small but perfectly adequate apartments in a 2008-built block on the hill above Mala Plaža. Request a room with a view and be prepared for plenty of stairs and small hot-water cylinders. There's a playground for little kids on the shared front terrace.

MIDRANGE

Hotel Albatros (☎ 423 264; www.albatros-hotels.com; Steva Đakonovića bb; new block low-high s €32-39, d €48-60; ☒ wi-fi) The reception is a treasure trove of 1970s period gems: octagonal booths, descending pipes holding drop lights, brown roof with bubbly light fixtures, disinterested staff smoking behind the counter. Eschew the cheaper rooms in the dingy older block in favour of the clean but faded facilities of the 'new' block. Best of all, the hotel has its own beach divided into clothed and naked sections.

ourpick **Hotel Dolcino** (☎ 422 288; www.hotel dolcino.com; Hazif Ali Ulqinaku bb; s/d/q/ste €40/50/60/70; ☒) You can't quibble over the exceptionally reasonable prices of this modern business-orientated minihotel in the centre of town. The quieter rooms at the back have spacious terraces, although the small front balconies are great for watching the passing parade.

Dvori Balšića & Palata Venecija (☎ 421 457; www.real estate-travel.com; Stari Grad bb; s/d/q/apt €75/100/140/190; ☒ wi-fi) If you've ever fancied being king of the castle, these grand stone palazzos in the Old Town should satisfy the urge. The sizeable rooms all have kitchenettes, romantic sea views and stucco and dark wood interiors.

Eating

If you're keen to cook, hit the traditional **market** (Gjergj Kastrioti Skënderbeu bb) at the top end of town or the **Mex supermarket** (Ulcinjski Moreplovci bb; ☗ 7am-10pm Mon-Sat, 7am-8pm Sun) down by the beach.

Restaurant Pizzeria Bazar (☎ 421 639; Hazif Ali Ulqinaku bb; mains €4-10) An upstairs restaurant that's a great idling place when the streets below are heaving with tourists. People-watch in comfort as you enjoy a plate of *lignje na žaru* (grilled squid), the restaurant's speciality.

Restaurant Dolcino (☎ 422 288; Hazif Ali Ulqinaku bb; mains €4-14) The Italian restaurant at the Hotel Dolcino occupies a smartly furnished room on the 1st floor overlooking the street. Despite the designer stone walls and leather chairs, the prices are reasonable, with most dishes (including pizza and pasta) under €10.

Restaurant Teuta (☎ 431 442; Stari Grad bb; mains €5-11) The food's good but it's all about the views at this traditional restaurant overlooking Mala Plaža from the battlements of the Old Town.

Other options:

VISITING MOSQUES

Unlike in some parts of the Islamic world, respectful non-Muslims are usually welcome to visit mosques in Montenegro, although some mosques don't allow women or have separate areas set aside for them (if you're unsure, ask for permission before entering). Mosques are primarily a place for prayer and most are kept purposefully plain so as not to distract the faithful – so there's usually not a lot to see inside anyway. The interiors of some are decorated with geometric patterns or Arabic calligraphy but the representation of people or animals is strictly forbidden. What they all have in common is a prayer niche aligned at the centre of the wall facing Mecca.

If you're keen to visit, a few simple protocols should be followed. Clothing should be loose and should cover the body: shorts, singlets, short skirts and tight jeans are a no-no and women will often cover their heads. Shoes must be removed and mobile phones switched off. Devout Muslims are required to ritually cleanse themselves before entering for prayer, so there's usually a fountain or tap near the entrance. Non-Muslims aren't expected to do so. Don't distract anyone praying by wandering around or talking loudly inside the mosque – in fact, don't enter at all if group prayers or other community activities are taking place.

Ristorante Pizzeria Gallo Nero (☎ 315 245; Kadi Hysen Mujali bb; mains €4-14) Friendly service and a good Italian menu comprising pasta, pizza and grills.
Bella Vista (☎ 402 088; Hazif Ali Ulqinaku bb; mains €4-17) Yet more pizza, pasta and fish dishes. Good for an early breakfast or late-night drink and snack.

Drinking & Entertainment

The Mala Plaža promenade buzzes on summer nights when it's lined with teenagers hanging out. All the bars get packed and fast food is served hand over fist.

Caffe Princ (Hazif Ali Ulqinaku bb) Where the young and hip hang out, this place thinks it's too cool to serve *rakija* yet it has a good vibe and popular pool table.

Dona Bar (Hazif Ali Ulqinaku bb) If this chic little cafe-bar wasn't in the Balkans, its deco curves, red glittery furniture and soft pink lighting might have you thinking you'd stumbled into a gay bar. It isn't one, of course, despite them playing Barbra Streisand when we visited.

Rock (Hazif Ali Ulqinaku bb; ⊗ 7am-3am) A worthy attempt at an Irish pub with dark wood and electric candles adding to the atmosphere.

Millennium Summer Nightclub (Ulcinjski Moreplovci bb) Like it says on the label. DJs pump out the tunes on this large flat area below the city walls in summer.

Getting There & Away

The **bus station** (☎ 413 225) is on the northeastern edge of town just off Bulevar Vëllazërit Frashëri. Services head to Bar (€2.50, 30 minutes, six daily), Podgorica (€7, one hour, daily) and Shkodra (€4.50, 90 minutes, daily).

Minibuses head to Shkodra at 9am and 3pm (or when they're full) from the car park beside Ulcinj's market (about €5).

AROUND ULCINJ
Velika Plaža & Ada Bojana
Велика Плажа и Ада Бојана

The appropriately named **Velika Plaža** (Big Beach) starts 4km southeast of Ulcinj and stretches for 12 sandy kilometres. Sections of it sprout deckchairs but there's still plenty of space for solitude. To be frank, this large flat expanse isn't quite as picturesque as it sounds and the water is painfully shallow – great for kids but you'll need to walk out a fair way for a decent swim.

On your way to Velika Plaža you'll pass the murky **Milena canal** where the local fishermen use nets suspended from long willow rods

attached to wooden stilt houses. The effect is remarkably redolent of Southeast Asia. There are more of these contraptions on the banks of the **Bojana River** at the other end of Velika Plaža.

A bridge leads over the river to **Ada Bojana**, as peculiar a place as you're likely to find in Montenegro. It was apparently formed around a shipwreck between two existing islands in the river mouth, which eventually gathered enough sediment to cover around 520 hectares and create 3km of sandy beach. During its Yugoslav heyday it became one of Europe's premier nudist resorts, with the island completely given over to the footloose and fancy-threads-free. In summer, a barricade is erected to restrict access to hotel guests but you'd have to be totally committed to the lifestyle to want to stay in the neglected accommodation that's currently offered.

Both Velika Plaža and Ada Bojana are in the developers' sights. While a wrecking ball wouldn't go astray at Ada Bojana, the plans to lease 100 hectares for a 2500-bed luxury (presumably clothed) resort could bring environmental strain to an important habitat for shore birds. Still, that's nothing compared to the 25,000 beds mooted for Velika Plaža. Plans are afoot to create biking and walking tracks to the best birdwatching areas where you may also spot sea turtles.

SLEEPING & EATING

Casa Agata (☎ 455 025; Velika Plaža–Ada Bojana Rd, Štoj; apt €20-40; ⊗) Agata is the name of the delightful matriarch whose lack of English is negated by her son's fluency. This large house surrounded by oleanders and lush gardens has 12 apartments. While they're literally a little rough around the edges (some of the joinery isn't great), they're kept very clean and tidy and they all have en suites and balconies. It's a good homely option, only 250m from the beach.

Autocamp Tomi (Velika Plaža–Ada Bojana Rd, Štoj; car, tent, 2 adults & kids €20, apt €70) There's no point trying to call ahead as the lovely elderly couple who run this peaceful campsite don't speak a word of English. There are a handful of simple but spacious apartments available as well as plenty of shady spots to pitch a tent and a decent ablutions block with both squat and sit-down options.

ourpick Riblja Čorba (☎ 401 720; Bojana River; mains €6-10) Not actually in Ulcinj but well worth the 14km drive, this memorable fish restaurant is one of several that jut out over the Bojana River just before the bridge to Ada Bojana. The name means 'fish soup' and their broth is indeed sublime: thick with rice and served in a metal pot that will fill your bowl twice over.

Lake Šas Шаско Језеро

If you've got your own wheels and fancy getting well off the beaten track, this pretty area near the Albanian border makes for a pleasant and peaceful drive. Take the road leading northwest from Ulcinj. After 17km you'll reach the large village of Vladimir where a marked turn-off to the right leads to the lake. After 2km you'll see to your right the ruins of the once great Zetan city of **Svač** (Šas). Park here and cut across the rough football (soccer) pitch to its top left corner where you'll find the beginnings of a rocky path. Make sure you're wearing proper shoes as the track is quite rough and there are a lot of thorns.

There's not a lot remaining here apart from some sections of wall and the shells of a couple of buildings, one of which was obviously a church. The town was razed by the Mongols in 1242 and then again by the Ottomans in the 16th century, after which it was abandoned to the dragonflies, bees and butterflies. It's now a rustically beautiful spot, completely unbothered by tourists, offering broad views over the plains towards the Rumija Mountains.

Jump back in the car and continue to follow the signs to the lake, which is 3km further. At the end of the road a left fork leads uphill to a large abandoned building that offers the best lake views. **Lake Šas** (Šasko jezero) covers 364 hectares and is lined with a muddy border of reeds and water lilies, making it an important habitat for the 240 species of bird that are found here. In winter it attracts both dedicated birdwatchers and Italian hunters.

Below the viewpoint is the character-filled **Restaurant Shasi** (☎ 069-592 873; mains €5-13), a rambling stone complex built into the cliff that even has its own waterfall. It's a lovely and quiet spot where the staff spring into action when you arrive and fish soup is served with delicious corn damper. Shasi's specialities are eel, mullet and carp, caught from the pier at the bottom of their yard.

Central Montenegro

You can't really say you've been to Montenegro if you haven't visited the region that has always been its physical, spiritual and political heartland. A distinct Montenegrin (as opposed to Serbian) identity formed here from the crucible of resistance to Ottoman hegemony represented by Lovćen, the black mountain. As the Ottoman Empire waned, Montenegro spread first into these lands and it's here that the independent Montenegrin spirit remains strongest.

To reach central Montenegro from the coast you'll first have to skirt two wonderful national parks that provide every excuse for a back-to-nature diversion. Mountainous Lovćen and voluminous Lake Skadar don't have much in common apart from their natural gorgeousness, but these important habitats shelter many species that have a hard time surviving in modern Europe, including bears, wolves and the Dalmatian pelican. For mammals of the two-legged variety, both parks provide ample opportunity for active pursuits, whether that be hiking, mountain biking, swimming, windsurfing or kayaking.

Behind the parks are the two capitals, the ancient current one (Podgorica, founded by the Romans) and the newer former one (Cetinje, the royal city). Together they offer the chance to get better acquainted with Montenegrin art and history in their richly endowed galleries and museums.

Continue into the hinterland and you'll reach Ostrog Monastery. In a country with a seemingly endless supply of religious sites, none comes close to Ostrog either in spiritual significance or sheer impressiveness.

Central Montenegro may not quite have the pulling power of the coast but it still packs a punch.

HIGHLIGHTS

- Marvelling at the majesty of both the mountains and the monument at the **Njegoš Mausoleum** (p122)
- Diving through Montenegrin history and culture in **Cetinje's museums** (p123)
- Gazing in wonder at the improbable cliff-face construction of **Ostrog Monastery** (p133)
- Cruising the sparkling waters of **Lake Skadar** (p126)
- Feasting on the sublime seafood and serene setting of **Rijeka Crnojevića** (p127)
- Travelling between the sheer cliffs and green depths of the **Piva Canyon** (p136)

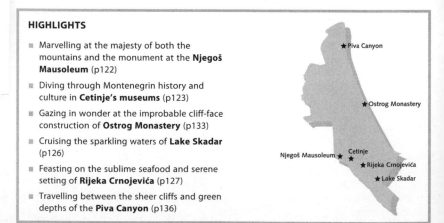

★ Piva Canyon

★ Ostrog Monastery

Njegoš Mausoleum ★ Cetinje ★
★ Rijeka Crnojevića

★ Lake Skadar

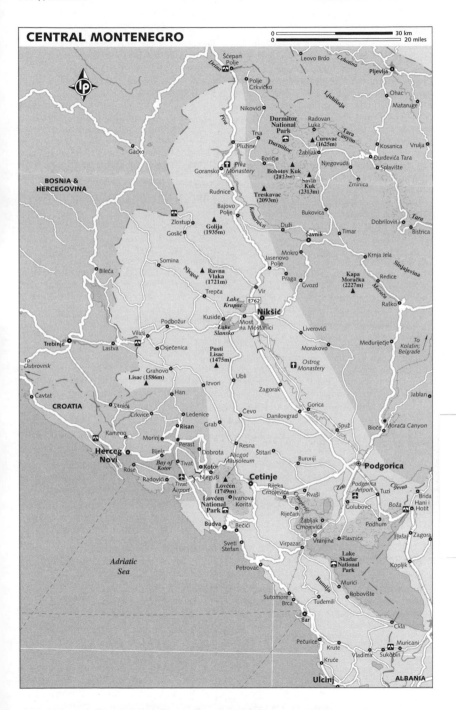

CENTRAL MONTENEGRO

0 — 30 km
0 — 20 miles

BOSNIA & HERCEGOVINA

CROATIA

Adriatic Sea

ALBANIA

Šćepan Polje
Polje Crkvičko
Nikovići
Leovo Brdo
Cehotina
Pljevlja
Ohac
Mataruge
Ljubišnja

Drina
Piva

Durmitor National Park
Trsa
Plužine
Durmitor
Žabljak
Boriče
Radovan Luka
Ćurovac (1625m)
Tara Canyon
Kosanica
Vrulja
Đurđevića Tara
Splavište

Piva Monastery
Goransko
Rudnice
Bobotov Kuk (2523m)
Savin Kuk (2313m)
Njegovuđa
Žminica

Bajovo Polje
Treskavac (2093m)
Duži
Bukovica
Dobrilovina
Tara
Bistrica

Zlostup
Goslić
Golija (1935m)
Šavnik
Timar
Krnja Jela

Somina
Bileća
Njegoš
Ravna Vlaka (1721m)
Mokro
Jasenovo Polje
Praga
Gvozd
Kapa Morača (2227m)
Redice
Sinjajevina
Morača
Raško

Trepča
Vir
E762
Lake Krupac
Nikšić
Liverovići
Kuside
Luke Slansko
Most na Moštanici
Podbožur
Vilusi
Lastva
Osječenica
Pusti Lisac (1475m)
Morakovo
Međurječje
To Kolašin; Belgrade

Trebinje
To Dubrovnik
Ostrog Monastery
Ubli
Grahovo Lisac (1586m)
Izvori
Zagorak
Gorica
Jablan

Cavtat
Sitnica
Crkvice
Han
Ledenice
Čevo
Danilovgrad
Spuž
Bioče
Morača Canyon

Kameno
Morinj
Risan
Grab
Resna
Štitari
Buronji
Podgorica

Herceg Novi
Bijela
Perast
Dobrota
Njegoš Mausoleum
Podgorica Airport
Tuzi
Brida Hani i Hotit

Rose
Radovići
Tivat
Kotor
Njeguši
Cetinje
Rijeka Crnojevića
Rvaši
Zeta
Čijevna
Boža

Tivat Airport
Lovćen (1749m)
Lovćen National Park
Ivanova Korita
Riječani
Golubovci
Podhum

Budva
Bečići
Žabljak Crnojevića
Ljašar
Zagora

Sveti Stefan
Virpazar
Vranjina
Plavnica
Kopljik

Petrovac
Rumija
Lake Skadar National Park
Murici
Bobovište

Sutomore
Brca
Tuđemili
Ckla

Bar
Pečurice
Krute
Vladimir
Muricani
Sukobin

Kruče
Ulcinj

Climate

Extremes in temperature are more likely in this region than on the coast. Podgorica is scorching in summer and can reach into the 40s, although the average maximum for July and August is 33°C. The coldest month is January, when the average ranges between 2°C and 9°C, but it can fall below freezing any time from November to March. October through to December is the wettest period but these months still see more sunny than rainy days. Summer afternoons are prone to sudden tropical-style deluges and thunderstorms.

In the mountains the climate is considerably cooler. The average annual temperature of Ivanova Korita in Lovćen National Park is only 6°C.

Getting There & Away

The main route from the coast to Cetinje leaves the Adriatic highway between Budva and Bečići. An alternative is the scenic back road, which climbs up the mountain behind Kotor and heads through Lovćen National Park.

The second major route from the coast heads through Virpazar and on to Podgorica and can be accessed from Petrovac or via a toll tunnel starting near Sutomore, north of Bar. Another scenic drive links Ulcinj to Lake Skadar near the Albanian border.

From the north, the main highway heads along the Morača River to Podgorica. A major secondary road connects Durmitor National Park to Nikšić, while a back road heads west and crosses the Piva River near Plužine, north of Nikšić.

Regular bus services ply all of the major routes. You can reach central Montenegro by train from Bar in the south or from Kolašin, Mojkovac or Bijelo Polje in the north.

A ROYAL ROUND TRIP

From Cetinje a 53km, day-long circular mountain-biking route follows asphalt roads through Lovćen National Park. You'll ascend 890m in your first 20km to the entrance of the Njegoš Mausoleum, where you can stop for the views and a bite to eat. It's mainly downhill from here, heading in the direction of Kotor before looping through Njeguši and back to Cetinje.

For flights to Podgorica or road connections from Nikšić to Bosnia and Hercegovina or from Podgorica to Albania, refer to the Transport chapter (p163).

Getting Around

Podgorica is the bus hub and has regular services to Cetinje, Nikšić and Virpazar. Trains are only possible between Podgorica and Virpazar. There's no public transport to Ostrog Monastery, Lovćen National Park, Rijeka Crnojevića or the south shore of Lake Skadar.

LOVĆEN NATIONAL PARK ЛОВЋЕН

Directly behind Kotor is **Mt Lovćen** (1749m, pronounced 'lov·chen'), the black mountain that gave Crna Gora (Montenegro) its name (crna/negro means 'black', gora/monte means 'mountain' in Montenegrin and Italian respectively). This locale occupies a special place in the hearts of all Montenegrins. For most of its history it represented the entire nation – a rocky island of Slavic resistance in an Ottoman sea. The old capital of Cetinje nestles in its foothills and many of its residents head up here for picnics during summer.

Two-thirds of the national park's 6220 hectares are covered in woods, particularly the black beech that gives it its moody complexion. Even the rockier tracts sprout wild herbs such as St John's wort, mint and sage. The park is home to various types of reptile, 85 species of butterfly and large mammals such as brown bears and wolves. The 200 avian species found here include regal birds of prey such as the peregrine falcon, golden eagle and imperial eagle (but you'll be looking for a long time for the two-headed variety featured on the Montenegrin flag). Several species migrate between here and Lake Skadar.

The mountains are criss-crossed with well-marked hiking paths and mountain-biking trails, which can be accessed from Kotor, Budva or Cetinje, and the Coastal Mountain Traversal (see the boxed text, p80) runs straight through it. If you're planning on hiking, come prepared as the temperature is an average of 10°C cooler than on the coast and Lovćen's prone to sudden changes in summer. Despite the high average rainfall, water supplies are limited as the moisture quickly leeches into the karstic limestone.

Lovćen's star attraction is the magnificent **Njegoš Mausoleum** (Njegošev Mauzolej; admission €3) at the top of its second-highest peak, Jezerski Vrh (1657m). Take the 461 steps up to the entry where two granite giantesses guard the tomb of Montenegro's greatest hero (see p29). Inside under a golden mosaic canopy a 28-ton Petar II Petrović Njegoš rests in the wings of an eagle, carved from a single block of black granite by Croatian sculptor Ivan Meštrović. The actual tomb lies below and a path at the rear leads to a dramatic circular viewing platform providing the same spectacular views that caused George Bernard Shaw to exclaim 'Am I in paradise or on the moon?'. A photographer stationed near the entrance has a stash of folk costumes and a computer set up to print out quirky instant souvenirs (€5).

The park's main hub is **Ivanova Korita** near its centre, where there are a few eateries and (in winter) a 150m-long ski slope. Here you'll also find the **National Park Office** (☎ 033-761 128; www .nparkovi.cg.yu; ☒ 9am-5pm Apr-Oct, shorter hr in winter), which offers accommodation in four-bed bungalows (€40). If you're planning some serious walking, buy a copy of the *Lovćen Mountain Touristic Map* (scale 1:25,000), available from the office and park entries.

Near the northern edge of the park is the village of **Njeguši**, an endearing place that's famous for two things: being the birthplace of Petar II Petrović Njegoš and for making the country's best *pršut* (smoke-dried ham). You'll see dishes branded 'Njeguški' on menus throughout the country whether the produce originated from this tiny spot or not.

If you're driving, the park can be approached from either Kotor or Cetinje (entry fee €2). The back route between the two shouldn't be missed (see the boxed text, p88). Tour buses are the only buses that head into the park.

CETINJE ЦЕТИЊЕ
☎ 041 / pop 15,137

Rising from a green vale surrounded by rough grey mountains, Cetinje (pronounced 'tse·ti·nye') is an odd mix of former capital and overgrown village where single-storey cottages and stately mansions share the same street. Several of those mansions – dating from times when European ambassadors rubbed shoulders with Montenegrin princesses – have become museums or schools for art and music.

The city was founded in 1482 by Ivan Crnojević, the ruler of the Zeta state, after abandoning his capital near Lake Skadar to the Ottomans.

Orientation & Information

Cetinje's main street is pretty Njegoševa, a partly pedestrianised thoroughfare lined with interesting buildings including the **Presidential Palace** and various former embassies marked with plaques (check out the unusual **French embassy** at the corner of Ulica Jovana Tomaševića). Everything of significance is in the immediate vicinity, including banks and the **post office** (☎ 232 026; Njegoševa bb).

Accident & Emergency Clinic (Hitna pomoć; ☎ 233 002; Vuka Mićunovića 2)

Tourist information (☎ 078-108 788; Novice Cerovića bb; ☒ 8am-8pm Mon-Sat, 9am-5pm Sun) No English spoken, but you can buy souvenirs and Cetinje guidebooks (€10).

Sights
MUSEUMS

The **National Museum of Montenegro** (Narodni muzej Crne Gore; all museums adult/child €8/4; ☒ 9am-5pm, last admission 4.30pm) is actually a collection of five museums housed in a clump of important buildings. A joint ticket will get you into all of them or you can buy individual tickets at each site.

Two are housed in the former parliament (1910), Cetinje's most imposing building. The fascinating **History Museum** (Istorijski muzej; ☎ 230 310; Novice Cerovića 7; adult/child €3/1.50) is very well laid out, following a timeline from the Stone Age to 1955. There are few English signs but the enthusiastic staff will walk you around and give you an overview before leaving you to your own devices. Bullet holes are a theme of some of the museum's most interesting relics: there are three in the back of the tunic that Prince Danilo was wearing when assassinated; Prince Nikola's standard from the battle of Vučji Do has 396; while in the communist section there's a big gaping one in the skull of a fallen comrade.

Upstairs you'll find the equally excellent **Art Museum** (Umjetnički muzej; adult/child €3/1.50). There's a small collection of icons, the most important being the precious 9th-century *Our Lady of Philermos*, traditionally believed to be painted by St Luke himself. It's spectacularly presented in its own blue-lit 'chapel', but the Madonna's face is only just

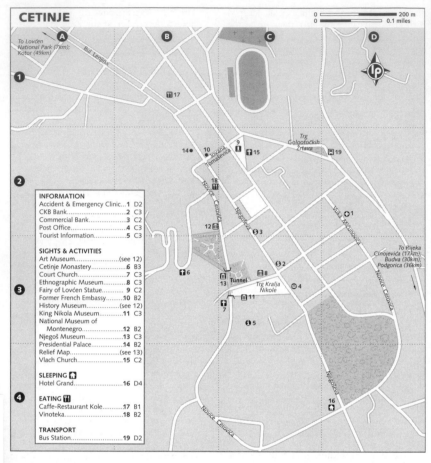

CETINJE

0 ————— 200 m
0 ————— 0.1 miles

To Lovćen
National Park (7km);
Kotor (49km)

Buf Lenjina

Trg
Golgotockih
Zrtava

Jovana
Tomaševića

Novice Cerovica

Njegoševa

Vuka Mićunovića

To Rijeka
Crnojevića (17km);
Budva (30km);
Podgorica (36km)

Tunnel

Trg Kralja
Nikole

Novice Cerovica

Njegoševa

Novice Cerovica

INFORMATION
Accident & Emergency Clinic...**1**	D2
CKB Bank...............................**2**	C3
Commercial Bank..................**3**	C2
Post Office............................**4**	C3
Tourist Information................**5**	C3

SIGHTS & ACTIVITIES
Art Museum.....................(see 12)	
Cetinje Monastery.................**6**	B3
Court Church........................**7**	C3
Ethnographic Museum...........**8**	C3
Fairy of Lovćen Statue............**9**	C2
Former French Embassy.........**10**	B2
History Museum................(see 12)	
King Nikola Museum.............**11**	C3
National Museum of	
Montenegro.......................**12**	B2
Njegoš Museum...................**13**	C3
Presidential Palace................**14**	B2
Relief Map......................(see 13)	
Vlach Church.......................**15**	C2

SLEEPING
Hotel Grand.........................**16**	D4

EATING
Caffe-Restaurant Kole...........**17**	B1
Vinoteka.............................**18**	B2

TRANSPORT
Bus Station..........................**19**	D2

visible behind its spectacular golden casing mounted with diamonds, rubies and sapphires. Elsewhere in the gallery all of Montenegro's great artists are represented, with the most famous (Milunović, Lubarda, Dado Đurić etc) having their own separate spaces. Expect a museum staff member to be hovering as you wander around.

While the hovering at the Art Museum is annoying, the **King Nikola Museum** (Muzej kralja Nikole; ☎ 230 555; Trg Kralja Nikole; adult/child €5/2.50) can be downright infuriating. Entry is only by guided tour, which the staff will only give to a group, even if you've prepaid a ticket and they have nothing else to do. Still, this 1871 palace of Nikola I, last sovereign of Montenegro, is worth the hassle. Although looted

during WWII, enough plush furnishings, stern portraits and taxidermied animals remain to capture the spirit of the court.

Opposite the National Museum, the castle-like **Njegoš Museum** (Njegošev muzej; ☎ 231 050; Trg Kralja Nikole; adult/child €3/1.50) was the residence of Montenegro's favourite son, prince-bishop and poet Petar II Petrović Njegoš. The hall was built and financed by the Russians in 1838 and housed the nation's first billiard table, hence the museum's alternative name, Biljarda. The bottom floor is devoted to military costumes, photos of soldiers with outlandish moustaches and exquisitely decorated weapons – these people clearly loved their guns. Upstairs are displayed Njegoš's personal effects, including his bishop's cross and garments, documents, fabulous furniture and, of course, the billiard table.

When you leave the museum turn right and follow the walls to the glass pavilion housing a fascinating large-scale **relief map** (adult/child €1/50c) of Montenegro created by the Austrians in 1917. If it's closed you can peer through the windows.

Occupying the former Serbian Embassy, the **Ethnographic Museum** (Etnografski muzej; Trg Kralja Nikole; adult/child €2/1) is the least interesting of the five but if you've bought a joint ticket you may as well check it out. The collection of costumes and tools is well presented and has English notations.

CETINJE MONASTERY
ЦЕТИЊСКИ МАНАСТИР

It's a case of three times lucky for the **Cetinje Monastery** (Cetinjski manastir; ☎ 231 021; ☉ 8am-6pm), having been repeatedly destroyed during Ottoman attacks and rebuilt. This sturdy incarnation dates from 1785, with its only exterior ornamentation being the capitals of columns recycled from the original building founded in 1484.

The chapel to the right of the courtyard holds the monastery's proudest possessions: a shard of the True Cross (the *pièce de résistance* of many of Europe's churches) and the mummified right hand of St John the Baptist. The hand's had a fascinating history, having escaped wars and revolutions and passed through the hands of Byzantine emperors, Ottoman sultans, the Knights Hospitallers, Russian tsars and Serbian kings. It's now housed in a bejewelled golden casket by the chapel's window, draped in heavy fabric and with an icon of the Baptist at its, ahem, foot. The casket's only occasionally opened for veneration so if you miss out you can console yourself with the knowledge that it's not a very pleasant sight.

The monastery **treasury** (admission €2; ☉ 8am-4pm) is only open to groups but if you are persuasive enough and prepared to wait around, you may be able to get in. It holds a wealth of fascinating objects that form a blur as you're shunted around the rooms by one of the monks. These include jewel-encrusted vestments, ancient handwritten texts, icons (including a lovely Syrian *Madonna and Child*) and a copy of the 1494 *Oktoih* (Book of the Eight Voices), the first book printed in Serbian. The crown of

14th-century Serbian king Stefan Uroš III Dečanski (who was deposed by his son, murdered and became a Serbian saint) is covered in pearls, large precious stones and priceless Byzantine-style enamels.

If your legs, shoulders or cleavage are on display you'll either be denied entry or given an unflattering smock to wear.

COURT CHURCH ДВОРСКА ЦРКВА

Built in 1886 on the ruins of the original Cetinje Monastery, cute little **Court Church** (Dvorska crkva; Novice Cerovića bb) has a lovely gilded iconostasis but its main claim to fame is as the burial place of Cetinje's founder, Ivan Crnojević, and Montenegro's last sovereigns. If Nikola I and Milena were unpopular after fleeing the country during WWI, dying in exile in Italy, they received a hero's welcome when their bodies were returned and interred in these white-marble tombs in 1989 during a three-hour Orthodox service. While still a part of communist Yugoslavia, a quarter of Montenegro's population were reported to have attended and the royal couple's son Prince Nicholas (a Parisian architect) and his fashion-designer wife Francine were mobbed by adoring royalist fans.

VLACH CHURCH ВЛАШКА ЦРКВА

Vlach people can be found throughout the Balkans and much of Central and Eastern Europe. They're believed to be the remnants of the Roman population (either ethnically Latin or Romanised Illyrians) who retreated into the less accessible areas as the Slavs poured in from the north. In Montenegro they formed seminomadic shepherding communities, moving their flocks between summer and winter pastures. While in neighbouring states they retain their own Latin-based language and customs to a greater or lesser degree, in Montenegro they appear to have been assimilated into the Slavic population; anyone identifying as Vlach in the 2003 census was included under the 0.35% listed as 'other'.

One echo of their presence is the sweet **Vlach Church** (Vlaška crkva; Baja Pivljanina bb). While its present appearance dates from the 19th century, it was actually founded around 1450 and therefore predates the Montenegrin founding of Cetinje. The original structure was made of thatch daubed in mud, a far cry from the sumptuous gilded iconostasis (1878) that's the centrepiece of the church today.

OFF WITH THEIR HEADS

Decapitated heads were once a common sight in Europe; up until 1802 those of executed criminals were still being displayed on London's Temple Bar. However, the Montenegrins' fondness for chopping off and displaying bits of their enemies was legendary and continued into the 20th century.

The hill above Cetinje Monastery was the repository of many such gruesome trophies, mainly taken from the shoulders of Ottoman Turks. Soldiers would proudly display their own collections as testimony to their prowess in battle. To be fair, the Ottomans shared the same taste in battle souvenirs, so the Montenegrins would often remove the heads of fallen comrades rather than allow the enemy to do it. A Russian officer who stumbled while fighting alongside Montenegrin allies in the early 19th century was startled by a friendly but deadly serious offer to prematurely remove his head lest he be captured.

After the capture of Herceg Novi from the French, it's reported that the Montenegrins used the French general's head as a football. When General Marmont remonstrated with Vladika (later Saint) Petar I about the custom, he was told that he could hardly complain as the French had recently chopped off the heads of their own king and queen.

Prince Nikola issued an edict against the practice in 1876, and visiting dignitaries were spared from such macabre sights in the capital. Montenegrin soldiers made do with only removing ears and noses instead, a tradition that continued right up to WWI.

Take a closer look at the fence around the church: it's made from 1544 barrels of guns taken from the Ottomans during the wars at the end of the 19th century. On the small square in front stands the bronze **Fairy of Lovćen statue**. It was erected in 1939 to commemorate the expatriates who were returning from America to fight for Montenegro during WWI when their boat was sunk near Albania; 350 of them died.

Sleeping & Eating

Cetinje seems to expect its visitors to flit in and out on tour buses. Accommodation is limited and there are only a few proper restaurants. Come the weekend competing sound systems blast the cobwebs from the main street. If war broke out on a Saturday night you probably wouldn't hear it.

Hotel Grand (☎ 242 400; hotelgrand@cg.yu; Njegoševa 1; s €45-60, d €64-80, apt €120) Fading grandeur would be a more accurate moniker but aside from a few pigeons roosting in the walls, Cetinje's only hotel is a pleasant place to stay. The comfy beds, new linen and spongy carpet certainly help. Locals glam it up for afternoon drinks on the leafy terrace.

Vinoteka (☎ 068-555 771; Njegoševa 103; mains €2.20-5) The wood-beamed porch looking onto the garden is such a nice spot that the excellent and reasonably priced pizza and pasta feels like a bonus – the decent wine list even more so.

Caffe-Restaurant Kole (☎ 069-035 716; Bul Lenjina 12; mains €3-8) They serve omelettes, pizza and pasta at this snazzy modern eatery, but what's really great is the local treats. Try the *Njeguški ražanj*, smoky spit-roasted meat stuffed with *pršut* and cheese.

Getting There & Away

Cetinje's on the main highway between Budva and Podgorica and can also be reached by a glorious back road from Kotor via Lovćen National Park (see the boxed text, p88). The **bus station** (Trg Golootočkih Žrtava) is only two blocks from the main street but it doesn't have a timetable, ticket counter or even a phone. Buses leave every 30 minutes for Podgorica (€3) and at least hourly for Budva (€3).

LAKE SKADAR NATIONAL PARK
СКАДАРСКО ЈЕЗЕРО

The Balkans' largest lake, dolphin-shaped Skadar has its tail and two-thirds of its body in Montenegro and its nose in Albania. Covering between 370 and 550 sq km (depending on the time of year), it's one of the most important reserves for wetland birds in Europe. The endangered Dalmatian pelican nests here along with 256 other species, including a quarter of the global population of pygmy cormorants. You may spot whiskered terns making their nests on the water lilies. At least 48 species of fish lurk beneath its smooth surface, the most common of which are carp, bleak and eel. Mammals within the park's confines include otters, wolves, foxes, weasels, moles and groundhogs.

On the Montenegrin side, an area of 400 sq km has been protected by a national park since 1983. It's a blissfully pretty area encompassing steep mountains, hidden villages, historic churches, clear waters and floating meadows of water lilies.

Rijeka Crnojevića Ријека Црнојевића

The northwestern end of the lake thins into the serpentine loops of the Rijeka Crnojevića (Crnojević River) and terminates near the pretty village of the same name. When Montenegro was ruled from Cetinje, this is where the royals came to escape the black mountain's winter. It's a charming, tucked-away kind of place, accessed by side roads that lead off the Cetinje–Podgorica highway.

The village's main feature is the photogenic arched stone bridge constructed by Prince Danilo in 1854. There's a historical display in the **National Park Visitors Centre** (www.nparkovi .cg.yu; admission €1; ♥ 8am-4pm), which occupies four wooden huts that jut out over the river on stilts.

Kayak Montenegro's day trips from Herceg Novi take to the water here and paddle along the river to the lake (p78). It's also the starting point of a two-hour, 7.6km circular walking track that passes through the ruins of **Obod**, the site of the region's first printing press, and on to the **Obodska Cave** (Obodska Pećina) at the source of the river.

If you fall under Rijeka Crnojevića's spell and wish to stay, there are rooms available at **Kuća Perjanik** (☎ 067-478 440; r €30), one house back from the bridge. The garrulous owner has returned from Melbourne to fix up his ancestral home and although at the time of writing it was still a work in progress, the simple rooms are clean and tidy and should have en suites by the time this book is published. You can grab a simple meal and a cold beer downstairs.

You wouldn't expect it, but this sleepy village is home to one of Montenegro's best restaurants. **Stari Most** (☎ 033-239 505; fish per kg €25-45, 5-course set menu €40-50) is well located on the marble riverside promenade, looking to the old bridge from which it derives its name. Fish, particularly eel, is the speciality here and the fish soup alone is enough to justify a drive from Podgorica.

Virpazar Вирпазар

This sweet little town is what passes for the big smoke in these parts and it serves as the main gateway to the national park. It's centred on a pretty town square and a picturesque stone bridge across a river blanketed with water lilies and, disappointingly, litter. Looking over the town are two testaments to its bloody past: the ruins of **Besac castle**, the scene of a major battle with the Turks in 1702; and a striking **bronze sculpture** atop a watchtower memorialising the Partisans who lost their lives in WWII. The path leading to Besac is signposted from the road to Murići about 400m after the post office.

Most of the boat tours of the lake depart from Virpazar, so the tranquillity is briefly shattered at around 10.30am each day when the tour buses from the coast pull in. A 15km mountain-biking trail skirts around the Crmnica field, which lies between Virpazar and the tunnel to the coast. The route heads through oak forests and the tiny winemaking villages of **Boljevići**, **Limljani** and **Gluhi Do**.

Other charismatic villages to visit in the vicinity are **Godinje** (a cluster of interlocking stone houses in the hills to the southeast) and **Poseljani** (another stone village north of Virpazar that once had a complex of 14 cascading watermills). Many of the villagers set up stands along the main roads in summer selling homemade wine and *rakija* (brandy).

INFORMATION

Virpazar has no banks or ATMs.

Accident & Emergency Clinic (☎ 020-711 128)

National park kiosk By the marina; has no information but sells park entry tickets (€4 per day) and fishing permits (€5 per day).

Post office (☎ 020-711 165) Just past the Partisan sculpture.

FESTIVALS & EVENTS

Lake Skadar Day A one-day park-wide festival in the third week of June including a busy program of windsurfing, kayaking, sports fishing, hiking, mountain biking, ballooning, helicopter flights, birdwatching, exhibitions, cruises, music and sampling local produce.

Rural Fair Another chance to sample local wine, fruit, honey, music and dance in early September.

Festival of Wine & Bleak That's 'bleak' as in a type of fish, not Russian theatre. It's yet another chance (in December) to stuff yourself while tapping your toes to traditional music.

SLEEPING & EATING

Locals with budget-friendly rooms to rent often linger around the main square in the afternoons.

Pelikan Hotel (☎ 020-711 107; pelikanzec@cg.yu; r €52-75; 🐾) A well-run one-stop-shop offering accommodation, an excellent traditional restaurant (mains €5 to €12) and 2½-hour boat tours that explore the lake's northern reaches (€30). The rooms are clean and have nice views over the square but some of them are tiny.

Konoba Badanj (☎ 020-712 509; mains €7-12) A cool stone-walled interior with solid wooden beams, views of the river and interesting art make this an atmospheric eating option. The fish soup comes with big chunks of fish and delicious scone-like homemade bread.

GETTING THERE & AWAY

Virpazar doesn't have a bus station but buses on the Bar–Podgorica route stop here. The decrepit **train station** (☎ 020-441 435) is off the main road, 800m south of town. There are regular services to Bar (€2) and Podgorica (€2.50).

Murići Мурићи

The southern edge of the lake is the most dramatic, with the Rumija Mountains rising precipitously from the water. From Virpazar there's a wonderful **drive** (or 56km mountain-biking route) following the contours of the lake through the mountains and an enchanting (possibly even enchanted) chestnut forest. The road heads towards the Albanian border before crossing the range and turning back towards Ulcinj. About halfway along the lake a steep side road descends to the village of Murići, a cluster of traditional buildings set around a mosque.

This is one of the lake's best swimming spots. The water's clear, if a little weedy in places, and swarms of little fish follow your feet as you kick up the nutrients beneath. Keen hikers can start the Coastal Mountain Traversal from here (see the boxed text, p80).

The **Murići Vacation Resort** (☎ 069-688 288; www .nacionalnipark-izletistemurici.com; per person €35) is more smart school camp than Club Med. Simple log cabins nestle within an olive grove on the lakeshore and share a decent ablutions block with a separate bath and shower. The price includes a bed plus three meals in the shady outdoor **restaurant** (mains €5-9). They also organise **lake tours** (€16) that visit the islands and Virpazar. If you don't have your own transport to Murići, jump on the boat at Virpazar.

Islands

An archipelago of islands traces the southern edge of the lake and in true Montenegrin fashion, many of them shelter churches. **Grmožur**, closest to Virpazar, is topped by a fortress (1843) that was used mainly as a prison and nicknamed 'the Montenegrin Alcatraz'.

Both **Starčevo Monastery** and the island it rests on are named somewhat unflatteringly after the priest who founded the monastery in 1377; it translates as Old Man's Monastery. The complex includes the **Church of the Dormition** (Crkva Uspenja Bogorodice) and an accommodation wing surrounded by a stone wall. Both this monastery and its neighbour on the island of **Beška** were famous for producing religious scripts. Beška Monastery's **St George's Church** (Crkva Sv Đorđa) also dates from the 14th century, while the smaller **St Mary's Church** (Crkva Sv Marije) was built in 1440. Both contain only traces of once extensive frescoes. **Moračnik** is yet another island monastery dating from at least the early 15th century. Its **St Mary's Church** is watched over by a high tower.

It's not only nuns and monks that take to the islands. A colony of grey herons has made their home amongst the laurels of tiny **Omerova Gorica** between Beška and Moračnik.

On the other side of the causeway, in the swampy northeastern reaches of Lake Skadar, **Kom Monastery** stands on the island of **Ondrijska Gora**. Its **Church of the Dormition** (1415) has the best-preserved frescoes of any of the lake's many churches.

Boatmen from Virpazar and Murići offer island excursions for around €10 per hour.

Vranjina Врањина

The twin Vranjina hills are nicknamed Sofia Loren by the locals for reasons that become apparent when they're viewed from afar. The main **National Park Visitors Centre** (☎ 020-879 100; www.nparkovi.cg.yu; admission €2; ⏰ 8am-4pm) rests in the shade of their cleavage on the opposite side of the causeway leading to Podgorica from Virpazar. This modern facility has excellent displays about all the national parks, not just Lake Skadar, including lots of taxidermied critters and an ethnographic section with folk costumes and tools. It also sells park entry tickets (€4 per day) and fishing permits (€5 per day).

The complex also includes **Restoran Jezero** (☎ 020-879 106; mains €5-9), a reputable traditional restaurant with beautiful lake views that's owned by the Plantaže wine company. The surrounding area is Montenegro's main wine region; stock up at the **Plantaže store** (🕙 9am-4pm) built into a cave by the car park or look out for roadside stalls. In the busy months tour operators set up kiosks nearby. **Kings Travel** (☎ 020-202 800) hires row boats (€25/100 per hour/day) and speedboats with drivers (€60/300 per hour/day). **Pelikan Windsurf Klub** (🖳 069 077 869; www.pelikansurf.cg.yu) hires gear (€10 per hour) and gives lessons (€8 per hour plus €7 for equipment) from May to September.

The Vranjina walking trail leads to **St Nicholas' Monastery** (Manastir Sv Nikole), a 13th-century complex that's been destroyed in many wars; the current building dates from the 19th century. Just along the causeway are the remains of the 19th-century fortress **Lesendro**. The busy highway and railway tracks prevent safe land access to the site.

Plavnica Плавница

If you'd like to stay in the lap of luxury while within earshot of the lapping of the lake, **Plavnica Eco Resort** (☎ 020-443 700; www.plavnica .info; ste €180; 😵 🖳 🖳) is the de luxe option. The 'eco' claims only appear to stretch as far as the beautiful setting, but this upmarket complex has made an attempt to mirror traditional stone architecture and it's blissfully low-rise. There are only four lavishly furnished suites, each sleeping two adults and potentially a small child. The main focus is the large restaurant (mains €6 to €22), opening onto an impressive resort-style pool (day use €10, free with accommodation) set within an amphitheatre that's sometimes used for live performances.

The resort has a suitably glam boat that's used for lake tours, including a 3½-hour Saturday dinner cruise with a live band (€10 for the tickets, food and drink extra). There's a private marina where you can hire catamarans (€60 per hour), speedboats (€120 per hour) or simply kayaks (€4 per hour) and pedal boats (€5 per hour).

Head towards Podgorica from the National Park Visitors Centre and after 11km turn right at the large white war memorial in Golubovci and head back down in the direction of the lake for 6km. The resort's at the end of the road.

Žabljak Crnojevića
Жабљак Црнојевића

Standing forlorn on a lonely hillside surrounded by lush green plains with only some rather large snakes and spiders as occupants, are the enigmatic ruins of **Žabljak Crnojevića**. For a brief time, between the fall of Skadar (now Shkodra in Albania) and the founding of Cetinje, this was the capital of Zetan ruler Ivan Crnojević. Walking up from the small village at its base, the 14m-high, 2m-thick walls look intimidating enough, yet even these couldn't withstand the hammering the Ottoman invaders gave them in 1478 when the town was finally abandoned.

The site's a little hard to find but well worth the effort. Heading towards Podgorica from the main National Park Visitors Centre, turn left at the only set of traffic lights in Golubovci. You'll cross a one-way bridge and when you get to the next intersection where a choice is required, veer left. Continue for about 6km until you see a small bridge to your left. Cross the bridge and continue to the car park near the village. From the car park walk alongside the river until you see some stone stairs heading up amongst the houses to your left and follow your nose up past the village church and along the overgrown path.

PODGORICA ПОДГОРИЦА
☎ 020 / pop 136,473

Podgorica's never going to be Europe's most happening capital but if you can get past the sweltering summer temperatures and concrete apartment blocks, you'll find a pleasant little city with lots of green space and some decent galleries, restaurants and bars. If you have limited time it's probably not worth a special trip, but given that it's a major transport hub, why not leave your bags at the bus station and wander around for the day?

Orientation

Podgorica (pronounced '*pod*·go·ri·tsa') sits at the confluence of two rivers. West of the broad Morača is what passes for the business district. The smaller Ribnica River divides the eastern side in two. To the south is Stara Varoš, the heart of the Ottoman town, where you'll find a **Turkish clock tower** (Trg Bećir-Bega Osmanagića), **mosque** (Nemaljića bb) and the **ruins of fortifications** where the rivers meet. North of the Ribnica is Nova Varoš, an attractive, mainly low-rise precinct of late-19th/early-20th-century buildings

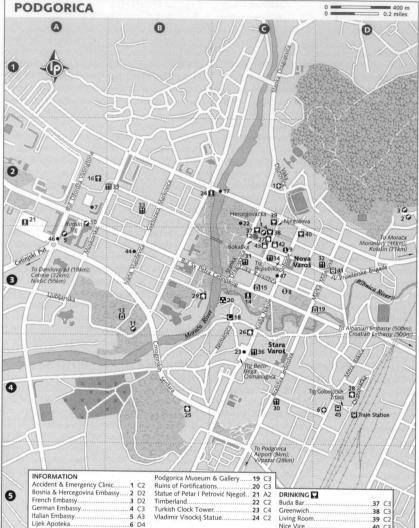

PODGORICA

INFORMATION

Accident & Emergency Clinic	1 C2
Bosnia & Hercegovina Embassy	2 D2
French Embassy	3 D2
German Embassy	4 C3
Italian Embassy	5 A3
Lijek Apoteka	6 D4
Montenegro Adventures	7 A2
Prva Bank	8 C3
Serbian Embassy	(see 29)
Tourist Organisation Podgorica	9 C3
UK Embassy	10 A2
USA Embassy	11 B3
www.club	12 C3

SIGHTS & ACTIVITIES

Dvorac Petrovića	13 B3
Equestrian Statue of Nikola I	14 C3
Galerija Centar	15 C3
Hram Hristovog Vaskrsenja	16 A2
Millenium Bridge	17 C2
Mosque	18 C3

Podgorica Museum & Gallery	19 C3
Ruins of Fortifications	20 C3
Statue of Petar I Petrović Njegoš	21 A2
Timberland	22 C2
Turkish Clock Tower	23 C4
Vladimir Visockij Statue	24 C2

SLEEPING

City Hotel	25 B4
Hotel Bojatours	26 C3
Hotel Eminent	27 C3
Hotel Evropa	28 D4
Hotel Podgorica	29 B3

EATING

Big Market	30 C4
Hong Kong II	31 C3
Laterna	32 D3
Leonardo	33 B2
Linea	34 C3
Little Market	35 B2
Maxi	36 C4

DRINKING

Buda Bar	37 C3
Greenwich	38 C3
Living Room	39 C2
Nice Vice	40 C3

ENTERTAINMENT

Kino Kultura	41 D3

SHOPPING

IPS	42 C3
RV Rakočević	43 C3

TRANSPORT

Adria Airlines	44 B3
Bus station	45 D4
Croatia Airlines	(see 44)
Jat Airways	(see 27)
Meridian	46 A3
Montenegro Airlines	47 C3

housing a lively mixture of shops and bars. At its heart is the attractive main square, Trg Republika.

Information

Accident & Emergency Clinic (Hitna pomoć; ☎ 124; Vaka Djurovića bb)

Lijek Apoteka (☎ 623 994; Mitra Bakića bb; ⦿ 7am-9pm) Pharmacy.

Montenegro Adventures (☎ 202 380; www.montenegro-adventures.com; Moskovska 63-64) The commercial wing of the nonprofit Centre for Sustainable Tourism Initiatives (www.cstimontenegro.org), with whom they share an office. They organise tours, accommodation and the like.

Prva Bank (Luka Karadžića bb) One of many bank branches with 24-hour ATMs in the central city.

Tourist Organisation Podgorica (TOP; ☎ 667 535; www.podgorica.travel; Slobode 47) Information on local sights, accommodation and services.

www.club (Bokaška 4; per hr €1.50; ⦿ 8am-2am) Decent cafe-bar with internet terminals.

Sights

Despite Cetinje nabbing most of the national endowment, the new capital's well served by the **Podgorica Museum & Gallery** (Muzej grada Podgorice; ☎ 242 543; Marka Miljanova 4; adult/child €5/1; ⦿ 9am-8pm). There's an interesting section on the city's history, which had its start around AD 100 as the Roman town of Doclea. Much of the museum's antiquities collection was exhumed from that site. The gallery features local big-hitters such as Dado Đurić and Petar Lubarda whose large canvas *Titograd* (1956) takes pride of place in the foyer.

The Centre for Contemporary Art operates two galleries in Podgorica. The bottom two floors of the once royal palace **Dvorac Petrovića** (☎ 243 513; Ljubljanska bb; admission free; ⦿ 8am-2pm & 4-9pm Mon-Fri & 10am-4pm Sat summer, 8am-8pm Mon-Fri & 8am-2pm Sat winter) are given over to high-profile exhibitions, while the top floor has an oddball collection of miscellanea (Indonesian batik, a metal palm tree from Iraq) that have the look of diplomatic gifts. The lovely grounds contain interesting sculpture, a tiny church and another exhibition space in the former guardhouse (Perjanički Dom). Temporary exhibitions are also staged in the small **Galerija Centar** (☎ 665 409; Njegoševa 2; admission free; ⦿ 9am-2pm & 5-9pm Mon-Fri, 10am-2pm Sat).

For a city formerly known as Titograd (literally 'Tito-city'), there is an inordinate number of royal sculptures dotted around its

many parks. The most imposing is the huge bronze **statue of Petar I Petrović Njegoš** standing on a black marble plinth on the Cetinje edge of town. A large **equestrian statue of Nikola I** struts grandly opposite the parliament at the head of a lovely park with manicured hedges and mature trees. You won't find Tito anywhere but there's a spectacularly cheesy sculpture of Russian singer **Vladimir Visockij** near the **Millennium Bridge**, pictured shirtless with a guitar and a skull at his feet.

A good indicator of the healthy state of Orthodoxy in Montenegro is the immense **Hram Hristovog Vaskrsenja** (Temple of Christ's Resurrection; Bul Džordža Vašingtona). It is still incomplete after 15 years' construction but its large dome, white stone towers and gold crosses are a striking addition to Podgorica's skyline.

If you're looking for something to entertain younger kids, **Timberland** (Stanka Dragojevića bb; admission €2; ⦿ 9am-11pm) is a small colourful playground in a park by the Morača River.

Sleeping

Most visitors to Podgorica are here for business, either commerce or government-related. Hotels set their prices accordingly and private accommodation isn't really an option.

Hotel Evropa (☎ 623 444; www.hotelevropa.cg.yu; Orahovačka 16; s €55-70, d/tr €90/120; 🛇 🖵 wi-fi) It's hardly a salubrious location, but Evropa is handy to the train and bus station and offers clean rooms with comfortable beds, writing desks and decent showers. Despite its diminutive size there's a sauna, fitness room and ample parking.

Hotel Bojatours (☎ 621 153; www.montenegrohotels.org; Kralja Nikole 10; s/d €80/115; 🛇 wi-fi) Going for a dash of chintzy elegance, this small hotel in a modern block has parquet floors, floral rugs, walnut veneer headboards and lots of artfully draped curtains. Try for room 301, a large bright double room with a terrace, or if you want to escape the traffic noise ask for one of the smaller rooms at the back of the building.

our pick **Hotel Eminent** (☎ 664 646; eminent@cg.yu; Njegoševa 25; s/d/tr €80/130/160, apt €90-140; 🛇 wi-fi) Given its location and excellent facilities, the Eminent seems to be set up for businesspeople keen on an after-work tipple. The front rooms can be noisy but the funky mezzanine apartments open on to a covered veranda at the back.

City Hotel (☎ 441 503; www.cityhotel-montenegro .com; Crnogorskih Serdara 5; s €88-158, tw €113, d €113-183, ste €220; 🞨 🖳 wi-fi) A business-orientated makeover in 2008 has thankfully kept the 1970s exterior angularity of this city-fringe hotel, while the surrealist art of Dado Đurić has prevented a total beige-out inside. There's a small gym, comfy furnishings and helpful English-speaking staff.

Hotel Podgorica (☎ 402 500; www.hotelpodgorica .cg.yu; Bul Sv Petra Cetinjskog 1; s €115-145, d €160-170, tw 170, ste €175-185; 🞨 🖳 wi-fi) A wonderful showcase of 1960s Yugoslav architecture, the Podgorica has been luxuriously modernised yet retains its period charm – the Pebblecrete exterior blending into stone the shade of Montenegro's mountains. The best rooms have terraces facing the river.

Eating

Head to the **little market** (Moskovska bb) or the **big market** (Bratstva Jedinstva bb) for fresh fruit and vegetables, and the large **Maxi** (Kralja Nikole bb; 🞧 7am-midnight Mon-Sat, 7.30am-3.30pm Sun) supermarket for other cooking supplies.

Linea (☎ 254 456; Trg Republike 22; mains €4.50-13; **V**) This attractive indoor and outdoor cafe serves decent breakfasts (omelettes, bacon and eggs), substantial sandwiches (€2.40) as well as the usual pasta, pizza and steak selections. The pear, walnut and gorgonzola salad makes a tasty change from all the grilled meat.

Hong Kong II (☎ 667 300; Stanka Dragojevića 14; mains €2.70-7.90) If your taste buds are crying out for variety, this inner-city restaurant serves a reasonable approximation of Chinese cuisine with a few standard Montenegrin grills thrown in to keep the locals happy. There's a big selection of chicken, pork and rice dishes, although the fried noodles look suspiciously like fettucine.

Laterna (☎ 232 331; Marka Miljanova 41; mains €4-13; 🞧 9am-midnight Mon-Sat; **V**) Farm implements hang from the rough stone walls creating a surprisingly rustic ambience for the centre of the city. A selection of meat and fish grills is offered, but it's hard to go past the crispy-based pizza – it's quite possibly Montenegro's best.

ourpick **Leonardo** (☎ 242 902; Svetozara Markovića bb; mains €4-13; **V**) Leonardo's unlikely position at the centre of a residential block makes it a little tricky to find, but the effort's well rewarded by accomplished Italian cuisine.

The pasta dishes are delicious and reasonably priced given the upmarket ambience, while the €4 pizzas should leave even those on a budget with a Mona Lisa smile.

Drinking & Entertainment

Buda Bar (☎ 067-344 944; Stanka Dragojevića 26; 🞧 8am-2am) A golden Buddha smiles serenely as you meditate over your morning coffee or search for the eternal truth at the bottom of a cocktail glass. This is one slick watering hole; the tent-like semienclosed terrace is the place to be on balmy summer nights.

Living Room (Njegoševa 37) There are loads of tables on the street but if you can handle the volume, the leather couches and chandeliers of the raised 'living area' are pretty cool.

Nice Vice (Slobode 84) Step through a wonky picture frame to a wine bar looking something like an English gentleman's library.

Greenwich (Njegoševa 29; 🞧 8am-3am) A pseudo-London pub where everyone ends up in the wee hours.

Kino Kultura (IV Proleterske Brigade 1; admission €2.50) The screenings aren't as regular as you might expect for the city's only cinema, but you may luck upon an English-language movie with Montenegrin subtitles.

Shopping

IPS (☎ 664 202; Njegoševa 28; 🞧 9am-9pm) The best selection of English-language books in the country, which isn't saying much.

RV Rakočević (☎ 067-840 882; Njegoševa 23; 🞧 8am-9pm Mon-Sat) If you're in the mood for a spot of *oro* (see p42), this is where you can find your fancy folk threads. A beautifully hand-embroidered, uniquely Montenegrin shirt will set you back somewhere between €60 and €150.

Getting There & Away

BUS

Podgorica's **bus station** (☎ 620 430; Trg Golootočkih Žrtava; 🞧 5am-10pm) has a left-luggage service, post office, ATM, restaurant and regular services to all major towns, including Nikšić (€3, one hour), Herceg Novi via Cetinje (€9, three hours), Kotor (€7, two hours), Bar (€7, 40 minutes) and Ulcinj (€7, one hour).

CAR

Avis (www.avisworld.com), **Europcar** (☎ 606 310; www .europcarcg.com), **Kompas** (☎ 244 117; www.kompas-car .com), **Rokšped** (☎ 620 000; www.roksped.com) and

Sixt (www.sixt.com) all have counters at Podgorica airport. Excellent local agency **Meridian** (☎ 234 944, 069-316 666; www.meridian-rentacar.com; Bul Džordža Vašingtona 85) also has a city office; one-day hire starts from €45.

TRAIN

Don't expect any English or a lot of help from the information desk at the **train station** (☎ 441 211; www.zeljeznica.cg.yu; Trg Golootočkih Žrtava 13; ⊙ 5am-11pm). Luckily, timetables are posted and fairly straightforward. Destinations include Bar (€3, one hour, 14 daily), Virpazar (€2.50, 40 minutes, 14 daily), Kolašin (€4.50, 90 minutes, three daily), Bijelo Polje (€5.80, 2½ hours, two daily) and Belgrade (€22, 7½ hours, four daily).

Getting Around

It's not difficult to get around town on foot but if you fancy trying a local bus, they cost 60c for a short journey. **Podgorica airport** (☎ 020-872 016) is 9km south of the city. Montenegro Airlines runs a shuttle bus (€3) between the airport and Trg Republike, timed around their flights. Airport taxis have a standard €15 fare to the centre but ordinary taxis should only charge about €8; try to grab one as they drop off passengers.

Alo Taxi (☎ 9700)

City Taxi (☎ 9711)

PLL Taxi (☎ 9705)

DANILOVGRAD ДАНИЛОВГРАД

☎ 020 / pop 5208

Little Danilovgrad, located 18km northwest of Podgorica, is well worth a short stop en route to Ostrog or Nikšić. There's a smattering of cafes on the main street, Ulica Baja Sekulića, which runs between two attractive squares.

The one nearest the Zeta River is dominated by an impressive socialist realist **monument** featuring two likely lads and a staunch woman topped by a red star. Below the monument there's a wonderful **sculpture garden** featuring dozens of interesting works carved out of white marble, ranging from the classic to the space-age.

In late August the three-day **River Zeta festival** (Rijekom Zetom) takes place featuring wooden raft and kayak races; diving, fishing and beauty contests; and an organic-food festival.

OSTROG MONASTERY
МАНАСТИР ОСТРОГ

Resting in a cliff face 900m above the Zeta valley, the gleaming white **Ostrog Monastery** (Manastir Ostrog) is the most important site in Montenegro for Orthodox Christians, attracting up to a million visitors annually. Even with its masses of pilgrims, tourists and trashy souvenir stands, it's a strangely affecting place.

Leaving the main Podgorica–Nikšić highway 19km past Danilovgrad, a narrow road twists uphill for 7km before it reaches the **Lower Monastery** (Donji manastir). In summer you'll be greeted with sweet fragrances emanating from the mountain foliage. **Holy Trinity Church** (Crkva Sv Trojice; 1824) has vivid frescoes and behind it is a natural spring where you can fill your bottles with deliciously fresh water and potentially benefit from an internal blessing as you sup it.

From here the faithful, many of them barefoot, plod up another two steep kilometres to the main shrine. Nonpilgrims and the pure of heart may drive directly to the upper car park. Halfway up, the beautiful stone walls of the little domed **Church of St Stanko the Martyr** (Crkva Sv Mučenika Stanka) gleam golden in the sunset.

The **Upper Monastery** (Gornji manastir; the really impressive one) is dubbed 'Sv Vasilije's miracle', because no one seems to understand how it was built. Constructed in 1665 within two large caves, it gives the impression that it has grown out of the very rock. Sv Vasilije (St Basil), a bishop from Hercegovina, brought his monks here after the Ottomans destroyed Tvrdoš Monastery near Trebinje.

Pilgrims queue to enter the atmospheric shrine where the saint's fabric-wrapped bones are kept. To enter you'll need to be wearing a long skirt or trousers (jeans are fine) and cover your shoulders. Most women also cover their heads with a scarf. It's customary to back out of the doorways and you'll witness much kissing of lintels and making of signs of the cross from the devout.

This idyllic place isn't without controversy. Radovan Karadžić christened his grandson here and several reports suggest that the monastery sheltered the former Bosnian Serb leader and alleged war criminal during his lengthy spell as a fugitive. This has always been strenuously denied; perhaps the matter will be settled now that Karadžić has finally been arrested. One of the only nonsmoking establishments in the country, the **guest house** (☎ 067-405 258; dm €4) near the Lower Monastery offers tidy single-sex dorm rooms, while in summer many pilgrims lay sleeping mats in front of the Upper Monastery.

There's no public transport but numerous tour buses head here from all of the tourist hot spots. Expect to pay about €15 to €20 for a day trip from the coast.

NIKŠIĆ НИКШИЋ
☎ 040 / pop 58,300

Montenegro's second-biggest city isn't high on most tourists' must-see lists and neither should it be. But if you fancy a blow-out in a lively student town, Nikšić (pronounced '*nik*·shich') has an array of establishments that offer a more genuine (not to mention cheaper) Montenegrin experience than the tourist-populated bars of Budva. What else would you expect in the town that produces Nikšićko Pivo, the nation's favourite beer? Eating and sleeping options are limited but they're also markedly cheaper – so much so that you might consider Nikšić as an alternative to staying in Podgorica, which is, after all, only 55km away.

Nikšić isn't just a university town; it's also one of Montenegro's main industrial centres, supporting a large steel mill and bauxite mine.

Orientation & Information
The main street, Njegoševa, is one of six roads coming together at a large roundabout at the bottom of town. You'll find banks with ATMs and pretty much everything else you need on this street.

Anita Travel Agency (☎ 200 598; Njegoševa 12; 🕑 8am-8pm Mon-Sat) Books rafting trips on the Tara River and air tickets.

Carev Most (☎ 213 551; Njegoševa 2) A small bookshop selling some English titles and road maps.

Hospital (☎ 244 111; Radoja Dakića bb)

Post office (☎ 244 452; Njegoševa bb; 🕑 7am-8pm Mon-Fri) Near the roundabout.

Uniprom Pharmacy (Trg Slobode; 🕑 8am-9pm Mon-Sat, 8am-2pm Sun)

Sights
Most of the historic buildings in Nikšić are clustered around the park near the main roundabout. King Nikola must have kept the country's builders busy as there's yet another

of his palaces here (adding to those in Cetinje, Podgorica and Bar). Now used as a **museum** (☎ 212 968; Trg Šaka Petrovića bb; adult/child €1/50c; 🕑 9am-1pm & 5-8pm Tue-Sat, 9am-noon Sun) it's badly in need of a renovation rescue to deal with the water stains and general decay. When we first visited (during the advertised opening hours) the place was locked up, but a second visit saw someone come running with a key seeming quite surprised to have a punter.

Start upstairs to the right in the prehistoric section (where there are various flints dating to the 3rd millennium BC) and progress past the bronze armour and iron spearheads to the lovingly decorated guns, jewel-encrusted armour and embroidered clothes in the ethnographic section. More recent history is covered by photographs and war memorabilia. Unfortunately, none of the explanations are in English, but you'll find that the graves of many of the fallen Partisan comrades represented here are in the nearby cemetery. Outside the museum you'll see examples of **stećci** (pronounced '*stech*·tsi'), mysterious carved stone monuments from the Middle Ages that are found throughout northern Montenegro and neighbouring Bosnia.

On top of the pine-covered hill next to the museum is the grand **Cathedral** (Saborna crkva; 1895), dedicated to St Vasilije of Ostrog (Sv Vasilije Ostroški). A central dome floods the interior with light and massive chandeliers hang from the ceiling. The exquisite iconostasis is painted in the more realistic style popular in the early 20th century, as opposed to the Byzantine look of the recent icons. Look out for the images of local saints Peter of Cetinje (Petar I Petrović, second from left) and Vasilije (second from right).

The heart of Nikšić is **Trg Slobode** (Freedom Sq), the large open area at the centre of Ulica Njegoševa. On summer nights what seems like the entire population – from the very young to the quite old – parade up and down the square. On one side is a hefty bronze **equestrian statue of King Nikola**, while the other side has a **fountain** set around a modern sculpture.

The original Nikšić formed within the walls of the **Onogošt fortress**, built on a rocky hill to the west of the current town. This was the site of a 4th-century Roman military base that was taken over by the Goths and fortified. Part of it has been restored and is used as a summer stage and cafe. From Ulica Njegoševa take Ulica Narodnih Heroja to the end, where you'll see the fortress ahead of you.

Activities

A 140km **mountain-biking trail** starts at Nikšić and heads east out of town before cutting north through remote villages and forgotten canyons and ending at the Tara River near Šćepan Polje. You'll need to be fit to attempt it as there are 3600m of ascents and descents involved.

The Montenegro Adventure Centre (see the boxed text, p103) can arrange **paragliding** in the vicinity.

Sleeping

Hotel Onogošt (☎ 246 014; onogost@cg.yu; Nika Miljanića 18; s/d €37/66) It's hard to imagine that this mammoth unrenovated Yugoslav-era hotel was ever full. While it's seen better days, it's still a surprisingly decent place to stay. Apart from the inevitable stains on the carpet, the rooms are clean and the bathrooms quite adequate. The front-desk staff are friendly and efficient (something you can't take for granted in state hotels of this vintage) and the location is excellent – close to the heart of things but far enough removed from the worst of the pandemonium on the streets. We're even perversely fond of the stridently yellow planters, couches and billowy curtains in reception.

Hotel Sindcel (☎ 212 591; fax 213 655; Danila Bojovića bb; s/d €45/50, apt €55-100) The Sindcel has some rough edges (shabby exterior, ill-fitting curtains, no proper shower cabinets, broken toilet seat), but the rooms are otherwise comfortable and very clean. It has a good location in a quiet residential street and the staff are very nice.

Eating

Proper restaurants are thin on the ground but there are plenty of places to grab a pizza or cheap snack.

Mex (Vuka Mićunovića bb; ☒ 7am-11pm Mon-Sat, 7am-8pm Sun) This big supermarket by the main roundabout has a good deli and fruit-and-veg selection.

Fontana (Njegoševa bb; snacks €1-3) A popular spot on the main drag for enjoying coffee, cakes and delicious ice cream. The blue-grey and chrome interior is a little like sitting in a classic Cadillac.

Konoba Portun (☎ 212 336; Njegoševa bb; mains €4-7; ☒ 8am-11pm) The centre's only proper restaurant is accessed by a dingy corridor

leading from the main street. The usual national specialities come in massive serves, accompanied by fries and vegetables.

Drinking

The main strip goes crazy on a Saturday night. There seems to be a higher concentration of bars and cafes on Njegoševa than anywhere else in the country and on the weekends most seem to operate under the assumption that the loudest is the best. On that criterion only, **Hemingway** and **Café Dodge** divvy up the gold and silver medals for their ear-bleeding techno, while the bronze goes to **Exit** (Trg Slobode) for its rousing (to the point of deafening) patriotic songs.

Caffe Cats (Nika Miljanića bb) A cool cafe-bar with funky furniture opposite the ruins of the space-age Dom Revolucije, once a grand testimony to communism and now collapsing in on itself under the weight of graffiti and neglect.

Camelot (Njegoševa bb) Although the name's Camelot, it's strictly Italian Renaissance scenes that are plastered over every surface of this cool-looking cafe serving €5 pizza and €2 (!!) cocktails. In the evening this is one of the few bars in which you can actually have a conversation.

De Bova (Novice Cerovića bb) Offers a decent pub feel, with photos of Jimmy Page and The Beatles on the walls.

Ibon (Trg Šaka Petrovića) Facing the park near the museum, this flash new cafe is a lovely spot for a morning coffee (a mere snip at 80c). Pizza's served inside amid smart leather seating and floaty curtains.

Getting There & Away

The modern **bus station** (☎ 213 018; Gojka Garčevića bb) is next to the main roundabout and has toilets, restaurants, an ATM and a left-luggage counter (€1). Buses to and from Podgorica (€3, one hour) are extremely frequent. Other domestic stops include Žabljak (€6, seven daily) and Kolašin (€5, every other day), and buses also cross the border to Trebinje (€5, three daily), Sarajevo (€17, three daily) and Belgrade (€25, five weekly).

While there is a train line running from Podgorica to Nikšić, it's not currently used for passengers. **Nik Taxi** (☎ 9733) is the local taxi service.

FROM PIVO TO PIVA

If you can drag yourself away from the Nikšićko *pivo* (beer), you'll find the Piva River just as satisfying. The route north from Nikšić meets the river after passing through 40km of verdant farmland. It then tangoes with the river until they both reach the border at Šćepan Polje, a popular rafting site (see p143). It's an extraordinarily beautiful drive and one not likely to be forgotten in a hurry.

The northern end of the river was blocked in 1975 by a 220m-high hydroelectric dam, flooding the Piva Canyon to create Lake Piva that reaches depths of over 180m. Great care was taken to move the **Piva Monastery** (Manastir Piva) from near the river's source to higher ground – a feat that took 12 years to complete. It's considered to be one of the most important religious sites in Montenegro and includes works by master fresco painters Longin and Kozma. The monastery was constructed between 1573 and 1586 with the permission of the Ottoman Grand Vizier who was a relative of its founder. The Muslim Vizier has been given the unusual honour of featuring in one of the church's frescoes with his head still attached to his body.

The road alongside the river is quite a feat of engineering in itself. It clings to the cliffs and passes through 56 small tunnels carved out of the stone in the years following WWII. After you pass the town of Plužine the route gets even more spectacular, with the steep walls of the canyon reflected in the deep green waters below. At Plužine it's possible (if there's no snow) to take a back road that cuts through Durmitor National Park to Žabljak (p143). An easier route from Nikšić to Žabljak passes through Šavnik.

AROUND NIKŠIĆ

Travelling west on the road to Trebinje in Bosnia, a large sign on the left (3.5km after the small roundabout on the edge of town) points to **Most na Moštanici**, an ancient Roman bridge. Make the most of this sign as there are no others once you leave the main road. Veer left after about 300m and head alongside the village. After a kilometre you'll see the bridge near a sweet little church, the inside of which is in a very poor state of repair. The bridge's five graceful arches span a ditch that's now completely dry: it seems that it's outlasted the river itself!

Heading in the same direction, a few kilometres past the turn-off to the bridge, look out for **Lake Slano** (Slansko jezero) to your left; there aren't any signs at all for this one. Although it's an artificial structure (there's a dam at one edge), its sparkling blue waters, low-lying islands and green borders make for a beautiful vista. There are few tiny villages on its shores but there's no straightforward route down to the water; take whatever turn-off you can find and wind your way down. You'll be unlikely to find more than a few people fishing or sunbathing on the shore.

More popular is **Lake Krupac** (Krupačko jezero), another dammed lake to the north-west of town, which is sometimes tagged 'Nikšić's sea'. It has a small sandy beach, a couple of beach bars, picnic spots under the poplar trees and pedal boats, jet skis and kayaks for hire. The waters are stocked with California trout.

There are four ski slopes at **Vučje** (☎ 040-213 262; day pass adult/child €10/5), 21km northeast of Nikšić on the back road to Šavnik.

Northern Mountains

This really is the full Monte: soaring peaks, hidden monasteries, secluded villages, steep river canyons and a whole heap of 'wild beauty', to quote the tourist slogan.

Locals will try to dissuade you from going anywhere other than Kolašin and Žabljak as these are the only towns that have a significant level of tourist infrastructure. This serves to give an off-the-beaten-track feel to almost any other place you might choose to explore, whether it be a small city like Bijelo Polje or a tiny village concealed within remote mountainous folds. Echoes of the Ottoman Empire can still be felt in places like Rožaje and Plav in the country's eastern reaches.

The mountainous north's premier attractions are its two national parks. Durmitor combines soaring peaks with the depths of the Tara Canyon, allowing for excellent skiing in winter and rafting in summer. Biogradska Gora shelters large swathes of ancient forest within the protecting arms of the Bjelasica Mountains. Both parks have well-marked paths that will lead you away from the trappings of civilisation within minutes. If you're after something more extreme, serious mountain lovers can take on the lofty reaches of Prokletije, the Accursed Mountains, themselves a candidate for national-park status.

However, you don't need to be an action hero to experience the beauty of this untamed region. Just hire a car for a few days and let the back roads lead you somewhere unexpected. Some parts may look remote on the map but don't underestimate how tiny Montenegro is. In a country this size you're unlikely to get lost for long – unless that's your desire.

HIGHLIGHTS

- Floating through paradise, rafting between the kilometre-plus walls of the **Tara Canyon** in Durmitor National Park (p143)

- Being dwarfed by the scale of the views enveloping the **Andrijevica–Kolašin road** (p148)

- Searching for wood nymphs in the primordial forest of **Biogradska Gora National Park** (p141)

- Time-warping to the 13th century as you step through the gates of the **Morača Monastery** (p138)

- People-watching as the evening promenade descends on **Rožaje's main street** (p146)

- Seeking that peaceful Eastern feeling between the mosques and mountains of **Gusinje** (p149)

★ Tara Canyon

Biogradska Gora National Park
★
Morača ★ ★ Andrijevica–Kolašin Road ★ Rožaje
Monastery
★ Gusinje

Climate

It shouldn't surprise anyone that this mountainous region is cooler than the rest of the country. In Žabljak, for instance, the annual average temperature is 5°C and from December through to March the average doesn't scrape above zero. The coldest month is January, averaging about -5°C, while the warmest is August at around 14°C. Even in the height of summer there are pockets of snow on Durmitor's highest peaks.

Kolašin is considerably warmer, ranging from a daily maximum of zero in January to 21°C in July and August.

Getting There & Away

The main highway between Podgorica and Belgrade cuts through Mojkovac and Bijelo Polje and is well served by buses. A major secondary road connects Nikšić to Durmitor National Park. You can travel to Kolašin, Mojkovac and Bijelo Polje by train from Serbia in the north or Podgorica and Bar in the south. For road connections with Serbia and Kosovo, refer to the Transport chapter (p167).

Getting Around

At Bijelo Polje the Podgorica–Belgrade highway joins another highway leading through Berane and Rožaje. Frequent buses take both of these routes. The road from Mojkovac to Žabljak is in excellent condition but gets twistier as it leaves the Tara Canyon and climbs into the mountains. This isn't a regular bus route. Plav is the most isolated town but it's also reached by a scenic road in good condition used by frequent buses to Berane. It's possible to circle the Bjelasica Mountains completely in a 136km loop. The most spectacular section is from Kolašin to Andrijevica, but it is prone to landslides in bad weather (see the boxed text, p148) and avoided by buses.

It's possible to travel between Kolašin, Mojkovac and Bijelo Polje by train.

MORAČA CANYON & MONASTERY
КАЊОН И МАНАСТИР МОРАЧА

Heading north from Podgorica it doesn't take long before the scenery becomes breathtaking. The main highway gets progressively more beautiful and more precarious as it follows the Morača River into a nearly perpendicular canyon, 300m to 400m deep. If you're driving, pull over in one of the viewing areas to enjoy it properly as this is an extremely busy and unforgiving stretch of road.

The river continues after the canyon recedes and near its banks, 46km from Podgorica, you'll find the **Morača Monastery** (Manastir Morača; 1252). Along with Ostrog (p133), Cetinje (p125) and Piva (see the boxed text, p136), this is one of the most important Orthodox monasteries in Montenegro, with some of its most accomplished religious art.

As you enter the walled compound into a garden courtyard where the bees from the monks' hives dance between the hydrangeas and roses, it's like stepping back into the 13th century. To the right, the small **St Nicholas' Church** (Crkva Sv Nikole) has faded frescoes on its facade that were once as vivid as those inside. You can still make out the Madonna and Child above the door and an archangel on either side.

The larger **Church of the Dormition** (Crkva Uspenja Bogorodice) also has external frescoes as well as beautiful doors inlaid with geometric patterns. In the vestibule there's a fascinating vision of Christ sitting in judgement, attended by saints. A slide of flames shoots the damned into hell where two-headed people-eating sea monsters do their worst. Look for the angels spearing little demons in the face with tridents to prevent them from tipping the scales of justice.

Inside the church the main image in the iconostasis, the *Virgin Enthroned with Child, Prophets and Hymnographers,* was painted by the celebrated master Đorđe Mitrofanović in 1617, the same year he completed the exterior frescoes. The other master at work here was Kozma, whose icon of *Saints Sava and Simeon* (1645) includes a border showing the construction of the monastery (the latter saint was the founder's grandfather). Also look out for the icon of St Luke by an unknown painter, depicting the apostle painting an icon of the Madonna and Child; this is probably a reference to the famous *Our Lady of Philermos* icon that now hangs in Cetinje's Art Museum (see p123).

KOLAŠIN КОЛАШИН
☎ 020 / pop 3000

Kolašin (pronounced 'ko·*la*·shin') is Montenegro's main mountain resort. Although the skiing's not as reliable as in Durmitor, Kolašin's much easier to get to (it's just off the main highway, 71km north of Podgorica)

NORTHERN MOUNTAINS

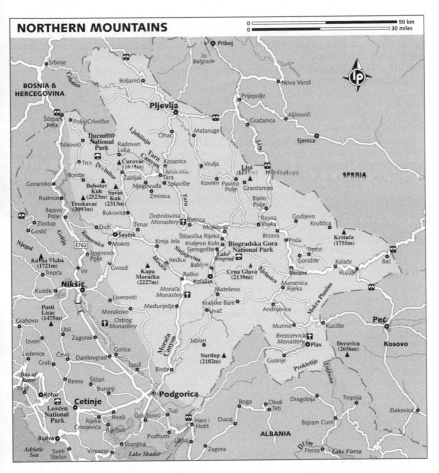

and has far ritzier accommodation offerings. Like most ski towns, it looks a lot prettier under a blanket of snow but even in summer it's a handy base for exploring Biogradska Gora National Park or other parts of the Bjelasica Mountains.

Orientation & Information

Most things of interest in this small town, including the banks and post office, are set around the two central squares (Trg Borca and Trg Vukmana Kruščiča) and the short street that connects them (Ulica IV Proleterske).

Cultural Centre (Dom kulture; Trg Borca 1; per hr €1; ☽ 10am-9pm Mon-Sat) Has an internet room upstairs, a small souvenir shop and a cinema (tickets €2).

Eco-tours Kolašin (☎ 860 700; www.eco-tours.cg.yu; IV Proleterske 5) Organises private accommodation, camping, mountain biking, fishing, rafting and jeep safaris.

Explorer Tourist Agency (☎ 864 200; www.montene gro explorer.cg.yu; Mojkovačka bb) Located near the bus station, this agency specialises in action-packed holidays. It can arrange hiking, skiing, rafting, mountain biking, canyoning, mountain climbing, jeep safaris, horse riding, paragliding and fishing expeditions. Mountain bikes can also be hired (€30/100 per day/week).

Regional Tourism Organisation (☎ 865 110; Trg Borca 2; ☽ 8am-4pm) You can tell this town's serious about tourism by this impressive wooden information centre that's very prominently located on the main street. The eager English-speaking staff can help arrange private accommodation, hotels, hiking, rafting, mountain biking and guided jeep tours (€70). They also rent out mountain bikes (€7/10/50 per half-day/full day/week).

Sights

Trg Borca features a stirring **Partisan statue** of a young man and woman marching forward, guns and communist flag aloft. They look like they're heading towards the **museum and gallery** (☎ 864 344; Trg Borca 1; admission free; 🕑 9am-1pm & 5-9pm Mon-Sat), a building once used for Partisan meetings. The collection mainly consists of photos and there aren't any English explanations, but the idealistic faces of the town's young comrades, many of whom lost their lives fighting the Nazis, are captivating. The gallery hosts interesting temporary exhibitions.

Activities

The **Jezerine ski centre** (☎ 069-379 418; www.jezerine.org; day pass €20) is located 10km east of Kolašin. The season lasts roughly from the New Year until the end of March. Gear can be hired for €12 to €20 per day.

Three marked **hiking paths** start from Trg Borca and head into the Bjelasica Mountains. From Jezerine ski centre there's a 16km, five-hour loop route through forest to **Mt Ključ** (1973m) and on to Eco Katun Vranjak (right) before heading back. If you're staying at the *katun* you can take another scenic trail that knocks off **Zekova Glava** (2117m) and passes **Lake Pešić** (Pešićko jezero), skirting beneath Bjelasica's highest peak. On the loop back it visits the spring that is the source of the Biogradska River before heading up **Troglava** (2072m). The 16km path is easy and well marked and should take less than five hours. For detailed descriptions and maps of both trails, pick up a copy of the *Mountains of Bjelasica* booklet (see the boxed text opposite).

A 93km **mountain-biking route** runs through remote countryside from Podgorica to Kolašin (see the boxed text, p80). There are plenty of places in Kolašin to hire bikes (see p139), so you could pick one up here, catch the train to Podgorica and cycle back over a few days.

MONTENEGRO'S MOST EXTRAORDINARY DRIVES

- Around the Bay of Kotor (p73)
- Kotor to Cetinje via Lovćen National Park (p88)
- Mojkovac to Žabljak along the Tara River (p145)
- Nikšić to Šćepan Polje along the Piva Canyon (p136)
- Plav to Andrijevica and over the mountains to Kolašin (p148)
- Podgorica to Kolašin along the Morača Canyon (p138)
- Virpazar to Ulcinj along the southern edge of Lake Skadar (p128)

Sleeping

For those establishments which vary their prices, the most expensive rates are during the ski season (especially around New Year) with a lower peak from June to August.

Eco Katun Vranjak (☎ 860 150; www.vilajelka.cg.yu; per person €15) This complex of wooden cabins near the ski field (at a height of 1750m) is the modern, traveller-friendly version of a *katun* (see the boxed text opposite), but it still provides an opportunity to eat traditional food, listen to folk songs, try your hand spinning wool, ride mountain horses (or bikes) and fall asleep to the sound of howling wolves. The family also have a small hotel in Kolašin and organise hiking and rafting trips.

our pick **Hotel & Restaurant Brile** (☎ 865 021; www.brile.info; Trg Borca bb; s/d/tr/q €32/64/98/130) Smart decor and comfy rooms are offered in this spotless family-run hotel on the main street. There's a sauna for an après-ski defrost and a restaurant downstairs serving warming comfort food like roasts, grilled meat, pizza and pasta (mains €3.50 to €11). They also rent out bikes and skis.

Hotel Čile (☎ 865 039; www.zlatnido.com; Braće Milošević bb; d/tr €46/69, apt €60-100) Although it's pronounced 'chilly', you'll be perfectly snug in this pleasant minihotel near the centre of town. The rooms are small but clean and while there's not a lot of English spoken, the owners provide a warm welcome. There are kitchenettes in the two- to five-bed apartments and some have jacuzzis.

Hotel Lipka (☎ 863 200; www.lipka.cg.yu; Mojkovačka bb; low-high s €50-120, d €60-190, tw €60-150, ste €95-270) Going for the designer-rustic look, this modern 72-room hotel is fitted out in wood and stone and liberally scattered with peasant artefacts – there's a spinning wheel in reception, should you get the urge. It's all finished to a very high and comfortable standard and the staff are delightful as well.

Bianca Resort & Spa (☎ 863 000; www.biancaresort.com; Mirka Vešovića bb; low-high d €119-288, ste €216-1440;

THIS IS MASSIF

The Bjelasica massif dominates northeastern Montenegro with 10 grand peaks higher than 2000m. The unfortunately named Crna Glava (literally a giant Black Head) is the highest at 2139m. Any preconception you may have of Montenegro's mountains as grey and barren will be shattered as the snows recede and reveal virgin forest (within the protected environs of Biogradska Gora National Park) and meadows teeming with wild flowers. In the higher pastures you'll find *katuns*, round thatched structures that have been used for centuries by seminomadic shepherds when they bring their flocks here in summer. It's a much more forgiving environment than the Orjen, Lovćen or Durmitor ranges and therefore easier to explore.

The best times for hiking are at the end of summer and in autumn when the forests are a mash of colours. Trails are easily accessed from the towns that encircle the mountain: Kolašin, Mojkovac, Bijelo Polje, Berane and Andrijevica. Some paths are detailed in the booklet *Mountains of Bjelasica – a Mountaineering Guide* (€3), available from the tourist office in Kolašin (p139) and the National Park Office at Lake Biograd (p142). There are six mountain huts that are usually only open on summer weekends or by prior arrangement – the tourist office and travel agencies (such as Montenegro Adventures, p131) should be able to help with this and arrange guides. Otherwise you may be able to camp by the *katuns*, but ask permission first. Be prepared for sudden drops in temperature and storms.

🎿) Take one large angular hotel with quirky hexagonal windows, completely gut it and give it the same rustic look as the Hotel Lipka (they were designed by the same people) and you end up with an atmospheric, idiosyncratic and first-rate ski resort. After a hard day's skiing you can sooth out any bumps and bruises in the luxury spa (massage per hour €55; day use of large indoor pool, sauna, Turkish bath and gym costs €40).

Eating

Vodenice (☎ 865 338; Dunje Dokić bb; mains €5-7) Vodenice offers a taste of traditional stodgy mountain food designed to warm your belly on cold nights. Ease back and let your arteries clog over a bowl of *cicvara* (a mixture of wheat, cream and cheese) or *kačamak* (the same with even more carbs courtesy of mashed potato).

Savardak (☎ 069-051 264; savardak@cg.yu; mains €9) Located 2.8km from Kolašin on the road to the Jezerine ski centre, Savardak serves traditional food in a traditional *katun*. Either eat in its atmospheric interior or sit at outdoor tables by the stream. Four-person apartments (€60) are available in a wooden chalet next door.

Getting There & Away

The **bus station** (Mojkovačka bb) is a shed on the road leading into town about 200m from the centre. There are regular services to Podgorica and Mojkovac.

At Kolašin's **train station** (☎ 441 400; www.zeljez nica.cg.yu) you'll see the town laid out below. It's a 1.5km walk to the centre. Eight trains pass through in each direction daily, stopping in Podgorica (90 minutes) and Mojkovac (10 minutes). Buy your tickets on the train.

BIOGRADSKA GORA NATIONAL PARK
БИОГРАДСКА ГОРА

Nestled within the Bjelasica mountain range, this pretty national park has as its heart 1600 hectares of virgin woodland – one of Europe's last three remaining primeval forests. King Nikola is to thank for its survival; on a visit in 1878 he was so taken by the beauty of Lake Biograd (Biogradsko jezero) that the locals gifted him the land and he ordered it to be preserved.

The main entrance to the park is between Kolašin and Mojkovac on the Podgorica–Belgrade highway. After paying a €2 entry fee you can drive the further 4km to the lake. It really is exquisitely pretty and oh-so-green. If you're knowledgable about such things, you'll be able to spot beech, fir, juniper, white ash, maple and elm trees. Occasional tour buses pull in, but a 10-minute stroll should shake the masses and quickly return you to tranquillity.

Most of the busloads will head directly to **Restoran Biogradsko Jezero** (mains €5.50-9.20). It has a wonderful terrace where you can steal glimpses of the lake through the trees as you tuck into a traditional lamb or veal dish.

You can hire row boats (€5 per hour) and buy fishing permits (€20 per day) from the **National Park Office** (☎ 020-865 625; www.nparkovi .cg.yu) by the car park. Nearby there's a **campsite** (small/large tent €3/5) with basic squat toilets; and a cluster of 11 new windowless **log cabins** (€20), each with two beds. The ablutions block for the cabins is much nicer.

From the car park, a 17km loop track heads up **Mt Bedovac** (1774m) for awesome lake views before tackling **Mt Razverše** (2033m). The route is well described in the *Mountains of Bjelasica* booklet (see the boxed text, p141) and, apart from a couple of steep climbs, it's a fairly straightforward six-hour hike.

If you don't have a car, the nearest bus stop is near the park entrance an hour's walk away (Kraljevo Kolo) and the nearest train station is a 90-minute walk (Štitarička Rijeka).

MOJKOVAC МОЈКОВАЦ
☎ 050 / pop 4200

Despite being on the doorstep of two national parks, you're unlikely to spot many tourists in Mojkovac (pronounced '*moy*·ko·vats') – at least not yet. The Czech government has fronted up cash for a major environmental effort to clean up the legacy of centuries of silver, lead and zinc mining; that serene lake reflecting the mountains beside the highway is actually a stew of toxic waste. There are also multimillion-dollar plans to construct a new ski centre nearby. At the moment Mojkovac's main attraction is as a cheap base for exploring the Bjelasica Mountains or before following the Tara River into Durmitor National Park.

The centre of town is a triangular square with a pretty little park and a large pompous statue. Surrounding it is a slew of decaying apartment blocks which, despite the grimness, residents have made an effort to decorate with flower gardens. On the approach to town there's a war memorial resembling a giant tooth.

A steep but easy-to-follow path leads from the centre of Mojkovac on a 17km (six-hour) loop through the surrounding mountains; take trail 310 and return on 319 and then 301. Halfway along it passes the Džambas mountain hut, which can be used as a base for other hikes outlined in the *Mountains of Bjelasica* booklet (see the boxed text, p141).

Orientation & Information
Everything is laid out around the square (Trg Ljubomira Bakoča), including a bank and post

office at its pointy end and an unmarked internet cafe in a brick lean-to next to a red-and-yellow-painted cafe nearby.

Sleeping & Eating
Eating options are limited to a couple of shabby-looking restaurants and *pekaras* (bakeries) near the bus station selling the ubiquitous *burek*. The square has two grocery stores and several cafe-bars, some of which serve cake and ice cream.

Hotel Dulović (☎ 472 615; fax 474 710; Trg Ljubomira Bakoča bb; s/d/tr €20/40/57) Hidden in the corner of the square behind the park, this midsize hotel is a strictly perfunctory affair that's personality-less but clean. There's a restaurant downstairs that provides a decent cooked breakfast.

Hotel Palas (☎ 478 339; centromobil@cg.yu; Podgorica–Belgrade Hwy; s/d/tr/apt €22/40/54/100) Montenegro's pointiest hotel has the form of a set of interconnecting triangles collapsing into each other like a matryoshka doll. The rooms are clean and serviceable in an early-1980s kind of way, but it's certainly no palace.

Getting There & Away
Mojkovac is well connected for public transport with its **bus station**, on the highway near the centre of town, a major stop on the Podgorica–Belgrade route. There's no ticket office so you'll need to buy tickets on the bus. The **train station** (with daily services to Podgorica, Kolašin and Bijelo Polje) is harder to find. Take the road between the Hotel Palas and the cemetery. Veer left past the timber yard and keep going to the southern outskirts of town. When you reach it you might be forgiven for thinking it was bombed by NATO – most of the windows are smashed and it's covered in graffiti.

DURMITOR NATIONAL PARK
ДУРМИТОР
☎ 052 / pop 4900

Magnificent scenery ratchets up to stupendous in this national park, where ice and water have carved a dramatic landscape from the limestone. Some 18 glacial lakes known as *gorske oči* (mountain eyes) dot the Durmitor range, with the largest, **Black Lake** (Crno jezero), a pleasant 3km walk from Žabljak. The rounded mass of **Međed** (The Bear; 2287m) rears up behind the lake flanked by others of the park's 48 peaks over 2000m, including the highest,

Bobotov Kuk (2523m). In winter (December to March) Durmitor is Montenegro's main ski resort, and in summer it's a popular place for hiking, rafting and other active pursuits.

The park is home to enough critters to cast a Disney movie as well as purportedly the greatest variety of butterflies in Europe. The golden eagle is the king of the 163 species of bird, and about 50 types of mammals roam the woodlands. It's very unlikely you'll spot the bears and wolves, which is either good or bad thing depending on your perspective. We were assured that the wolves are only dangerous if they're really starving at the end of a long winter.

Orientation & Information

Durmitor National Park covers the Durmitor mountain range and a narrow branch heading east along the Tara River towards Mojkovac. West of the park, the Tara forms the border with Bosnia and joins the Piva River near Šćepan Polje.

Žabljak, at the eastern edge of the range, is the park's principal gateway and the only town within its boundaries. It's not very big nor is it attractive, but it has a supermarket, post office, bank, hotels and restaurants, all gathered around the car park masquerading as the main square.

Internet (Božidara Žugića bb, Žabljak) In an unmarked wooden hut next to Restaurant Durmitor.

National Park Visitors Centre (☎ 360 228; www .nparkovi.cg.yu; ☺ 7am-2pm autumn & spring, 8am-6pm winter & summer) On the road to the Black Lake, this centre includes a wonderful micromuseum focusing on the park's flora and fauna. The knowledgable English-speaking staff answer queries and sell local craft, fishing permits (river/lake €15/10), maps (€8) and hiking guides.

Summit Travel Agency (☎ 361 502; anna.grbovic@ cg.yu; Njegoševa bb, Žabljak) Owner Anna Grbović speaks good English and can arrange jeep tours (€100 for up to three people), rafting trips (see right) and mountain-bike hire (€2/10 per hour/day).

Žabljak Tourist Centre (Trg Durmitorskih Ratnika, Žabljak) This wooden hut in the car park below Hotel Žabljak may be able to help out with maps and advice in winter, but when we visited in the height of the summer season there was no sign of life.

Sights & Activities

TARA RIVER & CANYON
КАЊОН И РИЈЕКА ТАРА

Slicing through the mountains at the northern edge of the national park like they were made from the local soft cheese, the Tara River forms a canyon that at its peak is 1300m deep. By way of comparison, Colorado's Grand Canyon is only 200m deeper. A **rafting** jaunt along the Tara River is one of the sure-fire things that enduring Montenegro memories are made of.

This is one of the country's most popular tourist activities, with various operators running trips daily from May to October. There are some rapids but don't expect an adrenaline-fuelled white-water experience. You'll get the most excitement in May when the last of the melting snow revs up the flow.

The 82km section that is raftable starts from Splavište, south of the impressive 150m-high Tara Bridge (see the boxed text, p144), and ends at Šćepan Polje on the Bosnian border. The classic two-day trip heads through the deepest part of the canyon on the first day, stopping overnight at Radovan Luka, where there's a motel and a campsite. Most of the day tours from the coast traverse only the last 18km – this is outside the national park and hence avoids hefty fees. You'll miss out on the canyon's depths but it's still a beautiful stretch, including most of the rapids. Coaches on day trips from the coast follow the spectacular road along the Piva River (see the boxed text, p136), giving you a double dose of canyon action.

At **Šćepan Polje** you'll find rafting operators set up along the river. If you have your own wheels you can save a few euros and avoid a lengthy day tour by heading directly here. **Tara Tour** (☎ 069-086 106; www.tara-tour.com) offers an excellent half-day trip (with/without breakfast and lunch €30/40) and has a cute set of wooden chalets with squat toilets and showers in a separate block; accommodation, three meals and a half-day's rafting cost €55. Another good operator is **Kamp Grab** (☎ 083-200 598; www.tara-grab.com), with lodgings blissfully located 18km upstream at Brstanovica.

Summit Travel Agency (left) offers a range of tours out of Žabljak starting from Splavište (half-/one-/two-day tour €50/110/200). The park fees bump up the price but you'll get to see the heart of the canyon. If you can find nine friends, a two-day trip on a wooden raft can be arranged (€3000).

If you'd rather stay dry and admire the canyon from afar, the best view is from the top of **Mt Ćurevac** (1625m). It's not signposted and is pretty hard to find without a local in tow, but a taxi from Žabljak should get you there for €10 (one way).

HIKING

Durmitor is one of the best-marked mountain ranges in Europe. Some suggest it's a little too well labelled, encouraging novices to wander around seriously high-altitude paths that are prone to fog and summer thunderstorms. However, as the national park staff point out, the longest walks can be done in a (lengthy) day and there shouldn't be a problem if you're sensibly prepared. That means checking the weather forecast before you set out, sticking to the tracks and preparing for sudden drops in temperature.

It costs €2 per day to use the park and paths can be as easy as a 4km stroll around the Black Lake. A more substantial hike is to the two **Škrčka Lakes** (Škrčka jezera), in the centre of a tectonic valley, where you can stay overnight in a mountain hut (see opposite) and enjoy magnificent scenery.

Durmitor and the Tara Canyon by Branislav Cerović (€12 from the National Park Visitors Centre) is a great resource for mountaineers and serious hikers.

SKIING & SNOWBOARDING

On the slopes of **Savin Kuk** (2313m), 5km from Žabljak, you'll find the main ski centre. The 3.5km run starts from a height of 2010m and is best suited to advanced skiers. Even in the

---

THE BRIDGE & ITS BUILDER

The elegant spans of the Tara Bridge were completed just as WWII was starting. At the time it was the largest concrete arched vehicular bridge in Europe. Its 365m length is carried on five sweeping arches, the largest of which is 116m wide.

In May 1942, with large numbers of Italian and German troops stationed in Žabljak, the Partisan command gave the order to blow up the bridge. The honour went to one of its engineers, Lazar Jauković, who planted the bomb that destroyed his beautiful creation. Jauković was captured by the Italians and Četniks (Serb royalists) and executed on the remains of his bridge. When it was rebuilt in 1946, Jauković's bravery was acknowledged by a plaque that still stands on the bridge today.

---

height of summer Savin Kuk wears a pocket of snow. On the outskirts of town near the bus station, **Javorovača** is a gentle 300m ski slope that's good for kids and beginners. A third centre at **Mali Štuoc** (1953m) was being renovated at the time of research. It offers terrific views over the Black Lake, Međed and Savin Kuk and slopes to suit all levels of experience.

One of the big attractions for skiing here is the cost: day passes are around €15, weekly passes €70 and ski lessons between €10 and €20. You can rent ski and snowboard gear from **Sport Trade** (☎ 069-538 831; Vuka Karadžića 7, Žabljak) for €10 per day.

The season runs from December to March, peaking around New Year.

DOBRILOVINA MONASTERY

МАНАСТИР ДОБРИЛОВИНА

Near the eastern boundary of the national park, 28km from Mojkovac, this 17th-century **monastery** has an idyllic setting in lush fields hemmed in by the mountains and Tara River. If you knock at the accommodation wing, a black-robed nun will unlock the church but only if she's satisfied that you're appropriately attired. Dedicated to St George (Sv Đorđe), it has some lovely frescoes inside.

Sleeping

ŽABLJAK ЖАБЉАК

Summit Travel Agency (p143) can help source private accommodation starting from around €10 per person. Most of the giant Yugoslav-era hotels were either closed for renovations when we visited or deserved to be.

Autokamp Mlinski Potok Mina (☎ 069-497 625; site per person €3, bed €10) With a fabulously hospitable host (there's no escaping the *rakija* shots), this campsite above the National Park Visitors Centre is an excellent option. When we visited, the toilet block was a work in progress but the six showers and clean sit-down toilets are already a step up from most Montenegrin camping options. The owner's house can sleep 12 guests in comfortable wood-panelled rooms and he has another house sleeping 11 by the Black Lake.

Hotel Javor (☎ 361 337; vladoprof@hotmail.com; Božidara Žugića 8; s/d/tr €26/52/78) There's not a lot of English spoken, but you'll find eight cosy rooms with TVs, minibars and en suites.

MB Hotel (☎ 361 601; Tripka Đakovića bb; s/d/villa €30/57/100; wi-fi) In a quiet back street halfway

---

DETOUR: PLJEVLJA

The road over the vertigo-inducing Tara Bridge, 23km west of Žabljak, heads north to Pljevlja (pronounced…actually, don't even bother trying). This is Montenegro's third-largest city, with a population of 21,400. Although it has ancient roots (Roman and before that Illyrian), it's now given over to heavy industry and has a large coalmine and thermal powerplant.

Pljevlja's main sights both date from the 16th century. The 1569 **Hussein Pasha Mosque** (Husein Pašina Džamija; ☎ 052-323 509; Vuka Kneževića bb) is the most beautiful mosque in Montenegro and also boasts the highest minaret in the Balkans (42m). Its interiors are unusual as they're painted with elaborate frescoes featuring geometric patterns and floral motifs; see the boxed text on p117 for information on visiting mosques. **Holy Trinity Monastery** (Manastir Sv Trojice; ☎ 052-325 025), dating from 1537, is also sumptuously painted.

---

between the town centre and the bus station, this little hotel offers modern rooms, English-speaking staff and an attractive restaurant and bar. The restaurant even has a nonsmoking section – something even less likely to be seen in these parts than wolves.

NATIONAL PARK

The staff at the National Park Visitors Centre (p143) should be able to give you information about **mountain huts**. There's a 20-bed hut located between the large and small Škrčka Lakes (€5) and another one near Lake Sušica (Sušičko jezero); don't expect electricity or running water. You can pitch a tent nearby, or indeed anywhere appropriate within the park (small/large tents €3/5).

our pick **Eko-Oaza Suza Evrope** (☎ 067-511 755; eko-oaza@cg.yu; Dobrilovina; cottage €50) Situated 25km west of Mojkovac at the beginning of the arm of the park that stretches along the Tara River, this 'eco-oasis' consists of four comfortable wooden cottages, each sleeping five people. From here you can hike up the mountain and stay overnight in a hut near the glacial Lake Zaboj (Zabojsko jezero; 1477m).

Eating & Drinking

Restaurant Durmitor (☎ 069-657 316; Božidara Žugića bb, Žabljak; meals €2-9; ⏱ 7am-11pm) Offers home cooking at its best in what is just a small wooden hut seating 20. At this size a cosy winter atmosphere is guaranteed.

National Eco Restaurant (☎ 361 337; Božidara Žugića 8, Žabljak; mains €3-10) A great place to try traditional mountain food, such as lamb or veal roasted 'under the pan' (€24 per kilogram). It's all locally sourced and hence organic without trying very hard.

Čudna Šuma (Vuka Karadžića bb) Somehow managing to be rustic and hip at the same time, this is easily Žabljak's best cafe-bar.

Getting There & Away

All of the approaches to Durmitor are spectacular. The most reliable road to Žabljak follows the Tara River west from Mojkovac. In summer this 70km **drive** takes about 90 minutes. If you're coming from Podgorica the quickest way is through Nikšić and Šavnik but the road can be treacherous in winter. The main highway north from Nikšić follows the dramatic Piva Canyon to Šćepan Polje. A back road cuts through the park from Plužine.

There's a petrol station near the **bus station** (☎ 361 318) at the southern end of Žabljak on the Nikšić road. Buses head to Belgrade (€25, nine hours, two daily) and Podgorica (€9.50, 3½ hours, three daily). In summer the Podgorica buses go through Nikšić, while in winter they take the Mojkovac–Kolašin route.

BIJELO POLJE БИЈЕЛО ПОЉЕ
☎ 050 / pop 15,900

Montenegro's fourth-largest city, Bijelo Polje (pronounced 'bi·*ye*·lo *po*·lye') was once part of the evocatively named Sandžak of Novi Pazar, the Ottoman-controlled region that separated Montenegro from Serbia until 1912. Today 42.4% of the town's population still identify their ethnicity as Bosniak or Muslim, 36.3% as Serb and 16.1% as Montenegrin. It's one of the most diverse cities of Montenegro with mosque minarets and church bell towers sprouting in nearly equal profusion.

Predating the Ottoman invasion is the 12th-century **Church of Sts Peter and Paul** (Crkva Sv Petra i Pavla; Kneza Miroslava bb); it's signposted to the left

of the main road coming from Mojkovac. It's a lovely little church despite the jarring steeple grafted onto it. Inside, the remains of frescoes contrast with the bright red of the episcopal throne and a modern iconostasis.

The broad Lim River skirts the somewhat shabby town centre, where you'll find lots of cafe-bars, pizzerias, banks and the **post office** (Tomaša Žižića 2). The **bus station** (☎ 432 219) is nearby on the main road, with services to all neighbouring towns and in both directions on the Podgorica–Belgrade highway. There's a large **train station** (☎ 478 560) on the highway 2.5km north of town with services to Podgorica (€6, 10 daily) and Belgrade (€17, six daily).

A recommended option for both a bed and a feed is **Hotel & Restaurant MB Dvori** (☎ 488 571; Podgorica–Belgrade Hwy; s/d €35/50; 🔀) on the western approach to town. The building has an attractive antique ambience with little gables, wooden shutters and terracotta tiling, but the rooms are sparkling new and very comfortable. Needless to say, the ones looking over the fields at the back are preferable to those facing the highway. The restaurant does excellent crispy-based pizza; try the eponymous one, featuring *pršut* (smoke-dried ham), pancetta, egg, olives and local cheese.

Walking trail 309 leading into the Bjelasica Mountains starts at the bus stop at nearby Ravna Rijeka (see the boxed text, p141). If you're taking the road to Berane, after 14km you'll spot the picturesque interlocking circles of **St John's Church** (Crkva Sv Jovana; Ribervina bb). The road signs date it from the 9th to 11th centuries, but in reality it's a recent construction built on earlier foundations. There's nothing much inside: only a temporary altar and a few modern icons.

ROŽAJE РОЖАЈЕ
☎ 051 / pop 9200

Rožaje is Montenegro's most easterly town, nestled within the mountainous folds bordering Serbia and Kosovo. Ninety-three per cent of its population are Muslim and the song of muezzins can regularly be heard echoing from its minarets. It's fascinating to sit by the main square and watch the evening promenade. While this social ritual is common to every town in Montenegro, here you'll spot plenty of men strolling together arm in arm and some (but by no means most) women wearing hijabs (head coverings).

With a backdrop of rocky cliffs and plenty of old wooden houses achieving a look bordering on designer decrepitude, Rožaje could be very pretty indeed. The main thing preventing that happening is the scandalous state of the Ibar River, which seems to be used as the main waste disposal. Plastic bags full of household refuse line its banks as it gurgles through town.

Orientation & Information

Rožaje's main street is Ulica Maršala Tita, which is car-free in the middle, forming the town square. The Ibar River (more an overgrown stream) runs along one side of it, while on the other a cliff leads up to the highway and the upper section of town. The streets leading into the centre are narrow and parking can be difficult to find.

Hamas Pharmacy (☎ 271 700; Maršala Tita bb; ⏲ 8am-8pm)

Internet Café Download (Mustafa Peđancia bb)

Police (Maršala Tita 41)

Post office (Maršala Tita bb)

Tourist Organisation (Turistička organizacija; ☎ 270 158; Maršala Tita bb) Hidden behind the Fontana cafe on the main square; don't expect any English or much information from this local tourist bureau.

Sights

The main **mosque** (Mustafa Peđancia bb) has an elegant dome and twin minarets. Tiling in geometric patterns completely covers the interior and includes an image of the Kaaba in Mecca above the prayer niche. Further along the same street, the 17th-century **Kurtagića Mosque** (Kurtagića Džamija; Mustafa Peđancia 14) is testimony to the horrors of 1960s stone cladding. An attractive wooden minaret is a reminder of its venerable age, as are the extremely low doors leading inside. During the late '90s both mosques provided shelter for refugees from neighbouring Kosovo.

Near the mosques, **Ganića Kula** (☎ 067-503 915; Trg IX Crnogorske Brigade bb) is a good example of the sort of residential tower that was once common in this area and across the border in Kosovo and northern Albania. Not just a defence against invaders, *kula*s were particularly useful for protecting the menfolk during interfamily blood feuds. There are gun slits on the bottom floor and only small barred windows on the next two. The wooden top floor provides a little more comfort, with bigger windows and a carved balcony. There's

a small collection of artefacts inside but the tower is only opened by arrangement – you'll need to call ahead and try your luck.

Activities
There are two sets of ski slopes on the highway between Berane and Rožaje. **Lokve** is 15km from Rožaje on Smiljevica Mountain. There are two short runs here and you'll only pay €8 for a day pass and €2 for the chairlift. **Turjak** is only 9km from town, at the bottom of the Hajla massif (2403m), and has a 250m and a 700m run.

Theoretically the Tourist Organisation (opposite) should be able to arrange mountain guides for hiking or horse-riding excursions in the surrounding mountains during summer.

Sleeping
The Tourist Organisation (opposite) has a brochure summarising the few local motels and private apartments.

Motel Grand (☎ 069-465 539; Berane–Rožaje Hwy; s/d €12/24) There's nothing grand about this place, located on the highway 2.5km west of town, but it is a perfectly adequate and wonderfully cheap place to lay your head. The rooms are small and reasonably clean.

Hotel Duga (☎ 278 266; Berane–Rožaje Hwy; s/d/tw/tr €15/30/30/45) Slightly grander than the Grand and very nearby, Hotel Duga's dark wooden trim and flower boxes give it an old-fashioned homely feeling, as do the friendly staff. There's a popular restaurant on the front terrace that serves pasta and traditional grills.

our pick **Hotel Rožaje** (☎ 240 000; hotelrozaje.cg.yu; Maršala Tita bb; s €50, d €90-110, tr €110, apt €150; ✷ ☃ ▣ wi-fi) Yet another crazy angular hotel, this distinctive wonky M-shaped one has been bought by a Turkish company seemingly intent on recapturing the glamour of the Ottoman age. The rooms have opulently draped curtains, thickly embroidered bedspreads and attractive en suites with see-through vanities. The basement hides a wonderful heated swimming pool and Turkish bath.

Eating & Drinking
Supermarket Mesara (Maršala Tita 4; ☼ 8am-11pm) A handy place to stock up on cooking supplies.

Fontana (Maršala Tita bb; snacks €1-3) On the main square, Fontana is the place for coffee, cakes and delicious ice cream.

Ćevabdžinica Mek (Mustafa Pećancia bb; mains €1-3; ☼ 6am-11pm) This cheapie has a great position overlooking the river by the bridge leading from the main square. As well as ćevapčići (grilled skinless sausages), they serve tasty steaks and salads. It's best to focus on the food and flower boxes, rather than the grimy tablecloths.

Hotel Rožaje (☎ 240 000; Maršala Tita bb; mains €3.50-9.50) You won't find a flasher restaurant in Rožaje than the one on the ground floor of the main hotel, but despite the sparkling chandeliers it's quite reasonably priced. A smart café-bar spills over onto the main square.

Tajson Caffe (Maršala Tita bb; ☼ 7am-midnight) At first we thought this place was called 'The Best Of Caffe' as that's what all the signage says. It actually is the best of Rožaje's cafe-bars and its comfy couches provide a ringside seat for the promenade on the main square.

Getting There & Away
From Rožaje the main highway continues into Serbia, 22km to the northeast. On a windy road heading southeast is Montenegro's only border crossing with Kosovo.

The **bus station** (☎ 271 115) is on the highway above the town centre. There are regular services to Podgorica (€9, 10 daily) and international destinations including Peć (€5, four daily), Belgrade (€13, nine daily), Niš (€15, daily) and Novi Sad (€16, two daily).

PLAV ПЛАВ
☎ 051 / pop 3615
Although only 33km as the crow flies, there's a border and a whole heap of mountains between Rožaje and Plav, necessitating an 83km drive through Berane and Andrijevica. From Andrijevica the road follows the Lim River through lush fields as the imposing Prokletije Mountains (Montenegro's highest) begin to reveal themselves. As if knowing that such beauty demands a mirror, picturesque **Lake Plav** (Plavsko jezero) has positioned itself to provide it. It's devastatingly pretty, with swarms of tiny fish swimming between the reeds and water lilies lining its edges, and a chorus of birds and frogs singing of their contentment to call it home.

The human occupants seem rather less appreciative, judging by the amount of rubbish washing into it from the township. The lakeside road passes a crop of massive turreted

---

DRIVER ON THE STORM

An excerpt from the author's journal:

'The back road from Andrijevica to Kolašin starts beautifully, twisting up and up, the views expanding all the time. Hang on, what's with those dark clouds coming into view? That tingling in my ears is ominous. I always get tingly ears when there's a thunderstorm approaching and there's been one every day since I've been in the mountains. At about this time of day, now I think of it.

'The road's still climbing. Those old people gathering wild herbs wouldn't be here if a storm was brewing, surely. Still I'm heading up and up. Maybe I should speed up. I don't really want to be stuck in an oversized tin can at close to 2000m if a storm's about to break. But that view! Must…resist…urge…to…stop…and…take…photo. Resistance futile. Surely an extra five minutes isn't going to hurt.

'Quick snap then – BAM – the first thunderclap. Back in car. Heading down other side of the pass now. BOOM. Torrential rain. Road not wide enough for two motorbikes to pass without a bit of argy-bargy. CRASH. Windows fogging up. Precipitous drops on either side. I open the windows despite the rain and get a lightning illuminated view of incredible peaks to my left. Mustn't look – too dangerous. Can't not look – too beautiful. So that's a massif? It's massive. KABOOM. Oh God, I'm going to die up here. Electrocuted in a Hyundai Getz – not a good look. Is it just me or is this road getting worse? Yep, that'll be a landslide to my left that's taken out half the road. That's it, I'm definitely going to die. How long will it take for my family to realise?

'Hang on, perhaps the rain's lifting. I think it is, yes. Maybe I won't die after all. I've only travelled 30km in about an hour but I think I'll live. Hang on, what's that blocking the road ahead? A massive log. Damn, damn, damn – don't make me drive all the way back through Bijelo Polje again! What to do, what to do? Oh thank God, there's a 4WD. I normally hate 4WD drivers but I freaking love these ones.

'How can I get to Kolašin?' I try to say in Montenegrin but in my agitated state who knows what comes out.

'You speak English, yes? Follow us.'

'Thank you Lord. These are possibly the nicest 4WD drivers in the entire world. God bless Montenegrin 4WD drivers! Another half an hour driving virtually cross-country on metal roads and I'm in Kolašin. My Hyundai Getz coped probably better than I did. Time to find a bar and raise a glass of *rakija* in celebration.'

---

houses that either take their inspiration from fairy tales or nightmares, take your pick.

Like Rožaje, Plav is a predominantly Muslim town, with 79% of the people identifying their ethnicity as Bosniak or Muslim and a further 9% as Albanian. It seems to produce some very unusual characters, such as the overweight shirtless fellow with the prodigious moustache wandering around with red braces attached to his shorts; or the busty blond waitress (equal parts Bet Lynch and Candy Darling) who clears leftover cans, serviettes and food from her tables directly into the Plav River.

Orientation & Information

Plav is another of those towns that don't believe in street names, so you'll have to follow your nose through the twisting laneways of its hilly *čaršija* (old market area). The post office has an ATM attached and is near the main roundabout leading down to the *čaršija*. **Prima Apoteka** (☎ 252 500; Čaršija bb; ☷ 8am-8pm Mon-Sat, 10am-6pm Sun) is a pharmacy located a little further down the hill. The area around the bus station is called Racina.

Sights & Activities

The minarets of four mosques are the most prominent feature of the centre. The most imposing is the **Sultana Mosque** (Džamija Sultanija; 1909) to the left of the roundabout. It's the only one completely made out of stone and is capped by a set of large and small domes. Nearby is the 1471 **Old Mosque** (Stara Džamija), which is easily spotted by its decorated wooden minaret.

If you continue down from the roundabout to the main street, turn right and head up the hill, you'll reach perhaps the most interesting **mosque**. A slender minaret made of geometrically arranged panels of wood extends from a steeply pitched and tiled roof, which in turn is mounted on a solid stone base with a beautifully carved enclosed wooden porch. Intricate floral motifs are carved on the door.

Slightly up the hill is the **Redžepagića Kula** (1671, although possibly 16th century), another defensive tower like the one in Rožaje (p146). The bottom two floors have stone walls over a metre thick, capped by a wooden storey with lovely carved balconies.

The **pier** extending over the lake is a good spot to swim from, or you can hire paddle boats (€2 per hour) or kayaks (€1 per hour) nearby.

Sleeping & Eating

Decent accommodation and eating options are extremely limited, with nothing worth recommending in Plav itself. At the time of research the large state-owned complex by the lake was closed. For private accommodation try **Meridijan 10** (☎ 255 005), a travel agency opposite the bus station; the staff are friendly but they don't speak any English. The **covered market** in the centre of the *čaršija* is a good place to stock up on fruit and vegetables.

Lovac (☎ 251 392; Gusinje Rd; s/d €15/30) Only 500m past the turn-off to Gusinje, Lovac has basic rooms above a modest restaurant.

Eko Turističko Nazalje Aqua (☎ 069-889 759; admirs@cg.yu; Gusinje Rd; r/bungalow €30/50) Hugging the lake's western shore near the beginning of the road to Gusinje, this complex offers simple free-standing bungalows (sleeping up to four people) and a handful of rooms with three single beds. It's a simple set-up but reasonably comfortable. Upstairs, the restaurant offers lake views to accompany pizza, pasta, salad, fish and meat dishes (€3.50 to €8).

Slastičara Racina (Racina bb; snacks €1-2) A humble but friendly bakery and takeaway, which serves delicious cakes, fruit salads, *burek* and pizza.

Getting There & Away

Regular services from Berane (€2.90) pull into the **bus station** (☎ 069-653 732) on the main road. Less frequent buses head to Rožaje (€5, daily), Podgorica (€10, five daily), Ulcinj (€15, daily) and across the border (via Rožaje) to Peć (€7, daily).

AROUND PLAV
Holy Trinity Monastery, Brezojevica
Манастир Св Тројице, Брезојевица

On the approach to Plav, in the first village before the lake, Brezojevica Monastery (Manastir Brezojevica) is a study in rural tranquillity. Meadows of yellow and purple flowers line the riverbank broken by the occasional abandoned stone building. If you're looking for a picnic spot, you could do a lot worse.

Holy Trinity Church (Crkva Sv Trojice) has had a tough life. The present structure was built in the 16th century on 13th century foundations but was damaged during WWII and left to decay, used only by the local Orthodox community for funerals. It's a testimony to the religious revival of recent years that the monastery is being restored. There's a brand new stone gate leading from the highway, topped by a shiny golden Orthodox cross. Over the door of the church is an image of the Holy Trinity dating from 1998: Jesus is dressed as a medieval Serbian king while his Father resembles Ian McKellen's Gandalf. There's more artistic merit in the faded remains of the 16th-century frescoes inside, although the only subject that's easy to discern is the *Dormition of the Mother of God* over the door.

Gusinje Гусиње

It's difficult to understand why Plav has such a shabby, frontier-town feel when Gusinje (pronounced '*gu*·si·nye'), 10km further towards nowhere, is such a tidy and laid-back place. The setting is idyllic, surrounded by verdant farmland hemmed in by the rugged majesty of the Prokletije Mountains. You could easily lose a whole day exploring the back roads and villages either by bicycle or car.

While the 1700-strong community is overwhelmingly Muslim, the town's two mosques coexist comfortably with both an Orthodox and a Catholic church. The most impressive architecturally is the **Vizier's Mosque** (Vezirova Džamija; 1626). This stone structure has a carved wooden porch and minaret that are similar to the mosques in Plav but better preserved. It's interesting to note the four prominent communist graves in the little cemetery.

In the centre of Gusinje you'll find a post office, ATM, cafes and plenty of options for pizza or *burek*.

Prokletije Mountains Проклетије

Widely tipped to become Montenegro's fifth national park sometime soon, the Prokletije Mountains are a large expanse of wilderness forming the border with Albania and Kosovo. More ambitious still, plans are afoot for the whole mountain range to be declared a cross-border Balkans Peace Park.

It's a bit ironic really, as both the Slavic and Albanian versions of its name mean 'accursed', a reference to the harsh environment of these jagged peaks. They reach their highest point at Jezerski Vrh (2694m) on the Albanian side of the border and also include Montenegro's loftiest peak Kolac (2534m).

This magnificently scenic area may well rate as one of Europe's least explored.

From both Gusinje and Plav, yellow signs point to various walking tracks and give both the distance and estimated time required for each. Within a few hours you can reach glacial lakes and mountain springs. If you're interested in doing some serious mountaineering, it's best to talk to one of the agencies specialising in adventure tourism, such as Black Mountain (p78) or Montenegro Adventures (p131), as you'll need help in arranging guides, accessing mountain huts and dealing with red tape if you wish to cross the Albanian border.

Directory

CONTENTS

Accommodation	151
Activities	152
Business Hours	155
Children	155
Climate Charts	158
Customs Regulations	158
Dangers & Annoyances	158
Discount Cards	159
Embassies & Consulates	159
Festivals & Events	159
Food	159
Gay & Lesbian Travellers	159
Holidays	160
Insurance	160
Internet Access	160
Legal Matters	160
Maps	161
Money	161
Post	161
Shopping	161
Solo Travellers	161
Telephone	161
Time	162
Tourist Information	162
Travellers with Disabilities	162
Visas	162
Women Travellers	162

ACCOMMODATION

The main accommodation types available are hotels or private accommodation rentals. Camping grounds operate in summer and some of the mountainous areas have cabin accommodation in 'eco' villages or mountain huts. The country's only hostels were up for sale at the time of research.

BOOK ACCOMMODATION ONLINE

For more accommodation reviews and recommendations by Lonely Planet authors, check out the online booking service at www.lonelyplanet.com. You'll find the true, insider low-down on the best places to stay. Reviews are thorough and independent. Best of all, you can book online.

PRACTICALITIES

- *Vijesti* (The News), *Dan* (The Day), *Republika* (The Republic) and *Pobjeda* (Victory) are all daily newspapers.

- *Monitor*, a weekly news magazine, joins local-language versions of international titles on the news-stands.

- RTCG (Montenegrin Radio TV) is the state broadcaster, with a radio station and two TV channels.

- In total there are four national free-to-air TV channels and eight regional channels.

- There are dozens of independent radio stations based around the country.

- Montenegro uses standard European electricity (220V to 240V/50Hz to 60Hz).

- Plugs are of the round two-pin variety which is the norm for continental Europe.

- The video system in Montenegro is PAL.

- The metric system is used for weights and measurements (see conversion chart on the inside front cover).

Prices are very seasonal, peaking in July and August on the coast. Some places require minimum stays (three days to a week) during these times and there are often discounts for longer bookings. In the ski resorts the high season runs from January through to March, with the absolute peak around New Year. Smaller establishments on the coast may close during winter. Where the prices vary according to the season we've listed a range from the cheapest low-season price through to the most expensive high-season rate for each room category. Where there's no range given, you won't find any difference between weekend and weekday rates.

For the purposes of this book, reviews are listed in budget order; midrange accommodation is defined as being between €30 and €90 per night for the cheapest option, with anything below this labelled as budget and anything above, top end. An additional tourist tax (less than €2 per night) will be added to the rate for all accommodation types when you go to pay.

Tariffs usually include breakfast, towels, basic toiletries and (unless otherwise mentioned in the reviews) en suites. Most midrange rooms will also have a TV set, fridge and air conditioning *(klima)* – except for in the mountains where cooling isn't necessary and heaters are provided in winter. Top-end establishments will usually have direct-dial telephone access, minibars and, in the very best establishments, fluffy robes, slippers, safes, swimming pools, health spas and 24-hour room service. Ironically, you're more likely to get a free wireless internet connection in a midrange hotel than a top establishment (where you'll have to pay for it). Often the signal is only available in certain parts of the building.

In the reviews we've often listed websites, but where they're not available we've included email addresses and failing that, fax numbers. Be warned that many Montenegrin businesses are not adept at keeping their websites up to date or replying to emails.

If you don't mind spending a few extra euros in order to save yourself some hassle, specialist travel agencies will arrange things on your behalf and take a cut on the booking. The better ones can arrange village homestays and for mountain huts to be opened. Try Black Mountain (p78), Montenegro Adventures (p131), So Montenegro (opposite) or the local agencies mentioned at the beginning of each town's Sleeping listings.

Camping & Caravan Parks

Facilities at camping grounds tend to be basic, often with squat toilets and limited water. The national parks have cabin-style accommodation but most camping grounds don't. Charges are a combination of a nightly rate per vehicle, size of tent, number (and age) of guests and whether you require power or not. Camping grounds are most common along the coast (including the Bay of Kotor) and near Žabljak.

During summer, when shepherds in the mountainous areas take their flocks to the higher meadows, you can ask permission to pitch your tent next to one of their traditional *katun* dwellings.

Hotels

The recent tidal wave of development has seen hotels large and small spring up in the popular destinations. They usually have some form of restaurant attached and offer the option of half- or full-board (breakfast plus one or two meals).

In Montenegro, a hotel spa centre is called a 'wellness centre' and a double bed is referred to as a 'French bed' *(francuski ležaj)*. We've only used the room type 'suite' in our reviews when there's a completely separate living space offered. In the case of what some hotels call 'junior suites' (ie a living area in the same room as the bed) we've included these within the 'double' price range.

Podgorica hotels are consistently pricey (they're targeted at suits) but you'll find more of a range of establishments on the coast. Generally, the further you travel from Budva, the cheaper the average price. Tourist-focused Žabljak and Kolašin are the most expensive of the northern centres, but you'll find good deals in the other towns.

Private Accommodation

The cheapest options in any given town are almost always private rooms and apartment rentals. These can be arranged through travel agencies or, in season, you may be approached at the bus stop or see signs hanging outside the houses (they often read 'Sobe/Zimmer/Rooms'). Some local tourist offices publish handy guides to private accommodation. Rooms in local homes shouldn't be hard to find but some places will require minimum stays in high season. Don't expect an en suite.

Apartments will always have their own bathroom and at least a kitchenette. Generally speaking, you'll get what you pay for. The cheaper options are usually a bit rougher, further from the attractions and don't have views. In most cases there shouldn't be a problem with cleanliness.

If you're armed with a bit of charm, an adventurous spirit, an unfussy attitude and a few words in the local lingo, it should be possible to turn up in remote villages and ask if anyone has any rooms to rent for the night.

ACTIVITIES

With such a focus on its physical environment it's only natural that Montenegro has plenty of active pursuits on offer. Along the coast there's the usual selection of water sports, including swimming, kayaking, fishing and diving. Inland, the iconic attraction is rafting on the Tara River but there are also hundreds of kilometres of mountain-biking and hiking tracks to explore. Skiing is the big winter attraction.

The best time for a well-rounded roster of adventures is May and early June when the spring melts add thrills to a rafting trip and the wild flowers are bursting into bloom. Sea and air temperatures are highest in July and August but you'll be battling the crowds on the beaches. September and October are also good options, especially if you like your hikes accompanied by a blazing backdrop of autumn colour. October is also when the wonderful Adventure Race Montenegro (p159) is held.

Rafting, kayaking, skiing and short hikes can be easily arranged when you get to Montenegro, but hooking up with other activity operators can be tricky due to language difficulties, lack of permanent offices and out-of-date websites. Luckily there are some excellent travel agencies that will do the legwork for you. If you're planning an action-intensive holiday, it is well worth considering the following agencies:

Black Mountain (p78; ☎ 321 968; www.montenegro holiday.com)

Montenegro Adventure Centre (see the boxed text, p103; ☎ 067-580 664; www.montenegrofly.com)

Montenegro Adventures (p131, ☎ 202 380; www .montenegro-adventures.com)

So Montenegro (☎ 020-3039 5651 in England; www .somontenegro.co.uk) London-based agency that can construct a customised action-packed tour.

Birdwatching

Budding ornithologists can grab the binoculars and peer at the waders in Lake Skadar (p126), Lake Šas (p119) and Lake Plav (p147) or watch the big birds of prey showing off in the mountainous zones.

Boating

If you have an inkling to potter around Montenegro's waters under your own steam (or sail), you'll be sorely disappointed unless you're dripping in cash. Licences are required to skipper a boat, so rentals tend to target the luxury crowd and include a crew. You can arrange this in Kotor (p86), Budva (p99) and Vranjina (p128) or Plavnica (p129) on Lake Skadar.

Otherwise, you'll have to content yourself with a novelty paddle boat or annoy your fellow holidaymakers on a jet ski, both of which are readily available on the coast.

Cycling

With so many mountains you'd think that mountain biking would be on the agenda and you'd be right. The National Tourist Office has been working hard with the regional mountain clubs to develop a network of marked routes, the result of which is the *Wilderness Biking Montenegro* pamphlet (downloadable from www.montenegro .travel/xxl/en/brochures/index.html). The pamphlet outlines five 'top trails' and the mother of all mountain tracks, the 14-day, 1276km **Tour de Montenegro** that circles the entire country. This should only be attempted by those with arses and thighs carved from granite as 30km of climbing is involved.

The easiest and shortest of the trails takes four to five days and covers 262km with only 1.3km of climbing. It starts in Cetinje and heads down to Lake Skadar, following its south shore before doubling back over the Rumija Mountains to Ulcinj. It then heads up the coast to Bar and cuts inland to return to Cetinje via Virpazar.

The others in the pamphlet are a nine-day (595km) trail looping north from Herceg Novi; an eight-day (382km) route through the northern mountains from Nikšić; a nine-day (455km) trip through the eastern mountains starting at Mojkovac; and a nine-day (474km) exploration of the central parts of the country beginning at Podgorica.

For a single day's cycling, consider the loop track from Cetinje through Lovćen National Park (see the boxed text, p122) or through Crmnica field from Virpazar (p127). A longer jaunt is the 93km trail between Kolašin and Podgorica (p140) – you can catch the train for the return journey.

The easiest places to find bikes for hire are Herceg Novi, Kolašin and Žabljak.

Diving

Not all the landscape, wildlife and history here is above ground. Montenegro's azure waters hide caves, shelves, springs and thousands of years' worth of shipwrecks – those Ulcinj pirates were busy chaps and WWII added to the collection. Visibility ranges from 10m to 25m but is usually around 15m. The best

---

RESPONSIBLE DIVING

Please consider the following tips when diving and help preserve the ecology and beauty of the reefs:

- Never use anchors on the reef, and take care not to ground boats on coral.
- Avoid touching or standing on living marine organisms or dragging equipment across the reef. Polyps can be damaged by even the gentlest contact. If you must hold on to the reef, only touch exposed rock or dead coral.
- Be conscious of your fins. Even without contact, the surge from fin strokes near the reef can damage delicate organisms. Take care not to kick up clouds of sand, which can smother organisms.
- Practise and maintain proper buoyancy control. Major damage can be done by divers descending too fast and colliding with the reef.
- Take great care in underwater caves. Spend as little time within them as possible, as your air bubbles may be caught within the roof and thereby leave organisms high and dry. Take turns to inspect the interior of a small cave.
- Resist the temptation to collect or buy corals or shells or to loot marine archaeological sites (mainly shipwrecks).
- Ensure that you take home all your rubbish and any litter you may find as well. Plastics in particular are a serious threat to marine life.
- Do not feed fish.
- Minimise your disturbance of marine animals. *Never* ride on the backs of turtles.

---

times to dive are from the middle of May until September when the surface water is up to 25°C, dropping to 16°C under 30m (you'll need a 7mm neoprene wetsuit). The main fauna you're likely to spot are swarms of young dentex, gilt-head bream and the occasional lobster or sea turtle.

You'll find diving operators in Herceg Novi (p78), Dobrota (p83), Budva (p100), Pržno (p106) and Ulcinj (p116). From Herceg Novi it's possible to do a 'night dive' during the daytime in the large former submarine dock on the Luštica Peninsula.

Expect to spend between €50 and €130 for a day's diving.

Hiking

Thanks to the enthusiastic amateurs at mountain clubs all over the country, Montenegro has an excellent network of hiking tracks. Areas such as the Orjen, Bjelasica and Prokletije mountains have route-marking to rival the national parks.

The main difficulty serious walkers and mountaineers will face is access to accommodation on longer expeditions. Mountain huts are available in some places but it isn't easy for the independent traveller to access them or to find out, for example, which ones were wiped out in last winter's avalanche. As the mountain clubs are volunteer-based, finding an English-speaker to provide assistance and arrange for a hut to be unlocked is challenging. National park and regional tourist offices aren't much help either. This is where the services of one of the adventure-focused travel agencies (see p78) can be useful. They can also arrange experienced guides from the local club.

Whether you're armed with a tent or just planning a day walk, make sure you're well prepared for sudden changes in temperature and storms. It's sensible to check the weather forecast before heading out. Because of the karstic nature of much of the terrain, water supplies can be limited.

The National Tourist Office has a downloadable brochure on some of the most spectacular walks (see the boxed text, p80). See also p80 for more information on walks on Mt Orjen, p86 for tracks leaving from Kotor, p99 for Budva, p122 for Lovćen National Park, p127 for Rijeka Crnojevića, p140 for Kolašin, p141 for Biogradska Gora National Park, p142 for Mojkovac, p144 for Durmitor National Park, p145 for Bijelo Polje and p150 for the Prokletije Mountains.

Kayaking

Herceg Novi–based Kayak Montenegro (p78) is the market leader, offering kayaking tours of the Bay of Kotor and Lake Skadar from Rijeka Crnojevića. Although it's still at the ideas stage, the agency has been considering instigating a multiday kayak safari, leaving from Herceg Novi and travelling the entire way down the coast to the Bojana River. If formalities regarding crossing in out and of Albania can be resolved, the trip would then follow the river to Lake Skadar, paddle the entire length of the lake and end at Rijeka Crnojevića.

Very experienced white-water kayakers can take on the rapids on some of Montenegro's rivers. The 56km ride along the Morača from Redice to Podgorica includes grade IV and V white-water sections, with one unrunable siphon near the middle.

The 93km ride from Gusinje to Bijelo Polje on the Lim River is a little easier, but still has a grade V rapid heading out of Berane. These are both suitable for kayaking between April and June. A 20km section of the Tara River at the eastern edge of Durmitor National Park is strictly off limits at all times because of the danger involved, but the remaining 104km can be kayaked between April and September.

A €75 national park fee applies for access to the 60km of the Tara Canyon, which can be done as a two-day trip. You'll find more details in a pamphlet available at the Kolašin tourist office (p139).

Basic kayaks can be hired for around €5 per hour from Herceg Novi (p78), Budva (p99), Bečići (p102), Sveti Stefan (p105), Pržno (p106), Plavnica on Lake Skadar (p129), Lake Krupac near Nikšić (p136) and Lake Plav (p149).

Paragliding

Montenegro has plenty of precipices from which you can hurl yourself off and while hang-gliding is yet to take off, paragliding is starting to soar; see the boxed text on p103 for details.

Parasailing

If you want the feeling of flying without having to jump off anything, you might like to try the expensive but less vertigo-inducing option of parasailing at Herceg Novi (p78) or Bečići (p102).

Rafting

This is Montenegro's premier active drawcard. At present, commercial rafting is only established on the Tara River and once you've experienced the spectacular canyon you'll understand why; see p143 for details.

Skiing

Montenegro's ski season roughly lasts from December to March, with the peak time being around New Year. The most glamorous ski resorts are at Kolašin, 10km from the Jezerine ski centre (p140). However, the best skiing is in Durmitor National Park where there are three slopes close to Žabljak (p144) with options for beginners or serious skiers. There are smaller runs near Nikšić (p136) and Rožaje (p147), while cross-country skiing can be undertaken in Lovćen and Durmitor National Parks.

Day passes are reasonably priced, ranging from €15 to €20 for the main slopes and around €10 for the secondary locations. Gear can be hired for around €10 to €20 per day.

BUSINESS HOURS

Business hours in Montenegro are a relative concept. Even if hours are posted on the doors of museums or shops, don't be surprised if they're not heeded. Banks and post offices are usually open from 8am to 5pm Monday to Friday and until noon Saturday. Shops in busy areas often start at around 8am or 9am and close at a similar time in the evening. Sometimes they'll close for a few hours in the late afternoon. Restaurants open at around 8am and close around midnight, while cafebars may stay open until 2am or 3am.

In this guide we've only listed opening hours for those businesses where they differ substantially from the hours listed here.

CHILDREN

Children are more likely to be fussed over than frowned upon anywhere you might go in Montenegro. Hotels, restaurants and cafes all warmly welcome children, and we've even seen the occasional young teenager boogying with their parents at beachside nightclubs. For many parents this is half the battle won.

However, special facilities for children are more limited. Better hotels may have cots available, but it's best to check in advance. The same goes for car seats at rental car agencies or taxi companies. Car seats aren't

RESPONSIBLE HIKING

To help preserve the ecology and beauty of Montenegro, consider these tips when hiking.

Rubbish

- Carry out *all* your rubbish. Don't overlook easily forgotten items, such as silver paper, orange peel, cigarette butts and plastic wrappers. Empty packaging should be stored in a dedicated rubbish bag. Make an effort to carry out rubbish left by others.

- Never bury your rubbish: digging disturbs soil and ground cover and encourages erosion. Buried rubbish will likely be dug up by animals that may be injured or poisoned by it. It may also take years to decompose.

- Minimise waste by taking minimal packaging and no more food than you will need. Take reusable containers or stuff sacks.

- Sanitary napkins, tampons, condoms and toilet paper should be carried out despite the inconvenience. They burn and decompose poorly.

Human Waste Disposal

- Contamination of water sources by human faeces can lead to the transmission of all sorts of nasties. Where there is a toilet, please use it. Where there is none, bury your waste. Dig a small hole 15cm (6in) deep and at least 100m (320ft) from any watercourse. Cover the waste with soil and a rock. In snow, dig down to the soil.

- Ensure that these guidelines are applied to a portable toilet tent if one is being used by a large trekking party. Encourage all party members, including porters, to use the site.

Washing

- Don't use detergents or toothpaste in or near watercourses, even if they are biodegradable.

- For personal washing, use biodegradable soap and a water container (or even a lightweight, portable basin) at least 50m (160ft) away from the watercourse. Disperse the waste water widely to allow the soil to filter it fully.

- Wash cooking utensils 50m (160ft) from watercourses using a scourer, sand or snow instead of detergent.

Erosion

- Hillsides and mountain slopes, especially at high altitudes, are prone to erosion. Stick to existing trails and avoid short cuts.

- If a well-used trail passes through a mud patch, walk through the mud so as not to increase the size of the patch.

- Avoid removing the plant life that keeps topsoils in place.

legally required, but given the dangers on the roads you might consider bringing your own. Highchairs are the exception rather than the rule at restaurants. Black Mountain (p78) hires travel cots (€20 per week) and highchairs (€15 per week).

You won't find children's menus but the ubiquitousness of kid-friendly favourites like pasta, pizza and hot chips (fries) makes meal time easy. Babysitting services are only offered in the most exclusive five-star hotels.

Disposable nappies (especially Pampers and Huggies) are easy to come by, but biodegradable versions aren't. Infant formula is available in the bigger supermarkets, but it's a good idea to bring a few days' supply with you. The main brands are Bebelac and Nestle and you can sometimes find Aptamil as well.

You'll rarely see anyone breastfeeding in public, but given that this is strongly encouraged here you're unlikely to strike negative reactions.

Medical care is generally very good, but language difficulties can present a problem. Every town has a medical centre ('Dom

Fires & Low-Impact Cooking

- Don't depend on open fires for cooking. The cutting of wood for fires in popular trekking areas can cause rapid deforestation. Cook on a lightweight kerosene, alcohol or Shellite (white gas) stove and avoid those powered by disposable butane gas canisters.
- If you are trekking with a guide and porters, supply stoves for the whole team. In alpine areas, ensure that all members are outfitted with enough clothing so that fires are not a necessity for warmth.
- If you patronise local accommodation, select those places that do not use wood fires to heat water or cook food.
- Fires may be acceptable below the tree line in areas that get very few visitors. If you light a fire, use an existing fireplace. Don't surround fires with rocks. Use only dead, fallen wood. Remember the adage 'the bigger the fool, the bigger the fire'. Use minimal wood, just what you need for cooking. In huts, leave wood for the next person.
- Ensure that you fully extinguish a fire after use. Spread the embers and flood them with water.

Wildlife Conservation

- Do not engage in or encourage hunting.
- Don't buy items made from endangered species.
- Don't attempt to exterminate animals in huts. In wild places, they are likely to be protected native animals.
- Discourage the presence of wildlife by not leaving food scraps behind you. Place gear out of reach and tie packs to rafters or trees.
- Do not feed the wildlife as this can lead to animals becoming dependent on handouts, to unbalanced populations and to diseases.

Camping on Private Property

- Always seek permission to camp from landowners.

Environmental Organisations

- The Podgorica-based Centre for Sustainable Tourism Initiatives (www.cstimontenegro.org) is a nongovernment, nonprofit organisation founded in 2006 that's involved with developing responsible and sustainable tourism in Montenegro. It works with small local operators to set up profitable and sustainable businesses which bring employment to the area. Their commercial wing, Montenegro Adventures (p131), organises tours and accommodation.

zdravlja'). They generally have a separate section for children with two waiting rooms: one for kids with potentially contagious infections (sniffles etc) and one dealing with broken bones and the like.

Older offspring should have a blast in Montenegro, with the relatively safe environment allowing them off the leash a little. You may find that they're kicking a ball around with the local scallywags in no time. The opposite is true for toddlers and small children as a generally lower standard of safety regulations (missing railings, unfenced pools etc)

means you'll have to keep a closer eye on them. You'll struggle to get pushchairs along the cobbled lanes and stairways in the older towns and you'll often find yourself having to trundle them along dangerous roads due to parked cars blocking the footpaths.

Any hurdles you may strike will be insignificant compared to the wonderfully family-friendly atmosphere, fresh air and gently lapping Mediterranean waters that Montenegro provides. Lonely Planet's *Travel With Children* offers further tips for hitting the road with the brood in tow.

CLIMATE CHARTS

In Montenegro it's possible to reach an altitude of 1700m within 10km of the coast, so wild variances in climate are to be expected. You'll find a summary of what to expect at the beginning of each regional chapter and a general discussion of the best times to travel on p16.

Like most of the Mediterranean region, Montenegro's coast enjoys balmy summers and mild winters. The warmest months are July and August, when the temperature ranges from 19°C to 29°C (average lowest to average highest).

The coldest month is January, ranging from 4°C to 12°C. July gets the most sunshine (338 hours) and December has the least (106 hours).

The water temperature ranges from a chilly but hardly frigid 13°C in January and February to 25°C in August.

In the mountainous interior the temperatures are considerably cooler, with the exception of the plain around Podgorica which sizzles in summer. January temperatures range from -7°C to 2°C, while even in August, the warmest month, the average minimum temperature is a nippy 9°C, although the maximum is around 23°C. Spectacular afternoon thunderstorms are quite common in summer.

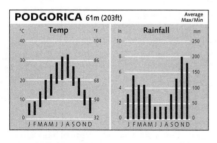

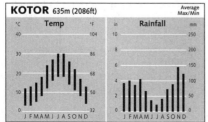

CUSTOMS REGULATIONS

In a bid to stop tourists from neighbouring countries bringing all their holiday groceries with them, Montenegro now restricts what food can be brought into the country but the odd chocolate bar isn't going to be an issue.

It's not permitted to take more than €2000 out of the country. If you're entering with a big wad of cash or travellers cheques and think you might have more than €2000 left when you leave, it's best to complete a currency declaration form on arrival or you may find your money confiscated on departure.

Drug laws are similar to most other European countries. Possession or trafficking of drugs could result in a lengthy jail sentence (see p160).

When you enter the country you need to receive an entry stamp in your passport. If you don't, you may be detained or charged a fine when you seek to leave for entering the country illegally.

DANGERS & ANNOYANCES

Montenegro's towns are generally safe places. You'll see children playing unsupervised on the streets and young women walking alone at night or even hitchhiking (not to say that we necessarily recommend these things).

Montenegro's roads, on the other hand, can be treacherous. They're generally in good condition but many are narrow and have sheer drops on one side. The main hazard is from other motorists who have no qualms about overtaking on blind corners while talking on their mobile phones or stopping in the middle of the road without warning. There's plenty of random tooting – don't let it faze you. It's best to keep your cool and stick to the speed limit as the traffic police are everywhere.

Chances are you'll see some snakes if you're poking around ruins during summer. Montenegro has two types of venomous vipers but they'll try their best to keep out of your way. If bitten, you will have time to head to a medical centre for the antivenom but you should head there immediately. Water snakes are harmless.

Check with the police before photographing any official building they're guarding.

Since Montenegro is in an active seismic zone, earthquakes strike from time to time, with the last major one that caused a loss of life occurring in 1979.

A major annoyance is the amount of time spent waiting for waiters, particularly when it comes time to pay your bill. Virtually everyone smokes – pretty much everywhere except for churches and (usually) buses.

DISCOUNT CARDS

The Euro<26 discount card (www.euro26 .rs) can provide holders with discounts on rail travel, air travel with Jat Airways and Montenegro Airlines, and some selected hotels. For other discounts on rail passes, see p168.

EMBASSIES & CONSULATES

For a full list, see www.vlada.cg.yu/eng/mini nos/. The following embassies and consulates are all in Podgorica unless otherwise stated:

Albania (Map p130; ☎ 020-652 796; Zmaj Jovina 30)
Bosnia and Hercegovina (Map p130; ☎ 020-618 105; Atinska 58)
Croatia Podgorica (Map p130; ☎ 020-269 760; Vladimira Ćetkovića 2); Kotor (Map p85; ☎ 032-323 127; Šušanj 248)
France (Map p130; ☎ 020-655 348; Atinska 35)
Germany (Map p130; ☎ 020-667 285; Hercegovačka 10)
Italy (Map p130; ☎ 020-234 661; Bulevar Džordža Vašingtona 83)
Serbia (Map p130; ☎ 020-402 500; Hotel Podgorica, Bulevar Svetog Petra Cetinjskog 1)
UK (Map p130; ☎ 020-205 460; Bulevar Sv Petra Cetinjskog 149)

GOVERNMENT TRAVEL ADVICE

The following government websites offer travel advisories and information on current hot spots. At the time of research there were no major advisories concerning travel to Montenegro.

- **Australian Department of Foreign Affairs & Trade** (☎ 1300 139 281; www.smarttraveller.gov.au)

- **British Foreign & Commonwealth Office** (☎ 0845-850 2829; www.fco .gov.uk)

- **Canadian Department of Foreign Affairs & International Trade** (☎ 1800 267 8376; www.dfait-maeci.gc.ca)

- **New Zealand Ministry of Foreign Affairs & Trade** (☎ 04-439 4000; www.safetravel.govt.nz)

- **US Department of State** (☎ 1888 407 4747; http://travel.state.gov)

USA (Map p130; ☎ 020-225 417; Ljubljanska bb)
The following countries are represented from offices in nearby countries:
Australia (☎ 011-330 3400; Čika Ljubina 13, Belgrade, Serbia)
Canada (☎ 011-306 3000; Kneza Miloša 75, Belgrade, Serbia)
Ireland (☎ 1-301 4960; Bank Center, Gránit Tower, Szabadsag ter 7, Budapest, Hungary)
The Netherlands (☎ 011-202 3900; Simina 29, Belgrade, Serbia)

FESTIVALS & EVENTS

The municipal tourist authorities put a lot of emphasis on events to lure travellers to their towns. These range from song contests and theatre festivals aimed at those who speak the local language to superstar concerts to build the area's reputation throughout the region and world. Most coastal towns host summer festivals and the former Venetian towns have a tradition of masked carnivals. Details of local festivals and events are provided throughout the destination chapters. See also p18 for some top picks.

Active types should consider entering the **Adventure Race Montenegro** (www.adventureracemon tenegro.com; 1-/2-day entry €120/200). This two-day event in early October combines outdoor pursuits (kayaking, mountain biking, trekking and orienteering), brilliant scenery, environmental awareness and fundraising for local charities.

FOOD

Reviews in this guidebook are listed in budget order, according to the price of the least expensive dish. We haven't listed per-kilogram prices for fish restaurants but a standard portion is around 200kg to 250kg; ask for a rough price before you choose a fish if you're unsure. Budget mains can be had for less than €5, while midrange mains should be less than €10; mains above €10 are labelled as top end in this book. Refer to the Food & Drink section (p44) for more details.

GAY & LESBIAN TRAVELLERS

Where's the party? The answer's nowhere. Although homosexuality was decriminalised in 1977, you won't find a single gay or lesbian venue in Montenegro. Don't be fooled by all the men walking arm-in-arm, or hand-in-hand in the Albanian areas.

DIRECTORY

Attitudes to homosexuality remain hostile and life for gay people is extremely difficult, exacerbated by the fact that most people are expected to live at home until they're married.

Many gay men resort to online connections (try www.gayromeo.com) or take their chances at a handful of cruisy beaches. These include Njivice near Herceg Novi, Jaz Beach near Budva (far left-hand side), Pržno near Tivat (far left-hand side) and below the ruins of Ratac near Bar.

HOLIDAYS

Public holidays in Montenegro include the following:

New Year's Day 1 January
Orthodox Christmas 7 and 8 January
Orthodox Easter Monday date varies, usually April
Statehood Day 13 July
Labour Day 1 May
Independence Day 21 May

INSURANCE

A watertight travel insurance policy covering theft, loss and medical problems is recommended. While theft isn't a huge problem, rental cars are sometimes targeted by opportunists and Montenegro's roads aren't the world's safest. There are plenty of policies to choose from – compare the fine print and shop around.

Some policies specifically exclude designated 'dangerous activities' such as scuba-diving, parasailing, paragliding, white-water rafting, skiing and even hiking. If you plan on doing any of these things (a distinct possibility in Montenegro), make sure the policy you choose covers you fully and includes ambulances and emergency medical evacuation. See p173 for more information on medical insurance, and p171 for car insurance.

If you need to make a claim, ensure you obtain and keep all relevant documentation. This may involve a police report in case of theft and invoices for medical expenses incurred. Some policies ask you to call back (reverse charges) to a centre in your home country where an immediate assessment of your problem is made.

Worldwide travel insurance is available at www.lonelyplanet.com/travel_services. You can buy, extend and claim online any time – even if you're already on the road.

INTERNET ACCESS

Most towns have internet cafes, although they can be surprisingly difficult to find. You won't pay more than €2 per hour for a terminal. Top-end hotels usually have wall sockets for you to access a dial-up connection in your room; expect to pay a steep call rate. Wireless is becoming more common but often doesn't penetrate to every part of the hotel and may be limited to the reception area. One of the sweeteners of the Porto Montenegro project for residents of Tivat (p90) is free wireless access throughout the town.

Throughout this book we've used the 🖳 symbol for accommodation providers that have a computer linked to the internet for guests to use. Places that have a wireless connection (whether or not they charge for it) are marked 'wi-fi'. Where both are available you'll see ' 🖳 wi-fi'.

See p19 for some handy websites about Montenegro.

LEGAL MATTERS

Obviously, while you are in Montenegro you're covered by Montenegrin law. If you're arrested, you have the right to contact your country's embassy or consulate (see p159) and arresting officers have a responsibility to help you to do so. They're also required to immediately notify you of the charges you're facing in a language you understand and to inform you that you're not required to give any statement. You have the right to a defence counsel of your own choosing during any interrogation.

A lower court can choose to detain you for three months pending trial, while a higher

---

LEGAL AGE

- To vote – 18
- To drive – 18
- To purchase alcohol – 18
- To drink alcohol – no limit
- To have sex (with an opposite- or same-sex partner) – 14

Travellers should note that they can be prosecuted under the law of their home country regarding age of consent, even when abroad.

court can extend this for a further three months. Minors may not be held for more than 60 days. The Montenegrin constitution enshrines a right to a fair and public trial with a defence, legal aid if required and a presumption of innocence. Montenegro has outlawed the death penalty but if you're caught with drugs you may face a lengthy stint in a local jail.

You are required to register with local police within 24 hours of arriving in Montenegro and whenever you change address. Accommodation providers usually do this on your behalf (which is the reason you're asked to hand over your passport when you arrive at a hotel).

The Canadian Government travel advisory warns against incidences of traffic police asking for money upfront for alleged violations, which is a situation that travellers have alerted us to in the past. If this happens to you, Canada's very sensible advice is to ask for a full explanation of the situation from the officer and, if it's not forthcoming, to ask to speak to your embassy. During our recent research we didn't experience or hear of any travellers that had been approached for bribes.

MAPS

Unless you're planning on doing a lot of driving on back roads, the maps in this book should be adequate. Magic Map's *Montenegro road map* (1:370,000) is widely available and has enlargements of the coast and major towns.

Detailed maps for hikers heading to the Lovćen, Durmitor or Bjelasica mountains are recommended in the destination chapters.

MONEY

Montenegro uses the euro (€) and all prices quoted in this book are in that currency (see Quick Reference on the inside front cover for exchange rates with other leading currencies at the time of research). You'll find banks with ATMs in all the main towns, most of which accept Visa, MasterCard, Maestro and Cirrus. ATMs tend to dish out big notes which can be hard to break. Don't rely on restaurants, shops or smaller hotels accepting credit cards. **Western Union** (www.westernunion .com) transfers can be made at most banks and major post offices.

For an indication of what you should expect to spend while in Montenegro, see p16. Tipping isn't expected although it's common to round up to the nearest euro.

POST

Every town has a post office that locals use for paying their bills, so you should be prepared for horrendous queues. Parcels should be taken unsealed for inspection. You can receive mail, addressed poste restante, in all towns for a small charge. International postal services are slow

SHOPPING

Montenegro offers plenty of potential liquid souvenirs, such as *vranac* or *krstač* wine and various types of *rakija* (see p45). Other specifically Montenegrin ideas include filigree jewellery, religious icons and embroidered folk costumes.

SOLO TRAVELLERS

Lone sharks will face no particular difficulties in Montenegro, although you're likely to pay a little more in accommodation than those travelling in couples or with a pack. Some meals will be better off shared, however you won't get too many strange looks if you're dining alone.

TELEPHONE

After declaring independence Montenegro was given its own country code (☎ 382) and a new set of local codes. Partly because of the changes, many businesses advertise their mobile numbers (starting with ☎ 06) instead of land lines.

The international access prefix is ☎ 00 or + from a mobile phone. Press the *i* button on public phones for dialling commands in English. Post offices are the best places to make international calls; phonecards don't give enough time for a decent call.

Local SIM cards are a good idea if you're planning a longer stay. The main providers

---

EMERGENCY NUMBERS

- Ambulance ☎ 124
- Fire service ☎ 123
- Police ☎ 122

are T-Mobile, M:tel and Promonte; they have storefronts in most towns.

TIME

Montenegro is in the Central Europe time zone (an hour ahead of GMT). Clocks go forward by an hour for daylight saving at the end of March and return to normal at the end of October. Outside the daylight-saving times, when it's midday in Montenegro it will be 3am in Los Angeles, 6am in New York, 11am in London, 9pm in Sydney and 11pm in Auckland. Montenegrins use the 24-hour clock, so hours will be listed as '9-17' rather than '9am-5pm'.

TOURIST INFORMATION

Official tourist offices are hit and miss (see the individual towns for details). Some have wonderfully helpful English-speaking staff and a good supply of free material while others have none of the above. Thankfully the National Tourist Office is more switched on and its website (www.montenegro.travel) is a great resource for travellers. It doesn't have a public office but you can dial ☎ 1333 at any time to receive tourist information from multilingual staff.

TRAVELLERS WITH DISABILITIES

The mobility-impaired will find the cobbled lanes and numerous stairways extremely challenging. There are very few specific facilities for either travellers or residents with disabilities. Some of the top-end hotels have wheelchair-accessible rooms.

VISAS

Visas are not required for citizens of most European countries, Australia, New Zealand, Singapore, South Korea, Israel, Canada and the USA. In most cases this allows a stay of up to 90 days. If your country is not covered by a visa waiver, you will need a valid passport, verified letter of invitation, return ticket, proof of sufficient funds and proof of medical cover.

Transport

CONTENTS

Getting There & Away   **163**
Entering The Country   163
Air   163
Land   167
Sea   169
Getting Around   **170**
Bicycle   170
Bus   170
Car & Motorcycle   170
Hitching   172
Local Transport   172
Train   172

This chapter deals with both getting to Montenegro and getting around while you're there. In today's Montenegro neither presents much of a challenge, even to a rookie traveller.

GETTING THERE & AWAY

Whether you choose to fly, train, ferry or drive, it's not difficult to get to Montenegro these days. New routes are continually being added to the busy timetable at the country's two airports, although at present no low-cost, no-frills carriers are represented. It's sometimes cheaper and more convenient to make your way from neighbouring countries, especially Croatia. Dubrovnik's Čilipi airport is very close to the border and the Adriatic's most beautiful city makes an impressive starting point to a Montenegro holiday. If you're

---

THINGS CHANGE...

The information in this chapter is particularly vulnerable to change. Check directly with the airline or a travel agent to make sure you understand how a fare (and ticket you may buy) works and be aware of the security requirements for international travel. Shop carefully. The details given in this chapter should be regarded as pointers and are not a substitute for your own careful, up-to-date research.

---

chasing a discount fare, easyJet (www.easyjet.com) flies to Split from London's Gatwick airport, Bristol and Geneva.

Flights, tours and rail tickets can all be booked online at www.lonelyplanet.com/travel_services.

ENTERING THE COUNTRY

Entering Montenegro doesn't pose any particular bureaucratic challenges. In fact, the country's dead keen to shuffle tourists in. Unfortunately, Croatia seems less happy to let them go, if the long waits at their side of the Adriatic highway checkpoint are any indication. This is the only border crossing where you're likely to face a delay; if you've got to get somewhere at a certain time, it pays to allow an hour.

Passport

Make sure that your passport has at least six months left on it. You'll need a visa if you're not from one of the many countries with a visa-waiver arrangement (see opposite). There are no particular nationalities or stamps in your passport that will deny you entry.

AIR
Airports & Airlines

Montenegro's largest and most modern airport is immediately south of the capital **Podgorica** (TGD; ☎ 020-872 016; www.montenegroairports.com/podgorica/). The entire south of the country and everywhere as far north as Kolašin is within 100km of this airport. If you're wondering about the airport code, the TGD is a hangover from Podgorica's previous name Titograd. Locals sometimes call it Golubovci airport as it's close to a village with that name. The airport's safety record is blemished only by a small plane skidding while landing in snowy conditions in 2005; there were no serious injuries.

The second international airport at **Tivat** (TIV; ☎ 032-617 337; www.montenegroairports.com/tivat/) is well positioned for holidaymakers heading to the Bay of Kotor or Budva and now welcomes over half a million passengers annually. Despite its mountainous surrounds and a runway that ends only 100m from the water,

CLIMATE CHANGE & TRAVEL

Climate change is a serious threat to the ecosystems that humans rely upon, and air travel is the fastest-growing contributor to the problem. Lonely Planet regards travel, overall, as a global benefit, but believes we all have a responsibility to limit our personal impact on global warming.

Flying & Climate Change

Pretty much every form of motorised travel generates CO_2 (the main cause of human-induced climate change) but planes are far and away the worst offenders, not just because of the sheer distances they allow us to travel but because they release greenhouse gases high into the atmosphere. The statistics are frightening: two people taking a return flight between Europe and the US will contribute as much to climate change as an average household's gas and electricity consumption over a whole year.

Carbon-Offset Schemes

Climatecare.org and other websites use 'carbon calculators' that allow travellers to offset the level of greenhouse gases they are responsible for with financial contributions to sustainable-travel schemes that reduce global warming – including projects in India, Honduras, Kazakhstan and Uganda.

Lonely Planet, together with Rough Guides and other concerned partners in the travel industry, supports the carbon-offset scheme run by climatecare.org. Lonely Planet offsets all of its staff and author travel.

For more information check out our website: www.lonelyplanet.com.

---

there has never been an accident here in the airport's nearly 40-year history.

Montenegro's de facto third airport is actually in neighbouring Croatia. **Dubrovnik airport** (DBV; ☎ 020-773 100 in Croatia; www.airport-dubrovnik.hr) is a modern facility only 12km from the border and the closest airport to Herceg Novi. More commonly referred to locally as Čilipi airport, it's used by over a million travellers annually.

The word for airport in Montenegrin is *aerodrom* (АЕРОДРОМ). This was also used in Croatia until independence but in a fit of French-style linguistic nationalism the official Croatian term has been changed to a direct translation of the words for 'air' and 'port', *zračna luka* – a potential trap for English speakers.

Montenegro Airlines is the national carrier, running a small fleet of 102- to 116-seater planes. Apart from the skid at Podgorica airport mentioned above, its safety record has been unsullied during its 10 years of operation. It has code-share agreements with Adria Airways, Austrian Airways and Malév.

AIRLINES FLYING TO/FROM MONTENEGRO & DUBROVNIK

As you can see from the following list, literally dozens of airlines fly into Montenegro or neighbouring Dubrovnik from all over Europe. Some of them only operate in the busy summer months or reduce their services substantially at other times.

Adria Airways (airline code JP; Map p130; ☎ 020-201 201; www.adria-airways.com; Ivana Vujoševića 46, Podgorica) Flies from Ljubljana and Sarajevo to Podgorica.

Aer Lingus (airline code EI; ☎ 0818-365 000 in Ireland; www.aerlingus.com) Flies from Dublin to Dubrovnik in summer.

Aerosvit (airline code VV; ☎ 044-496 7975 in Ukraine; www.aerosvit.com) Flies from Kiev to Tivat.

Air One (airline code AP; ☎ 199 20 70 80 in Italy; www.flyairone.it) Flies from Rome to Dubrovnik.

Atlant-Soyuz Airlines (airline code 3G; ☎ 495-436 7045 in Russia; www.atlant-soyuz.ru) Flies from Moscow to Tivat.

Austrian Airlines (airline code OS; ☎ 020-606 170; www.austrian.com) Flies from Vienna to Podgorica and from Vienna and Zagreb to Dubrovnik.

Austrojet (airline code AUJ; www.austrojet.at) Flies from Banja Luka to Tivat.

Blue1 (airline code KF; ☎ 09-630 003 in Finland; www.blue1.com) Flies from Helsinki to Dubrovnik.

British Airways (airline code BA; ☎ 0844-493 0787 in UK; www.britishairways.com) Flies from London's Gatwick airport to Dubrovnik.

Croatia Airlines (airline code OU; Map p130; ☎ 020-201 201; www.croatiaairlines.com; Ivana Vujoševića 46, Podgorica) Flies from Zagreb to Podgorica and from Amsterdam, London, Paris, Rome, Split, Zagreb and Zurich to Dubrovnik.

Estonian Air (airline code OV; ☎ 640 1163 in Estonia; www.estonian-air.com) Flies from Tallinn to Dubrovnik in summer.

Flybe (airline code BE; ☎ 0871 700 2000 in UK; www .flybe.com) Flies from Birmingham and Exeter to Dubrovnik.

Flyglobespan (airline code Y2; ☎ 0871-971 1440 in UK; www.flyglobespan.com) Flies from Edinburgh to Dubrovnik.

Germanwings (airline code 4U; ☎ 0870-252 1250 in UK; www.germanwings.com) Flies from Berlin, Cologne, Dresden, Dublin, London (Stansted) and Verona to Dubrovnik.

Iberia Airlines (airline code IB; ☎ 902-400 500 in Spain; www.iberia.com) Flies from Madrid to Dubrovnik.

Jat Airways (airline code JU; www.jat.com) Budva (Map p99; ☎ 033-451 641; Mediteranska 2); Podgorica (Map p130; ☎ 020-664 750; Njegoševa 25) Flies from Belgrade and Niš (summer only) to Tivat and from Belgrade to Podgorica.

Jet2.com (airline code LS; ☎ 0871 226 1 737 in UK; www.jet2.com) Flies from Belfast and Leeds to Dubrovnik.

Malév Hungarian Airlines (airline code MA; ☎ 06-40 212121 in Hungary; www.malev.hu) Flies from Budapest to Podgorica and Dubrovnik.

Montenegro Airlines (airline code YM; www.monte negroairlines.com) Budva (Map p99; ☎ 033-454 900; Slovenska Obala bb); Podgorica (Map p130; ☎ 020-664 411; Slobode 23) Flies from Belgrade, London (Gatwick), Milan, Moscow, Niš (summer only) and Paris (Charles de Gaulle) to Tivat. Also from Belgrade, Frankfurt, Ljubljana, London, Paris, Rome, Vienna and Zurich to Podgorica.

Moskovia Airlines (airline code 3R; Map p97; ☎ 033-455 967; www.ak3r.ru; Mediteranska 23, Budva) Flies from Moscow to Tivat and Podgorica.

Norwegian Air Shuttle (airline code DY; ☎ 815 21 815 in Norway; www.norwegian.no) Flies from Oslo to Dubrovnik.

Rossiya Airlines (airline code FV; ☎ 495-995 2025 in Russia; www.rossiya-airlines.ru) Flies from St Petersburg to Tivat.

S7 Airlines (airline code S7; ☎ 033-459 706; www .s7.ru) Flies from Moscow to Tivat and Podgorica.

SkyEurope (airline code NE; ☎ 02-3301 7301 in Slovakia; www.skyeurope.com) Flies from Bratislava, Prague and Vienna to Dubrovnik.

Thompsonfly (airline code BY; ☎ 0871-231 4691 in UK; www.thompsonfly.com) Flies from London (Gatwick and Luton) and Manchester to Dubrovnik.

TUIfly (airline code X3; ☎ 01805 757 510 in Germany; www.tuifly.com) Flies from Hannover, Munich and Stuttgart to Dubrovnik.

Ukraine International Airlines (airline code PS; ☎ 044-581 5050 in Ukraine; www.flyuia.com) Flies from Kiev to Tivat (summer only).

Ural Airlines (airline code U6; ☎ 343-345 3645 in Russia; www.uralairlines.ru) Flies from Yekaterinburg to Tivat (summer only).

Tickets

Domestic flights from within Europe can be pricy, so it pays to shop around. The best deals are often found on the internet, either directly from the airline's site or through a booking site (see below). It's also worth checking with a reputable travel agency in your home city as they often get access to special discounted fares.

If you're coming from outside Europe, chances are you'll get a reasonably priced add-on sector on a longer fare from a partner airline of one of the major airline alliances such as Star Alliance (represented in Montenegro/Dubrovnik by Austrian Airlines, Adria Airways, Blue1 and Croatia Airlines) or Oneworld (British Airways or Malév Hungarian Airlines).

INTERCONTINENTAL (RTW) TICKETS

Round-the-world (RTW) fares can be a good option if you're travelling a long distance and want to make multiple stops along the way. The segments are serviced by different airlines and usually require all of the travelling to be in the same direction. Both Star Alliance (www.star alliance.com) and Oneworld (www.oneworld .com) offer RTW tickets including Montenegro. Another alternative is Star Alliance's Europe Airpass or Oneworld's Visit Europe, which allow multiple stops in Europe combined with

---

ONLINE TICKETS

Some recommended websites to book air tickets include those listed below. They usually levy a booking fee on any flights bought, but even if you don't buy through them, their software can be very useful for checking that the flight prices offered to you by other travel agents are the best ones available.

- www.ebookers.com
- www.expedia.com
- www.flybudget.com
- www.itasoftware.com
- www.lonelyplanet.com/travel_services
- www.opodo.com
- www.orbitz.com
- www.statravel.com
- www.travelocity.com

a ticket originating from a different continent. Oneworld's Circle Trip Explorer allows you to travel multiple continents while not necessarily heading all of the way around the world. All of the journeys must be in the same circular direction and the pricing alters depending on the number of continents visited.

All of these fares can be booked on the respective alliance's website, or the individual airlines (or your travel agent) can arrange the booking.

Australia

If you're coming all the way from Australia it's unlikely that you'll only want to stop in Montenegro, so it's worth checking the prices of round-the-world or other intercontinental tickets (see p165).

Flights to Europe via Asia are shorter and cheaper than flying through the USA but it will still take more than 24 hours to get to Montenegro. It's possible to fly the entire way from Sydney to Dubrovnik by British Airways, stopping in Singapore, although you will have to get yourself between London's Heathrow and Gatwick airports for your connecting flight. Expect to pay upwards of A$2900 unless you find a special fare. **Qantas** (☎ 13 13 13; www.qantas.com) or other Oneworld airlines may be used for some segments.

However, you may find it's cheaper to source a discount return fare to London (or any other major European hub) on any of the many carriers flying these routes and then arrange your Montenegrin connection separately (see opposite for connections from London). Remember to allow a reasonable gap between flights in case there's a delay; airlines don't take responsibility for missed connections that aren't part of their booking. Also, for London in particular, you'll need to factor in time to get between airports. Most flights from Australia arrive in Heathrow but no flights to Montenegro depart from there and all of London's airports are far apart.

STA Travel (☎ 134 782; www.statravel.com.au) and **Flight Centre** (☎ 133 133; www.flightcentre.com .au) are reliable travel agencies for booking flights, with branches all over Australia. It's well worth getting a quote from an agent for a relatively obscure destination such as Montenegro, as many airlines that don't fly there directly (such as Qantas) don't include it as a destination on their website even though code-share arrangements may be available.

For example, at the time of research the Flight Centre site was showing a fare from Sydney to Podgorica flying Qantas and Austrian Airlines for less than A$2400.

Canada

From Toronto, Montreal, Ottawa, Calgary and Vancouver you can pick up an Austrian Airlines flight to Vienna and then transfer to Podgorica or Dubrovnik. It takes less than nine hours to fly from Toronto to Vienna and then a further hour to your final destination.

As in other countries, **Flight Centre** (☎ 1877 967 5302; www.flightcentre.ca) is a good source for competitive quotes.

Continental Europe

There is a huge array of flights available to get you to Montenegro from within Europe, although some are restricted to the summer months. Prices vary widely and can be surprisingly high. To give you an idea, an Adria Airways return flight from Ljubljana to Podgorica taking less than an hour each way can be €740 to €1030.

Montenegro's popularity with its northern Slavic cousins can be seen in the number of carriers servicing the former Soviet Union. From Moscow you have the choice of Atlant-Soyuz, Montenegro, Moskovia and S7 Airlines. From St Petersburg you can catch a direct flight on Rossiya Airlines and from Yekaterinburg you can take Ural Airlines. The Ukrainian capital Kiev is serviced by both Aerosvit and Ukraine International Airlines. Estonian Air flies from Tallinn.

From northwestern Europe you can pick up a direct flight from Oslo (Norwegian Air Shuttle), Helsinki (Blue1) or Amsterdam (Croatia Airlines) to Dubrovnik. Central Europe offers lots of options, with direct flights from Banja Luka (Austrojet), Belgrade (Jat Airways, Montenegro Airlines), Berlin (Germanwings), Bratislava (SkyEurope), Budapest (Malév), Cologne (Germanwings), Dresden (Germanwings), Frankfurt (Montenegro Airlines), Hannover (TUIfly), Ljubljana (Adria Airways, Montenegro Airlines), Munich (TUIfly), Niš (Jat Airways, Montenegro Airlines), Paris (Croatia Airlines, Montenegro Airlines), Prague (SkyEurope), Sarajevo (Adria Airways), Split (Croatia Airlines), Stuttgart (TUIfly), Vienna (Austrian Airlines, Montenegro Airlines, SkyEurope), Zagreb (Austrian Airlines,

Croatia Airlines) and Zurich (Croatia Airlines, Montenegro Airlines).

If you're coming from Southern Europe, you can head to Rome (Air One, Croatia or Montenegro Airlines), Milan (Montenegro Airlines), Verona (Germanwings) or Madrid (Iberia Airlines).

New Zealand

As with Australia (opposite), it pays to investigate round-the-world fares or find a cheap return fare to Europe and add on a separate Montenegrin connection. From New Zealand it's a similar distance to fly to Europe via Asia or the Americas, making a round-the-world trip even more practical and expanding the choice of carriers.

A British Airways fare from Auckland to Dubrovnik starting with a code-share flight to Hong Kong on Cathay Pacific can cost upwards of NZ$3400. All up, expect a marathon travelling time of more than 24 hours to get to your destination.

Reputable travel agencies include **STA Travel** (☎ 0800 474 400; www.statravel.co.nz) and **Travel Smart** (☎ 0800 622 000; www.travelsmart.co.nz).

UK & Ireland

Flights from the UK to Montenegro take a little less than three hours. Montenegro Airlines currently has regular flights from London's Gatwick airport to either Tivat or Podgorica, while British Airways and Croatia Airlines fly to Dubrovnik, also from Gatwick. Standard fares are around the £300 to £400 mark, although you might find significant specials in the low season.

During the warm months travel directly to Dubrovnik from Dublin (Aer Lingus), Belfast (Jet2.com), Edinburgh (Flyglobespan), Manchester (Thompsonfly), Leeds (Jet2.com), London Stansted (Germanwings), London Luton (Thompsonfly), London Gatwick (Thompsonfly), Birmingham (Flybe) and Exeter (Flybe). If you get in early enough for the cheaper carriers, the fares may be around £80 to £200.

Good travel agencies for arranging flights include **STA Travel** (☎ 0871 230 0040; www.statravel .co.uk) and **Trailfinders** (☎ 0845 058 5858; www .trailfinders.com). It's worth checking **Avro Flights** (☎ 0871 423 8550; www.avro.co.uk), a web-based agency specialising in cheap fares from the UK.

Bargain-hunters should also investigate taking **easyJet** (www.easyjet.com) from Gatwick to the Croatian city of Split, which arrives early enough for you to undertake the lengthy bus journey to Montenegro (allow a whole day as you may need to catch a bus to Dubrovnik and then change buses for Herceg Novi – see p168). Another option is to fly from Stansted to Bari (on the east coast of Italy) with **RyanAir** (www.bookryanair.com) and catch the ferry to Bar (p169).

USA

British Airways has flights from New York, Atlanta, Tampa and Orlando to London's Gatwick where you can transfer to a flight to Dubrovnik. From New York the cost is upwards of US$1000. Austrian Airlines flies from New York and Chicago to Vienna, where you can connect to either Podgorica or Dubrovnik for around US$1500 or more. The flight from New York to Vienna takes about 8½ hours with another hour for the connecting flight.

For quotes on complicated fares try **Flight Centre** (☎ 1866 967 5351; www.flightcentre.us) or **STA Travel** (☎ 0800 781 4040; www.statravel.com).

LAND

Montenegro may be a wee slip of a thing but it borders five other states: Croatia, Bosnia and Hercegovina, Serbia, Kosovo and Albania. You can easily enter Montenegro by land from any of its neighbours.

Bicycle

There are no problems bringing a bicycle into the country. There are not many cyclists here so road-users are not cycle savvy – and remember that there's a 'Monte' in the country's name for a reason.

If you want to bring your own bike, most airlines allow you to put a bicycle in the hold for a surprisingly small fee. You can either take it apart and pack all the pieces in a bike bag or box, or simply wheel it to the check-in desk, where it should be treated as a piece of check-in luggage. You may have to remove the pedals and turn the handlebars sideways so that it takes up less space in the aircraft's hold; check all this with the airline before you pay for your ticket. If your bicycle and other luggage exceed your weight allowance, ask about alternatives or you may find yourself being charged a small ransom for excess baggage.

TRANSPORT

Bus

There's a well-developed bus network linking Montenegro with the major cities of the former Yugoslavia and onwards to Western Europe and Turkey. Podgorica is the main hub but buses stop at many coastal towns as well. From Herceg Novi, for example, there are buses to Dubrovnik (€8, two hours, two daily), Sarajevo (€22, seven hours, four daily) and Belgrade (€30, 13 hours, nine daily).

From Ulcinj there's a daily bus to Shkodra (€4.50, 90 minutes) and three to Prishtina (€22.50, eight hours). Minibuses head to Shkodra at 9am and 3pm from the car park beside Ulcinj's market (about €5).

There are daily connections from Sarajevo (€18, five hours, daily), Međugorje (€18, three hours, two daily) and Mostar (€15, three hours, two daily) to Dubrovnik.

At the border, guards will often enter the bus and collect passports, checking the photos as they go. Once they're happy with them they return them to the bus conductor who will return them as the driver speeds off. Make sure you get yours back and that it's been stamped.

Car & Motorcycle

Crossing into Montenegro with a private or hire car won't pose any problems as long as you have all of your papers in order. You must have vehicle registration/ownership documents and a locally valid insurance policy such as European Green Card vehicle insurance. Be sure to check your hire car insurance cover as some Western European companies will not cover you for travel in Montenegro.

On 15 June 2008 the Montenegrin Government introduced an eco-tax on all road vehicles. The funds raised will be used for the implementation of environmental preservation and protection projects. Foreign nationals must pay the tax when entering Montenegro by car. The fees range from €10 (for most cars with a capacity of up to eight passengers) to €150 (for coaches) and are determined according to the make and size of the vehicle. The eco-sticker obtained upon payment of the tax is valid for one year and must be displayed on the inside of the front windscreen in the upper right-hand corner.

From the major border crossings with Croatia, Serbia, Kosovo and Albania you won't have to drive more than 25km to find a petrol station or assistance with mechanical repairs. From the Bosnian crossings don't expect to find anything before Nikšić.

There have been incidences of problems involving cars with Montenegrin plates in Croatia. During our research we had our car spat upon by a group of youths as we stopped at an intersection near Dubrovnik's Old Town. There are also reports of cars being keyed while parked on the road. If you do drive a Montenegrin hire car into Dubrovnik you're strongly advised to park in one of the official car parks near the Old Town – and it may pay to keep the windows up while you're driving.

For more information see p170.

Train

Montenegro's only passenger train line starts at Bar and heads into Serbia (p172). Two to four trains head between Podgorica and Belgrade daily (€22, 7½ hours) with one continuing on to Novi Sad. You'll find timetables on the website of **Montenegro Railways** (Željeznica Crne Gore; ☎ 020-441 211; www.zeljeznica.cg.yu).

From Belgrade it's possible to connect to destinations throughout Europe. The Serbian Railways website (www.serbianrailways.com) has timetables and lists special offers. Sample 2nd-class one-way fares include:

Destination	Frequency	Duration	Cost (€)
Bucharest	daily	14hr	70
Budapest	2 daily	7hr	15
Munich	2 daily	17hr	118
Venice	daily	16hr	69
(incl sleeper & breakfast)			
Vienna	2 daily	11hr	70 (return)

Montenegro can be included as part of the **Eurail** (www.eurail.com) Select Pass, which offers varying days of rail travel over a two-month period in three, four or five neighbouring countries. Adult prices range from €319 (five days, three countries) to €1235 (15 days, five countries). There are youth discounts for those 25 years old and younger.

InterRail (www.interrailnet.com) passes can only be used by European residents of more than six months' standing. The Global Pass allows free train travel in 30 countries (including Montenegro) during a certain period of time. Some are valid over a continuous period of time, while others are more flexible. Prices depend on age and class; youth passes for those younger than 25 are cheaper than adult passes, and child passes are 50% less than adult. For some examples of prices, a Global Pass valid for five days in a 10-day period costs €249/159 per adult/youth, or €599/399 for one continuous month. Terms, conditions and occasional surcharges may apply on certain trains.

The Balkan Flexipass from **Rail Europe** (www.raileurope.com) covers rail travel in Montenegro, Serbia, Macedonia, Bulgaria, Greece, Romania and Turkey. It covers travel in 1st class only, and costs from US$283 for five days' travel in one month to US$591 for 15 days' travel in one month. Discounted passes are available for both youth (under 26) and seniors (over 60); with five days' travel costing US$166/226 respectively and 15 days' travel costing US$356/475.

If you plan to travel extensively by train, it is worth getting hold of the *Thomas Cook European Rail Timetable*, which gives a complete listing of train schedules, reservation information and indicates where supplements apply. It's updated monthly and available from Thomas Cook outlets or by order online via www.thomascookpublishing.com.

Albania

There are two main crossings: Sukobin is between Shkodra and Ulcinj while Hani i Hotit is between Shkodra and Podgorica. If you're paddling about on Lake Skadar, remember that the border runs through the lake and be careful not to cross it. Because of problems with trafficking (of cigarettes, drugs and women), the Montenegro police do patrol the lake; in June 2008 they were accused of firing on Albanian fishermen who were alleged to be fishing with dynamite. The same caution should be applied while hiking in the Prokletije Mountains.

Bosnia & Hercegovina

Two main checkpoints link Nikšić to Trebinje (Dolovi) and to Srbinje (Šćepan Polje). There's a more remote crossing halfway between the two at Vratkovići and another in the Kovač Mountains in the far north.

Croatia

Expect delays at the busy checkpoint on the Adriatic highway between Herceg Novi and Dubrovnik. You can avoid them by taking a detour down the Prevlaka Peninsula to the sleepy Kobila border post. From the Croatian

---

> **FLIGHT-FREE TRAVEL**
>
> If you fancy a guilt-free, carbon-neutral journey from London to Montenegro, log on to www.seat61.com and click on Montenegro on the side navigation. You'll find detailed instructions on how to get from London to Belgrade by train and then connect through to Montenegro, including departure times, fares and travel-pass information.

---

side you turn right off the highway a few kilometres before the main border crossing and pass through Pločice and Vitaljina. The road rejoins the highway on the Montenegro side just before Igalo.

Kosovo

There's only one crossing here, on the road between Rožaje and Peć.

Serbia

The busiest crossing is north of Bijelo Polje near Dobrakovo, followed by the checkpoint northeast of Rožaje and another east of Pljevlja. The train crosses at the Dobrakovo border.

SEA

Ferry services connect Montenegro (Bar and Kotor) with Italy (Bari and Ancona).

Montenegro Lines (☎ 030-303 469; www.montenegrolines.net) has boats from Bar to Bari (€60, 10 hours, three weekly, nearly daily from July to September) and Ancona (€72, 16 hours, twice weekly from July to early September). Cars cost €68 to €90 and cabins are an additional €12 to €68 depending on the type and season.

Azzurra Line (☎ 080-592 8400 in Italy; www.azzurraline.com) has weekly ferries heading between Bar and Bari (deck passage €48, seat €55, cabins €67 to €91, car €78; 10 hours) and between Kotor and Bari (deck passage €55, seat €65, cabin €75 to €189, car €72; nine hours) but only from June/July to September. If you're transporting a car into Montenegro there's an additional €6.50 fee.

Jadrolinija (www.jadrolinija.hr; ☎ 071-20 71 465 Ancona; ☎ 080-52 75 439 Bari; ☎ 051-211 444 Rijeka) runs a service from Bari to Dubrovnik (346KN to 477KN, eight hours, one to four weekly). Prices are for a deck seat; cabins and couchettes cost more and bringing a car costs an extra 50% of the price.

GETTING AROUND

BICYCLE

Cyclists are a rare species even in the cities and there are no special bike lanes on the roads. Don't expect drivers to be considerate and wherever possible, try to get off the main roads.

However, the outlook for cyclists isn't as grim as it sounds. The National Tourist Office has developed a series of wilderness mountain-biking trails (see p153), making a two-wheeled tour of Montenegro an excellent proposition. As most of the country is mountainous, you'll have to be exceedingly fit to attempt it.

The key to a successful bike trip is to travel light, and don't overdo it on the first few days. Even for the shortest and most basic trip it's worth carrying the tools necessary for repairing a puncture. You might want to consider packing spare brake and gear cables, spanners, Allen keys, spare spokes and strong adhesive tape. At the risk of stating the bleeding obvious, none of the above are much use unless you know what to do with them. Maintenance is also important (and obvious): check over your bike thoroughly each morning and again at night when the day's touring is over. Take a good lock and always use it when you leave your bike unattended.

The wearing of helmets is not compulsory but is certainly advised.

A seasoned cyclist can average about 80km a day, but this depends on the terrain and how much weight is being carried. Again, don't overdo it – there's no point burning yourself out during the initial stages.

BUS

The local bus network is extensive and reliable. Buses are usually comfortable and air-conditioned; they're rarely full. It's usually not difficult to find information on services and prices from the bus station. Most have details prominently displayed, although they're not always up to date. As with many service-industry types in Montenegro, some station staff are more helpful than others. Where English isn't spoken they'll usually write down the price and time of the bus for you.

It's a bit cheaper to buy your ticket on the bus rather than at the station, but a station-bought ticket theoretically guarantees you a seat. Reservations are only worthwhile for international buses, at holiday times and where long-distance journeys are infrequent. Luggage carried below is charged at €1 per piece.

Smoking is forbidden on buses and this rule is generally enforced. The standard of driving is no better or worse than that of anyone else on the roads. Many bus drivers once drove trucks.

CAR & MOTORCYCLE

Independent travel by car or motorcycle is an ideal way to gad about and discover the country; some of the drives are breathtakingly beautiful (see the boxed text, p140). Traffic police are everywhere, so stick to speed limits and carry an International Driving Permit (see opposite).

Allow more time than you'd expect for the distances involved as the terrain will slow you down. You'll rarely get up to 60km per hour on the Bay of Kotor road, for instance. The standard of roads is generally fair with conditions worsening in rural areas, especially in winter and after bad weather. Many roads are under construction, so there are often delays and detours. A particularly notorious road is the Podgorica–Belgrade highway as it passes through the Morača Canyon, which is often made dangerous by bad conditions and high traffic. It's a good idea to drive defensively and treat everyone else on the road as a lunatic – when they get behind the wheel, many of them are. That said, no matter how much they toot at you or overtake on blind corners, you should avoid confrontation.

The only toll in Montenegro is the Sozina tunnel between Lake Skadar and the sea (€2.50 per car) and you will also be charged to drive your vehicle into the national parks (see the destination chapters for details).

Automobile Associations

The **Automobile Association of Montenegro** (AMSCG; ☎ 020-225 493) offers roadside assistance, towing and repairs. The roadside assistance number is ☎ 987.

UK motoring organisations such as the **Automobile Association** (www.theaa.com) and the **RAC** (www.rac.co.uk) have excellent information on their websites, with driving tips and conditions for all the countries of the Western Balkans.

Bring Your Own Vehicle

As long as you have registration/ownership papers with you and valid insurance cover, there should be no problem driving your car into Montenegro. You'll need to purchase an eco-sticker on arrival, which is valid for a year (see p168). If your vehicle has obvious signs of damage the border guards should provide you with a certificate that must be produced upon leaving to prove that the damage didn't occur inside the country.

Driver's Licence

It's recommended that you arrange an International Driving Permit from your home country before the trip. Although many rental companies will hire out a car based on your foreign driver's licence, there's no assurance that a traffic cop will accept it and it doesn't pay to give them any excuse to fine you

Fuel & Spare Parts

Filling up is no problem in any medium-sized town but don't leave it until the last drop as there are few late-night petrol stations. Diesel, unleaded 95 and 98 octane are easy to find. Spare parts for major makes will be no problem in the cities, and mechanics are available everywhere for simple repairs.

Hire

It's not difficult to hire a car in the bigger towns. Budva, in particular, is overflowing with options. The major European car-hire companies have a presence in various centres including the airports, but the local alternatives are often cheaper. If you're coming from North America, Australia or New Zealand, ask your airline if it has any special deals for rental cars in Europe. You can often find very competitive rates.

Avis (www.avisworld.com)
Budget (☎ 031-321 100; www.budget.com)
Europcar (☎ 032-671 894; www.europcarcg.com)
Kompas (☎ 020-244 117; www.kompas-car.com)
Meridian Rentacar (☎ 020-234 944; www.meridian
-rentacar.com) A reliable local option with offices in Budva,
Bar and Podgorica; one-day hire starts from €45.
Rokšped (☎ 020-620 000; www.roksped.com)
Sixt (www.sixt.com)

Insurance

Third-party insurance is compulsory and you'll need to be able to prove you have it in order to bring a car into Montenegro (see p168). In general you should get your insurer to issue a Green Card (which may cost extra), an internationally recognised proof of insurance, and check that it lists all the countries you intend to visit. You'll need this in the event of an accident outside the country where the vehicle is insured. The European Accident Statement (known as the 'Constat Amiable' in France) is available from your insurance company and is copied so that each party at an accident can record information for insurance purposes. The Association of British Insurers (www.abi.org.uk) has more details. Never sign accident statements you cannot understand or read – insist on a translation and sign that only if it's acceptable.

Some insurance packages (particularly those covering rental cars) do not include all European countries and Montenegro is often one of those excluded – make sure you check this before you rent your car. When you're renting a car, ensure you check all aspects of the insurance offered, including the excess (you may wish to pay extra to reduce it) and rules regarding where you may or may not drive it (on dirt roads, for example).

Parking

Local parking habits are quite carefree, so it's possible you can be blocked in by someone double-parking next to you. Sometimes parking that looks illegal (eg on footpaths) is actually permitted.

Road Rules

As in the rest of continental Europe, people drive on the right-hand side of the road and overtake on the left. Keep right except when overtaking, and use your indicators for any change of lane and when pulling away from the kerb. You're not allowed to overtake more than one car at a time, whether they are moving or stationary (eg pulled up at a traffic light). School buses can't be overtaken when they stop for passengers to board or alight. Vehicles entering a roundabout have right of way. Standard international road signs are used.

You are required by law to wear a seatbelt (including in the back seat if they're fitted), drive with dipped headlights on (even during the day) and wear a helmet on a motorbike. Children's car seats aren't compulsory but kids under 12 and intoxicated passengers are not allowed in the front seat. Using a mobile

TRANSPORT

phone while driving is prohibited, although plenty of people do it anyway. Driving barefoot is a no-no. These offences could result in fines of between €20 and €300. Penalties for drink-driving are severe and could result in jail time. The legal limit is 0.05% of alcohol in your bloodstream. Police can issue an on-the-spot fine but cannot collect payment (see p160 for advice on what to do if asked for money).

Standard speed limits are 50km/h in built-up areas, 80km/h outside built-up areas and 100km/h on fast roads. Often the limit will change several times on a single stretch of the road because of the mountainous conditions. Excessive speeding (30km over the limit) could lead to your driver's licence being temporarily confiscated.

Cars must carry a set of replacement bulbs, a first-aid kit and a warning triangle.

If you're involved in an accident resulting in major injury or material damage to your or another vehicle, you're legally obliged to report it to the police.

HITCHING

Hitching is never entirely safe and we wouldn't recommend it, but it is a common practice in Montenegro. Wherever you are, there's always a risk when you catch a ride with strangers. It's safer to travel in pairs and to let someone know where you're planning to go. Once you've flagged down a vehicle, it's safer if you sit next to a door you can open. Ask the driver where they are going before you say where

you are going. Trust your instincts if you feel uncomfortable about getting in, and get out at the first sign of trouble. You can find more pointers at www.bugeurope.com/transport /hitch.html and information on ride sharing at http://europe.bugride.com/, www.hitchhik ers.org and www.bugeurope.com.

LOCAL TRANSPORT

Most Montenegrin towns, even Podgorica, are small enough to be travelled by foot. Podgorica is the only city to have a useful local bus network, costing 60c per trip. Taxis are easily found in most towns. If they're not metered, be sure to agree on a fare in advance. Taxi boats are a common sight during summer and can be hailed from the shore for a short trip along the coast or to one of the islands. They're harder to find outside the high season; look for them at the marinas.

TRAIN

Montenegro Railways (Željeznica Crne Gore; ☎ 020-441 211; www.zeljeznica.cg.yu) runs the only passenger train line, heading north from Bar and crossing the country before disappearing into Serbia. The trains are old and stiflingly hot in summer, but they're priced accordingly and the route through the mountains is spectacular. Useful stops include Virpazar, Podgorica, Kolašin, Mojkovac and Bijelo Polje. In January 2006 a failure in the breaking system caused a train to derail in the Morača Canyon, killing 43 people and injuring hundreds more.

Health

CONTENTS

Before You Go   **173**
Insurance   173
Recommended Vaccinations   173
Internet Resources   173
In Transit   **173**
Deep Vein Thrombosis (DVT)   173
Jet Lag & Motion Sickness   174
In Montenegro   **174**
Availability & Cost of Health Care   174
Infectious Diseases   174
Traveller's Diarrhoea   174
Environmental Hazards   174
Travelling with Children   174

Travel health depends on your predeparture preparations, your daily health care while travelling and how you handle any medical problem that develops. The standard of medical care in Montenegro is high, and all foreigners are entitled to emergency medical aid at the very least.

BEFORE YOU GO

Prevention is the key to staying healthy while abroad. A little planning before departure, particularly for pre-existing illnesses, will save trouble later: see your dentist before a long trip, carry a spare pair of contact lenses and glasses, and take your optical prescription with you. Bring medications in their original, labelled, containers. A letter from your physician describing your medical conditions and medications, including generic names, is also a good idea. If you are carrying syringes, be sure to have a physician's letter with you documenting their necessity.

INSURANCE

If you're an EU citizen, you will be covered for most emergency medical care except for emergency repatriation home. Citizens from other countries should find out if there is a reciprocal arrangement for free medical care between their country and Montenegro. If you do need health insurance, strongly consider a policy that covers you for the worst possible scenario, such as an accident requiring an emergency flight home. Find out in advance if your insurance plan will make payments directly to providers or if it will reimburse you later for any overseas health expenditures. The former option is generally preferable, as it doesn't require you to pay out of pocket in a foreign country.

RECOMMENDED VACCINATIONS

The World Health Organization (WHO) recommends that all travellers should be covered for diphtheria, tetanus, measles, mumps, rubella and polio, regardless of their destination. Since most vaccines don't produce immunity until at least two weeks after they're given, visit a physician at least six weeks before departure.

INTERNET RESOURCES

The WHO's publication *International Travel and Health* is revised annually and is available online at www.who.int/ith. Other useful websites include the following:

www.mdtravelhealth.com Travel-health recommendations for every country; updated daily.

www.fitfortravel.scot.nhs.uk General travel advice for the layperson.

www.ageconcern.org.uk Advice on travel for the elderly.

www.mariestopes.org.uk Information on contraception and women's health.

IN TRANSIT

DEEP VEIN THROMBOSIS (DVT)

Blood clots may form in the legs during plane flights, chiefly because of prolonged immobility. The longer the flight, the greater the risk. The chief symptom of DVT is swelling of or pain in the foot, ankle or calf, which is usually (but not always) on just one side. When a blood clot travels to the lungs, it may cause chest pain and breathing difficulties. Travellers with any of these symptoms should immediately seek medical attention.

To prevent the development of DVT on long-distance flights you should walk about the aircraft cabin, contract the leg muscles while sitting, drink plenty of fluids and avoid alcohol.

JET LAG & MOTION SICKNESS

To avoid jet lag (which is common when crossing more than five time zones) try drinking plenty of nonalcoholic fluids and eating light meals. Upon arrival, get exposure to natural sunlight and readjust your schedule (for meals, sleep and so on) as soon as possible.

Antihistamines such as dimenhydrinate (Dramamine) and meclizine (Antivert, Bonine) are usually the first choice for treating motion sickness. A herbal alternative is ginger.

IN MONTENEGRO

AVAILABILITY & COST OF HEALTH CARE

Good health care is readily available in Montenegro and for minor illnesses pharmacists can give valuable advice and sell over-the-counter medication. They can also advise when more specialised help is required and point you in the right direction. The standard of dental care is usually good, but it is sensible to have a dental check-up before a long trip.

INFECTIOUS DISEASES

Tick-borne encephalitis is spread by tick bites. It is a serious infection of the brain and vaccination is advised for those in risk areas who are unable to avoid tick bites (such as campers and hikers). Two doses of vaccine will give a year's protection, three doses up to three years'.

TRAVELLER'S DIARRHOEA

If you develop diarrhoea, be sure to drink plenty of fluids, preferably an oral rehydration solution (eg dioralyte). A few loose stools don't require treatment, but if you start having more than four or five stools a day, you should start taking an antibiotic (usually a quinolone drug) and an antidiarrhoeal agent (such as loperamide). If diarrhoea is bloody, persists for more than 72 hours, or is accompanied by fever, shaking, chills or severe abdominal pain, you should seek medical attention.

ENVIRONMENTAL HAZARDS

Heat Exhaustion & Heatstroke

Heat exhaustion occurs following excessive fluid loss with inadequate replacement of fluids and salt. Symptoms include headache, dizziness and tiredness. Dehydration is already happening by the time you feel thirsty – aim to drink sufficient water to produce pale, diluted urine.

To treat heat exhaustion, replace lost fluids by drinking water and/or fruit juice, and cool the body with cold water and fans. Treat salt loss with salty fluids such as soup or Bovril, or add a little more table salt to food than usual.

Heatstroke is much more serious, resulting in irrational and hyperactive behaviour and eventually loss of consciousness and death. Rapid cooling by spraying the body with water and fanning is ideal. Emergency fluid and electrolyte replacement by intravenous drip is recommended.

Sea Urchins

Watch out for sea urchins around rocky beaches; if you get some of their needles embedded in your skin, olive oil will help to loosen them. If they are not removed, they could become infected. As a precaution wear rubber shoes while walking on the rocks or bathing.

Snake Bites

To avoid getting bitten by snakes, do not walk barefoot or stick your hands into holes or cracks. Half of those bitten by venomous snakes are not actually injected with poison (envenomed). If bitten by a snake, do not panic. Immobilise the bitten limb with a splint (eg a stick) and apply a bandage over the site firmly, similar to a bandage over a sprain. Do not apply a tourniquet, or cut or suck the bite.

Get medical help as soon as possible so that antivenom can be administered if necessary.

TRAVELLING WITH CHILDREN

All travellers with children should know how to treat minor ailments and when to seek medical treatment. Make sure the children are up to date with routine vaccinations, and discuss possible travel vaccines well before departure, as some vaccines are not suitable for children under one year.

In hot moist climates any wound or break in the skin is likely to let in infection. The area should be cleaned and kept dry.

Remember to avoid contaminated food and water. If your child has vomiting or diarrhoea, lost fluid and salts must be replaced. It may be helpful to take rehydration powders for reconstituting with boiled water.

Children should be encouraged to steer clear of dogs and other mammals because of the risk of rabies and other diseases. Any bite, scratch or lick from a warm-blooded, furry animal should be thoroughly cleaned straight away. If you think there is any possibility that the animal is infected with rabies, immediate medical assistance should be sought.

HEALTH

Language

CONTENTS

Pronunciation	176
Accommodation	177
Conversation & Essentials	177
Directions	178
Emergencies	178
Health	178
Language Difficulties	179
Numbers	179
Paperwork	179
Question Words	179
Shopping & Services	179
Time & Dates	180
Transport	180
Travel with Children	181

Montenegrin belongs to the western group of the South Slavic language family. Other languages in this group include Serbian, Croatian, Bosnian and Slovene.

Montenegro's break from the union of Serbia and Montenegro in 2006 (created after the breakup of former Yugoslavia in 1991) has had an impact on the language. Though the official language is now referred to as Montenegrin, in linguistic terms it's not really different from Serbian, Croatian or Bosnian (all formerly known as 'Serbo-Croatian'). The variants are so similar that they are effectively dialects of the one language, with only slight variations in pronunciation and vocabulary. Furthermore, Serbian, Croatian, Bosnian and Albanian are also recognised in Montenegro's Constitution as languages in official use. Albanian, however, is completely unrelated to the four Slavic languages and constitutes a branch of its own within the wider Indo-European language family. It is spoken mainly in the southeastern parts of the country, along the borders with Albania and Kosovo. On the coast you might find that some knowledge of Italian comes in handy as well.

You can enrich your travel experience in Montenegro by using the more extensive language content of Lonely Planet's *Croatian Phrasebook*, which will be fully understood throughout Montenegro. For Albanian, consult Lonely Planet's *Eastern Europe Phrasebook*. For information on food and dining, including lots of useful culinary terms and phrases to help you when eating out, check out p48.

PRONUNCIATION

Written Montenegrin is phonetically consistent, meaning that every letter is pronounced and its sound will not vary from word to word. With regard to the position of stress, only general rules can be given: in most cases the accent falls on the first vowel in a word, and the last syllable of a word is normally not stressed. You don't need to worry about this though, as the stressed syllable is indicated with italics in our pronunciation guides.

Montenegrin can be written in both the Roman and Cyrillic alphabets, and both are in official use. In this chapter we've only given the Roman alphabet in translations, as it tends to dominate nowadays, especially in the tourist areas. However, it's also worth familiarising yourself with the Cyrillic alphabet (opposite), in case you come across it on menus, timetables or street signs.

Many letters in the Montenegrin Roman alphabet are pronounced just like in English. In the following list, specific Montenegrin letters are given along with their pronunciation and their closest English-letter equivalents (as used in our pronunciation guides in this chapter). Note also that the letter 'r' can be used as a vowel (eg *pršut* pr·shut).

c	ts	as the 'ts' in 'cats'
ć	ch	as the 'tu' in 'future'
č	ch	as the 'ch' in 'chop'
đ	j	as the 'j' in 'jury'
dž	j	as the 'dj' in 'adjust'
j	y	as the 'y' in 'young'
lj	ly/l'	as the 'lli' in 'million'
nj	ny/n'	as the 'ny' in 'canyon'
š	sh	as the 'sh' in 'hush'
ž	zh	as the 's' in 'pleasure'

CYRILLIC	SOUND	PRONUNCIATION
А а	a	short as the 'u' in 'cut'; long as in 'father'
Б б	b	as in 'but'
В в	v	as in 'van'
Г г	g	as in 'go'
Д д	d	as the 'd' in 'dog'
Ђ ђ	j	as in 'joke'
Е е	e	short as in 'bet'; long as in 'there'
Ж ж	zh	as the 's' in 'measure'
З з	z	as in 'zoo'
И и	i	short as in 'bit'; long as in 'marine'
Ј ј	y	as in 'young'
К к	k	as in 'kind'
Л л	l	as in 'lamp'
Љ љ	ly/l'	as the 'lli' in 'million'
М м	m	as in 'mat'
Н н	n	as in 'not'
Њ њ	ny/n'	as the 'ny' in 'canyon'
О о	o	short as in 'hot'; long as in 'for'
П п	p	as in 'pick'
Р р	r	as in 'rub' (but rolled)
С с	s	as in 'sing'
Т т	t	as in 'ten'
Ћ ћ	ch	as in 'check'
У у	u	short as in 'put'; long as in 'rule'
Ф ф	f	as in 'fan'
Х х	h	as in 'hot'
Ц ц	ts	as in 'cats'
Ч ч	ch	as in 'change'
Џ џ	j	as the 'j' in 'judge'
Ш ш	sh	as in 'shop'

ACCOMMODATION
I'm looking for a ...
Tražim ...   tra·zhim ...
  camping ground
  kamp   kamp
  guesthouse
  privatni smještaj   pri·vat·ni smyesh·tai
  hotel
  hotel   ho·tel
  youth hostel
  omladinsko prenoćište   om·la·din·sko pre·no·chish·te

Where's a (cheap) hotel?
  Gdje se nalazi (jeftin)   gdye se na·la·zi (yef·tin)
    hotel?   ho·tel
Do you have any rooms available?
  Imate li slobodnih   i·ma·te li slo·bod·nih
    soba?   so·ba

Do you have a ...?
Imate li ...?   i·ma·te li ...
  bed
  krevet   kre·vet
  single room
  jednokrevetnu sobu   yed·no·kre·vet·nu so·bu
  double/twin bedroom
  dvokrevetnu sobu   dvo·kre·vet·nu so·bu
  room with a bathroom
  sobu sa kupatilom   so·bu sa ku·pa·ti·lom

How much is it ...?
Koliko košta ...?   ko·li·ko kosh·ta ...
  per night
  za noć   za noch
  per person
  po osobi   po o·so·bi

MAKING A RESERVATION
(for written and phone inquiries)

From ...	*Od ...*	od ...
To ...	*Do ...*	do ...
Date	*Datum*	da·tum
credit card	*kreditna karta*	kre·dit·na kar·ta
number	*broj*	broy
expiry date	*rok važenja*	rok va·zhe·nya

I'd like to book ...
  Želim da rezervišem ...
  zhe·lim da re·zer·vi·shem ...
In the name of ...
  Na ime ...
  na i·me ...
Please confirm availability and price.
  Molim potvrdite ima li slobodnih soba i cijenu.
  mo·lim pot·vr·di·te i·ma li slo·bod·nih so·ba
  i tsi·ye·nu

May I see it?
  Mogu li da vidim?   mo·gu li da vi·dim
Where is the bathroom?
  Gdje je kupatilo?   gdye ye ku·pa·ti·lo
Where is the toilet?
  Gdje je toalet?   gdye ye to·a·let
I'm leaving today.
  Ja odlazim danas.   ya od·la·zim da·nas

CONVERSATION & ESSENTIALS
Montenegrin has both polite and informal modes of address (indicated in this chapter by the abbreviations 'pol' and 'inf'). Use the polite form when addressing older people, officials or service staff.

LANGUAGE

Hello.	Zdravo.	zdra·vo
Goodbye.	Do viđenja.	do vi·je·nya
Yes.	Da.	da
No.	Ne.	ne
Please.	Molim.	mo·lim
Thank you.	Hvala.	hva·la
You're welcome.	Nema na čemu.	ne·ma na che·mu
Excuse me.	Oprostite.	o·pro·sti·te
Sorry.	Žao mi je.	zha·o mi ye
Just a minute.	Samo momenat.	sa·mo mo·me·nat

Where are you from?
Odakle ste/si? (pol/inf)   o·da·kle ste/si
What's your name?
Kako se zovete?   ka·ko se zo·ve·te (pol)
Kako se zoveš?   ka·ko se zo·vesh (inf)
My name is ...
Zovem se ...   zo·vem se ...
I'm from ...
Ja sam iz ...   ya sam iz ...
Do you like ...?
Da li volite ...?   da li vo·li·te ... (pol)
Da li voliš ...?   da li vo·lish ... (inf)
I (don't) like ...
Ja (ne) volim ...   ya (ne) vo·lim ...

DIRECTIONS
Where is ...?
Gdje je ...?   gdye ye ...
What's the address?
Koja je adresa?   ko·ya ye a·dre·sa
Can you show me (on the map)?
Možete li da mi   mo·zhe·te li da mi
pokažete (na mapi)?   po·ka·zhe·te (na ma·pi)
Go straight ahead.
Idite pravo naprijed.   i·di·te pra·vo na·pri·yed
Turn left.
Skrenite lijevo.   skre·ni·te li·ye·vo
Turn right.
Skrenite desno.   skre·ni·te des·no
at the corner
na uglu   na u·glu
at the traffic lights
na semaforu   na se·ma·fo·ru

SIGNS

Ulaz	Entrance
Izlaz	Exit
Otvoreno	Open
Zatvoreno	Closed
Zabranjeno	Prohibited
Toaleti/WC	Toilets/WC
Muški	Men
Ženski	Women

EMERGENCIES

Help!
Upomoć!   u·po·moch
There's been an accident!
Desila se nezgoda!   de·si·la se nez·go·da
I'm lost.
Izgubio sam se.   iz·gu·bi·o sam se (m)
Izgubila sam se.   iz·gu·bi·la sam se (f)
Leave me alone!
Ostavite me na miru!   o·sta·vi·te me na mi·ru
Call a doctor!
Zovite ljekara!   zo·vi·te lye·ka·ra
Call the police!
Zovite policiju!   zo·vi·te po·li·tsi·yu

---

behind	iza	i·za
in front of	ispred	i·spred
far (from)	daleko (od)	da·le·ko (od)
near	blizu	bli·zu
next to	pored	po·red
opposite	nasuprot	na·su·prot

bay	zaliv	za·liv
beach	plaža	pla·zha
bridge	most	most
canyon	kanjon	ka·nyon
castle	zamak	za·mak
cathedral	katedrala	ka·te·dra·la
church	crkva	tsr·kva
island	ostrvo	os·tr·vo
lake	jezero	ye·ze·ro
mausoleum	mauzolej	ma·u·zo·ley
monastery	manastir	ma·nas·tir
mountain	planina	pla·ni·na
mountain hut	katun	ka·tun
national park	nacionalni park	na·tsi·o·nal·ni park
old town	stari grad	sta·ri grad
palace	palata/dvor	pa·la·ta/dvor
river	rijeka	ri·ye·ka
ruins	ruševine	ru·she·vi·ne
sea	more	mo·re
(main) square	(glavni) trg	(glav·ni) trg
summer house	ljetnikovac	lyet·ni·ko·vats
tower	kula	ku·la

HEALTH
I'm ill.
Ja sam bolestan.   ya sam bo·le·stan (m)
Ja sam bolesna.   ya sam bo·le·sna (f)
I've been injured.
Ja sam povrijeđen.   ya sam po·vri·ye·jen (m)
Ja sam povrijeđena.   ya sam po·vri·ye·je·na (f)
It hurts here.
Boli me ovdje.   bo·li me ov·dye

I'm ...
Ja imam ...
ya *i*·mam ...

asthmatic	*astmu*	*ast*·mu
diabetic	*dijabetes*	di·ya·*be*·tes
epileptic	*epilepsiju*	e·pi·*lep*·si·yu

I'm allergic to ...
Ja sam alergičan/alergična na ... (m/f)
ya sam a·*ler*·gi·chan/a·*ler*·gich·na na ...

antibiotics	*antibiotike*	an·ti·bi·*o*·ti·ke
penicillin	*penicilin*	pe·ni·*tsi*·lin
bees	*pčele*	*pche*·le
nuts	*razne orahe*	*raz*·ne o·ra·he
peanuts	*kikiriki*	ki·ki·*ri*·ki

antiseptic	*antiseptik*	an·ti·*sep*·tik
aspirin	*aspirin*	as·*pi*·rin
condoms	*kondomi*	kon·*do*·mi
contraceptive	*sredstva za kontracepciju*	*sreds*·tva za kon·tra·*tsep*·tsi·yu
diarrhoea	*proliv*	*pro*·liv
medicine	*lijek*	*li*·yek
nausea	*mučnina*	much·*ni*·na
sunscreen	*krema za sunčanje*	*kre*·ma za *sun*·cha·nye
tampons	*tamponi*	tam·*po*·ni

LANGUAGE DIFFICULTIES
Do you speak (English)?
Govorite/Govoriš li (engleski)? (pol/inf)
go·vo·ri·te/*go*·vo·rish li (*en*·gle·ski)
Does anyone here speak (English)?
Da li neko govori (engleski)?
da li *ne*·ko *go*·vo·ri (*en*·gle·ski)
What's this called in Montenegrin?
Kako se ovo zove na crnogorskom?
ka·ko se *o*·vo *zo*·ve na tsr·*no*·gor·skom
What does ... mean?
Šta znači ...?
shta *zna*·chi ...
I (don't) understand.
Ja (ne) razumijem.
ya (ne) ra·*zu*·mi·yem
Could you write it down, please?
Možete li to da napišete?
mo·zhe·te li to da *na*·pi·she·te

NUMBERS
0	*nula*	*nu*·la
1	*jedan*	*ye*·dan
2	*dva*	dva
3	*tri*	tri
4	*četiri*	*che*·ti·ri
5	*pet*	pet
6	*šest*	shest
7	*sedam*	*se*·dam
8	*osam*	*o*·sam
9	*devet*	*de*·vet
10	*deset*	*de*·set
11	*jedanaest*	ye·*da*·na·est
12	*dvanaest*	*dva*·na·est
13	*trinaest*	*tri*·na·est
14	*četrnaest*	che·*tr*·na·est
15	*petnaest*	*pet*·na·est
16	*šesnaest*	*shes*·na·est
17	*sedamnaest*	se·*dam*·na·est
18	*osamnaest*	o·*sam*·na·est
19	*devetnaest*	de·*vet*·na·est
20	*dvadeset*	*dva*·de·set
21	*dvadeset jedan*	*dva*·de·set *ye*·dan
22	*dvadeset dva*	*dva*·de·set dva
30	*trideset*	*tri*·de·set
40	*četrdeset*	che·tr·*de*·set
50	*pedeset*	pe·*de*·set
60	*šezdeset*	shez·*de*·set
70	*sedamdeset*	se·dam·*de*·set
80	*osamdeset*	o·sam·*de*·set
90	*devedeset*	de·ve·*de*·set
100	*sto*	sto
1000	*hiljadu*	*hi*·lya·du

PAPERWORK
name	*ime*	*i*·me
nationality	*nacionalnost*	na·tsi·o·*nal*·nost
date of birth	*datum rođenja*	*da*·tum ro·*je*·nya
place of birth	*mjesto rođenja*	*mye*·sto ro·*je*·nya
sex/gender	*pol*	pol
passport	*pasoš*	*pa*·sosh
visa	*viza*	*vi*·za

QUESTION WORDS
Who?	*Ko?*	ko
What?	*Šta?*	shta
What is it?	*Šta je?*	shta ye
When?	*Kada?*	*ka*·da
Where?	*Gdje?*	gdye
Which?	*Koji/Koja/Koje?* (m/f/n)	*ko*·yi/*ko*·ya/*ko*·ye
Why?	*Zašto?*	za·*shto*
How?	*Kako?*	*ka*·ko
How much?	*Koliko?*	ko·*li*·ko

SHOPPING & SERVICES
I'm just looking.
Ja samo razgledam.
ya *sa*·mo *raz*·gle·dam
I'd like to buy (an adaptor plug).
Želim da kupim (utikač za adapter).
zhe·lim da *ku*·pim (u·*ti*·kach za a·*dap*·ter)

May I look at it?
Mogu li to da pogledam?
mo·gu li to da po·gle·dam

How much is it?	*Koliko košta?*	ko·li·ko kosh·ta
It's cheap.	*To je jeftino.*	to ye yef·ti·no
It's too expensive.	*To je preskupo.*	to ye pre·sku·po
I like it.	*Sviđa mi se.*	svi·ja mi se
I'll take it.	*Uzeću ovo.*	u·ze·chu o·vo

Do you accept ...?
Da li prihvatate ...?
da li pri·hva·ta·te ...

| **credit cards** | *kreditne kartice* | kre·dit·ne kar·ti·tse |
| **travellers cheques** | *putničke čekove* | put·nich·ke che·ko·ve |

more	*više*	vi·she
less	*manje*	ma·nye
bigger	*veći/veća/ veće* (m/f/n)	ve·chi/ve·cha/ ve·che
smaller	*manji/manja/ manje* (m/f/n)	ma·nyi/ma·nya/ ma·nye

Where's ...	*Gdje je ...?*	gdye ye ...
a bank	*banka*	ban·ka
the church	*crkva*	tsrk·va
the city centre	*centar grada*	tsen·tar gra·da
the ... embassy	*... ambasada*	... am·ba·sa·da
the hospital	*bolnica*	bol·ni·tsa
the market	*pijaca*	pi·ya·tsa
the museum	*muzej*	mu·zey
the police	*policija*	po·li·tsi·ya
the post office	*pošta*	posh·ta
a public phone	*javni telefon*	yav·ni te·le·fon
a public toilet	*javni toalet*	yav·ni to·a·let
the tourist office	*turistički biro*	tu·ris·tich·ki bi·ro

TIME & DATES

What time is it?
Koliko je sati? ko·li·ko ye sa·ti
It's (one) o'clock.
(Jedan) je sat. (ye·dan) ye sat
It's (10) o'clock.
(Deset) je sati. (de·set) ye sa·ti

in the morning
ujutro u·yu·tro
in the afternoon
poslijepodne po·sli·ye·pod·ne
in the evening
uveče u·ve·che

today	*danas*	da·nas
tomorrow	*sjutra*	syu·tra
yesterday	*juče*	yu·che

Monday	*ponedjeljak*	po·ne·dye·lyak
Tuesday	*utorak*	u·to·rak
Wednesday	*srijeda*	sri·ye·da
Thursday	*četvrtak*	chet·vr·tak
Friday	*petak*	pe·tak
Saturday	*subota*	su·bo·ta
Sunday	*nedjelja*	ne·dye·lya

January	*januar*	ya·nu·ar
February	*februar*	feb·ru·ar
March	*mart*	mart
April	*april*	ap·ril
May	*maj*	mai
June	*jun*	yun
July	*jul*	yul
August	*avgust*	av·gust
September	*septembar*	sep·tem·bar
October	*oktobar*	ok·to·bar
November	*novembar*	no·vem·bar
December	*decembar*	de·tsem·bar

TRANSPORT
Public Transport
What time does the ... leave/arrive?
U koliko sati kreće/stiže ...?
u ko·li·ko sa·ti kre·che/sti·zhe ...

boat	*brod*	brod
bus	*autobus*	a·u·to·bus
plane	*avion*	a·vi·on
train	*voz*	voz

I'd like a ... ticket.
Htio/Htjela bih jednu ... kartu. (m/f)
hti·o/htye·la bih yed·nu ... kar·tu

one-way	*jednosmjernu*	yed·no·smyer·nu
return	*povratnu*	po·vrat·nu
1st class	*prvorazrednu*	pr·vo·raz·red·nu
2nd class	*drugorazrednu*	dru·go·raz·red·nu

I want to go to ...
Želim da idem u ... zhe·lim da i·dem u ...
The train has been delayed.
Voz kasni. voz kas·ni
The train has been cancelled.
Voz je otkazan. voz ye ot·ka·zan

the first	*prvi*	pr·vi
the last	*poslednji*	pos·led·nyi
platform	*peron*	pe·ron
ticket office	*blagajna*	bla·gai·na
timetable	*red vožnje*	red vozh·nye
station	*stanica*	sta·ni·tsa

Private Transport

I'd like to hire a/an ...
Htio/Htjela bih da iznajmim ... (m/f)
*hti-*o/*htye*-la bih da *iz*-nai-mim ...

bicycle	*bicikl*	bi-*tsi*-kl
car	*automobil*	a-u-to-*mo*-bil
4WD	*džip*	jip
motorbike	*motocikl*	mo-to-*tsi*-kl

ROAD SIGNS

Opasno	Danger
Obilaznica	Detour
Ulaz	Entry
Izlaz	Exit
Ulaz Zabranjen	No Entry
Zabranjeno Preticanje	No Overtaking
Zabranjeno Parkiranje	No Parking
Jedan Pravac	One Way
Uspori	Slow Down
Putarina	Toll

Is this the road to ...?
Je li ovo put za ...?   ye li *o*-vo put za ...
Where's a service station?
Gdje je benzinska   gdye ye *ben*-zin-ska
stanica?   *sta*-ni-tsa
Please fill it up.
Pun rezervoar molim.   pun re-zer-*vo*-ar *mo*-lim
I'd like ... litres.
Treba mi ... litara.   *tre*-ba mi ... *li*-ta-ra

diesel	*dizel gorivo*	*di*-zel *go*-ri-vo
petrol	*benzin*	*ben*-zin

(How long) Can I park here?
(Koliko dugo) Mogu ovdje da parkiram?
(ko-*li*-ko *du*-go) *mo*-gu *ov*-dye da *par*-ki-ram
I need a mechanic.
Treba mi automehaničar.
tre-ba mi *a*-u-to-me-*ha*-ni-char

Also available from Lonely Planet:
Croatian Phrasebook

The car/motorbike has broken down (at ...)
Automobil/Motocikl se pokvario (u ...).
a-u-to-*mo*-bil/mo-to-*tsi*-kl se pok-*va*-ri-o (u ...).
The car/motorbike won't start.
Automobil/Motocikl neće da upali.
a-u-to-*mo*-bil/mo-to-*tsi*-kl ne-che da *u*-pa-li
I have a flat tyre.
Imam probušenu gumu.
i-mam *pro*-bu-she-nu *gu*-mu
I've run out of petrol.
Nestalo mi je benzina.
ne-*sta*-lo mi ye ben-*zi*-na
I've had an accident.
Imao/Imala sam saobraćajnu nezgodu. (m/f)
i-ma-o/*i*-ma-la sam sa-o-bra-chai-nu nez-go-du

TRAVEL WITH CHILDREN

Are children allowed?
Da li je dozvoljen pristup djeci?
da li ye *doz*-vo-lyen *pri*-stup *dye*-tsi

Do you have (a/an) ...?
Imate li ...?
i-ma-te li ...
   baby change room
   sobu za povijanje beba
   so-bu za po-*vi*-ya-nye *be*-ba
   car baby seat
   sjedište za dijete
   sye-dish-te za di-*ye*-te
   child-minding service
   usluge čuvanja djece
   u-slu-ge *chu*-va-nya *dye*-tse
   children's menu
   dječji jelovnik
   dyech-yi ye-*lov*-nik
   (disposable) nappies/diapers
   pelene (za jednokratnu upotrebu)
   pe-le-ne (za yed-*no*-krat-nu *u*-po-tre-bu)
   (English-speaking) babysitter
   dadilju (koja govori engleski)
   da-di-lyu (*ko*-ya *go*-vo-ri en-*gle*-ski)
   highchair
   visoku stolicu za bebe
   vi-so-ku *sto*-li-tsu za *be*-be
   infant milk formula
   hranu za bebe
   hra-nu za *be*-be
   potty
   nošu
   no-shu
   pusher/stroller
   dubak
   du-bak

LANGUAGE

Glossary

aerodrom – airport
autocamp – camping ground for tents and caravans
Avars – Eastern European people who waged war against Byzantium from the 6th to 9th centuries

bb – in an address the letters 'bb' following a street name (eg Jadranski put bb) stand for *bez broja* (without number), indicating that the building has no street number
Bokelj – inhabitant of Boka Kotorska (Bay of Kotor)
Bosniak – Slavic Muslim, not necessarily from Bosnia
burek – heavy pastry stuffed with meat or cheese

čaršija – old market area
Cattaro – Venetian name for Kotor
ćevapčići – small spicy beef or pork sausages
čojstvo i junaštvo – literally 'humanity and bravery' (ie the concept of chivalry present in Montenegrin culture)
crkva – church
Crna Gora – Montenegrin name for Montenegro (literally 'black mountain')

dnevna karta – day ticket
dolazak – arrivals
dom – dormitory, mountain cottage or lodge
Dom kulture – cultural centre
Dom zdravlja – medical centre
donji (m), **donja** (f) – lower
Duklja – early Serbian state considered a precursor of Montenegro
džamija – mosque

galerija – gallery
garderoba – left-luggage office
Glagolitic – ancient Slavic alphabet (precursor of the Cyrillic alphabet) created by Greek missionaries Cyril and Methodius
gora – mountain
gornji (m), **gornja** (f) – upper
gorske oči (literally 'mountain eyes') – name for glacial lakes in the mountainous regions
grad – city
guslar – singer/composer of epic poetry accompanied by the *gusle*
gusle – one-stringed folk instrument

hajduk – Balkan outlaw during the period of Ottoman rule
hammam – Turkish bathhouse
Hitna pomoć – emergency clinic

Illyrians – ancient inhabitants of the Adriatic coast, defeated by the Romans in the 2nd century BC
ispod sača – (meat) roasted under a metal lid covered with hot coals

jelovnik – menu
jezero – lake

kanjon – canyon
karst – highly porous limestone and dolomitic rock
karta – ticket
katun – traditional shepherds' mountain hut
kino – cinema
klapa – a traditional form of unaccompanied singing from Dalmatia
klima – air conditioning
kolo – lively Slavic round dance in which men and women alternate in the circle
konoba – the traditional term for a small, intimate dining spot, often located in a cellar; now applies to a wide variety of restaurants; usually a simple, family-run establishment
kula – a blocky tower-like house built for defence
Kulturni centar – cultural centre

mali (m), **mala** (f) – little
manastir – monastery
millet – system of administration in the Ottoman Empire that allowed subject peoples religious autonomy
most – bridge
muzej – museum

novi (m), **nova** (f) – new

obala – waterfront
odlazak – departures; also *polazak*
oro – traditional Montenegrin circle dance
ostrvo – island

palačinke – pancakes
Partisans – communist-led WWII resistance fighters
pekara – bakery
pivo – beer
plaža – beach
polazak – departures; also *odlazak*
polje – field
pršut – smoke-dried ham
put – path; road; trail

račun – bill; cheque
rakija – fruit brandy
ražnjići – small chunks of pork grilled on a skewer
restoran – restaurant
rijeka – river
rruga – Albanian word for 'street' (used in Ulcinj street names)

šetalište – walkway
sladoled – ice cream
sobe (pl) – rooms (available for hire)
stara maslina – literally 'old olive', a famous 2000-year-old tree in Bar
stari (m), **stara** (f) – old
Stari Grad – Old Town
stećci – mysterious carved stone monuments from the Middle Ages found throughout northern Montenegro
sveti (m), **sveta** (f) – saint

trq – square
turbofolk – version of Serbian music, a mix of folk and pop

ulica – street
Uspenje Bogorodice – literally 'the falling into sleep of the mother of God', an Orthodox feast similar to the Catholic concept of the Assumption

veliki (m), **velika** (f) – large
Vlachs – Central and Eastern European people believed to be the remnants of the Roman population (either ethnically Latin or Romanised Illyrians)
vladika – prince-bishop
vrh – peak; summit

xhami – Albanian word for 'mosque'

Zakonik – legal code (historic term)
Zdravstvena stanica – medical centre or emergency clinic
Zeta – early Serbian state considered a precursor of Montenegro
Zimmer – German word for 'rooms' (available for hire)

The Authors

PETER DRAGIČEVIĆ   Coordinating Author

After a dozen years working for newspapers and magazines in both his native New Zealand and Australia, Peter finally gave in to Kiwi wanderlust, giving up staff jobs to chase his typically antipodean diverse roots around much of Europe. While it was family ties that first drew him to the Balkans, it's the history, natural beauty, convoluted politics, cheap *rakija* and, most importantly, the intriguing people, that keep bringing him back. He's contributed to over a dozen Lonely Planet titles, including writing the Macedonia and Albania chapters for the previous edition of the *Eastern Europe* guide.

CONTRIBUTING AUTHORS

Will Gourlay wrote the History chapter. Will ate his first *ćevapčići* at a child's birthday party at Melbourne's Yugoslav consulate in the mid-'70s. Some 25 years later he made his first foray into the Balkans and was immediately hooked on the region, its history and its diverse cultures. Subsequent trips to Montenegro and parts thereabouts have only served to heighten his addiction and that of his family. A travel junky with tertiary degrees in history and editing, Will has worked as a commissioning editor for Lonely Planet for several years. He is contemplating learning the *gusle* and spends entire days dreaming of the opal seas, chalky hills and plump pomegranates of the Boka Kotorska.

Vesna Marić wrote the Gateway City: Dubrovnik chapter. Vesna was born in Bosnia and Hercegovina while it was still a part of Yugoslavia, and she has never been able to see Croatia as a foreign country. A lifetime lover of Dalmatia's beaches, pine trees, food and wine, she found researching this chapter a true delight.

LONELY PLANET AUTHORS

Why is our travel information the best in the world? It's simple: our authors are passionate, dedicated travellers. They don't take freebies in exchange for positive coverage so you can be sure the advice you're given is impartial. They travel widely to all the popular spots, and off the beaten track. They don't research using just the internet or phone. They discover new places not included in any other guidebook. They personally visit thousands of hotels, restaurants, palaces, trails, galleries, temples and more. They speak with dozens of locals every day to make sure you get the kind of insider knowledge only a local could tell you. They take pride in getting all the details right, and in telling it how it is. Think you can do it? Find out how at **lonelyplanet.com**.

Behind the Scenes

THIS BOOK

This is the 1st edition of Lonely Planet's *Montenegro*. It was researched and written by Peter Dragičević. Vesna Marić wrote the Gateway City: Dubrovnik chapter and Will Gourlay wrote the History chapter. The Health chapter was adapted from material originally written by Dr Caroline Evans. This guidebook was commissioned in Lonely Planet's London office, and produced by the following:

Commissioning Editors Will Gourlay, Fiona Buchan
Coordinating Editor Branislava Vladisavljević
Coordinating Cartographer Jolyon Philcox
Coordinating Layout Designer Pablo Gastar
Managing Editor Bruce Evans
Managing Cartographer Mark Griffiths
Managing Layout Designer Laura Jane
Assisting Editor Helen Yeates
Assisting Cartographers Alex Leung, Andras Bogdanovits
Cover Designer Pepi Bluck
Project Manager Rachel Imeson

Thanks to Melanie Dankel, Huw Fowles, Quentin Frayne, Jennifer Garrett, James Hardy, Clara Monitto, Fabrice Rocher, Celia Wood

THANKS

PETER DRAGIČEVIĆ

A huge thanks to all the wonderful people who helped me along the way, especially my beloved Dragičević cousins, Hayley and Jack Delf, Goran and Jadranka Marković, Dragana Ostojić, Slavko Marjanović, Danica Ćeranić, Kirsi Hyvaerinen and David Mills. Extra special thanks to Milomir Jukanović and to my enthusiastic editor Will Gourlay.

WILL GOURLAY

Thanks to Moge and Jason who pushed so hard for this book to get a green light; also to author extraordinaire Peter for doing such an outstanding job; and to Brana for all of her regional and linguistic expertise. Finally, extra special thanks to Claire, Bridget and Tommy, my co-adventurers in Montenegro and parts thereabouts, and my all-time favourite Balkan travel companions. *Hajdemo!*

VESNA MARIĆ

Hvala to Maja Gilja, my mother, Toni and Marina Ćavar, Ružica, Stipe, Ante, Dana and Loreta Barać. Also *hvala* to Kristina Hajduka, and Janica and Matej. Thanks to Gabriel and all the travellers I chatted to along the way. Thanks also to Anja Mutić and William Gourlay.

ACKNOWLEDGMENTS

Many thanks to the following for the use of their content:

Globe on title page ©Mountain High Maps 1993 Digital Wisdom, Inc.

SEND US YOUR FEEDBACK

We love to hear from travellers – your comments keep us on our toes and help make our books better. Our well-travelled team reads every word on what you loved or loathed about this book. Although we cannot reply individually to postal submissions, we always guarantee that your feedback goes straight to the appropriate authors, in time for the next edition. Each person who sends us information is thanked in the next edition – and the most useful submissions are rewarded with a free book.

To send us your updates – and find out about Lonely Planet events, newsletters and travel news – visit our award-winning website: **lonelyplanet.com/contact**.

Note: we may edit, reproduce and incorporate your comments in Lonely Planet products such as guidebooks, websites and digital products, so let us know if you don't want your comments reproduced or your name acknowledged. For a copy of our privacy policy visit lonelyplanet.com/privacy.

THE LONELY PLANET STORY

Fresh from an epic journey across Europe, Asia and Australia in 1972, Tony and Maureen Wheeler sat at their kitchen table stapling together notes. The first Lonely Planet guidebook, *Across Asia on the Cheap*, was born.

Travellers snapped up the guides. Inspired by their success, the Wheelers began publishing books to Southeast Asia, India and beyond. Demand was prodigious, and the Wheelers expanded the business rapidly to keep up. Over the years, Lonely Planet extended its coverage to every country and into the virtual world via lonelyplanet.com and the Thorn Tree message board.

As Lonely Planet became a globally loved brand, Tony and Maureen received several offers for the company. But it wasn't until 2007 that they found a partner whom they trusted to remain true to the company's principles of travelling widely, treading lightly and giving sustainably. In October of that year, BBC Worldwide acquired a 75% share in the company, pledging to uphold Lonely Planet's commitment to independent travel, trustworthy advice and editorial independence.

Today, Lonely Planet has offices in Melbourne, London and Oakland, with over 500 staff members and 300 authors. Tony and Maureen are still actively involved with Lonely Planet. They're travelling more often than ever, and they're devoting their spare time to charitable projects. And the company is still driven by the philosophy of *Across Asia on the Cheap*: 'All you've got to do is decide to go and the hardest part is over. So go!'

Internal photographs: Bertrand Gardel/Hemis/Corbis p54 (#1); Peter Dragičević p55 (#3), p59 (#3); Rafael Estefania p56 (#1); Graham Lawrence/Photolibrary p56 (#2); Diomedia/Photolibrary p58 (#1), p60 (#1); Tony P Eveling/Photolibrary p59 (#2); all other photographs by Lonely Planet Images, and by Patrick Horton p53, p57 (#3), (#4); Shannon Bruce Nace p54 (#2). All images are the copyright of the photographers unless otherwise indicated. Many of the images in this guide are available for licensing from Lonely Planet Images: www.lonelyplanetimages.com.

Index

A

accommodation 151-2, *see also*
  ecolodges, *katuns*, mountain huts
activities 18, 152-5, *see also individual*
  activities
Ada Bojana 118
Adriatic coast 94-119, **95**
  climate 96
  history 95-6
  itineraries 20-1
  travel to/from 96
  travel within 96
Adventure Race Montenegro 159
air travel
  airlines 163-5
  airports 163-5
  carbon-offset schemes 164
  deep vein thrombosis 173-4
  jet lag 174
  tickets 165-6
  to/from Dubrovnik 163-7
  to/from Montenegro 163-5
Albanian language 114, 176
animals 62-5, *see also individual species*
archaeological sites, *see* ruins
architecture 42, *see also kulas*, palazzos
area codes 161, *see also inside front*
  cover
art galleries, *see* museums & galleries
arts 41-3, *see also individual arts*
ATMs 161
Austria-Hungary 31, 32, 33, 74, 81
Avar people 25

B

Balkan Wars 33
Balkans Peace Park 64, 65, 150
Balšić family 26-7, 28, 96
Bar 110-13, **111**
  accommodation 112
  drinking 113
  emergency services 111
  entertainment 113
  festivals 112
  food 112-13
  medical services 111
  sights 111-12
  tourist offices 111
  travel to/from 113
  travel within 113

bars 46
basketball 40
Bay of Kotor 73-93, **75**, 4, 11
  climate 75
  history 74-5
  itineraries 20-1
  travel to/from 75-6
  travel within 76
beaches 18
  Ada Bojana 118
  Bečići 102
  Belani 90
  Buljarica 107
  Dobreč 93
  Drobni Pijesak 109
  itineraries 23
  Jaz Beach 102
  Krtole 92
  Ladies' Beach 116
  Lučice 107
  Luštica Peninsula 93
  Mala Plaža 116
  Miločer 106
  Mirišta 93
  Mogren 98
  Morinj 81
  Murići 128
  Pržno (Luštica Peninsula) 93
  Pržno (Sveti Stefan) 106
  Rafailovići 102
  Queen's Beach 106
  Slovenska 98-9
  St Mark's Island 92
  Šušanj 111
  Sveti Stefan 103-5, **104**, 6, 54-5
  Velika Plaža 118
  Žanjice 93
bears 62, 122, 143
Bečići 102-3
bicycle travel
  to/from Montenegro 167
  within Montenegro 170
Bijelo Polje 145-6
Biogradska Gora National Park 64,
  141-2, 8
birds 62-5, *see also individual*
  species
birdwatching 153
  Ada Bojana 118
  Lake Šas 119

Lake Skadar National Park 126-9
  Velika Plaža 118
Bjelasica Mountains 141
Black Lake 142, 8
Blue Grotto 93
boating 153, *see also* jet skis, yachting
  Bečići 102
  Budva 100
  Herceg Novi 78
  Kotor 86
  Lake Krupac 136
  Lake Plav 149
  Lake Skadar 126-9
  Petrovac 108
  Plavnica 129
  Rafailovići 102
  Sveti Stefan 105
  Vranjina 129
boat tours
  Herceg Novi 78
  Kotor 86
  Murići 128
  Petrovac 108
  Plavnica 129
  Tivat 90-1
  Virpazar 127
boat travel, *see also* ferries, taxi boats
  to/from Montenegro 169-70
  within Montenegro 172
Bojana River 62, 118
Boka Kotorska, *see* Bay of Kotor
Boka Navy Day 86
Boka Night 87
books, *see also* literature
  history 19, 26, 27, 28, 29, 31, 33,
    34, 35, 40
  politics 34, 35
  travel 19, 29, 37
border crossings 163, 169
Brezojevica Monastery 149
bridges
  Most na Moštanici 136
  Tara Bridge 144, 60
Budva 96-102, **97**, **99**, 6
  accommodation 100-1
  activities 99-100
  beaches 98-9
  drinking 101-2
  emergency services 97
  entertainment 101-2

Budva *continued*
  festivals 100
  food 101
  Greek myths 98
  internet access 97
  medical services 97
  shopping 102
  sights 97-9
  tourist offices 97
  tours 99-100
  travel to/from 102
  travel within 102
bus travel
  to/from Montenegro 168
  within Montenegro 170
business hours 155, *see also inside front cover*
Byzantine Empire 24, 25, 26

C
cafes 46, **54**
camping 152
canyons
  Morača Canyon 138, **8**
  Piva Canyon 136
  Tara Canyon 143-4, **58**
car travel, *see also* drives
  dangers 158
  driving licenses 171
  hire 171
  insurance 171
  organisations 170
  road rules 171-2
  to/from Montenegro 168
  within Montenegro 170-2
carnivals, *see* festivals
cathedrals, *see* Catholic churches, churches
Catholic churches 39
  Church of the Birth of our Lady 89
  St Anthony's Church 90
  St Eustace's Church 83
  St Jerome's Church 78
  St John's Church (Budva) 98
  St John's Church (Prčanj) 89
  St Mary Koleđata Church 86
  St Matthew's Church 83
  St Nicholas' Church (Bar) 112
  St Nicholas' Church (Perast) 82

St Nicholas' Church (Prčanj) 89
St Tryphon's Cathedral 86
caves
  Blue Grotto 93
  Obodska Cave 127
cell phones 161
Cervantes, Miguel de 28, 116
Cetinje 123-6, **124**, **57**
  accommodation 126
  food 126
  medical services 123
  museums 123-5
  sights 123-6
  tourist offices 123
  travel to/from 126
Cetinje Monastery 125
children, travel with 155-7
  food 48
  health 174-5
churches, *see also* Catholic churches
  Archangel Michael's Church 78
  Court Church (Cetinje) 125
  Elijah's Church 107
  Holy Sunday Church 107
  Holy Trinity Church (Budva) 98
  Holy Trinity Church (Island of Flowers) 92
  Lake Skadar islands 128
  Nikšić Cathedral 134
  Our-Lady-of-the-Rock Church 82, **10**
  St John's Church (Stari Bar) 114
  St Luke's Church 86
  St Mary's Church 90
  St Mary's in Punta 98
  St Nicholas' Cathedral (Ulcinj) 115-16
  St Nicholas' Church (Kotor) 86
  St Nicholas' Church (St Nicholas' Island) 103
  St Roko's Church 90
  St Sava's Church 98
  St Thomas' Church 107
  Sts Peter & Paul Church (Bijelo Polje) 145-6
  Sts Peter & Paul Church (Risan) 81
  Temple of Christ's Resurrection 131
  Vlach Church 125-6
cinema 41-2
clans 29
climate 16, 75, 96, 122, 138, 158
Coastal Mountain Traversal 80
consulates 159
costs 16, *see also inside front cover*

credit cards 161
Crnojević family 27-8
Crnojević River 127
Crno jezero 142, **8**
Croats 25, 74, 84, 90
cruises, *see* boating, boat tours
culture 36-43
customs regulations 158
cycling, *see* bicycle travel, mountain biking
Cyrillic alphabet 25, 26, 39, 176, 177

D
Dalmatian pelican 63, 126
dance 42, *see also* oro
Danilovgrad 133
deep vein thrombosis 173-4
development projects 65, 90, 92, 96, 102, 118
diarrhoea 174
Đilas, Milovan 34
Đukanović, Milo 35
disabilities, travellers with 162
diving 153-4
  Bay of Kotor 78
  Budva 100
  Dobrota 83
  Lapčići 103
  Petrovac 108
  Pržno (Sveti Stefan) 106
  responsible travel 154
  Ulcinj 116
Dobreč 93
Dobrilovina Monastery 144
Dobrota 83-4
drinks 45-6, *see also rakija*, wine
  customs 48
  language 49-50
drives 140
  Bay of Kotor 76, 140, **75**, **4**, **11**
  dangers 158
  itineraries 22
  Kotor–Cetinje 88, 140, **59**
  Mojkovac–Žabljak 140, 145
  Nikšić–Šćepan Polje 136, 140
  Plav–Andrijevica 140, 148
  Podgorica–Kolašin 138, 140, **8**
  Virpazar–Ulcinj 128, 140
driving licenses 171
Drobni Pijesak 109
Dubrovnik 35, 66-72, **67**, **68**
  accommodation 69-71
  activities 69
  beaches 69

000 Map pages
000 Photograph pages

drinking 71
entertainment 71-2
food 71
internet access 66
medical services 66
shopping 66, 72
sights 66-69
tourist offices 66
travel to/from 72
Duklja 25, 26, see also Zeta
Durmitor Mountains 142
Durmitor National Park 64, 142-5, 6
accommodation 143, 144-5
activities 143-4
drinking 145
food 145
internet access 143
shopping 143
sights 143-4
tourist offices 143
tours 143
travel agencies 143
travel to/from 145

E
eagles 62, 122, 143
earthquakes 29, 61, 74, 78, 86, 97,
    107, 114, 115, 116, 158
ecolodges 17-18
economy 37-8
electricity 151
embassies 159
emergencies, see inside front cover
encephalitis 174
endangered species 62-3, see also
    Dalmatian pelican, eagles
environmental issues 65, see also
    sustainable travel
ethnicity 38-9
EU membership 35, 36
events, see festivals, sporting events
exchange rates, see inside front cover

F
Fašinada 82
ferries 76, 113
festivals 18, 159, see also sporting
    events
Boka Navy Day 86
Boka Night 87
Fašinada 82
Festival of Mediterranean Song
    100
Hitting a Cock 82
International Fashion Selection 86

International Folklore Festival 100
International Klapa Festival 82
Lake Skadar Day 127
Mimosa Festival 79
River Zeta Festival 133
Sunčane Skale 79
Theatre Town 100
Traditional Kotor Carnival 86
film 41-2
fishing 63, 64
Budva 100
Durmitor National Park 143
Kolašin 139
Kotor 86
Lake Krupac 136
Lake Skadar 126, 127, 128, 129
Lake Slano 136
Petrovac 108
Vranjina 128
food 44-52, 159
cafes 46, 54
celebrations 46
customs 48
fast food 47
language 48-52
restaurants 46-7
vegetarian travellers 47-8
football (soccer) 40
fortresses
Besac 127
Budva Citadel 97-8
Fortemare 78
Haj-Nehaj 113
Kanli-Kula 78
Kastio 108
Lesendro 129
Mamula Island 81
Onogošt 134
Španjola 78
freedom of press 39
frescoes 43

G
galleries, see museums & galleries
gay travellers 159-60
geography 61
geology 61
glacial lakes 142, 150
Gospa od Milosti 92
Gospa od Škrpjela 82, 10
Greek myths 98
Greeks 24, 95
guns 36, 124
Gusinje 149
gusle 41, 42

H
Haj-Nehaj fortress 113
health 173-5
insurance 173
vaccinations 173
websites 173
heat exhaustion 174
heat stroke 174
herbs 65
Herceg Novi 76-80, **77**, 11
accommodation 79
activities 78
drinking 79
entertainment 79
festivals 79
food 79
internet access 76
sights 76-8
tourist offices 76
tours 78
travel to/from 79
travel within 80
hiking 154, 155
Bijelo Polje 146
Biogradska Gora National Park
    141, 142
Bjelasica Mountains 141
Budva 100
Coastal Mountain Traversal 80
Durmitor National Park
    143, 144
Herceg Novi 78
Kolašin 140
Kotor 86
Ladder of Cattaro 86
Lapčići 103
Lovćen National Park 122
Mojkovac 142
Mt Orjen 80
Murići 128
Praskvica Monastery 107
Prokletije Mountains 150
responsible travel 156-7
Rijeka Crnojevića 127
Rožaje 147
history 24-35
Adriatic coast 95-6
Bay of Kotor 74-5
books 19, 26, 27, 28, 29, 31, 33,
    34, 35, 40
hitching 172
holidays 160
Holy Sunday Island 107
horse riding 139, 147
hotels 152

I

icons 43
Illyrians 24, 74
immigration 163
independence 15, 34, 35
insurance
    health 173
    travel 160
    vehicle 171
International Fashion Selection 86
International Folklore Festival 100
International Klapa Festival 82
internet access 160
internet resources 19
    health 173
    online tickets 165
Islam 39, 41
islands
    Ada Bojana 118
    Holy Sunday Island 107
    Island of Flowers 92
    Katič 107
    Lake Skadar 128
    Mamula Island 81
    Our-Lady-of-Mercy Island 92
    Our-Lady-of-the-Rock Island 82, 10
    St George's Island 82
    St Mark's Island 92
    St Nicholas' Island 103
    Sveti Stefan 103-5, **104**, 6, 54-5
itineraries 4, 20-3
    beaches 23, **23**
    drives 22, **22**
    highlights 20, **20**
    national parks 21, **21**
    off-the-beaten-track 23, **23**
    sustainable travel 23, **23**
Ivanova Korita 123

J

Jaz Beach 102
jeep tours 139, 143
jet lag 174
jet skis
    Budva 102
    Herceg Novi 78
    Kaluđerovina 93
    Krtole 93
    Lake Krupac 136
    Sveti Stefan 105
    Ulcinj 116

000 Map pages
000 Photograph pages

K

Kaluđerovina 92-3
Karadžić, Radovan 133
Katič 107
katuns 140, 141
kayaking
    Bay of Kotor 78
    Bečići 102
    Budva 100
    Herceg Novi 78
    Kaluđerovina 93
    Krtole 93
    Lake Krupac 136
    Lake Plav 149
    Plavnica 129
    Pržno (Sveti Stefan) 106
    Rafailovići 102
    Rijeka Crnojevića 127
    Sveti Stefan 105
King Nikola 31-2, 96, 124, 125, *see also* palaces
Kingdom of Serbs, Croats & Slovenes 32, 33, 74, 96
Kolašin 138-41
konobas 46, 47
Kosovo 15, 27, 28, 34, 35, 146
Kotor 84-9, **85**, 5, 53, 54
    accommodation 87-8
    activities 86
    drinking 88-9
    entertainment 88-9
    festivals 86-7
    food 88
    internet access 84
    medical services 84
    shopping 89
    sights 84-6
    tourist offices 84
    tours 86
    travel to/from 89
Krtole 92-3
kulas 42, 146, 149

L

Ladder of Cattaro 86
Ladies' Beach 116
Lake Skadar Day 127
Lake Skadar National Park 64-5, 126-9, 7
    accommodation 127, 128, 129
    churches 128
    festivals 127
    food 127, 128, 129
    islands 128
    medical services 127

monasteries 128
    tourist offices 127, 128
lakes
    Black Lake 142, 8
    glacial lakes 142, 150
    Lake Biograd 141-2
    Lake Krupac 136
    Lake Pešić 140
    Lake Plav 147, 149
    Lake Šas 119
    Lake Skadar 126-9
    Lake Slano 136
    Škrčka Lakes 144
language 41, 176-81
    Albanian 114, 176
    Cyrillic alphabet 25, 26, 39, 176, 177
    food & drink 48-52
    Montenegrin 41, 176-81
    street names 114
Lastva 89-90
legal matters 160-1
lesbian travellers 159-60
literature 41, *see also* books
littering 65, 146, 147
Lovćen National Park 64, 122-3
Lučice Beach 107
Luština Peninsula 92-3

M

magazines 151
Mamula Island 81
maps 161
measures 151, *see also inside front cover*
medical services 174, *see also* health
metric conversions, *see inside front cover*
Miločer Beach 106
Milošević, Slobodan 35
Mirišta 93
mobile phones 161
Mojkovac 142
monasteries
    Brezojevica Monastery 149
    Cetinje Monastery 125
    Dobrilovina Monastery 144
    Gradište Monastery 110
    Holy Trinity Monastery (Pljevlja) 145
    Lake Skadar islands 128
    Monastery of St Michael Archangel 92
    Morača Monastery 138, 9
    Ostrog Monastery 133-4, 12, 57

INDEX

Piva Monastery 136
Podmaine Monastery 100
Podostrog Monastery 100
Praskvica Monastery 106-7
Reževići Monastery 110
Savina Monastery 78
St George's Monastery 82
St Nicholas' Monastery 129
money 16, 159, 161, *see also inside front cover*
Montenegrin language 41, 176-81
Montenegrin Orthodox Church 30, 33, 38-9
Morača Canyon 138, 8
Morača Monastery 138, 9
Morača River 138
Morinj 81
mosques 39, 117
    Bijelo Polje 145
    Hussein Pasha Mosque 145
    Kryepazarit Mosque 116
    Kurtagića Mosque 146
    Lamit Mosque 116
    Mezjah Mosque 116
    Old Mosque (Plav) 148
    Omerbašića Mosque 114
    Pasha's Mosque 116
    Plav Mosque 149
    Podgorica Mosque 129
    Rožaje Mosque 146
    Sultana Mosque 148
    Vizier's Mosque 149
motion sickness 174
motorcycle travel, *see* car travel
mountain biking 80, 153
    Durmitor National Park 143
    Herceg Novi 78
    Kolašin 140
    Lapčići 103
    Lovćen National Park 122
    Mt Orjen 80
    Murići 128
    Nikšić 135
    Tour de Montenegro 153
    Virpazar 127
mountain huts 80, 141, 142, 144, 145, 150, *see also* katuns
mountains, *see also* drives
    Bjelasica Mountains 141
    climate 122, 138
    Durmitor Mountains 142
    Mt Lovćen 122
    Mt Orjen 80
    Prokletije Mountains 150
    Rumija Mountains 128

travel to/from 122, 138
travel within 122, 138
Murići 128
museums & galleries
    Archaeological Museum (Budva) 98
    Art Museum (Cetinje) 123-4
    Cetinje Monastery treasury 125
    Dvorac Petrovića 131
    Ethnographic Museum (Cetinje) 125
    Gallery & Museum Tivat 90
    History Museum (Cetinje) 123
    King Nikola Museum 124
    Kolašin Museum & Gallery 140
    Maritime Museum (Kotor) 84-6
    Museum of Modern Art (Budva) 98
    National Museum of Montenegro 123-5
    Nikšić Museum 134
    Njegoš Museum 124
    Perast Museum 82
    Podgorica Museum & Gallery 131
    Red Commune Memorial House 108
    Regional Museum (Herceg Novi) 78
    Reževići Monastery 110
    Stari Bar 114
    Ulcinj Museum 115
music 42, *see also* gusle
Muslims 38, 145, 146, 148, 149

N
Napoleon 30, 31, 74
National Museum of Montenegro 123-5
national parks 64-5, *see also* Balkans Peace Park
    Biogradska Gora National Park 64, 141-2, 8
    Durmitor National Park 64, 142-5, 6
    itineraries 21
    Lake Skadar National Park 64-5, 126-9, 7
    Lovćen National Park 64, 122-3
NATO bombing 34
Nemanjić dynasty 26, 27
newspapers 39, 151
Nikšić 134-5
Njegoš
    life 29, 31
    literary work 31, 41
    Njegoš Mausoleum 122-3, 59
    Njegoš Museum 124
Njeguši 123

O
Obod 127
Obodska Cave 127

olive trees 64, 114
online tickets 165
oro 42, 132
Ostrog Monastery 133-4, 12, 57
Ostrvo Cvijeća 92
Ottoman Empire
    history 26-33, 74, 96
    sights 78, 114, 129
Our-Lady-of-Mercy Island 92
Our-Lady-of-the-Rock Island 82, 10

P
painting 43
palaces
    Dvorac Petrovića 131
    King Nikola's Palace (Bar) 112
    King Nikola's Palace (Cetinje) 124
    King Nikola's Palace (Nikšić) 134
    Presidential Palace (Cetinje) 123
palazzos 82, 83
paragliding 155
    Bečići 103
    Herceg Novi 78
    Kolašin 139
    Nikšić 135
parasailing 155
    Bečići 102
    Herceg Novi 78
    Rafailovići 102
Partisans 33, 34
passports 163, *see also* visas
Paštrović clan 96, 107, 109, 110
Perast 82-3, 9, 56
Petrovac 107-9, **108**
    accommodation 109
    activities 108
    drinking 109
    entertainment 109
    festivals 109
    food 109
    internet access 107
    medical services 107
    shopping 109
    sights 107-8
    tours 108
    travel to/from 109
    travel within 109
Petrović dynasty 30, 33
Petrović, Nikola *see* King Nikola
Petrović, Petar I 30-1
Petrović, Petar II *see* Njegoš
phonecards 161
pirates 28, 116
Piva Canyon 136
Piva Monastery 136

Piva River 136
planning 16-19, 159, *see also* itineraries
plants 63-5, *see also* olive trees
Plav 147-9
Plava Špilja 93
Plavnica 129
Pljevlja 145
Plužine 136
Podgorica 34, 129-33, **130**
  accommodation 131-2
  drinking 132
  entertainment 131, 132
  food 132
  internet access 131
  medical services 131
  shopping 132
  sights 131
  tourist offices 131
  travel to/from 132-3
  travel within 133
population 38, 75
postal services 161
Prčanj 89
prince-bishops 29-31, 100
private accommodation 152
Prokletije Mountains 150
Pržno (Luštica Peninsula) 93
Pržno (Sveti Stefan) 105, 106

Q
Queen's Beach 106

R
radio 151
Radovan Luka 143
Rafailovići 102-3
rafting 155
  Durmitor National Park 143
  Herceg Novi 78
  Kolašin 139
  Lapčići 103
  Tara River 143-4, **58**
rakija 45, 46, 127
Raška 25, 26
recycling 65
religion 25, 26, 38-9, 74, 84, 95
  Islam 39, 41
  Montenegrin Orthodox Church 30, 33, 38-9
  Serbian Orthodox Church 26, 27, 29, 30, 33, 38-9

000 Map pages
000 Photograph pages

responsible travel 17-19, *see also* sustainable travel
  diving 154
  hiking 156-7
restaurants 46-7, *see also konobas*
Rijeka Crnojevića 127, **7**
Rijeka Reževići 110
Risan 81-2
River Zeta Festival 133
rivers, *see also* canyons
  Bojana River 62, 118
  Crnojević River 127
  Morača River 138
  Piva River 136
  Tara River 143-4, **58**
  Zeta River 133
road rules 171-2
Roman Empire
  history 24-5, 74, 95
  sights 81, 92, 107, 136
Rose 93
Rožaje 146-7
ruins
  Besac 127
  Island of Flowers 92
  Lesendro 129
  Mother of God of Ratac Monastery 111
  Obod 127
  Petrovac 107
  Podgorica 129
  Risan 81
  Stari Bar 113-14, **10**
  Svač 119
  Žabljak Crnojevića 129
Rumija Mountains 128
Russia 29, 30, 31, 34, 74

S
safe travel 158
  hitching 172
  road rules 171-2
Šavnik 136
Šćepan Mali 30
Šćepan Polje 143
sea urchins 174
Serbia
  history 25, 26, 27, 29, 32-3
  Montenegrin-Serb relations 15, 36, 37
  Serbia & Montenegro, union of 35
  Serbian Orthodox Church 26, 27, 29, 30, 33, 38-9
  Serbs 25, 38, 74

shopping 161
skiing 155
  Durmitor National Park 144
  Kolašin 140
  Rožaje 147
  Vučje 136
Škrčka Lakes 144
Slavs 25
snakes 63-5, 158, 174
snowboarding 144
soccer 40
software piracy 38
solo travellers 161
Splavište 143
sporting events 159
  Adventure Race Montenegro 159
  International Aerobics Weekend 109
  Port Cup 112
  Swimming Marathon 112
  Tour de Montenegro 153
sports 40, *see also individual sports*
St George's Island 82
St Mark's Island 92
St Nicholas' Island 103
stara maslina, see olive trees
Stari Bar 113-14, **10**
stećci 43, 134
Stoliv 89
street names 114
sustainable travel 164, 169, *see also* responsible travel
  carbon-offset schemes 164
  ecolodges 17-18
  itineraries 23
  Montenegro Adventures 131
Svač 119
Sveta Nedjelja 108
Sveti Đorđe 82
Sveti Marko 92
Sveti Nikola 103
Sveti Stefan 103-5, **104**, **6**, **54-5**
  accommodation 105
  activities 103-5
  food 105
  travel to/from 105

T
Tara Bridge 144, **60**
Tara Canyon 143-4, **58**
Tara River 143-4, **58**
taxi boats 76, 79, 82, 96, 102, 113
telephone services 161
time 162
Tito, Josip Broz 33, 34

Titograd, *see* Podgorica
Tivat 90-2, **91**
    accommodation 91-2
    activities 90-1
    festivals 92
    food 91-2
    sights 90
    tourist offices 90
    travel to/from 92
    travel within 92
Tour de Montenegro 153
tourist information 87, 112, 162
tours, 78, 91, 139, 143, *see also* boat
    tours, jeep tours
Traditional Kotor Carnival 86
train travel
    to/from Montenegro 168-9
    within Montenegro 172
trekking, *see* hiking
tribes 29
Turks, *see* Ottoman Empire
TV 151

U
Ulcinj 114-18, **115**, **55**
    accommodation 117
    activities 116

drinking 118
    entertainment 118
    food 117-18
    internet access 115
    medical services 115
    sights 115-16
    travel to/from 118

V
vaccinations 173
vegetarian travellers 47-8
Velika Plaža 118
Venetian Republic
    history 27, 28, 29, 30, 31, 74,
        95, 96
    sights 78, 84, 97, 107, 113, 114
video systems 151
Virpazar 127-8
visas 162, *see also* passports
Vlach people 125
*vladika*s 29-31, 100
Vranjina 128-9
Vučje 136

W
walking, *see* hiking
war crimes 36, 81, 133

warrior culture 36
    beheadings 32, 126
    weapons 36, 124
wars of the '90s 35, 146
water polo 40
water shortages 65, 96
weather 16, 75, 96, 122, 138, 58
websites, *see* internet resources
weights 151, *see also inside front cover*
wildlife, *see* animals, plants
wine 45, 127, 129
wolves 62, 122, 127, 143
women in Montenegro 40
women travellers 162
World Heritage Sites, *see* Durmitor
    National Park, Kotor

Y
yachting 78, 86
Yugoslavia 33-5, 75, 96

Z
Žabljak 143-5
Žabljak Crnojevića 129
Žanjice 93
Zeta 25, 26, *see also* Duklja
Zeta River 133

MAP LEGEND
ROUTES

Tollway	Mall/Steps
Freeway	Tunnel
Primary	Pedestrian Overpass
Secondary	Walking Tour
Tertiary	Walking Tour Detour
Lane	Walking Trail
Under Construction	Walking Path
Unsealed Road	Track
One-Way Street	

TRANSPORT

Ferry	Rail
Metro	Rail (Underground)
Monorail	Tram
Bus Route	Cable Car, Funicular

HYDROGRAPHY

River, Creek	Water
Intermittent River	Lake (Dry)
Reef	Mudflats

BOUNDARIES

International	Regional, Suburb
State, Provincial	Ancient Wall
Marine Park	Cliff

AREA FEATURES

Airport	Land
Area of Interest	Mall
Beach, Desert	Market
Building	Park
Cemetery, Christian	Rocks
Cemetery, Other	Sports
Forest	Urban

POPULATION

○ CAPITAL (NATIONAL)	◉ CAPITAL (STATE)
● Large City	● Medium City
● Small City	○ Town, Village

SYMBOLS

Sights/Activities
- Beach
- Canoeing, Kayaking
- Castle, Fortress
- Christian
- Diving, Snorkeling
- Golf
- Islamic
- Jewish
- Monument
- Museum, Gallery
- Point of Interest
- Pool
- Ruin
- Skiing
- Trail Head
- Zoo, Bird Sanctuary

Eating
- Eating

Drinking
- Drinking
- Café

Entertainment
- Entertainment

Shopping
- Shopping

Sleeping
- Sleeping
- Camping

Transport
- Airport, Airfield
- Border Crossing
- Bus Station
- Cycling, Bicycle Path
- General Transport
- Parking Area
- Petrol Station
- Taxi Rank

Information
- Bank, ATM
- Embassy/Consulate
- Hospital, Medical
- Information
- Internet Facilities
- Police Station
- Post Office, GPO
- Telephone
- Toilets

Geographic
- Lighthouse
- Lookout
- Mountain, Volcano
- National Park
- Pass, Canyon
- Picnic Area
- River Flow
- Shelter, Hut
- Waterfall

LONELY PLANET OFFICES

Australia
Head Office
Locked Bag 1, Footscray, Victoria 3011
☎ 03 8379 8000, fax 03 8379 8111
talk2us@lonelyplanet.com.au

USA
150 Linden St, Oakland, CA 94607
☎ 510 250 6400, toll-free 800 275 8555
fax 510 893 8572
info@lonelyplanet.com

UK
2nd fl, 186 City Rd,
London EC1V 2NT
☎ 020 7106 2100, fax 020 7106 2101
go@lonelyplanet.co.uk

Published by Lonely Planet Publications Pty Ltd
ABN 36 005 607 983

© Lonely Planet Publications Pty Ltd 2009

© photographers as indicated 2009

Cover photograph: Sveti Stefan and Adriatic coastline, Montenegro, Graham Lawrence/Photolibrary. Many of the images in this guide are available for licensing from Lonely Planet Images: www.lonely planetimages.com.

Printed by Fabulous Printers Pte Ltd
Printed in Singapore

Mixed Sources
Product group from well-managed forests, controlled sources and recycled wood or fibre
www.fsc.org Cert no. SGS-COC-005002
© 1996 Forest Stewardship Council
FSC